December 12, 1991

To Majority Leader Dick Gephardt,
with deep appreciation for your
strong support of the Conversion Law
of 1990 ("Division D" of the
Defense Authorization Act), and the
hope that 1992 will see stronger
Congressional action on Conversion.

John Tepper Marlin

Building a Peace Economy

Published in cooperation with the
Council on Economic Priorities

Building a Peace Economy

Opportunities and Problems of Post–Cold War Defense Cuts

Betty G. Lall
and John Tepper Marlin

WITH

Eugene Chollick and Domenick Bertelli

AND

Michael Barsa, Anna DePalo,
Josh Leventhal, Dana McGrath,
Matthew Paice, Robert Trager, and Dawn Zuroff

Westview Press
BOULDER • SAN FRANCISCO • OXFORD

Copyright © 1992 by the Council on Economic Priorities

Published in 1992 in the United States of America by Westview Press, Inc., 5500 Central Avenue, Boulder, Colorado 80301-2847, and in the United Kingdom by Westview Press, 36 Lonsdale Road, Summertown, Oxford OX2 7EW

A CIP catalog record for this book is available from the Library of Congress.
ISBN 0-8133-8433-8

Printed and bound in the United States of America

The paper used in this publication meets the requirements
of the American National Standard for Permanence of Paper
for Printed Library Materials Z39.48-1984.

10   9   8   7   6   5   4   3   2   1

Contents

Acknowledgments

This book is part of a program of work on the peaceful use of military resources that the Council on Economic Priorities (CEP) has been engaged in for more than two decades. We therefore have many debts to acknowledge. Above all, we thank the John D. and Catherine T. MacArthur Foundation for a foresighted 1989 writing grant that resulted in a much longer study on which this book is based. We also express our deep appreciation for related additional support from the Ira and Miriam Wallach Foundation, the Joyce Mertz-Gilmore Foundation, Ploughshares Fund, Rockefeller Family Associates, Rena Shulsky, and Malcolm Wiener.

Eugene Chollick was a crucial resource in bringing this work to completion. A conscientious and skilled research associate at CEP, he worked with Betty G. Lall on Chapters 1-3 and handled the desk-top publishing challenges throughout the book. Interns Michael Barsa (Stanford University), Dana McGrath (Middlebury College), and Mary Robinson (Claremont College) assisted with Chapters 1-3. Consultants Kosta Tsipis and Archon Fong (MIT) contributed to Chapter 3.

Domenick Bertelli, a talented Harvard undergraduate, took a year off to help with Chapters 4-8. Anna DePalo (Harvard-Radcliffe), Josh Leventhal (Carleton College), Matthew Paice (London School of Economics), Gautam Rana (Wharton School, University of Pennsylvania), Robert Trager (Middlebury), and Dawn Zuroff (Barnard) contributed to these chapters. Hans Bos (NYU Graduate School of Public Administration) assisted with the computer work.

Our book has benefited greatly from the editorial input of Alice Tepper Marlin (executive director and founder of CEP), Carolyn Seely Wiener, and our copy editor, Patrick Vance. Matthew Held, Lynn Arts, and Mary Kay Scott of Westview Press were helpful in providing, interpreting, and gracefully modifying their guidelines for readying this book for publication.

Very helpful comments on both the original study and the manuscript of this book were provided by Dennis Flanagan (former editor of *Scientific American*), John E. Lynch (former associate director of the Office of Economic Adjustment, Department of Defense, and more recently vice chairman, Economic Development Authority, Fairfax County, Va.), and Peter Rose (formerly with the Office of Technology Assessment).

Helpful comments on the manuscript of the original study were contributed by Marc Baldwin (Research Department, United Auto Workers), William Hartung (office of the New York State Attorney General), and Robert Rauner (director, Office of Economic Adjustment, Department of Defense).

We are also grateful for helpful comments on portions of the book by Greg Bischak (National Commission on Economic Conversion and Disarmament), Joseph Cartwright (Office of Economic Adjustment, Department of Defense), Michael Closson (Center for Economic Conversion), Gus Comstock (assistant to Ohio's former Gov. Richard Celeste), Lewis Franklin (TRW), Natalie Goldring (Defense Budget Project), Richard Greenwood (recently retired from the International Association of Machinists), Paul Grenier (former CEP research associate), Prof. Michael Intriligator (Center for International and Strategic Studies, UCLA), Lawrence Korb (Brookings Institution), Jack Mendelsohn (Arms Control Association), Stanley Moses (Hunter College), Milo Nordyke (Lawrence Livermore National Lab), Jack Sheinkman (Amalgamated Clothing and Textile Workers Union), Beth Smith (University of Missouri), and Janet Stone (Center for Economic Conversion).

Betty G. Lall is primarily responsible for Chapters 1-3 and John Tepper Marlin for the Introduction and Chapters 4-8.

Betty G. Lall
John Tepper Marlin

Introduction

Coping with Defense Cuts

The ascendance of Mikhail Gorbachev to power in 1985 set in motion a stunning series of changes that in the fall of 1991 spelled an irreversible shift toward a new European and world order. The European satellites and at least three of the 15 former Soviet republics are now independent, while the remaining 12 are being reconstituted as a loose federation with varying degrees of affiliation.

Some argue that the Reagan military buildup hastened these changes. Others believe the Soviet changes were caused by long-standing and inexorable economic and political pressures within the Soviet Bloc and that the U.S. paid an unnecessarily high price for the buildup.

Whatever one's views about why the Cold War ended, the changes mean the U.S. can bring home hundreds of thousands of troops that were stationed in Europe to defend against Soviet aggression. As President George Bush made clear in September 1991, the U.S. can now accept a panoply of nuclear-disarmament proposals that were on the Soviet agenda. Like the Soviets and Europeans, we face a formidable challenge: *How can we make the smoothest possible transition to civilian use of newly released military resources, especially the physical and human resources that have been devoted to defense production?*

This book is designed to be a practical guide to such potential reuse for planners, union and company officials, community leaders, government officials, and others who are, or will be, affected by the transition. The aim of the authors is to provide information and guidelines to help these people make the required economic adjustment.

Conversion Yesterday: Swords to Plowshares

This book may be seen as an expansion on the Biblical theme, to be found in the Books of Isaiah and Micah, of converting swords into plowshares at the conclusion of war.

Benjamin the Blacksmith

Imagine Benjamin the Blacksmith living near Jerusalem in the Kingdom of Judah in the time of the prophets, 740 B.C., selling plowshares to farmers.

One day terrible news arrives: "The King of Damascus has sent an army against us. It is now only a few days' march distant." The fears of those in the region generate a fierce demand for swords, spears, and shields. Benjamin becomes a local hero as he and his assistants sweat day and night hammering at his forge; he is paid handsomely by the wealthy prince of the region, who decides the time has come to make use of the family treasure to preserve his position.

Fortunately, the Syrian invaders are confronted and retreat. Benjamin goes back to the less glamorous and less-well-paid job of providing farmers with plowshares, pails, and pruning hooks. He confides to his wife: "The farmers aren't as good customers as the prince. Few of them are loyal to me. Another blacksmith sells a plowshare for a lower price, and the farmers will take off a day or more to travel there and save some money. Of course, most of them don't have much savings. They tend to buy only when they have had a good harvest. I just hope I can sell some iron implements to the prince's steward."

This situation corresponds closely enough to the reconversion era in the U.S. after World War II. Benjamin undertakes three basic tasks common to all conversion situations (though in modern market economies individual efforts are supported in varying degrees by market sanctions and incentives). He:

1. *Adjusts his goals.* He reorients his production and marketing goals from selling military goods to a single buyer (the "prince") to the trickier one of selling to multiple civilian businesses ("farmers") or civilian government agencies (the "prince's steward").
2. *Retrains his assistants.* Having changed his goals, Benjamin retrains those of his assistants who haven't made farmers' implements before. An alternative open to him is to release (lay off) his assistants and hire new ones with more experience or talent selling to, and producing inexpensively for, farmers.
3. *Changes the organization of his shop.* Plowshares and pruning hooks are not made to be as sharp as swords and spears, but must be more durable. Pails have to be made to hold water, whereas shields do not. Benjamin changes his tools and production techniques.

Aaron the Armorer

Now consider Benjamin's son Aaron, who starts work in 734 B.C., when Syria and Israel both threaten Judah. Isaiah correctly prophesies that Judah should fear its would-be ally, the sprawling and cunning Assyrian Empire. The local prince takes the prophets seriously, so for the next 33 years Aaron devotes all of his working hours to making weapons for the prince's soldiers. He becomes a full-time armorer, a high-priced blacksmith.

When Aaron the Armorer has sold the prince two swords for every one of the prince's soldiers, he experiments with new technology to give Judah's fighters an edge in battle and, not coincidentally, keep up demand for his weapons.

"Your excellency," he tells the prince, "you owe it to your loyal soldiers to buy my new weapons. They can hardly be compared to the primitive ones I sold you in prior years, when I was a mere novice at making weaponry. My new swords are double-edged, giving the user a 2-to-1 advantage on the battlefield. I also use a unique combination of metals and firing techniques to craft swords and spears that we call our line of Superweapons — stronger, sharper, more flexible than any others available, with a virtually unshakeable custom grip. Your officers will also benefit from the added self-respect they obtain by having gold plating, pearls, and semi-precious stones on the handles."

This works for many years. Then in 701 B.C. the Assyrian army unsuccessfully attempts to take Jerusalem. Its general decides to head back to Nineveh. The prince is blunt: "You have been a trooper, Aaron, and your Superweapons really are fine. But the Assyrians are gone, and I've worked out a deal with them that should keep them from bothering us again during my lifetime. But it's going to cost me. Frankly, I'm broke and I can't spend any more money on your new weapons."

Aaron is crestfallen. Like his father, in moments of perplexity he talks through his situation with his wife. "Sara," he frets to her, "it hardly seems fair. Jerusalem resisted takeover because we had superior weaponry, and I'm the best armorer in the region. How does the prince reward me? He's cutting me off! I'll have to learn a whole new business. Dad at least had *experience* making plowshares and pruning hooks. Even he will tell you the plowshares business is the pits. You have to sell to farmers one by one. They don't have much ready cash and want credit. The prince paid well and on delivery. At best, I'll be working for less money and less status. At worst, I will be out of work or underemployed because no one wants to risk buying my plowshares and finding they crack before the first season is over. The joke among the farmers is that my plowshares will have pearl handles. Imagine, I save their skins and they laugh at me."

The next day, Phoenician traders offer Aaron a tempting way out. "We'll buy your Superweapons. We can resell them easily in Babylon and many other countries." Aaron is excited about the opportunity to make his weapons for export, but word of this reaches the prince, who visits the smithy with a stern, and sensible, warning: "There is no way I'm going to let you make Superweapons for the Phoenicians. They might fall into the hands of those who could become enemies of Judah. Forget it. Pay a little more attention to the prophets."

Aaron's situation is much like that of U.S. (and Soviet and European) defense contractors in 1991. Many of them have little experience in civilian work and most of them see it as a risky, possibly unprofitable activity. Exporting arms is a way out for the contractors, used in the 1970s after the Vietnam War, but as the Gulf War in latter-day Assyria showed, it's a solution full of hazards for the world.

Conversion Options

Let us review the options open to Aaron and his assistants, and the prince.

Aaron: Do We Diversify or Not?

"The basic question," Aaron sums up in a blunt dialog with his assistants, "is whether or not we should diversify our business. Diversification simply means adding new skills and products to our existing business. We have been making weapons. Diversifying would mean adding some farm implements or other civilian products to what we produce.

Yes? "If we *do* decide to diversify, what do our skills best suit us to produce? (Farm implements is an obvious answer, but not the only one.) Are all you assistants adaptable, with retraining, to a new business of this kind? Might the prince send us someone to teach us the new skills we need? Might the prince's steward hire us for some kind of work, for example to make improvements on the prince's lands – especially since he has opposed our making weapons for sale to the Phoenician traders? Is there possibly a market among the wealthier farmers for extra-strong or extra-flexible plowshares? Are any of our inventories of metal usable in a new business? Can the unsold weapons be made into something useful to the farmers or other civilians? What about the blacksmith shop itself – might it be better used for something else? Might the prince advance some money to set up a new business?

No? "If we *don't* diversify, you all must know that the end of the war means our weapons sales will probably drop off pretty quickly. If we can't find new customers, I won't be able to keep paying you all at the same rate, and sooner or later I'll have to let some of you go."

The assistants, galvanized by the prospect of being without work, agreed that looking for outlets for diversification was a high priority. Some of them offered to go with Aaron to appeal to the prince for help.

The Prince: Do I Intervene or Not?

Aaron and his assistants call on the prince: "You got us into this situation," they argue. "We have been working for you making weapons so long that we don't know how to do anything else. If you won't let us make weapons for export, at least send us someone to train us to do something else, or give us some money so we can learn a new skill and start a new business, or give us some other work to do." After they left, the prince ruminated with his steward:

Yes? "If we *do* intervene to help them, where will it end? Other people will want similar 'economic-adjustment' help when things go badly. Can I afford to help everyone? No, because when the villagers are poor, I am poor too. Why are these armorers so special, anyway? Maybe because they are all in one place and they have families who depend on them. Could we find something useful for them to do on my lands, like making an iron gate or a fence? How much money do they need to make the transition to a new line of work? How long would they need help for? Would it be in my interest to advance them some money to start a new business?

No? "If we *don't* intervene, I am going to see another part of their village become poor. These good workers could become discouraged and then their poverty will add a blight to this region. They do need help to learn something new and get started in a different kind of work. It won't cost me that much to provide them with instruction and get them started."

Isaiah and the Economic Consequences of Peace. As the prince was thinking things over, he remembered words he had heard from the prophet Isaiah, about converting swords to plowshares.

"Isaiah wants us to put war behind us," mused the prince. "Making weapons is itself an act of war. Even if our clearest way to prosperity were to make weapons for other countries to use, it would be wrong. Supporting new work for those who made weapons is right. It may also lead to even greater prosperity. But it's more than an issue of Profit and Loss; it's also one of Prophet and Laws."

The Prince's Decision. The prince decided to help Aaron and his assistants. Whether he did this strictly out of economic self-interest or was motivated also by religious concerns is shrouded by the veils of time.

Conversion Today

This book is not about how to decide whether or not to close a base or terminate a weapon-system contract – the modern equivalent of the decision to stop buying swords and shields. Rather, this book addresses the kinds of questions facing Aaron and the prince in 700 B.C., once the decision to cut defense spending has been made.

We address these issues as they are confronted 2,600 years later by U.S. companies, workers, investors, and community leaders who are seeing their source of income drop because of U.S. defense cuts. These issues come under the broad heading of "conversion."

Narrowly Defined (Plant) Conversion

In recent years the word conversion in the United States has been used by some in the narrowest sense, to mean *mandated, employee-driven retooling of a defense plant for civilian reuse.* Those who use the word in the narrow sense see conversion as a labor and infrastructural rebuilding issue rather than simply as an economic-development issue. They favor planning for conversion while the wolf of contractor layoffs is still roaming the woods, before it has reached the community's door.

This narrow concept of conversion is embodied in a bill – described further in Chapter 6 – first introduced in the U.S. Congress by Sen. George McGovern in 1963 and more recently adoptedby Rep. Ted Weiss (D-NY). It requires alternative-use labor-management planning committees in every major defense-contract facility. Prof. Seymour Melman, who for decades taught industrial engineering at Columbia University, has from the beginning been the bill's most ardent proponent.

A broader concept of conversion envisions a general, voluntary move to plan for the transition to peace at the local level and encourages every community and company affected by defense cuts to consider the three tasks Benjamin undertook at war's end in our story. A mandatory labor-management planning process is not considered likely to lead to a useful plan quite apart from the low probability that it could ever become law. We therefore favor the broad approach.

No recent U.S. examples exist of a process that fits the narrow definition of conversion. What we do find is successful company diversification – expansion of non-military production – efforts with decisions made at the company, not the plant, level. These diversification efforts are not always successful. Defense-industry managers are not well trained for competition in a commercial marketplace; their background is better suited for alternative (non-military) government work.

Similarly, worker retraining and placement are most efficiently undertaken at the community, not the plant, level. Defense workers who must move to civilian work face likely cuts in their income and a need to learn marketing and cost-control skills (which are not so needed in a quality-first defense-industry environment); they learn the new skills faster by moving to a new civilian employer. Factories often aren't physically appropriate for civilian production.

So conversion in the narrow sense of mandated labor-management planning to retool a defense plant in advance of the decision to cut defense spending is a distinctly unlikely prospect. Instead, defense contractors usually devote their attention to getting more defense work. If they face cuts, they generally do not attempt to retool a factory but either opt to sell it and lay off workers or to diversify internally at the company level. Defense workers not summarily dismissed are typically screened, trained, and moved to civilian facilities in a *different* location (disruptive though this may be for the workers and economically stressful for the communities they lived in). Aerospace companies such as Boeing historically have kept their military and civilian operations distinct and have been more willing to move their employees from civilian to military work than in the other direction.

Laid-off employees have little choice but to find new work, and many of them do. The main problems are the transitional pain, the residual group of workers who do not easily find new jobs, and the economic impact on their community of the drop in workers' incomes.

Broadly Defined Conversion and the 1990 Law

We use the term "conversion" throughout this book mostly as a broad, general description of the process of moving from a military to a civilian mode of production and other activities. This is the way the word is most often used by the U.N., Soviets, Chinese, and Europeans — and increasingly by Americans..

As will be made clear in Chapter 5, we strongly advocate voluntary advance planning for civilian activities by companies (diversification) and communities (economic adjustment/development). But we believe it is not useful to restrict the word "conversion" to a narrow definition, especially since the implied legislative goal is politically difficult to achieve.

Because U.S. advocates of mandatory advance planning for civilian reuse preempted the word conversion to describe what they favored, their corporate and governmental opponents have avoided the word completely, reacting not only to the advance-planning requirement but also to the word "conversion" itself.

One alternative word that has some support is "economic adjustment" — a term introduced in 1961 with the creation of the Office of Economic Adjustment in the Pentagon; it conveys working with economic-development techniques to ameliorate economic disruptions caused by changes in defense spending, *after* they have been decided.

Thus, as we discuss in more detail in Chapter 6, alternatives to Rep. Weiss's conversion bill avoided using the word "conversion" at all. Rep. Sam Gejdenson (D-CT) favors planning at the community (not the plant) level, and introduced a bill to promote "diversification." Rep. Nick Mavroules (D-MA) opposes plant-level mandatory planning and introduced a bill promoting "economic adjustment." Rep. Mary Rose Oakar (D-OH) used yet another term, "economic stabilization," and threw in all four labels in the long title to the successful compromise bill she introduced in 1990.

Broader concepts of conversion won the day politically with the passage of the first U.S. conversion legislation, the 1990 Conversion Law, which Washington insiders call Division D of the National Defense Authorization Act for Fiscal Year (FY) 1991, as discussed in Chapter 6. The 1990 Conversion Law deals with the economic impact of defense cuts only at the community level after cuts have been made. It does not fund any advance planning before it can be shown that jobs are being lost — a community must show that substantial defense layoffs have already occurred or are probably about to occur to be eligible to apply for a share of the $200 million that the 1990 Converson Law appropriated to help communities and workers adjust to defense cuts (the wolf of layoffs must be at the door).

Experience suggests that this 1990 Conversion Law is in harmony with mainstream U.S. political reality. Community-based organizations have been finding that American voters support their military establishment and have no *a priori* predisposition to cut it back. Their interest in cutting defense spending stems from the rapid decline in external threats, from evidence of excessive spending gets a hearing when linked to the decline in external threats and need to reduce the Federal budget deficit.

Similarly, companies engaged in defense work have no predisposition to convert; their interest in the subject comes from a sense that defense cuts are inevitable. Community leaders will lobby against defense cuts in their region but will support conversion once defense cuts are made, rallying around to help the laid-off workers who are the casualties of peace.

What's in This Book

The book is organized both by type of affected group (in Chapters 1-7) and by affected area (in Chapter 8). Chapter 1 describes likely budget cuts and strategies defense contractors are using to adjust to the downturn in military spending, from layoffs to diversification. Chapter 2 presents the impact of defense reduction on employment at military bases and nuclear weapons complexes. Chapter 3 details changes at the main National Laboratories where much military research and development, especially on nuclear weapons, has been conducted—Lawrence Livermore, Los Alamos, and Sandia. Chapter 4 shows the impact of defense cuts on U.S. states and localities. The *Vulnerability Index* and *Defense Dislocation Index* are described and applied. Chapter 5 describes some exemplary or representative state and local conversion programs and their record where available. Chapter 6 describes the 1990 Conversion Law and proposed additional programs for economic assistance to workers or localities most hurt by defense cuts. Chapter 7 describes what some organizations have done to advance conversion. We describe key national organizations and their activities, and list contacts. This chapter shows how individuals can work through these organizations. It also shows the role of organizations that are primarily motivated, like Isaiah, by noneconomic goals.

Chapter 8 is the focus of much of our research. After a few pages of explanation, it reviews the status of conversion in each state plus the District of Columbia and Puerto Rico. The first page of each state profile provides conversion *Benchmarks* including estimates of cuts, the Vulnerability Index, and CEP's unique *Defense Dislocation Index*, a measure of the likely impact of defense cuts. It also provides a prime-contract *Trend* chart, and *Spending* data by the top five prime contractors and by the top 10 spending sites. The first page also provides a map of military installations in each state. The remaining pages of each profile cover the *Overall Health of the Economy* against which military cuts can be evaluated, *Defense and the Economy* relating the military budget in each state to its overall economy, *State Legislative Initiatives* where relevant (contacts and phone numbers are provided both in the text and in the notes to the state profiles), and *Community Surveys* describing the situation in the most affected cities and base sites.

1

Impact of Cuts on Contractors and Labor

With the collapse of the Soviet Union as a unified state, the major threat to America's post-World War II national security has virtually disappeared. Weapons spending may now be significantly cut, along with troop strength. These events occur at a time when deficits and debt threaten the country's economic well-being, so that such budget cuts would presumably be welcomed by both the Administration and Congress. Such optimistic assumptions, however, may not necessarily be realized.

Former Defense Secretary Robert McNamara is one of several authorities on the defense establishment who advocates a 50 percent cut in the defense budget over a period of ten years. The proposed FY (Fiscal Year) 1992 Department of Defense budget sent up to Congress by the President was $290.8 billion.

One difficulty with cutting the defense budget is its size and complexity. Military contracting is a massive business, with the Department of Defense buying goods and services from a quarter of a million firms each year for everything from aircraft carriers, to fuel, to "Pampers" for resale at base commissaries. A Defense Department Management Report predicting savings of $71.7 billion from terminating 13 weapons systems from FY 1992 to FY 1997, was challenged by the General Accounting Office, which reported that "most of the savings estimates ... were based primarily on management judgments and not supported by historical facts or empirical cost data."[1] Thus, some skepticism may be necessary about such predictions until they are actually realized.

There are also countervailing considerations. Companies conducting weapons research and producing military hardware for the Department of Defense may face a loss of lucrative contracts and income. Significant numbers of workers at weapons plants will have to be laid off and many local communities will consequently face the prospect of shrinking tax income.

The process of scaling back the huge military establishment, particularly reducing the number of weapons to be produced, is likely to be slow. Weapons contracts cannot necessarily be severed precipitously by the Department of

Defense and members of Congress are likely to resist the economic ax falling on their constituencies. There will be considerable pressures to go slow in scaling back purchases of weapons, research and development, and weapons production.

Shifting from high to lower military spending is aided by the necessity to reduce the national budget and the hundreds of billions of dollars of deficits and cumulative debts that the Government piled up during 40 years of the Cold War. The Congress and the Bush Administration, after much negotiation, reached agreement in October 1990 on how much the military budget should be scaled back over the next several years. The agreement was a major step by Congress and the Administration to put the defense sector on an equally constrained footing with the rest of the Federal budget. Ironically, events overtook the agreement and what in 1990 seemed a victory to contain defense spending is one year later looking more like a protective shield against deeper budget cuts.

Defense Budget Trends in the 1990s

An important effect of the hammering out of the 1990 agreement may be that both the Administration and Congress will approach in a more disciplined way than they have in recent years, the whole exercise of the architecture of the Federal budget.

Key Industry Official Looks at the Future

Pursuant to the 1990 agreement, Congress set targets for spending for national defense, international programs, and domestic programs for FY 1991. As Geoffrey K. Bentley of Textron Defense Systems described the new situation, "there is no horsetrading, no reallocations that can be done, no robbing Peter to pay Paul or of taking money out of one major account and putting it in another account."[2] Given these Congressional restrictions, the battle within the Department of Defense will be over which parts of the its budget will be cut.

As Bentley put it: "During the 44 years of the Cold War, what we did on the downticks was to reduce and delay programs, stretch and cut, but we would never (or very rarely) cancel or terminate programs. Now we are looking at a new world order and a new way of doing business where clearly budgeting is driving planning. So, terminations and cancellations will be the name of the game."[3]

Bentley told the Electronic Industries Association: "We are back to the kind of budget as a percentage of the Gross National Product that we have not seen since the 1930s where we were spending about $15 billion in real terms, in today's dollar, for defense. ... Our national defense has grown by a factor of twenty, and the economy by a factor of about six."[4]

Bentley also pointed out that several weapons systems will be terminated, including the F-14D aircraft, Army Helicopter Improvement Program, Phoenix missile, M-88A2 recovery vehicle, F-14E aircraft, Apache helicopter, M-1 tank, and Maverick missile.[5]

Job Loss from Defense Cuts

Given the predicted reductions in the defense budget, job losses would occur not only at the Department of Defense but in defense companies throughout the country. The Manufacturer's Alliance for Productivity and Innovation (MAPI) estimated that 650,000 jobs (163,000 per year) would be lost from 1990 to 1994 as a result of "planned defense cuts." The manufacturing sector of the economy may be hit the hardest, according to MAPI.[6] It reported that "while defense-related output in 1990 made up 3.5 percent of total private production it accounted for a much larger share of manufacturing, 6.7 percent."[7] Industries affected include metals, electrical machinery, the transportation sector, and heavy machinery.

The top-to-bottom review of America's military spending programs by Congress and the Department of Defense over the next few years will result in a leaner and somewhat smaller military force. How lean depends in part on the extent of improved U.S.-Soviet relations, whether other perceived military threats become real, and on Congressional action to reduce the Federal deficit through defense budget cuts.

In a shrinking market, small contractors may leave the defense business or merge with larger companies. A few firms may diversify by buying nondefense companies, or expand on their own, and some may invest capital to develop arms control verification technology. Others may attempt the most ambitious — entry into new commercial markets.

Distribution of Military Spending

Less than half the money Congress appropriates for the U.S. military establishment finds its way into communities and industries in the U.S.[8] Sen. Nunn (D-GA), Chair of the Senate Armed Services Committee, pointed out that the remaining funds are used to support troops and military installations overseas. Many members of the military are stationed at bases in Europe, the Middle East, Asia, and the South Pacific, and some are in Central America. This distribution is likely to change as troops come home from Europe and Asia.

In the U.S., almost 30 percent of the military budget goes to developing and producing weapons. Members of Congress work hard to persuade the Department of Defense to award contracts to companies employing their constituents. To understand some of the impact of weapons production on the U.S. economy and on companies and workers, we provide data on the distribution of contracts for procurement of weapons throughout the 435 Congressional Districts (CDs). Twenty-five CDs received over $1 billion each in prime contract awards from the Department of Defense in FY 1988 for weapons procurement. Table 1.1 below, provides the amount awarded in each of these districts.

Of the 25 Congressional Districts in 13 states receiving the largest awards for defense contracts, nine are in California; two each are in Connecticut, Massachusetts, Texas, and Virginia; and one each is in Colorado, Florida, Maine, Mississippi, Missouri, New York, Ohio, and Washington. All but three of these CDs are coastal states. About 72 percent of the approximately $80 billion appropriated by Congress in FY 1988 for weapons purchases were contracts awarded to companies in 25 CDs of the 435 nationwide. Seventy-two CDs received over $500 million in contracts for the procurement of weapons, and 266 received between $100 million and $500 million.

The data on the distribution of prime contract awards point to a major shift in the geography of industry in the U.S. since the end of World War II. In 1945 many of the major defense companies were situated in the country's heartland, for example, Illinois, Indiana, Michigan, Ohio, and Pennsylvania. Today, companies producing for the military are mostly in New England, the Southeast, the Southwest, and the West. To illustrate this change,in the Midwestern states of

Table 1.1

Congressional Districts with over $1 Billion in Prime Contract Awards, FY 1988

Rank	State	C.D.	$ Millions
1	Virginia	1	$5,316
2	Missouri	2	$4,548
3	California	42	$3,686
4	California	27	$3,642
5	Massachusetts	5	$3,424
6	Texas	12	$3,072
7	California	12	$2,998
8	New York	4	$2,926
9	Colorado	5	$2,437
10	Florida	11	$2,386
11	Washington	7	$2,018
12	Mississippi	5	$1,984
13	Virginia	10	$1,955
14	Ohio	2	$1,930
15	Connecticut	3	$1,873
16	California	39	$1,799
17	Connecticut	2	$1,696
18	California	41	$1,337
19	California	35	$1,333
20	Texas	26	$1,329
21	California	31	$1,220
22	Maine	4	$1,147
23	Massachusetts	8	$1,135
24	California	21	$1,123
25	California	44	$1,086
	Total		$57,453

Sources: Defense Department, *Civilian and Active Duty Personnel by State and Congressional Dist.* and Military Spending Research Services, *Prime Contracts , FY 1988.*

Indiana, Iowa, Michigan, and Wisconsin, there were no Congressional Districts receiving military contracts totalling over $500 million in 1988.

Impact of Cuts on Subcontractors

Boeing, McDonnell Douglas, and General Dynamics are household words to those interested in military matters, but they are the tip of the iceberg in the defense industrial base. They and the other companies on the Defense Department's Top 100 Prime Contractor list subcontract out to tens of thousands of smaller firms throughout the country. The Small Business Administration tracks 170,000 small defense contractors.[9] An average of 50 percent of the work on a prime contract is jobbed out. The vast subcontracting web on a big program like Northrop's "Stealth" bomber spans the 50 states and most congressional districts.

When prime contractors complete their orders for the Department of Defense, their subcontractors often are affected. To gain some insight as to how such subcontractors are affected, the Council on Economic Priorities sent a questionnaire to a group of them in 1990 to learn their views.[10] Ninety-two firms responded. They are diverse in terms of size, though all of them employed at least 100 persons each. Over one-fourth employed more than 1,000 workers. The subcontractors were heavily involved in defense work, with half relying on the Department of Defense to take at least 50 percent of their output. None of the firms was totally dependent on defense for its viability. Thirty-three sold between 25 and 50 percent of their output to the Department of Defense and the rest sold up to 25 percent. These percentages had not changed substantially during the previous five years.

The companies were asked about the importance of their subcontracts with the Defense Department's prime contractors. Thirty-eight said they were not a big factor, 40 said the contracts were important, and only 14 said very important. These 14 companies sold over 50 percent of their output for military purposes.

Most of the companies were not unionized and thus their workers would not have union assistance when jobs were lost.

The respondents divided on the commercial application of their defense work. Fifty-three said no commercial application was involved and 35 said they had a division producing civilian versions of their defense work. About half the subcontractors said they thought the state and Federal governments could play a constructive role in easing the transition from defense to non-defense work.

Despite its critical part in defense contracting, subcontracting is not tracked closely by state policymakers. The enormity and ever-shifting nature of the task are evidently daunting. The Defense Department's effort to keep abreast of subcontracting ended in 1974, with the Paperwork Reduction Act; California tried on its own but gave up in the mid-1980s.

Adjustment Strategies for Contractors

1980s Order Backlog May Cushion Uncertain Future

As to the future, Geoffrey Bentley's forecasting committee noted a sharp decline of R&D and more emphasis on commercial business. It predicted that military R&D would focus on:(1) recasting SDI as a high-tech program; (2) small mobile systems for light forces; and (3) standoff systems and unmanned vehicles; and (4) a return to research and advanced development and a move away from engineering development.[11]

An optimistic report on the defense industry's future was given by David C. Morrison in a March 13, 1990, article, "Cushions for Contractors," in the *National Journal*. He quoted Herbert F. Rogers, President of General Dynamics: "Are we in a downturn? Yes. Is it deep? No. Will we survive? Yes. Will we come out of it stronger? Yes."

The Commerce Department's *Industrial Outlook for 1990* reported that orders for military aircraft and parts fell. But it also reported that "a substantial amount of work on aircraft modernization programs and classified projects is helping to cushion the industry from the full force of cutbacks in new aircraft procurement."[12]

Layoffs

Given the huge military buildup throughout the 1980s, it is not surprising that significant numbers of layoffs began occurring in 1989. On February 13, 1989, in a cavernous hangar in Long Beach, CA, 5,000 McDonnell Douglas managers from the firm's defense and commercial operations were participating in a massive "groupthink" exercise to allocate half that many jobs among themselves. The country's largest defense contractor and 25th-ranked Fortune 500 company had begun to retrench. More recently the company announced an annual payroll cut of $700 million; 10-15,000 workers would be let go to meet the target.[13] Other major contractors took similar action. Hughes Aircraft pared 6,000 and is paying up to $5,000 per employee for coursework leading to other careers. Northrop began layoffs in anticipation of cutbacks in B-2 bomber money.[14]

New Sales to Foster

Contractors in the weapons-making business know that little stability exists in this industry. They accept the swings in defense purchases. Moreover, many companies know there are substantial backlogs of orders in both the aerospace and electronics sectors. Industry associations in the U.S. affected by proposed cuts in U.S. military spending note only a gradual decrease in the Department of Defense's procurement of weapons. One of them, the Aerospace Industries

Association, reports that its members have a substantial backlog of orders to fill, and have been preparing for the adjustment to declining military budgets.

According to the Association's president, Don Fuqua, 1989 was the beginning of a period of declining military sales although total orders for aerospace products continued to rise.[15] Sales rose to $117.6 billion in 1989, compared with $114.6 billion in 1988.[16] Orders also rose to a record $176.5 billion in 1989 and the backlog of unfilled orders totaled $246.8 billion.

Export sales of $32.1 billion in 1989 added to industry employment of 1,321,000 people, an increase of 4,000 people compared to 1988. The backlog of orders for aircraft engines and parts by the end of 1989 increased to $157.2 billion. The industry shipped 566 aircraft to foreign governments in 1989.[17] Total U.S. aircraft on order in 1989 rose to $89 billion. But, industry analysts point out that proposals by members of Congress to reduce the U.S. export of arms could discourage foreign sales.[18]

Getting on the Verification Bandwagon

With major treaties on conventional and strategic weapons completed, verification technology appears a promising field for some defense contractors. The Conventional Forces Reductions Europe (CFE) Treaty and the START Treaty on reducing strategic nuclear weapons, will require such verification technology. Companies like Martin Marietta and TRW are vying for markets in everything from microchip "license plates" on aircraft to gamma-ray detectors for inspecting mobile missiles. The long-negotiated Chemical Weapons Convention is likely to be completed in a few years. Once ratified, it will offer a large scope for intrusive verification of its very complex provisions. Companies such as Martin Marietta and TRW are vying for markets in everything from microchip "license plates" on aircraft, to gamma-ray detectors for inspecting mobile missiles.[19]

Easing the Transition for Labor

When military contracts end or threats of war recede, contractors search for ways of keeping their losses at a minimum. Usually their first action is to lay off workers. Unions representing workers in defense plants and industries face the difficult task of helping their members make a transition to jobs with other companies or seek training to extend their skills.

Several key unions represent the employees of defense companies and civilians employed by the U.S. Government at military bases or at the Department of Defense. The National Association of Machinists and Aerospace Workers; the United Auto Workers; the International Union of Electrical Workers; the Oil, Chemical, and Atomic Workers; the International Brotherhood of Electrical Workers; and the American Federation of Government Employees are among the largest and most prominent of AFL-CIO unions that serve defense workers.

Each of these unions has bargained with management regarding benefits workers would receive should the Government cancel defense contracts abruptly. These benefits have included special severance pay, assistance in locating new jobs, and compensation to relocate.

But many companies doing defense business are not in a position to help workers about to be laid off. This is especially true of small businesses, i.e., those with a workforce of less than 500. The U.S. Government has no comprehensive policy or program to assist the unemployed defense worker. The most important program for defense workers losing their jobs is the Displaced Worker Program, administered by the Department of Labor. The program provides retraining for workers who have lost their jobs due to industry or military cutbacks. Funding is also provided for basic needs.

As of mid-1991, reductions in defense spending and employment cutbacks by defense contractors have not been substantial. The Department of Labor reports that $36 million has been distributed to assist workers who are losing their jobs due to the retrenchment in military spending. Programs financed at the national level are needed to ease the transition from a period of high U.S. military activity to a period of preparedness for sustained peace.

A bill, H.R. 4977, dealing with government worker adjustments to cutbacks in defense spending was sponsored in the second session of the 101st Congress by Rep. Paul Kanjorski, chair of the Subcommittee on Human Resources of the House Post Office and Civil Service Committee. This proposed legislation would assist workers at military installations by providing a priority placement to such employees working at bases and other military installations. The bill would also provide job training for workers unable to find suitable work in their area of competence and experience. Congressman Lee Hamilton, from Indiana's 9th District, testified that H.R. 4977 would also offer "expanded health coverage following a base closure or realignment, supplemental severance allowance, and supplemental wage allowances for those who accept a full-time position with a lower wage."[20] Kanjorski's bill was not acted on before Congress went home in late October 1990. It has been reintroduced in 1991. According to Al Bilik, head of the AFL-CIO's Government Employees Department, it was passed in the House and is awaiting action in the Senate.

Another bill, to help non-government defense workers, was introduced as a compromise among several earlier bills by Rep. Mary Rose Oakar (D-OH), and was successfully ushered through the Congress by House Majority Leader Richard Gephardt (D-MO) and others. In 1990 the Council on Economic Priorities testified before three Congressional committees in favor of the bill. The 1990 Conversion Law, described at length in Chapter 6, provides $200 million to assist defense workers in private industry receive compensation and training if defense cutbacks prompt layoffs.

Worker Adjustment Programs enable contractors to soften the blow to employees by offering transitional education, training, and outplacement programs. Involving employees can also assist in the company's adjustment. Rockwell Corporation is credited by John Lynch, former associate director of the Defense Department's Office of Economic Adjustment, with doing an excellent job of trying to help its employees adjust to cuts in the B-1 bomber at their Palmdale facility during the late 1970s. Rockwell provided advance notice well before the shutdown and was very cooperative in assisting the overall community effort.[21] Such programs are discussed in greater detail in Chapter 5, on what communities can do.

In California, Rockwell, General Dynamics, Hughes Aircraft, Lockheed, McDonnell Douglas, Northrop, and TRW helped fund the Aerospace Human Resources Network. Recently shut down for lack of funds, it was run by the state's Employment Development Department, and offered free computerized job and retraining advice for white-collar aerospace employees; a program for blue-collar employees already exists.[22] Textron Corporation has devised a significant program to assist laid-off employees.

A less successful case involved General Electric, which opposed union efforts to make up for lost aircraft engine work at its massive Lynn, MA complex. Four thousand from the 14,000-strong workforce had been let go. Failing in its attempt to get the company to diversify, the union settled for what turned out to be a pioneering effort — the company helped found a retraining and outplacement center. Between April 1987, when the center opened, to May 1989, 1,231 of 2,000 enrollees had been placed in jobs paying them 92 percent of their exit wage.[23]

Selling the plant to employees, notably through Employee Stock Ownership Plans (ESOPs), can be good for the company and also for employees. Government incentives for this purpose are already in place, and some states like New York encourage ESOP growth. ESOPs develop incentives for worker productivity and do not require government outlays. A responsible ESOP plan will provide for adequate management and transition time.[24] A company can be sold to employees in parcels. For example, when the Ford plant closed in Oakton, CA, the servicing of fire trucks was taken over by employees who formed a business with county help.[25]

The Difficulties of Going Commercial

Contractors prosper when they manufacture and build highly complex and precise weapons systems. Cost is not so much a factor as performance, for if a weapon system fails, men and women are likely to die or be seriously injured and our prospects for winning the conflict are diminished.

Companies serving the military have always found the conversion to commercial business difficult. Some have changed their defense/commercial work mix but the crucial questions are: Have they done so by (1) merely losing volume on the military side; (2) buying up existing commercial companies; or (3) retraining and retooling people and plant to meet commercial demand? Honeywell's diversification is based on shedding its defense unit. Likewise for Ford and Chrysler.

Earlier studies in the 1960s and 1970s showed that the first step for defense companies when contracts ended, was to retrench and lay off workers.[26] Another step was to buy companies in the commercial area so as to diversify and maintain sales volume. With over 40 years of experience with the ups and downs of doing business with the Department of Defense, the experienced companies know a lot about downsizing and diversifying.

The Post-Vietnam Conversion Disappointments

Pulling out of Vietnam was bad news for about 1 million defense workers who were let go from 1969 to 1971. That prompted the Senate Government Operations Committee, under the stewardship of former Connecticut Sen. Abraham Ribicoff, to"begin exploring ways of converting the skills, products, and technology developed in our defense and space programs for civilian uses."[27] Ribicoff's Executive Reorganization and Government Research subcommittee polled corporations, labor leaders, and mayors to get a feel for the challenges that lay ahead. Boeing's answer highlighted the expectations of the biggest contractors.

> Boeing examined many of the civil systems markets during the five years following the end of the Vietnam War. These included in-depth studies of surface transportation, water management, waste disposal, and security systems. We find that each of these have elements consistent with our technical and systems management capabilities. However, we do not see either established national goals in these areas, consistent commitment to adequate funding, reasonable-size contracts of adequate duration, or contracting modes consistent with these (civilian markets).[28]

Usually, with only one customer to market products to, marketing in defense is not nearly as difficult as on the commercial side, where the tastes of millions of consumers can change rapidly and force marketing executives to keep their fingers constantly on the pulse of the marketplace. A veteran industry-watcher (and head of the Council of Economic Advisers in the Reagan Administration), Murray Weidenbaum, says "The same factors that make for success in the defense industry make it hard to compete in the commercial sector."[29] Grumman came up with the minivan before Chrysler, but could not match the automotive giant's marketing muscle. Without the assurance of one big, steady customer, big companies have to pinpoint a market and nurture a sales force that can go out and compete. That is getting harder and harder to do in some fields like electronics where the playing field is aswarm with nimble foreigners, long accustomed to servicing consumers.

A Tale of Two Companies: General Dynamics and Textron Move into the 1990s.

According to Lawrence Korb, Assistant Secretary of Defense for Manpower and Logistics in the Reagan Administration, "as the defense budget goes, so goes General Dynamics. If the defense budget goes down by 50 percent, General Dynamics goes down by 50 percent. It's hard to see how they will escape."[30]

This St.-Louis based company is a microcosm of the defense industrial base. Perennially a Top 10 contractor and 85 percent defense-dependent, it is well-diversified within defense, with contracts from all the service branches. It looks like the company is going to stick to its core businesses, whether it downsizes or not.

Companies like Textron are not as dependent on the Department of Defense, and have diversified. During the early 1950s, company founder Royal Little looked for ways to balance the ups and downs of commercial textile work. Soon Textron was into everything from eyeglasses to poultry and lingerie; its Bell subsidiary's "Huey" helicopters found service in Vietnam.

The philosophy of Textron has been to diversify and to limit the impact of the business cycle on the company. In the mid-1950s Textron moved away from textiles to industrial electronics because the latter had "tremendous application for both the military and civilian worlds." Today, of $7.4 billion in sales, 30 percent is in financial services, and 25 percent in the commercial area, e.g., auto parts and outdoor products. The remaining 45 percent is in aerospace, but the defense part is decreasing. Areas of sales include commercial helicopters, aircraft engines and components. Today its 57,000-strong workforce is scattered in 142 plants in 49 states and five foreign countries.

But Textron must face cuts on two major projects — the V-22 "Osprey" and the M-1 tank. Signalling to shareholders that indeed its strength lay in diversity, the company brought on the one-time CEO of Emerson Electronics — a company with limited defense exposure. In testimony before the House Small Business Subcommittee on Procurement, Tourism, and Rural Development, Textron's Director of Government and International Affairs, Steven Wein, emphasized that "defense reductions and program terminations that are implemented are done with sufficient notice to permit workers and companies with time to plan."[31]

The Recipe for Diversification

Can the Smaller Contractors Be Our Guides?

Imagine a voice-recognition device, developed for the intelligence community, marketed to daycare centers, banks, and housebound invalids. Those are just some of the possibilities Carl Guerriri is considering as he positions Electronic Warfare Associates, Inc., based in Vienna, VA.

With a key niche position supplying sophisticated simulation and voice-recognition equipment to the Department of Defense, Guerriri wanted to keep profit margins up in the waning years of the 1980s buildup. A system that can, in seconds, identify a voice as authorized or not, had several natural constituencies: banks with automatic teller machine (ATM) hutches, computer networks seeking to prevent unauthorized access, and daycare centers wanting to ensure that a caller phoning instructions is really the child's parent. Guerriri even thinks there is a demand for customized houses in which a handicapped individual could command lights to go on and off. The system would only respond to that person's voice. Said Guerriri "...there has always been this fence between [government and commercial] business and the other side was forbidden. Now we're allowed to cross that fence."[32]

Special concerns have been raised about the tens of thousands of smaller contractors making up the defense industrial base. Many may not have the wherewithal to test other waters. But their size could be their virtue — without the large bureaucracy and need for huge markets that daunt larger companies they can be more flexible. Furthering the process are clearinghouse-type meetings that have been set up by industry associations and state governments. Then Gov. Richard Celeste of Ohio hosted a January 1990 meeting for midsized contractors to broaden their horizons, especially in the technology crossover area. In mid-June 1990 the American Electronics Association did the same.

California-based Kavlico, with a background in sensors for missiles and aircraft, today sells more than half of its high-tech systems to automotive, ventilation, and heating concerns.[33] Its president, Michael Gibson, said that in the mid-1980s the company had to become proactive, to pursue aggressively new business, and to switch from producing small batches of state-of-the-art systems to mass production. Existing engineering staff, with the aid of an outside-recruited commercial sales force, wrought the needed changes. Sales doubled over the last three years and the payroll went from 250 to 600.

Charles Kaman, president of Kaman Aerospace (Connecticut) and an avid musician, personally spearheaded his company's early-1960s foray into guitar-making, one that took eight years to bear fruit. He saw the possibility of a high-quality, mass-produced guitar based on his engineers' superior knowledge of the physics of vibration. Result: the well-known Ovation guitar, a line that makes money to this day.

AAI Corp. of Maryland found a niche testing diagnostic equipment in hospitals. With a strong military background it plans to go on-site and test all makes and models of hospital diagnostic equipment. From the hospitals' vantage point that's cheaper than having all the original vendors come in.[34]

The path charted by Medina, OH-based Cletronics, Inc. is a diversification beacon. A manufacturer of magnetic parts used in military cameras, it moved into pacemaker accessories, blood monitors, electronic circuit boards, and ultimately into partnership with the prestigious Cleveland Clinic. Most interesting is the way it was done – in tandem with Ohio Gov. Richard Celeste's move to help that state's myriad small- to mid-sized defense contractors through seminars and linkups with state research centers. For Cletronics it was the relationship between the Edison Biotechnology Center that led to the contract for magnetic detection devices with the Cleveland Clinic. According to CEO David Sands, Cletronics has reduced its defense-dependency to 15 percent, from a high of 85 percent.

According to Robert DeGrasse, contributor to a major Department of Defense study on company conversion in 1985: "Ingredients for successful diversification include: (1) planning for change before cuts; (2) thorough market research; (3) an understanding of cost minimization; (4) using the existing workforce; (5) technology transfer; (6) persistence in the face of long-term payoff; and (7) committed leadership."[35] Persistence may be the most important quality. According to industrial reuse specialist Robert Ady of the Chicago-based Fantus Co., the process – from detailed assessments of the workforce and plant through industry screening – lasts an average of five years.[36]

Notes

1. *Department of Defense Budget—Observations on the Future Years Defense Programs*, U.S. General Accounting Office, April 1991, p. 4.

2. Geoffrey K. Bentley, *Overview of the Department of Defense Budget*, Textron Defense Systems, presentation to the Electronic Industries Association, March 26, 1991, p. 7.

3. *Ibid.*, p. 8.

4. *Loc. cit.*

5. *Ibid.*, p. 31.

6. *Defense Reductions and U.S. Manufacturing: What Cuts Mean for Jobs and Output in Specific Industries*, The Manufacturers' Alliance for Productivity and Innovation (MAPI), May 1991, p. iv.

7. *Loc. cit.*

8. Speech of Sen. Sam Nunn, U.S. Senate, March 22, 1990.

9. Mindy Fetterman and Denise Kallette, "Contractors All Scared Right Now," *USA Today*, June 7, 1990.

10. CEP Subcontractor Survey Questionnaire sent to Companies, July 1990.

11. Bentley, *loc. cit.*

12. *Industrial Outlook for 1990*, U.S. Department of Commerce.

13. "Top 100 Defense Contractors," *Research Report*, Council on Economic Priorities, May 1989.

14. *Loc. cit.*

15. *Aerospace Facts and Figures, 1990-1991*, Foreword, Don Fuqua, President, Aerospace Industries Association, p. 8.

16. *Loc. cit.*

17. *Ibid.*, p. 27.

18. *The U.S. Aerospace Industry and the Trend Toward Internationalization*, Aerospace Industries Association of America, March 1989, p. 9.

19. "Top 100...," *op. cit.*

20. Testimony submitted, June 19, 1990, before the House Post Office and Civil Service Subcommittee.

21. For more information: Frank Chabre, vice president, Human Resources,, North American Rockwell, El Segundo, CA, 213-414-1820.

22. Suomisto, Laurel, "Free Jobs Center Opens," *Outlook* (Santa Monica, CA), March 15, 1990.

23. Testimony of John T. Maguire, Codirector, Workers Assistance Center, Lynn, Massachusetts, before the House Banking Committee Subcommittee on Economic Stabilization, June 13, 1989.

24. Dotson Rader, "The Town that Saved Itself: Weirton, West Virginia," and Corey Rosen, "Employee Ownership as a Development Strategy," in Lynch, ed., *Plant Closures and Community Recovery*, National Council for Urban Economic Development, Washington, DC, 1990, pp. 52-53, 165-166.

25. Fawn McLaughlin and Charline O. Speck, "Preventing Job Losses–FMC Fire Truck Plant: Stanislaus County, California," in Lynch, ed., *op. cit.*, pp. 44-45.

26. *Economic Impact of Arms Control Agreements—Data Received from 370 Companies Engaged in Defense Work*, Subcommittee on Disarmament, Senate Committee on Foreign Relations, 1962.

27. Robert W. DeGrasse, "Corporate Diversification and Conversion Experience," in John Lynch, ed., *Economic Adjustment and Conversion of Defense Industries* (Boulder, CO: Westview, 1988), p. 92.

28. *Ibid.*, p. 92.

29. Philip Finnegan, Debra Polsky and David Silverberg, "Defense Realities Find Firms Examining New Markets," *Defense News*, March 26, 1990.

30. Leslie Wayne, "Arms Makers Gird for Peace," *The New York Times*, December 18, 1989, p. F-1.

31. *Testimony of Steven Wein, Director of Government and International Affairs, Textron, before the House Small Business Subcommittee on Procurement, Tourism, and Rural Development, on Review of Issues of Defense Industry Conversion*, Bristol, RI, May 18, 1990.

32. "Top 100 Defense Contractors," *op. cit.*

33. Louise McNeilly, "Braving the New World," *Plowshare* (Newsletter of the Center for Economic Conversion, Mountain View, CA), Winter 1990.

34. Ted Shelsby, "AAI Finds Health Care the Best Defense," *Baltimore Sun*, April 19, 1990, p. E-1.

35. *Economic Adjustment and Conversion*, Report prepared by the Economic Adjustment Committee and the Office of Economic Adjustment, Department of Defense, Washington, DC, 1985.

36. *Loc. cit.*

2

Impact on Bases and the Nuclear Weapons Complex

Military Bases and Nuclear Weapons Facilities

Uncle Sam is a very large property owner. Each of the 50 states provides land to the Federal Government for military bases and training facilities. In addition to these, an impressive array of naval and land bases is deployed in various parts of the globe. As of 1988 the U.S. maintained 871 military installations and properties within the U.S. and another 375 overseas. In the U.S., West Virginia had the fewest military facilities with two, and California the most with 105.[1] The cost of operating these bases worldwide amounts to approximately $17 billion a year.[2] In addition, the Department of Energy maintains several weapons facilities, including the seven plants to produce material for nuclear weapons. (See Chapter 3 for details on U.S. nuclear weapons laboratories.)

Every Congressional District in the U.S. houses government facilities connected with the military establishment. On behalf of their constituencies members of Congress compete for bases, contracts to build weapons, supply food, or construct military facilities.

The Dependency Syndrome

Military bases have become a way of life for many communities, providing jobs, tax revenue, local retail and service establishments, and indirectly, revenue for local facilities and merchants. This income can be crucial for the maintenance of schools, roads, police protection, and sanitation facilities.

Members of Congress win plaudits from voters when they bring home funds to build a military base or hospital, or a contract to produce bombers, tanks, and submarines locally. If a base is threatened by closure, community leaders and elected officials often lobby to keep the facility open.

When Robert McNamara became Secretary of Defense in the Kennedy Administration, he undertook a study of U.S. bases, and concluded that many were superfluous and could be converted to civilian use. McNamara closed or reduced activities at 954 military bases and industrial activities in the U.S. Approximately 220,000 civilian and military positions were eliminated.[3]

To manage base closing, in the early 1960s McNamara created the Office of Economic Adjustment (OEA) and housed it in the Department of Defense. The economic adjustment mission was broadened in May 1970 by the creation of the inter-agency Economic Adjustment Committee (EAC) composed of representatives from 18 departments and agencies. (See Table 2.1 below, for a full list of the members.)

Departments and agencies included on the EAC were the Departments of Agriculture, Commerce, Defense, Education, Energy, Health & Human Services, Housing and Urban Development, Interior, Justice, Labor, and Transportation. Agencies on the EAC which can also be helpful include the Council

Table 2.1
President's Economic Adjustment Committee
(May 1990)

Agriculture	La Verne Ausman	202-447-4581
Commerce	David McIlvin	202-377-2659
Defense	Robert M. Rauner	703-697-9155
	Paul J. Dempsey	703-695-1800
Army	Gordon M. Hobbs	703-695-0867
Navy	Frederick S. Starns	703-692-7076
Air Force	James F. Boatwright	202-695-3592
Defense Logistics	Roger Roy	703-274-6271
Education	Thomas E. Anfinson	202-732-5470
Energy	James Threeheld	202-586-5544
Health, Hum. Serv.	Ann Agnew	202-245-3400
Housing & Urb. Dev.	Carl D. Covitz	202-755-7123
Interior	Dr. Andrew Adams	202-343-5521
Justice	J. Michael Quinlan	202-724-6300
Labor	Dr. James Van Erden	202-535-0540
Transportation	Angelo P. Picillo	202-366-9724
Coun. Econ. Advisors	Carole Kitti	202-395-5012
Office of Management & Bud.	Daniel Taft	202-395-3285
Arms Control & Disarm. Agency	Daniel Gallick	202-647-1300
Environmental Protection Agency	Richard E. Sanderson	202-382-5053
General Services Administration	John Meade	202-535-7084
Small Business Administration	Gene Van Arsdale	202-653-6588
Office of Personnel Management	Len Klein	202-632-6005

Source: Office of Economic Adjustment, Defense Department.

on Economic Advisers, the Office of Management & Budget, the Arms Control and Disarmament Agency, Environmental Protection Agency, General Services Administration, the Small Business Administration, and the Office of Personnel Management.

In each community where a base was to close, the EAC organized a team which met with local officials, business and labor leaders, bankers, educational leaders, and heads of various economic enterprises. Together, these officials devised a plan for the reuse of the military base.

A critical factor in the degree of success of the economic adjustment plans was the ability of community leaders to work together and provide updated knowledge concerning plans for base reuse. Local bankers met — some for the first time — and arranged loans or other means of financing conversion of the base. OEA also provided planning grants for community groups charged with finding new tenants for a base. John Lynch, former associate director of OEA, reported that "the experience of numerous communities across the nation demonstrates that local areas can recover effectively from defense base closure dislocations."[4]

For 16 years OEA and EAC worked to facilitate the closing of military bases and other government defense facilities. Hundreds of bases were closed, including 60 major bases. In 1977, however, Congress mandated that its approval be secured for any base closure affecting 300 or more civilian employees of the Department of Defense. Moreover, it also required the Department "to comply with the procedural requirements of the National Environmental Policy Act for all base closure decisions." These Congressional obstacles were designed in part to prevent further base closure decisions.

Commission Recommends Base Closures

As the U.S. budget deficit grew and the Gramm-Rudman-Hollings law mandated a balanced budget by 1994, the Secretary of Defense proposed on May 3, 1988 that a Base Closing Commission be appointed,[5] and Congress agreed. The Commission, co-chaired by two former Congressional leaders, Sen. Abraham Ribicoff and Rep. Jack Edwards, met for several months and submitted a report on December 29, 1988 recommending that 86 military facilities and properties be closed, five partially closed, and 54 "experience a change, either an increase or a decrease as units and activities are relocated."[6] In its report the Commission stated that the annual savings resulting from its recommendations would be $694 millions.[7] The Secretary of Defense accepted all of the Commission's recommendations on January 5, 1989.

The law establishing the Commission stipulated that once it had concluded its work and made its recommendations, the Congress would be given only one choice — to accept or reject the Commission's recommendations as a whole. This provision removed painful decisions on specific cuts for many members of Congress. The law also specified that it would come into force 45 legislative days later unless overturned by a Resolution of Disapproval by Congress. No such resolution was passed.[8]

The Commission's recommendations affected 145 bases that have subsequently been closed, partially closed, or realigned. The Commission had also wanted to recommend actions to close or realign government-owned, contractor operated facilities which were not covered by the law. These include government plants such as those used by private companies, under contract with the Department of Defense. These facilities were not covered by the law, however. The Commission did recommend that such facilities be included in any future effort at base and facilities realignment.

Communities View Their Military Bases

Most military bases within the continental U.S. are located in the South (36.1 percent) and West (31.1 percent) and are usually in communities with a population of from 10,000 to 25,000. When a base closes or when a base is about to be located in a community for the first time OEA sends a representative to the town or city to assist with any problems that may have arisen or will presumably occur in the future.

From its creation in 1961, OEA has played a significant role in assisting communities about to lose a defense facility or, in the less common case, when the influx of military personnel in a community has caused crowding. During this period of over 30 years, OEA has found that establishing a base-community council is an essential instrument to facilitate good community-base relations.

In Virginia, for example, the Governor's office took an initiative and established the Virginia Military Advisory Council. This group focused on major questions and it created instruments to deal with them. One agreement concerned firefighting personnel and equipment. Another dealt with assistance to military personnel who remained in the community after their retirement. Provision of mutual support services to military personnel by the State Government included police and fire protection, refuse collection, transportation, public works infrastructure, education, waste water treatment, and drug abuse education. In a survey conducted, 254 respondents (65.6%) stated that impact aid was received, but many of the respondents (52.6%) felt that the aid did not meet the need created by the existence of the base. The Department of Defense's Economic Adjustment Office has a responsibility to report to Congress if aid supplied to communities is insufficient. The Congress thus must be informed by the EAC if additional appropriations are needed. In communities with a military installation, an average of almost 14 percent of students in kindergarten through the 12th grade were military dependents. Between 47.2% of communities in the West and 52.6% of those in the Northeast stated that impact aid provided by the military to defray educational costs of educating children of military families was insufficient.

The law establishing the Commission specifies that state and local governments must be consulted in the civilian reuse of the former military property.

Surplus property at military bases may be transferred or sold to other departments of the U.S. Government or state and local governments provided they pay fair market value for such property or facilities.

The Finances of Base Closures

In the 1960s and 70s, the EAC acted quickly to assist local communities to adjust to and take advantage of base closures. Between 1973 and 1980, the EAC granted an average of $85 million a year to help communities mitigate difficulties arising from base closures. These funds were used for such purposes as planning, building infrastructure, and providing municipal services.

The communities themselves played the major role in adjusting to base closures. They "assembled dedicated teams that not only drafted ambitious plans but also made their cases effectively to public agencies and private companies, often travelling extensively to do so... The communities went to great lengths to make themselves and the former bases attractive to investors and business. Roads were built, sewer pipe was laid, and services were improved."[10]

Beginning in the 1980s the Federal Government modified its approach. It has endeavored to realize as much of a return as possible on the disposal of assets. Unfortunately, this policy can conflict with the interests of the affected community, which would prefer that property be conveyed quickly so that adjustments to base closings can begin. When the Government decides to wait for the highest bids on property, it may delay and frustrate the community's plans for recovery.

A major problem confronting communities losing military bases is the loss of revenue. In the past this loss was alleviated in part by the EAC, which provided, between 1966 and 1986, over $500 million in adjustment assistance to communities affected by base closures.[11] Between 1975 and 1980 the Commerce Department's Economic Development Administration provided $57.5 million to 31 base redevelopment projects. In 1988 the assistance to communities decreased further with the Economic Development Administration providing only $12 million for such adjustment grants.

State development agencies have had to act where the U.S. Government has abandoned economic adjustment in cases of base closures. Every state today has a development agency with a budget ranging from $360,000 to over $180 million.[12] "These agencies provide technical and managerial assistance, trade promotion, financial aid, training programs, and tax incentives."[13] Some states maintain offices in foreign countries.

Congress Reacts Against Base Closures

On January 29, 1990, Secretary of Defense Dick Cheney, responding to the major changes taking place in Europe and the Soviet Union, recommended further reductions in the U.S. military establishment. He recommended that additonal military bases and installations be closed. Congress, reacting to the unilateral nature of the Secretary's actions, passed the Defense Base Closure and Realignment Act of 1990. The purpose of this Act was to halt any unilateral base closure actions of the Defense Secretary.[14]

On April 12, 1991 the Executive branch and the Congress agreed on the criteria against which the list of proposed military installation closures and realignments was to be measured. Four of the criteria concerned the military value of the installations; and others focused on the "number of years needed to recover the costs of closure and realignment; the economic impact on communities; the ability of the communities to support the forces to be housed in the particular localities; and the environmental impact."[15] In light of these criteria the Department of Defense was able to select 43 bases for closure and 28 for realignment.

Base Closure Criteria

As a result of negotiations and subsequent action by the Secretary of Defense and the Congress, base closure can take place under existing U.S law. Secretary Cheney made proposals on February 8, 1990 to streamline the base closure process. These included:

- Priority is given to criteria related to the military value of the base;
- Use of the OEA to calculate the economic impact of the proposed closure, including changes in employment at each base; and
- Consideration of key environmental factors.

The process of closing bases used by the Department of Defense also includes the establishment of a temporary account to fund the closure process. The General Services Administration has authority to sell and dispose of property. The proceeds of property sales are to be deposited in the base closure account where they will offset costs of implementing closures.

The Base Closure Commission recommended that the Department of Defense assist its employees affected by base closures, including especially the already existing Homeowners Assistance Program and the Priority Placement Program. Civilian employees of the Department who lose their jobs as a result of base closures should be guaranteed jobs within the Department at least at their current grade level.[16]

The Department of Labor has funds to assist personnel losing jobs as a result of the base closure process. To date little of the money has been used because layoffs have not occurred in large numbers.

Evaluation by General Accounting Office

As the 1990 Commission on Base Realignments and Closures was completing its report and providing guidance to the Department of Defense on its handling of this major adjustment, the General Accounting Office began a detailed evaluation of the Commission's work. This was requested by the Chairman and ranking minority members of the Senate and House Armed Services committees. The General Accounting Office's report criticized the Commission's work. It examined the recommendations for 15 base closures, representing some 90 percent of the savings estimated to result from the Commission's conclusions, and said the Commission had overestimated such savings by about $170 million out of a total of almost $700 million it said would result from the closures. The General Accounting Office reported, however, that "even considering the errors in base rankings and cost estimates, the recommendations are still sound and logical." The General Accounting Office concluded that the actions by the Department of Defense "represents a significant start in the process to propose bases for closure and realignment every other year for the next six years."[17]

The General Accounting Office also agreed with the Commission that "because the Department of Defense is already responsible for hazardous waste cleanup, these costs are not a consequence of the Commission's decisions to realign or close bases. The General Accounting Office also agreed that a more detailed examination of the economic impact on communities would have required more time than was available to the Commission.

Employment Impact Affects Thousands

As a result of the actions by the Base Closure Commission, it is estimated that approximately 7,718 civilian positions will be eliminated.[18] When bases are scheduled for closing, military personnel can be transferred to other bases or duties. But when civilians are involved, layoffs often occur. In both cases, the community loses revenue and thus its tax base is weakened.

The Public Employee Department of the AFL-CIO in January 1990 prepared for its members working at the Department of Defense and military installations, a comprehensive listing of programs available to Federal Civilian Employees who may be affected by the base closures. The document provides a discussion of these programs, gives specific instructions about steps to take for future employment,[19] and also discusses programs to assist states and localities. During the 1980s most Federal programs to help employees laid off because of base closures and other retrenchment were significantly cut back. Under the Base Closure and Realignment Act of 1988, however, "Congress authorized the Secretary of Defense to provide economic adjustment and community planning assistance if other funding sources are inadequate." The Public Employee Department of the AFL-CIO plans to lobby Congress to "help assure that sufficient funds are appropriated for dealing with the local impact of the coming base closures and reductions."[20]

Legislation sponsored by Rep. Paul Kanjorski (D-PA), would give laid-off civilian defense personnel first crack at vacancies at all Federal agencies, as well as extending their health benefits and giving them training assistance at a cost of $50 to $100 million. "We don't want the reaction to base closures to be so traumatic...as to inhibit base closures," said Kanjorski.[21] The Kanjorski bill is fashioned after the Trade Adjustment Assistance program for workers who lose jobs because of foreign competition.

Military personnel leaving the armed services and employees of defense contractors can receive assistance from the Department of Labor for training in new skills and be referred to jobs available through government programs or private industry. The Labor Department's program is the main channel of the Federal Government in providing a means to employment for those who fall victim to lay-offs due to changes in U.S. defense requirements. Since the Department of Defense plans to scale back military forces significantly, it will need to rely on the Labor Department's Manpower Training Programs throughout the period of shifting workers to help meet non-military needs.[22]

Base Conversion Works

Evidence compiled by the Department of Defense, reported by 100 communities that underwent adjustments over a 25-year period, indicates that base closings or conversions can be handled so that communities and workers do not suffer dramatically.[23]

- New Jobs Replaced Department of Defense Civilian Losses: Jobs lost as a result of base closings, numbered 93,424, but the gain in employment, 138,138, exceeded the loss by a substantial margin.
- New Educational Opportunities: Twelve four-year colleges, 32 post-secondary vocational technical institutes or community colleges, and 14 high-school "vocational-technical" programs were developed at the former bases. The "vo-tech" programs have been crucial in economic development plans for the affected communities.
- Student Enrollments: 53,744 college and post-secondary students, 7,864 secondary "vo-tech" students; and 8,110 trainees are being educated at 57 former bases.
- Industrial and Aviation Uses: Seventy-five former bases were turned into office-industrial parks; and 42 into municipal/general aviation airports. Table 2.2 below, provides a breakdown of community reuse of 100 converted bases.

Sacramento Plans for the Future

The case of Sacramento County in California typifies what confronts other communities faced with base closings. The Air Force will close Mather Air Force Base, which houses a wing of Strategic Air Command B-52s and a squadron of reserve tankers.

Local officials moved quickly on news of the planned 1992 shutdown, according to Paul Sileni of the city's Chamber of Commerce. The Mather Reuse Commission, formed in conjunction with Rep. Bob Matsui (D-CA), wants to

Table 2.2 The Record on Military Base Reuse

State	Bases Closed	Became: Schools	Industrial Parks	Public Use
Alabama	5	3	13	4
Alaska	1	–	–	4
California	8	2	2	13
Colorado	1	–	–	1
Florida	–	–	19	5
Georgia	2	–	5	4
Illinois	2	–	2	2
Indiana	2	2	7	1
Kansas	2	1	9	5
Louisiana	3	4	8	3
Maine	3	2	8	5
Maryland	1	–	30	–
Massachusetts	7	1	40	6
Michigan	1	–	7	2
Minnesota	3	1	2	3
Mississippi	1	–	3	1
Missouri	2	2	9	2
Montana	3	–	4	3
Nebraska	4	3	13	3
Nevada	1	1	2	1
New Hampshire	1	–	6	1
New Jersey	4	4	23	12
New Mexico	1	1	2	–
New York	7	–	13	9
North Carolina	1	–	3	2
Ohio	5	4	20	5
Oklahoma	1	1	4	1
Oregon	1	1	1	2
Pennsylvania	5	2	5	3
Puerto Rico	2	1	9	3
Rhode Island	2	–	13	1
South Carolina	1	–	7	2
South Dakota	1	–	1	–
Tennessee	1	–	3	2
Texas	9	7	27	14
Washington	1	–	4	1
Wisconsin	1	1	4	1
Total	100	44	339	125

Source: President's Commission on Economic Adjustment, 1986.

turn the base into a commercial airport.[24] While not minimizing the impact Mather's 5,000 employees and $150-million payroll have on the local economy, Sileni says its closure is not a life-and-death situation. Since the 1970s, defense-related work has declined from 15 percent of the regional economy to 6 percent.

With 6,000 acres and two landing strips that handle giant B-52s and C-5A cargo planes, the base is ideally suited for commercial reuse, according to Dick Wolgamott of the County Executive's Office. Since restrictive zoning kept developers from building to the edges of the base, no residential lobby against it has emerged, while a call to reduce air traffic congestion over San Jose and San Francisco has forced more regional air traffic to Sacramento.

A county official reported that if the city elects to use the base as an airstrip, the Air Force will turn it over for nothing, or for one dollar. If not, then the Air Force, with a mandate to get the best possible deal, could sell to the highest bidder. With California being such a population magnet, "developers would love to get their hands on the land," says Sileni. Several commercial airlines want to set up maintenance depots, and the State Forestry Department also has expressed interest in the facility.[25]

The General Accounting Office was asked by Congress to evaluate the recommendations of the Base Closure Commission. The General Accounting Office used four criteria related to the military value of the installations and four that addressed the number of years for the U.S. Government to recover the costs of closure and realignment. Based on these criteria the General Accounting Office found that the Army and the Air Force recommendations regarding closure or realignment were satisfactory. It was less satisfied with the Navy's process for reaching its decisions. As regards the Navy, the General Accounting Office concluded that the navy had excess berthing capacity which would justify reductions in naval bases.

The Nuclear Weapons Production Complex

A significant part of the U.S. weapons complex, less known to the outside world than military bases, is responsible for the testing and production of nuclear weapons.

From the beginning of the atomic age in 1945, nuclear weapons have been considered apart from the regular military budget. Because of the enormous destructive power of nuclear weapons, the Congress in 1945 established the Joint Committee on Atomic Energy with jurisdiction over all activities concerned with these weapons.

Later, when the Department of Energy was created, the Joint Committee was abolished and Congress created committees on energy in the House and Senate. The Department of Energy's budget of $10.9 billion for FY 1991 contained funding for the main defense functions of the Department: nuclear weapons testing and production. Production of plutonium and highly enriched uranium for over 40 years has enabled the U.S. to stockpile an enormous number of nuclear weapons now exceeding 25,000. The Soviet stockpile is comparable.[26]

Efforts to persuade the U.S. Government to seek an end or curtailment of nuclear weapons testing and production have failed. At present there are no plans by the Bush Administration to limit or reduce nuclear weapons stockpiles of the two major nuclear powers.

Action by the international community may eventually change the U.S. position. The Limited Test Ban Treaty (LTBT) of 1963 specifies that if over one-third of the signatories to the Treaty request a conference to change it from a limited to a comprehensive one (that would ban all testing), that conference must be held. The international organization, Parliamentarians Global Action, initiated such an effort and the conference began its deliberations in January 1991.[27] While such a change in the LTBT was recommended by a majority of U.N. members, the U.S., the Soviet Union, and United Kingdom have the power to veto such a move. The current position of the U.S. is to oppose any effort to negotiate a comprehensive ban on nuclear weapons testing or production.

Much of the work of the Department of Energy is shrouded in secrecy. The nature, amount and size of weapons tests are not made public. Nor are production figures for the nuclear weapons stockpile made available.

The culture of secrecy concerning all aspects of nuclear weapons testing and production may account in part for the disaster that now engulfs the nuclear weapons industry. As far back as March 25, 1986, Sen. John Glenn (D-OH) testified before the Senate Committee on Environment and Public Works that: "For over 40 years, Department of Energy and its predecessor agencies have self-managed, without oversight from other agencies, the treatment, storage, and disposal of defense-related wastes. Some of Department of Energy's waste disposal methods... have involved such questionable practices as draining liquid radioactive and hazardous wastes into unlined ponds, and dumping such solid waste into open, unlined trenches or burial grounds..."[28] The Senate Government Operations Committee estimated that the cost of the cleanup to the taxpayers may amount to $100 billion.[30]

Extent of Contamination and Possible Cleanup Costs

The Department of Energy announced in mid-1988 that 16 sites were contaminated with radioactive and chemical pollution[29] They are located in California, Colorado, Florida, Idaho, Missouri, New Mexico, Ohio, South Carolina, Tennessee, Texas, Washington, and the Marshall Islands. According to the Energy Department, the Hanford reactor complex, near Richland, WA might require $46.5 billion to be cleaned up, and the Savannah River reactor in South Carolina could involve $9.3 billion in cleanup charges.[30] An energy advisory group recommended new reactors be built at Savannah River because all three existing ones were too old.

Victor S. Rezendes, Director of the General Accounting Office's Energy Issues, Resources, Community and Economic Development unit, testified before the House Armed Services Committee in March 1990, and reported that 3,500 inactive waste sites throughout the complex needed to be cleaned up, with the cleanup cost estimated at $25 billion to $65 billion.[31] These cost estimates do not include the expense of disposing of radioactive waste. The time period required for these tasks is expected to be 20 years. Ground water at Department of Energy sites was contaminated with "hazardous radioactive material," some at levels hundreds to thousands of times above drinking water standards. The Department of Energy admitted having difficulty in finding a geological repository for the disposal of high-level radioactive waste. The General Accounting Office report, one of 35 it has issued on the issue since 1981, also said the Department of Energy's problems were "compounded by a management attitude in Department of Energy that emphasized the production of nuclear materials over environment, safety, and health concerns."[32] Sen. Cohen of Maine cited a report of 1988 and complained that "dumping radioactive and toxic materials cannot be continued for very long...there have been 40 years of neglect."[33]

Former Energy Secretary John Herrington conceded that "for 15 years this whole defense complex was allowed to go to seed...[and] that severe problems with safety, equipment, and management are wracking the nuclear weapons industry in the U.S." Herrington admitted that "neither he nor anyone else could say whether years of radioactive emissions from plants in Washington, Ohio, South Carolina, and Colorado, posed a risk to public health."[34] This major environmental problem prompted Rep. Pat Schroeder (D-CO) and Sen. Joe Biden (D-DE) to call for a "nuclear industry watchdog." Also in response to these disclosures, Idaho's Gov. Andrus banned shipments of plutonium-contaminated waste for storage at Idaho's National Energy Laboratory; and twelve Democratic members of Congress wrote to the President recommending that the nuclear plant at Savannah River be closed.[35]

The General Accounting Office report of June 13, 1990 covered three years of investigation.[36] It noted that the Energy Department had "estimated that its cleanup plan would cost about $19.1 billion from 1991 through 1995" and that "cost estimates will probably increase over the next five years." The General Accounting Office said the technologies that could reduce further cleanup costs "were years away from application" and that cleanup goals "will require a strong, nationwide commitment over the next 30 years." In another report the General Accounting Office found that "cost estimates ranged from $100 billion to over $155 billion, and that these costs could differ from the estimates due to lack of specific cleanup procedures, facility construction cost overruns, and the cost of building new production reactors." The General Accounting Office said "Department of Energy may not have sufficient technical expertise to accomplish all of the required tasks."

The Employment Impact of Prolonged Closures or Shutdowns

Most of the Energy Department installations are owned by the Government and operated by private contractors. Any employment impact would be mostly felt by these private contract employees.

The vast number of problems facing the nuclear weapons industry raises anew the question of whether the U.S. should seek an arms control agreement with the Soviet Union and possibly other nuclear powers to stop the production of fissionable material for use in nuclear weapons as well as stopping nuclear weapons production altogether. Only once, in the 1960s, was this question considered positively by U.S. policymakers. Given the active interest of the Soviet Union in arms control as well as the billions of taxpayer dollars required to start up and build new facilities, the time might be ripe for bringing this question before the Congress, the President, and the concerned public. Stopping production of nuclear weapons and the materials needed to make them does not eliminate the current stockpile. But negotiating a verifiable international agreement to stop production could become a giant step forward toward a nuclear weapons-free world. Considerable research has been conducted on how such an arms control measure would be verified.[37]

In addition to the efforts of the General Accounting Office to alert the Congress to health and safety problems at the weapons complex, the House of Representatives initiated an effort to urge the Reagan Administration to negotiate a plutonium production cutoff with the Soviet Union. Such an action would affect production of nuclear weapons and production materials such as uranium, plutonium, and tritium. The House rarely takes such arms control initiatives, and in this case the House advocates of a cutoff prevailed in a vote of 284 to 138 to urge negotiations. The Senate did not participate in this effort however.[38]

Notes

1. Department of Defense, "Defense 88" Published bimonthly by the American Forces Information Service, Alexandria, VA.

2. *The Great Base Closing Ploy*, Democratic Study Group, U.S. House of Representatives, March 24, 1990.

3. Lynch, John E., ed. *Economic Adjustment and Conversion of Defense Industries*, Westview Special Studies in Public Policy and Public Systems Management, Boulder, Colorado, 1987, pp. 16-17.

4. *Ibid.*, p.89.

5. *Base Closure and Realignment Act, Public Law 100-526.* October 24, 1988. Appendix B. Base Realignments and Closures, p. 38.

6. *Report of the President's Commission on Base Realignment and Closure*, December 29, 1988.

7. *Ibid.*

8. *Military Bases: An Analysis of the Commission's Realignment and Closure Recommendations*, U.S. General Accounting Office, Washington, DC, November 1989.

9. *Developing Exemplary Civilian-Military Relations*, EAC and OEA, Department of Defense, Washington, DC 20301-4000, July 1989.

10. *Ibid.*, p. 26.

11. *Loc. cit.*

12. *Ibid.*, p. 28.

13. *Loc. cit.*

14. *Military Bases: Observations on the Analyses Supporting Proposed Closures and Realignments, Report to the Congress and the Chairman, Defense Base Closure and Realignment Commission*, General Accounting Office, May 1991, p. 2.

15. *Ibid.*, p. 3.

16. *Ibid.*, p. 29.

17. *Ibid.*, p. 3.

18. *Loc. cit.*

19. *Military Base Closures, Federal Programs to Assist Civilian Employees and their Communities,* Public Employee Department, AFL-CIO, January 1990, p. 1.

20. *Loc. cit.*

21. *Ibid.*, pp. 3-20.

22. Rafshoon, Ellen, "Workers Riffed by Base Closings Could Pick from More Choices," *Federal Times*, June 18, 1990, p. 7.

23. *Twenty-five Years of Civilian Reuse*, EAC.

24. "Regional Responses to Defense Cuts," *Research Report*, Council on Economic Priorities, October 1989.

25. *Ibid.*, p. 3.

26. *Budget of the U.S. Government, Fiscal Year 1991, Atomic Energy, Senate-House Conference Agreement*, October 16, 1990, p. 90.

27. United Nations Special Session to consider transforming the Limited Test Ban Treaty of 1963 into a comprehensive treaty, New York, January 1991.

28. *Mixed Radioactive and Hazardous Waste Disposal Issues, Joint Hearing before the Subcommittee on Nuclear Regulation and Environmental Pollution of the Committee on Environment and Public Works*, U.S. Senate, 99th Congress, March 25, 1986, p. 3.

29. Reports on contamination of nuclear weapons facilities in *The New York Times*, December 3, 1989 (Rocky Flats, CO); December 10, 1989 (Pantex Plant, Amarillo, TX); and December 14, 1989 (Nevada Test Site; Idaho Chemical Processing Plant, Idaho Falls, ID; Savannah River Plant, Aiken, SC; and the Hanford Plant, Richland, WA).

30. *Ibid.*

31. *Statement of Victor S. Rezendes before the Defense Nuclear Facilities Panel, House Armed Services Committee*, March 15, 1990.

32. *Ibid.*, p. 5.

33. Hearings before the Senate Armed Services Committee, May-June 1989.

34. *Loc. cit.*

35. *Loc. cit.*

36. General Accounting Office, *Statement* of Norman J. Rabkin, National Security and International Affairs Division before the Subcommittee on Environment, Energy, and Natural Resources, Committee on Government Operations, House of Representatives, on Department of Defense Management of Hazardous Materials, June 28, 1990.

37. Frank Von Hippel, David Albright, and Barbara Levi, "Stopping the Production of Fissile Materials for Weapons," *Scientific American*, September 1985, p. 40.

38. *Arms Control Today*, August 1989, p. 31.

3

Impact on the National Labs

The Labs and the "New World Order"

The 1990s may focus on a new world order, less oriented to weapons building and more concerned with solving problems of energy, environment, income distribution, and employment throughout the world. How will U.S. weapons laboratories relate to this incipient new world order?

In the mid-1940s, the U.S. moved from the challenge of fighting a World War to waging a Cold War. With the hope that technology would provide effective weapons against potential adversaries, the nation's leaders initiated a rapid expansion of the scientific community. A major part of this effort was the growth of what are known today as the national nuclear weapons laboratories: Lawrence Livermore, Los Alamos, and Sandia.

The Los Alamos National Laboratory (Los Alamos) was created as part of the Manhattan Project during the World War II, while Lawrence Livermore National Laboratory (Livermore) was created in 1952 by the Atomic Energy Commission (AEC) and the University of California. The Sandia laboratory was expanded by AT&T in 1949, at the urging of President Harry Truman, to join the weapons research effort.

From their inception, the primary mission of these laboratories has been the advancement of nuclear-weapons technology. Since the first nuclear explosives were detonated over Japan, the pursuit of national security has meant, in considerable part, the ability to visit more destruction upon an enemy than he is able to deliver to the U.S. and its allies. The major role of the weapons laboratories has been to provide nuclear weapons designs that would most effectively and reliably meet the military requirements to accomplish this mission.[1]

Early History of the Labs

Two of the weapons laboratories, Los Alamos and Sandia, were built in the New Mexico desert, while the third, Livermore, is located in California. During the last 45 years, scientists and engineers at the labs have designed hundreds of different models of nuclear warheads, and have worked to optimize them for deployment on land, air, and sea.

While the bulk of work done at the labs initially had nuclear weapons as its focus, over the years actual research has broadened from bomb design to encompass many other scientific and engineering fields, including new energy technologies, magnetic and laser fusion, and biomedical research. However, research and development continue on new designs for nuclear weapons, nuclear weapons safety and reliability, and attempts to improve the basic understanding of the physics involved in nuclear explosions.

U.S. Nuclear Weapons Policy at a Crossroads

The future of the nuclear weapons labs and related facilities had not as of mid-1991 been raised as an important policy issue in Congress or the Executive branch. But with the Cold War ending and U.S. Government deficits rising, the continued presence of these facilities raises questions that the Executive branch and lawmakers in Congress need to address.

In the post-Cold War world, what purpose do the nuclear weapons labs fulfill? Are expenditures of over $10 billion annually to maintain these nuclear weapons labs, testing sites, and production plants, justified?

If the U.S. pursued a policy of negotiating arms control agreements with nuclear weapons powers and other countries to reduce the importance of nuclear weapons in national security, how would the weapons labs be affected?

What alternative options exist to place nuclear weapons stockpiles, weapons plants, and testing facilities in "mothballs" until the Executive branch and Congress can decide what future role, if any, they have in national and international security?

Would U.S. national security be enhanced if the nuclear powers agreed to negotiate agreements to stop nuclear weapons testing and halt production of these weapons?

Nuclear weapons facilities in the U.S. have been closed for some time due to contamination of the area surrounding such weapons facilities. As will be discussed later in this chapter, is the public interest best served by closing the plants and paying the billions for cleanup costs or must nuclear weapons production, testing, and stockpiling, continue? In short, given today's world what is the preferred policy for handling nuclear weapons issues?

The three weapons laboratories represent some of the greatest concentration of technical expertise and equipment in the country. They employ thousands of scientists and engineers, and house some of the most sophisticated computing equipment in the world. Their combined annual budget is $3 billion.

Since many of their present, nuclear-deterrence-oriented, activities may be curtailed, it remains for these scientific resources to be refocused on new tasks and national problems. The labs may have to adapt to changing global circumstances by modifying the direction of their research activities toward such problems as the energy and environmental crises.

The administrators of the laboratories have not been oblivious to these changes, and the laboratories have already broadened their activities to include a variety of non-nuclear programs, both military and civilian. In a recent report to the U.S. Senate, the director of Los Alamos pointed out that "this is an opportune time to re-examine the directions of the laboratories since... we face changing requirements for nuclear weapons as we are about to enter nuclear arms treaties with the Soviet Union."[2]

The fact that the laboratories are searching for alternative missions is a clear indication that there is political space in which to implement changes in the nation's research priorities. For the first time in four decades, the U.S. stands at a point at which the nation may decide to shift the attention of many scientists and engineers away from nuclear explosives to other, more socially productive, projects.

National Defense and the National Nuclear Labs

The largest funder of activities at the national labs is the Department of Energy, for which the national labs perform nuclear weapons research. The Department of Defense also sponsors a large number of non-nuclear weapons research projects.

Nuclear Weapons Research.

The lion's share of research programs at the weapons laboratories falls under the broad category of Department of Energy nuclear defense programs. These programs comprise 53 percent, 46 percent, and 62 percent of the total budgets of Los Alamos, Livermore and Sandia respectively.[3] Table 3.1 below provides funding details of the activities of the three labs' nuclear research programs. The total personnel force at the labs is 24,322 as of 1990. These programs cover a wide range of areas pertinent to nuclear defense; some deal with offensive destructive capability, while others aim to improve the safety and

Table 3.1
Funding of Nuclear Weapons Research, FY 1988*

	Los Alamos	Livermore	Sandia
Weapons Activities	$363.6	$380.2	$601.0
Verification and Control	30.7	24.1	43.2
Safeguards and Security	14.5	3.1	13.3
Materials Production	32.8	68.5	0.0
Defense Waste Management	8.5	13.1	25.0
Total DoE Defense	450.1	489.0	6826.
DoE Defense as % of total	53.0	46.3	62.1
Total Funding	$850.0	$1,055.6	$1,100.0

*-$Millions. *Source:* Lab national plans. Notes 4, 5, 6.

maintenance of nuclear weapons. Some of these programs will diminish with the reduced Soviet threat.

The labs conduct nuclear weapons research in five main areas: weapons activities, verification and arms control, safeguards and security, materials production, and defense waste management. Personnel for these research activities in 1990 totalled 7,658.

The major portion of research activity (about 80 percent of the Department of Energy nuclear defense program) falls under the "Weapons Activities" category. This is the category that would be most affected as a result of a reduced need for nuclear weapons. Weapons research, development, and testing programs aim to develop smaller and deadlier nuclear devices, insure that existing nuclear devices in the stockpile will continue to function as they age, and explore ways in which nuclear explosions may be used on new types of weapons.

The weapons labs have produced every design of nuclear bomb deployed in the country's arsenal. Los Alamos designs have included the W76 bomb, used on the Trident I submarine-launched missile, the W80-1, used on air-launched cruise missiles, and the W78 used on the Minuteman III Intercontinental Ballistic Missile (ICBM).[4] Livermore designs include the W48-artillery fired warhead and the W87 MX missile warhead.[5] While Los Alamos and Livermore are responsible for the design of the nuclear explosives, Sandia's primary role is "the weaponization of all nuclear explosives designed by Los Alamos or Livermore." Weaponization includes the development of the"safing, arming, fuzing, and firing [mechanisms]... use and control... aerodynamics and structures... and related testing and instrumentation" of bombs and re-entry vehicles."[6]

The labs also conduct underground nuclear warhead tests. To insure that old warheads still function per specification, such warheads are detonated from time to time. In addition, new bomb designs are verified by exploding prototypes. Scientists at Los Alamos test nuclear devices by exploding them in underground chambers at the Nevada Test Site. Sandia uses nuclear testing to explore the vulnerability of warheads to nuclear explosions.

Since it is becoming increasingly difficult to justify these intense efforts at building newer and better bombs, it is possible that these programs will diminish as the Cold War that spawned them wanes. The fate of other nuclear weapons programs, such as those described below, is not so clear. Moreover, support for nuclear weapons testing and weapons production continues to register below 50 percent of the American public.

Third-Generation Nuclear Weapons. In addition to pushing the limits of the relatively old nuclear bomb technology, the national labs are also involved in exploring advanced, so-called "third generation" applications of nuclear explosives. A major direction of research in this area is Nuclear Directed Energy Weapons (NDEWs). NDEWs, which received most of their momentum from the Reagan Administration's Strategic Defense Initiative (SDI), aim to direct the energy from a nuclear explosion in one direction to focus its energy more directly on a single target. NDEW programs at Livermore focus on the possibility of using a nuclear explosion to power an X-Ray laser. This weapon would focus a portion of the energy from the nuclear explosion into an X-ray laser beam that could travel long distances to destroy targets such as enemy missile boosters. NDEW programs at Los Alamos include a program that explores the possibility of using nuclear explosions to drive projectiles at very high velocities.

A third area in which all three national laboratories have large programs is Inertial Confinement Fusion (ICF). In ICF, a number of high power laser beams deliver a very large amount of energy to a very small fuel pellet whose atoms fuse as a result of the energy input from the beam. The aim of the program is to develop a system in which the energy released from the fusion of the fuel atoms will be greater than the energy in the beam needed to drive the fusion. If this point can be reached, designers envision significant civilian power applications for inertial fusion.

It is not clear how programs such as ICF and NDEW will be affected by the end of the Cold War. While it may seem that accumulating ever greater numbers of the same kinds of bombs that we have had for 40 odd years is a waste of resources, it is possible that some may be drawn by the appeal of challenging new technologies such as NDEWs and ICF.

According to officials at the national laboratories, "We must increase, not decrease, our research, development and testing requirements" in some areas of the nuclear defense program.[7] The category entitled "Verification and Control" technologies aim at improving the state of the art in monitoring the nuclear testing of other nations. Most countries, including the Soviet Union and the U.S., have ratified the Limited Test Ban Treaty which forbids testing in the atmosphere, under water, or in space. The verification programs develop sophisticated instrumentation to insure that all countries comply with the provisions of the test ban treaties and other arms control treaties, such as those to limit strategic nuclear missiles and warheads (START) and conventional weapons (CFE).

It is likely that arms control negotiations will continue to progress, and that the signing of a Comprehensive Nuclear Test Ban Treaty, which would ban nuclear weapons testing altogether, might be possible with increased Congressional interest. The Soviet position is supportive of a comprehensive ban. The Soviets are presently observing a unilateral moratorium imposed by public pressure from domestic environmental groups and may soon put heavy pressure on the U.S. to follow. Even as more and more agreements continue to be reached, more and more sophisticated verification technologies will be required. Thus, this area of the national labs' research will likely continue, and even expand.

Other categories included in the Department of Energy nuclear weapons programs are safeguards and security, materials production, and nuclear waste management. They account for a small but very important portion of the overall

nuclear weapons research and development program. The national laboratories are responsible for developing technologies to improve the production
of plutonium, which is used in nuclear weapons. These research programs deal
with keeping the production process as safe and secure as possible, developing
new techniques to refine and process the weapons-grade plutonium, and disposal and storage of the nuclear waste generated by the manufacture of the
refined plutonium.

These programs are necessary byproducts of the current nuclear weapons
production apparatus; they exist only to smooth and improve the manufacture
of warheads. Therefore, as the policy of nuclear deterrence is implemented by
smaller and more stable nuclear arsenals, research activities in support of the
warhead production programs may also be reduced..

Non-Nuclear Weapons Research

Research into directed-energy weapons is the labs' primary area of non-nuclear defense work. Similar in goals to the nuclear explosive driven X-Ray laser
described above, the national labs are also employed in a number of different,
non-nuclear, energy-beamed weapons projects. Sandia labs is engaged in a
number of beam weapons concepts, including microwave and electron beams.[8]
Los Alamos is conducting large research programs on Neutral Particle Beams
and Free Electron Lasers for the Strategic Defense Initiative Office.[9]
Livermore also conducts a Free Electron Laser program for the Defense
Advanced Research Projects Agency (DARPA).[10]

The purpose of these large, high-energy weapons projects is to explore
various possible systems for the much criticized SDI. Though the SDI program
was geared initially to develop an anti-ballistic missile system that could defend
against a large-scale nuclear assault by shooting down incoming missiles, the
program has shifted to ways to prevent missile attacks, such as the Scuds used
by Iraq in the recent Gulf War.

There are many other directions in which weapons research could continue.
For example, it is entirely possible that the national research focus will shift from
nuclear to non-nuclear weaponry. Even as the Soviets become less threatening,
the U.S. is redefining its national security requirements. Instead of the traditional East-West conflict scenarios, military planners are beginning to consider
a host of other possible enemies. The Middle East crisis precipitated by Iraq's
invasion of Kuwait demonstrates the potential for large-scale conflicts with
"smaller" nations. The old fears of Soviet tanks rolling into West Germany are
being replaced by new fears of small, third-world terrorist forces, drug dealer
armies, and the threat of Third World dictators.

We are being told that the battlefields of the future will no longer be the skies
above the earth and the fields of Central Europe, but rather the jungles of
third-world countries, the populous urban centers of the developed countries,
and the oil fields of the Persian Gulf. Such battles would not be fought with

nuclear bombs and laser beams, but rather with the old-fashioned conventional tools: rifles, tanks, helicopters, and airplanes.

The buzzword for these small-scale wars is Low Intensity Conflict. The national laboratories are already assisting in this new military focus with a host of research programs into non-nuclear weapons. New technology, they hope, will provide more sophisticated and destructive weapons to fight the battle against third world enemies.

All three national laboratories conduct research in advanced armor and anti-armor technologies. One branch of this area designs stronger tank armor, while the other designs shells that will penetrate armor more effectively.

Since testing actual warheads is an expensive undertaking, scientists prefer to use advanced computer simulations to predict the behavior of their designs. Los Alamos personnel have developed a sophisticated three-dimensional computer simulation code, called MESA, which accurately models the complex physics involved in warhead penetration of armor.[11] These computer codes will serve both those who design tank armor, and those who design the explosives to penetrate armor.

Current Low Intesity Conflict and counter-drug research is modest but significant, and may indicate a future research trend. Los Alamos is the most active of the national laboratories in this area, and its projects include a chemical detector for the Drug Enforcement Agency, a radar for U.S. customs, and a computer money flow model to detect illegal money laundering. In addition to these programs, Los Alamos proposes to conduct research into satellite detection of drug processing, biochemical cocaine detection, as well as other anti-narcotics programs.

The above examples demonstrate that the weapons laboratories are already involved in significant non-nuclear defense research. While defense budgets may shrink due to the decrease in strategic threat, the perception of smaller and more elusive threats from underdeveloped nations may well be used to justify support for continued weapons research. While it seems inevitable that nuclear weapons research will shrink from its present levels, the research emphasis may simply shift from nuclear to non-nuclear military activity. Given the ability of the labs generally with support from the Congress to formulate new research tasks, it is not likely that Congress will attempt to reduce its support for them in the near future.

Non-Nuclear Military Labs and Facilities The three major nuclear labs attract the attention of the American public because of their preeminence in the field of science and their preeminence in the field of nuclear weaponry. The Defense Department's complex of non-nuclear military labs is older, more diversified, and much more generously funded than the nuclear weapons labs. None is as large as the Energy Department's labs.

The Defense Department's research network covers the labs and research institutions with a budget over $6 billion a year. Many thousands of scientists and engineers are employed in them. The Air Force has 14 labs, the Army 38, and the Navy 24. One estimate is that about one-third, or 25, of these labs may be closed in the next five years. Perhaps as many as 5,000 jobs may be terminated.[12]

The Army has plans to close several of its labs and instead create large "corporate" labs. Labs in Fort Monmouth, NJ, St. Louis, MO, and Stanton, VA are slated for closure. Four to six thousand jobs could be eliminated as a result.

Non-Military Research at the Labs

Despite the close association of the Energy Department's labs with military research in the public's mind, 40 to 50 percent of the research done at the labs is non-military. Of this civilian research effort, most is energy research conducted for the Department of Energy. This area had been given more attention and funding in the 1970s, but suffered large cutbacks in the 1980s during the Reagan Administration.

Non-military research at the three nuclear weapons labs currently covers the following areas: fission energy, advanced nuclear, fossil fuel, conservation/renewable energy, basic energy research, nuclear waste, environmental/biological, and miscellaneous. The total amount spent on these activities in 1990 by the three labs was $658.2 million. At Livermore National Laboratory, for example, in FY 1990, non-military research involved over 2,000 people and some $300 million.[13]

Taken together, the programs at the three laboratories constitute a considerable research and development effort for improving existing energy sources, exploiting new energy supplies, and understanding the basic science involved in energy production. This effort, however, is modest and inadequate compared with the 1970s when the President and the Congress initiated expanded programs to deal with energy resources. Improvement of nuclear fission and fossil energy technologies, as well as the possibility of fusion energy, are active areas of non-weapons research.

Computer Capabilities. The computer capabilities at the national laboratories are among the most sophisticated available to scientific researchers.[14] Sandia has five Cray supercomputers, as well as seven IBM System/370 machines.[15] This advanced computing ability is a byproduct of the heavy nuclear weapons research at the labs. For years, the labs have numerically modelled the physical processes involved in nuclear explosions. Today, this competence could be applied to model complex physical systems and processes, such as nuclear energy plants, combustion engines, global climate systems, and biological structures. It would be highly appropriate for the U.S. Congress to focus on how these systems and processes can be shifted to meeting human and environmental needs of the society. Environmental committees of the Congress through hearings and research conducted by the Congressional Office of Technology Assessment could begin to focus on these emerging societal needs.

Change at the National Laboratories

It seems unlikely that the national nuclear laboratories will be able to continue their present course. The role of nuclear weapons eventually will become less prominent in the framework of U.S. national defense, and therefore the research dedicated to improving the nuclear arsenal will probably decline. Though not completely oblivious to the winds of change, the national weapons labs nonetheless may prefer their present research projects and, therefore, may be reluctant to face changing world realities:

> Our commitment to ensuring the nation's deterrent through nuclear weapons technology remains paramount. In our planning, we assume that nuclear weapons technology will remain the key program area in the Laboratory...[16]
>
> The primary program of the Laboratory will continue to be conducting research, development, and test activities associated with a nuclear design emphasis on all aspects of the phases of the nuclear weapon cycle and attendant national security tasks.[17]
>
> No significant change is anticipated in the level of effort of Defense Program activities. All programs are expected to maintain an essentially flat profile during the planning period.[18]

If the planning assumptions of the national weapons laboratories are incorrect, and the current emphasis on nuclear weapons research declines, the primary mission of the three laboratories will have gone the way of the dinosaur. It will be necessary to "convert" the laboratories to other research missions, shrink their size, or shut them down altogether. The nature of new research initiative will be determined by the capabilities of these research laboratories, as well as public priorities that will emerge as part of the overall science and defense policy of the nation. The views of the President and relevant Congressional committees will be extremely important.

Scientists and educators from all parts of the country need to become involved in these questions. The national labs discussed here are centered in one area—the Southwest (California and New Mexico). To put the country on the path of different goals, rather than the present concentration on nuclear weapons research, requires consideration by Congress. Also important is the involvement of additional groups of scientists, educators, and state legislators. Private groups, such as the Union of Concerned Scientists and the Federation of American Scientist, could consider a joint effort with their colleagues at the weapons labs on research and demonstration projects aiming at new missions for the post-Cold War era.

Criteria for Research Conversion

Though the exact future path of the weapons labs is unclear, several criteria seem to be useful in the evaluation of possible research directions. First, the laboratories ought to remain centers of excellence in applied research and engineering. Second, any future research projects should use, for the most part, existing personnel and resources at the national laboratories. If this can be done to a large extent the fear of job loss can be mitigated.

The three weapons laboratories have risen to their present stature largely because they have enjoyed steady and generous funding. Through this stable funding, the labs have been able to attract talented researchers and purchase the most sophisticated equipment. The continued funding has been possible because the labs' research mission, nuclear weapons research, has been an unquestioned national priority for some four decades.

If and when the laboratories shift their focus, any new research mission must be assured of similar long-term public support if it is to be successful. The high quality of the laboratories will be maintained only if new research missions can look forward to the level and continuity of support they have received in the past. Any new main research directions must work to solve problems that are recognized as a national priority, and for which there is broad public consensus to support for a period of many years.

In addition to continued funding, new research projects should use the mix of skills and equipment currently at the laboratories. This criterion is not a restrictive one, as the multidisciplinary labs presently employ a wide range of expertise. Typically, lab technical personnel are composed of scientists (chemists, physicists, mathematicians, and biologists), engineers, computer scientists, and lab technicians. These personnel possess the skills to explore and potentially solve a broad spectrum of problems.

New Prime Research Missions

Having established two of the criteria for future research priorities, which areas hold promise as candidates to fill the role of primary research missions for the weapons laboratories? Several of the existing programs described earlier address pressing national problems and could be expanded to utilize a larger portion of the laboratories' resources. Among them are energy, laser technology, global climatic change, environmental protection, and arms control verification.

Energy. Energy production and environmental degradation are two intimately related issues that the laboratories currently investigate. The future holds dwindling supplies of fossil fuels and a continually degenerating environment. Finding safe, clean, and cheap energy sources is a long-term technical problem that is rapidly becoming a national priority. For these reasons, energy research is a prime candidate to replace weapons research.

The weapons laboratories function under the direction of the Department of Energy, and many of the programs there already focus on energy research. There are many challenging and relevant problems in this field, and, given reliable public support, the existing programs could be easily expanded to fill the void left by decreased defense spending. The laboratories are already well poised to become national centers of energy research.

As the environmental crisis becomes an ever more pressing problem and energy shortages grow acute, cost-efficient renewable energy technologies will become a vital national goal. Currently, conservation, energy efficiency, and renewable energy programs consist of less than 2 percent of the activities of the national weapons laboratories, but the equipment and expertise exists to expand these critical areas of research. Much work remains to be done before sources of renewable energy such as the sun and geothermal differentials can be readily used for commercial energy production.

In addition, the laboratories may also expand their efforts in the area of civilian nuclear power generation. Currently, dominant efforts are in space-based reactors and nuclear waste disposal. New programs to improve the performance, operation, and safety designs of conventional nuclear reactors would be of benefit to the nation and could be easily undertaken.

Laser Technology. As a consequence of their work in SDI and other areas of nuclear and space technology, the national laboratories have an installed base of laser research and are currently world leaders in this area. Typical of the three labs, laser research and development represents about 25 percent of the programs at Livermore. Though most of the active areas of laser research involve high-energy beams for military application, the same basic skills and scientific knowledge can be applied to civilian uses such as inertial confinement fusion. Already, the labs are exploring the uses of lasers in uranium isotope separation for nuclear fuels (see above) and for underwater communication.

Though the uses of lasers in industry is still in its early stages, the potential uses of coherent light are almost limitless. Among other applications, lasers could be used for material fabrication, precision alignment, chemical and materials processing, and surgery. To speed the arrival of lasers as a practical tool, the labs could become national centers of laser research for civilian applications. Since the national labs already have a base of laser expertise, and this research requires the wide variety of interdisciplinary skills available at the labs, laser programs "could provide the long-term, multidisciplinary research program needed to assure continuation of the Laboratory [Livermore] as a major scientific research institution."[19]

Advanced Non-Nuclear Defense Technology. Though many want to see the national labs shift away from defense research, it is entirely possible they will simply shift from one area of weapons research to another. Though the days of aggressive nuclear weapons development seem to have gone, there is no guarantee that non-nuclear weapons will be subject to the same budget squeeze. In fact, an accelerated program in advanced conventional weapons technology could consume the resources freed by the decline in nuclear weapons research. As mentioned earlier, the laboratories already have extensive Department of Defense programs to explore new conventional weapons technologies. Before the laboratories move aggressively to expand work in conventional weapons, it would be necessary to have thorough Congressional oversight concerning the proper allocation of resources. During this period of budget cuts and rising domestic needs, it would be preferable to move the labs more out of the weapons business.[20]

Global Climatic Change. One possible area of research is global climate change. With the international attention given to pollution and environmental stability, the issue of global climate change is likely to receive increased attention for some time to come. The long-term influence of man's activities, especially in energy production and use is not well understood, and until recently has not attracted the systematic attention of researchers. Dangers such as global warming, however, are becoming more apparent with time, and work needs to be done before these phenomena are quantitatively understood.

To investigate quantitatively global climate change, scientists construct computer models of the ecosystem to predict future changes. The weapons labs are well equipped to perform this modelling work, as they house some of the most advanced supercomputers in the world and extensive computational expertise. This computational power could be applied to develop faster and more accurate climatic models and thus contribute fundamentally to the understanding of global environmental phenomena. Livermore currently conducts a small atmospheric modeling program; this program could be expanded and moved to include the other national labs.

Arms Control Verification. Developing technology for the verification of arms control agreements has increased as an important component of work at the labs. Al Narath, Sandia's President, told a Senate Committee that Sandia "has supported every arms control negotiation since the Limited Test Ban Treaty and has helped develop key technologies for the Nonproliferation Treaty and the START and nuclear testing negotiations. Our verification technology and related intelligence programs currently constitute about 12 percent of our work. This work is funded by the Department of Energy and other agencies and represents the largest aggregation of verification technology work at any facility in the world."[21] Narath also told Congress that the monitoring system at Votkinsk in the U.S.S.R. and much of the field instrumentation used for verifying the INF agreement, were developed at Sandia.

John Nuckolls, Livermore's Director, said "Our activities in support of the intelligence and verification communities include work on in-country seismic monitoring, tagging, nuclear detection, and chemical sampling."[22]

For verification of arms control agreements on strategic nuclear weapons, Nuckolls mentioned Livermore's development of tags and highly sophisticated detection devices. In the area of radiation detection, he mentioned work on "nonvisual" determination of the number of warheads contained in the payload section of MIRVed ballistic missiles, the discrimination of nuclear from conventional cruise missiles, and the detection of solid rocket propellant at prominently monitored rocket production facilities.

Los Alamos' Director, Siegfried Hecker, testified that his lab has been "active in the arms control verification business since the Limited Test Ban Treaty in 1963 when we started putting instruments on spacecraft and satellites in order to be able to monitor the verification requirements associated with the test ban treaty." His lab's arms control verification budget was $35 million in FY 1990.

Conclusion

While it seems clear that the weapons labs cannot continue to focus on intensive nuclear weapons research as they have done for decades, the nature of their future research directions is largely undetermined. The weapons labs represent a large body of expertise and equipment, and it is up to the national leadership, particularly the President, Congress, and public interest groups, to determine what this talent will be used to study and invent in the years to come. The talent and expertise of the personnel at the labs, given this wide range, can be used to explore a variety of technical problems.

The problems the labs will examine are a matter of public policy, i.e., a political issue more than a technical one. The labs are dependent on government funding, and thus it is up to the government and ultimately the people to determine which technical issues merit the expenditure of significant national resources. The Armed Services Committees of both houses of Congress are responsible for the oversight of the weapons labs. The Senate and House Energy Committees have virtually no role in the direction of funding for nuclear weapons. The Energy Committees, however, could be given some jurisdiction over the labs should Congress and the Administration decide to shift some resources from nuclear weapons activity to peaceful pursuits, such as the environment. These possibilities need to be explored.

The discussion above demonstrates that there is no shortage of problems to be solved; energy crisis, environmental change, and arms control, but also poverty, are examples of the most immediate and grave problems. The public and the Congress must set national priorities and thus determine how the national labs might apply their unique combination of skills.

Whatever the outcome of their deliberations, those who decide the future course should recognize that the weapons laboratories represent an irreplaceable national resource with the potential to provide solutions to the most pressing problems of our times. The fate of the weapons labs should not be decided out of hand, nor should this technical resource be squandered.

Notes

1. Interview with Milo Nordyke of Lawrence Livermore National Laboratory, August 14, 1990.

2. Siegfried S. Hecker, Director, Los Alamos National Laboratory, "Los Alamos National Laboratory: A Look at the Future," prepared Oral Statement to the U.S. Senate Committee on Armed Services, November 7, 1987.

3. See reference for chart in this chapter, entitled "Defense Funding Sources of the National Labs."

4. *Los Alamos National Laboratory Institutional Plan, FY 1989-FY 1994*, September 1989, p. 30.

5. *Lawrence Livermore National Laboratory Institutional Plan, FY 1989-FY 1994*, p. 18.

6. *Sandia National Laboratory Institutional Plan, FY 1989-FY 1994*, September 1989, p. 31.

7. *Sandia Plan, op. cit.*, p. 37.

8. *Livermore Plan, op. cit.*, p. 18.

9. *Los Alamos National Laboratory, Research Highlights, 1989*, p. 8.

10. Statement of Dr. James I. Davis, Executive Officer of Livermore, in a Senate Hearing for the Department of Defense Authorization for Appropriations for FY 1989, *Department of Energy Weapons Laboratories Role in Defense of the Technology Base*, March 18, 1988, p. 127.

11. *Los Alamos Highlights, op. cit.*, p. 30.

12. "Military Labs Hit by Funding Retreat," **Science**, July 12, 1991, p. 131.

13. *Livermore Plan, op. cit.*, September 1989, p. 90.

14. Livermore National Laboratory has two Cray-1's, two Cray-2's, a Cray X-MP, and a Cray Y/MP-32. *Livermore Plan, op. cit.*, p. 60.

15. *Sandia Plan, op. cit.*, p. 84.

16. *Los Alamos Plan, op. cit.*, p. 9.

17. *Livermore Plan, op. cit.*, p. 5.

18. *Sandia Plan, op. cit.*, p. 18.

19. Correspondence from Milo D. Nordyke, Livermore National Laboratory, June-September 1991.

20. Los Alamos houses five of Cray Research Inc.'s Cray X-MPs supercomputers, as well as four of the older Cray-1 supercomputers

21. Hearings before the Committee on Armed Services, U.S. Senate, March-June 1990, p. 884.

22. *Ibid.*, p. 895.

4

State and Local Impact

Isaiah was right to dream of peace. Peace is beneficial economically and spiritually. But while peace benefits the nation as a whole, the cuts in defense spending affect the livelihoods of some and not others. In the U.S., the transitional difficulties are concentrated in a relatively small number of affected communities.

The use of language in this chapter to the effect that defense cuts may have a negative impact on a locality should not be construed as in any way detracting from the desirability of peace or, generally speaking, defense cuts.

Impact of Defense Cuts on States

In 1989, long before the extent of the coming breakup of the Soviet empire became apparent, William Kaufmann of the Brookings Institution proposed reducing defense spending by almost half, to $160 billion (in 1990 dollars), by the end of the century. If the portion spent on procurement remained constant at about 27 percent, it would mean spending on procurement could drop from $81 billion to $43 billion.[1]

With an estimated 25,400 local jobs (including indirect and induced jobs as we discuss later in this chapter) tied to every $1 billion (in 1990 dollars) in defense procurement, such a procurement cut *could* mean a reduction of close to a million defense-dependent jobs during the 1990s, i.e. an average of close to 100,000 per year.[2] The reduced need for personnel in Europe could also mean the mustering out of an average of an additional 50,000 uniformed personnel per year.[3]

Nationwide, the cuts could substantially reduce jobs for America's six-million-plus defense workers. More than half of them (3.2 million people), work for private defense contractors; the rest are in the active-duty armed forces (2.1 million) or in civilian positions for the Department of Defense (1 million). Based on past experience, cuts in civilian defense-contractor workers will be faster and more dislocating than cuts in the career military.[4]

Which states will be most affected depends on (1) which bases and contracts are cut, (2) company defense dependence, discussed in Chapter 1, (3) community defense dependence, and (4) community economic strength.

Defense Dependence

Company and community defense dependence may be defined as the proportion of employment or income derived from military facilities and contracts. One way to gauge the potential impact of overall defense spending cuts is to look at state defense dependence. States most dependent on (that is, deriving 6 percent or more of income from) prime military contracts and bases in 1990 were Arizona, Colorado, District of Columbia, Hawaii, Maine, Maryland, Mississippi, Missouri, Utah, and Virginia.[5]

Information on defense spending comes primarily from the Pentagon and therein lies a serious measurement problem. Department of Defense contracts are identified by prime contractor and production location. However, over half of prime contract dollars are passed on to subcontractors. For example, the Lima, Ohio plant manufacturing the M-1 Abrams tank has 3,500 workers working under a subcontract to General Dynamics. In addition, this company puts out subcontracts that hire another 13,000 people at other companies. In fact, the bulk of the work is carried out by subcontractors because they tend to be smaller and pay less — but how many jobs are with subcontractors is subject to a wide range of estimates.[6]

Our discussion in this chapter assumes that most subcontractors are located fairly close to the primes. Location patterns of subcontractors suggest that this is generally (although far from always) the case. Moreover, workers might not live in the same state that they work in. For example, many workers at Electric Boat Co. in Groton, CT live in Rhode Island (and a few actually work at the company's Rhode Island subsidiary at Quonset Point), so that some of the negative impact that is attributed below to Connecticut may actually fall on nearby parts of Rhode Island.[7]

The Vulnerability Index

Defense-dependence estimates do not consider a state's economic situation. To capture this element and develop a number that takes into account both the state's dependence on defense income and its ability to weather military industry layoffs, we factor in the state unemployment rate. Since we want an index that weights approximately equally the potential for military cuts and the strength of the civilian economy, we give the figures equal weight and then add them.

Together they yield what CEP calls the Vulnerability Index (VI = defense dependence percent + unemployment percent). Among the 50 states plus DC and Puerto Rico, the number ranges from a high of 17.2 in Virginia and in Puerto Rico to a low of 4.8 in Nebraska. After Puerto Rico and Virginia, the most vulnerable are the District of Columbia, Mississippi, Massachusetts, Missouri, Alaska, Maine, Alabama, and Arizona.

This is a rough but serviceable measure of how vulnerable a state's economy is to defense cuts. The measure would not be meaningful in a state that had zero defense spending. But in fact, as can be seen from the state profiles in Chapter 8, every state has a defense presence that is significant in relation to the rest of the state economy. The state with the smallest defense-related employment is Vermont (6,000; see Table 4.1), and this employment level turns out to be quite significant for the state's Burlington region—especially since it represents half the level of a year or two before, the most rapid relative decline in any state.

The Defense Dislocation Index

We developed the Defense Dislocation Index (DDI) to go beyond assessing defense dependence and vulnerability, to factor in the amount of defense spending at risk, i.e., the amount likely to be cut. The DDI measures the cumulative effect of specific defense cuts on each state.

The DDI is derived by multiplying the Vulnerability Index by the ratio of likely cuts to total defense spending (DDI = VI x 10 x cuts/spending). But we didn't weight a dollar of spending on the uniformed services the same as a dollar spent on defense contracts, because the impact of these dollars on the affected communities differs.

The ultimate state and local impact of a loss in defense spending depends on the "multiplier effect." As $1 of new externally generated income such as Federal dollars flows into an area, the residents who get the money spend more. Then, as a result, other residents in the area who are beneficiaries of the increased spending also spend more. And so on. Thus every dollar invested in a region results in a larger increase in the final income of residents.

Employees of the initial recipients of defense money are called direct employees; employees of subcontractors are called indirect employees; employees of companies that benefit from the derived demand from defense spending (dry cleaners, supermarkets, and so forth) are called induced employees.

So cuts in the high earnings of defense-contractor employees who generate many indirect and induced jobs can have double the impact of cuts in relatively transient base personnel, who shop at their PX and generate few indirect and induced jobs.

The previously mentioned figure of 25,400 defense jobs per $1 billion in defense procurement already has a multiplier of 2.5 built into it; direct prime-contractor jobs are created at a rate of 10,160 per $1 billion of prime contracts. The comparable personnel multipliers are 1.2 for military personnel (who mostly live on the base) and 1.8 for civilian personnel (who are more likely to live off the base and spend more in the local economy).[9]

Likely cuts were calculated by adding up for each state the total value of prime contracts for each weapon system at risk based on the FY 1991 Conference Report on the Defense Appropriations Bill and the 1989 Eagle Eye database of MSRS, Inc., converting to community jobs at risk and adding the number of base personnel likely to be terminated or relocated, weighted according to the three multipliers. The result is shown in Table 4.1.[10]

Table 4.1
Defense Jobs in 1990 and DDI Rank, by State

	Base Personnel	Contractor Personnel	Defense-Dependent Jobs	DDI Rank (/52)
Alabama	44,502	49,223	192,000	25
Alaska	27,348	11,210	64,000	42
Arizona	33,709	86,372	262,000	3
Arkansas	13,786	7,966	39,000	12
California	292,955	566,734	1,842,000	10
Colorado	46,031	83,588	272,000	16
Connecticut	12,171	107,727	287,000	14
Delaware	6,282	2,433	15,000	40
District of Columbia	31,185	43,025	155,000	41
Florida	108,165	123,946	459,000	27
Georgia	83,020	46,025	238,000	33
Hawaii	59,793	13,002	116,000	47
Idaho	6,119	1,064	11,000	49
Illinois	56,512	34,011	166,000	15
Indiana	20,158	43,065	141,000	13
Iowa	2,068	12,547	35,000	31
Kansas	27,758	23,441	96,000	45
Kentucky	43,289	11,161	88,000	21
Louisiana	33,259	41,323	149,000	24
Maine	15,709	21,421	79,000	19
Maryland	76,383	111,277	396,000	9
Massachusetts	20,711	207,405	551,000	7
Michigan	19,350	34,541	116,000	11
Minnesota	3,921	44,430	118,000	22
Mississippi	24,750	36,298	127,000	37
Missouri	34,964	154,023	439,000	1
Montana	5,640	1,748	12,000	48
Nebraska	16,869	6,135	38,000	49
Nevada	11,384	4,641	27,000	26
New Hampshire	3,839	9,930	30,000	4
New Jersey	42,895	93,188	301,000	23
New Mexico	24,597	17,059	78,000	18
New York	47,466	173,600	502,000	6
North Carolina	85,865	30,859	190,000	39
North Dakota	11,932	2,521	22,000	46
Ohio	46,310	111,325	355,000	8
Oklahoma	49,620	15,791	113,000	35
Oregon	3,958	9,275	30,000	34
Pennsylvania	57,771	71,993	280,000	20
Puerto Rico	5,794	11,631	38,000	43
Rhode Island	8,281	14,094	48,000	32
South Carolina	57,228	17,745	125,000	29
South Dakota	8,044	904	13,000	49
Tennessee	16,593	30,242	100,000	17
Texas	171,835	231,949	822,000	2
Utah	27,103	23,207	103,000	28
Vermont	790	1,906	6,000	5
Virginia	197,673	201,138	805,000	36
Washington	84,671	62,257	251,000	30
West Virgina	2,307	5,719	18,000	44
Wisconsin	4,358	23,762	67,000	38
Wyoming	4,718	1,600	10,000	49
Total, All States	2,121,439	3,091,479	10,837,000	

Source: Derived from Department of Defense *Atlas*, FY 1990.[11]

number of base personnel likely to be terminated or relocated, weighted according to the three multipliers. The result is shown in Table 4.1.[10]

Some weapon systems were not fully represented. For example, the B-2 stealth bomber was in a research and development phase in FY 1989 and therefore doesn't appear in that year's Eagle Eye database.

The DDI shows how severely defense cuts are likely to hurt the economy of a state. Heaviest hit are: Missouri, Texas, and Arizona.

The most seriously affected state, Missouri, is an exception to the less defense-dependent situation of the Midwest compared to the Pacific states, the Southwest, and Northeast (see above). We project Missouri to be the most dislocated state in the nation—mostly because of its heavy dependence on the McDonnell Douglas plant in St. Louis that produces the F-15E "Eagle" fighter aircraft and other aircraft being cut.

Figure 4.1
Likely Impact of Defense Cuts by State

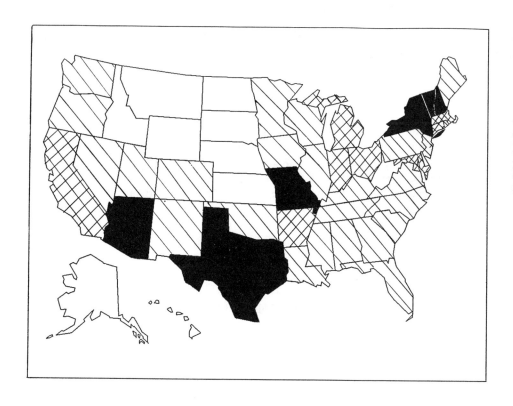

Defense Dislocation Index

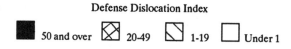

50 and over   20-49   1-19   Under 1

Impact of Defense Cuts on Localities

What is the local impact of cuts? With the same proviso that we raised in connection with state measures, i.e., that defense-contract data do not include adequate information on subcontracts, the most vulnerable companies and localities are those with a high defense dependence.

Defense Dependence

We have quite good information on which communities are getting the most defense money. The Department of Defense provides information on the ten places in each state that are the largest recipients of defense money, as sites of bases or defense contractors.

We find that the ones that received the most defense money in FY 1990 were, first, St. Louis, MO, followed by San Diego, CA, and Fort Worth, TX. Virginia had three sites in the top ten: Newport News, Norfolk, and Arlington. The other two states represented are Colorado and New York. These rankings were unchanged from FY 1989.

The Department of Defense data may not always identify the site correctly. A defense contract may be attributed to its headquarters location when the work is done at a different manufacturing location. But the numbers in Chapter 8 generally correspond to newspaper reports of defense contracts.

Impact of Cuts

Knowing which localities depend the most on defense spending is only a partial indicator of where the impact of defense cuts will be felt most keenly. The other question is what weapons systems and bases are scheduled for cutbacks. For example, 18 states were affected by the first round of defense-contract cuts in 1990. Some states like California and Arizona were hit harder than others:

- 6 contracts at risk in *California*: in Canoga Park, Downey, El Segundo, Huntington Beach, and Newport Beach
- 5 contracts at risk in *Arizona*: in Mesa, Tempe, and Tucson.
- 3 contracts at risk in each of *four states*: Connecticut, in East Hartford and Stratford; Indiana, in Indianapolis; Massachusetts, in Lowell and Lynn; Texas, in Dallas and Fort Worth.
- 2 contracts at risk in each of *three states*: Minnesota, in Minneapolis and Minnetonka; Pennsylvania, in Philadelphia and York; Washington, in Renton and Seattle.
- 1 contract at risk in each of *nine states*: Florida, in Stuart; Maryland, in Baltimore; Maine, in Saco; Michigan, in Warren; Missouri, in St. Louis; New Jersey, in Nutley; New Mexico, in Albuquerque; New York, in Bethpage; and Ohio, in Lima.

This listing doesn't take into account the size of the contracts; it simply shows how many communities in each state are bearing the brunt of the first round of cuts. Detailed information is provided for each community in Chapter 8.

Summary

Overall and in the long term, the economic effect of defense cuts will unquestionably be positive. Instead of making weapons that will be stored, destroyed, or (worst-case scenario) used, the economy will be generating goods and services that will raise the standard of living of U.S. citizens. Also, more people will be employed per dollar in the civilian sector than in the military one.

The costs of unemployment are high. Federal models suggest a 1 percent increase in unemployment reduces GNP by 2.5 percent and therefore the standard of living of all Americans. It reduces government revenues and increases spending on benefits — for example, layoffs of 100,000 employees a year would add $224 million to unemployment compensation outlays. Unemployment creates deficit and tax pressures as well as pockets of political resentment.

The most dislocated states are likely to be: Missouri, Texas, Arizona, New Hampshire, Vermont, New York, Massachusetts, Ohio, Maryland, and California; they all have a high Defense Dislocation Index.

At the local level, the places that receive the most defense money are St. Louis, San Diego, and Fort Worth, TX, and Washington, DC, followed by places in California, Colorado, New York, and Virginia. But defense cuts are concentrated in certain states, which vary in their ability to absorb newly unemployed workers.

The general picture is one of pockets in certain industrial states where dependence on defense spending is very high, while in some rural states it is very low.

Notes

1. In fact the proportion spent on procurement is likely to fall. Personnel reductions can only go so far and O&M costs will be hard to hold down as the average age of most military equipment increases (see Franklin Spinney, "Look What $2 Trillion Didn't Buy for Defense," *The Washington Post* , National Weekly Edition, November 14-20, 1988, p. 23). Procurement will probably be far less than $43 billion in a $150 billion dollar budget.

2. Estimated 25,400 jobs: The figure for defense procurement in aerospace and transportation contracts was calculated in June 1990 by Greg Bischak, then with Employment Research Associates in Lansing, MI and includes the multiplier effect on the local economy. An estimate of 50,000 jobs per $1 billion of *all* defense spending appeared in *The Wall Street Journal*, November 15, 1989; this figure is not necessarily inconsistent with Bischak's estimate because most military personnel earn less than civilians working on defense contracts. The above figures are also broadly consonant with other published estimates that 1 in every 16 people in the U.S. is dependent on defense spending for all or part of their income (e.g., Mark Thompson, *The Philadelphia Enquirer*, January 28, 1990). Figures used in 1988 by Franklin "Chuck" Spinney, a DoD

employee, suggest that about 20,000 "defense-related" jobs are dependent on each $1 billion in DoD spending; see Spinney, *loc. cit.* DoD's 1985 Economic Adjustment/Conversion Report suggests that about 23,000 people were employed in 1985 with each billion dollars spent on DoD procurement, which makes Bischak's 1990 number look, if anything, on the low side. See Joseph Cartwright and Edward A. Trott, Jr., "Defense-Related Employment for Selected Weapon Systems," Chapter 4 in John E. Lynch, ed., *Economic Adjustment and Conversion of Defense Industries* (Boulder, CO: Westview Press, 1987), p. 53. Nearly 1 million: $38 billion x 25,400 jobs/$billion = 965,200 jobs.

3. This figure for estimated troop reductions in Europe, from the Center for Defense Information, does not include reductions in personnel on ships in the region.

4. Defense workers: *Statistical Abstract of the U.S., 1990*, Table 552, p. 339. Past experience: For a chart showing the relative volatility of the defense-contract sector compared to the armed forces, see Figure 1 in Michael Renner, *Swords Into Plowshares: Converting to a Peace Economy* (Washington, DC: Worldwatch Institute, Paper 96, June 1990), p. 20.

5. The defense-dependence figures are derived by dividing a Department of Defense number for total defense spending by state by a Bureau of Economic Analysis figure for the total output of each state. Credit for first calculating this ratio appears to belong to Douglas Lee of the Washington Analysis Corporation, 1612 K Street, NW, Washington, DC; 202-659-8030.

6. Roughly half of defense-industry spending in the largest state, California, goes to prime contractors; the rest goes to subcontractors (see the section on California in Chapter 8). Slightly over half of defense-industry jobs were prime (37,000) vs. subcontracted (33,000) in Cartwright and Trott, *op. cit.*, p. 54. Lima plant data were provided in late 1990 by Gus Comstock, then assistant to former Ohio Gov. Richard Celeste. Smaller and pay less: *Business Week* in its cover story of July 3, 1990 claimed that three times as many jobs are generated by subcontractors as by primes.

7. Unfortunately, under the Nixon Administration the Office of Management and Budget eliminated collection of this information in the name of paperwork reduction. But as part of our research we surveyed prime contractors and found that a substantial portion of subcontractors were located in the same state or area. See also Michael Dee Oden, *A Military Dollar Really Is Different: The Economic Impacts of Military Spending Reconsidered* (Lansing, MI: Employment Research Associates, 1988), p. 36.

8. A monthly press release from the Bureau of Labor Statistics has the latest state unemployment data. To be included in this mailing, call the BLS at 202-523-1002. For the statistics in this chapter we used a two-month average from May 1990 to April 1991.

9. See John Tepper Marlin, "Who Is Hurt the Most by Defense Dept. Cuts?", *The New York Times*, News of the Week in Review, Letter, Sunday, September 8, 1991, p. 18.

10. MSRS is a private firm (the initials stand for Military Statistics Research Service) based in Middleburg, VA, that sells DoD data processed onto CD-ROM data under the trade name "Eagle Eye".

11. Columns 1 and 2 are derived from the Department of Defense *Atlas*, FY 1990. Column 2 is converted from dollars to jobs using the estimate of 10,160 prime contractor jobs per $1 billion (1990) of procurement. Column 3 provides a rounded estimate of total jobs (direct, indirect, and induced) in each state derived from defense spending: the number of uniformed base personnel is multiplied by 1.2, civilian personnel by 1.8, and contractor personnel by 2.5. See text for more explanation.

5

State and Local Strategies

One thing hasn't changed in 2,600 years: communities that depend on military production for their livelihood are ready for war but rarely for peace. The most common immediate reaction of many U.S. communities to impending plant or base closure is panicky lobbying by their Congressional representatives to prevent termination of the weapon or facility—what we might call the NIMDY (Not in My District Yet) Syndrome.

Parochial economic interests have distorted the U.S. defense debate and have tied up national resources that should be redirected to more productive uses. Blind lobbying for continued production of particular weapons is a costly way to buy time. Far better to confront changing economic realities with a plan for encouraging the emergence of new employers in the affected region.

In this chapter we offer some guidelines for community action at the state and local levels. Communities that undertake the kinds of programs outlined here (and described in more detail in Chapter 8) will likely experience a less painful transition to an economically healthier future.

A general summary of the implications of this chapter is that the states and localities most active in conversion usually have within them a community organization that is focusing on the issue and is successfully capturing the attention of government officials, usually by becoming part of a larger economic-development coalition. This chapter therefore overlaps somewhat with Chapter 7, where we discuss conversion activities and groups.

State Conversion Programs[1]

State and local "reconversion" initiatives and proposals were begun during and after World War II; the state and local economic-development profession can be said to have been born during this period. Conversion initiatives also started after the Korean War in 1953-55, and the Vietnam War in 1969-75.[2] The first Federal initiative, the creation of the Office of Economic Adjustment (OEA) in the Department of Defense in 1961, was designed to facilitate state and local planning.

Many communities that originally pressured their political representatives to prevent defense cuts have found they are better off without the defense work. For instance, between 1961 and 1986, the 93,000 jobs lost nationally from military base closures and realignments were replaced, with the OEA's and other Federal help, by nearly 140,000 new civilian jobs. That is, *three new jobs* replaced every *two* lost base jobs. Facilities were converted to such uses as vocational schools, machine shops and commercial airports.[3] True enough, communities more heavily reliant on military manufacturing may face greater problems than those reliant on bases, though steps we describe in this chapter can be taken to ameliorate the situation.

State Economic-Development Offices

States have economic-development offices that are supposed to confront regional recessions such as those of 1981-82. These offices grew from an average salary-and-operations budget of $5 million a year in 1984 to $22 million in 1988. But with the 1990-91 recession, half the states (including most in the Northeast) are so hobbled by budget deficits that they cannot adequately cope with existing problems, let alone the coming transitional retraining and development needs that will be created by defense cuts.

We strongly believe that Federal economic-adjustment programs are appropriate and essential for the hardest-hit communities, although the magnitude of the adjustment some states will have to face in the mid-1990s may be taking a while to register. A survey we conducted in early 1990 found that of 44 state officials (representing 25 states) responsible for economic planning and development, more than 80 percent did not believe additional Federal adjustment legislation to be "needed or desirable."

Yet in the fall of 1991, enough states showed interest in the $200 million assistance from the 1990 Conversion Law for the National Governors Association to sponsor a conference on conversion.

Innovative Conversion Programs in Ten States

State conversion programs are surveyed in detail in each of the state profiles in Chapter 8. In this section we summarize the most important state initiatives and programs. We have dropped some states where it seems the only conversion activities are bills that were vetoed by the governor (as in Colorado), or where the conversion initiatives are simply bills in the legislature (as in Delaware and Maryland), internal reports (Maryland), fairly traditional job-retention (as in Idaho and Michigan) or job-training and placement programs (as in Idaho and New Jersey). In some cases interesting statewide conversion initiatives are being undercut by state officials (Minnesota) and the most active programs are at the local level.

In making these judgments we are responding to strong requests from our advisers to provide the reader with some guidance in this area. We are relying on the most up-to-date information we could obtain in October 1991. In the rapidly changing 1990s, the wise reader will not rely entirely on the information provided here and before acting on it will call one or more of the organizations listed at the end of this chapter or Chapter 7.

California. In 1981 the state created the California Economic Adjustment Team to monitor the danger of plant closings and attempt to head off such closings through business-retention and revitalization programs. The Aerospace Human Resource Network office set up in Manhattan Beach in 1990 was closed in 1991 for lack of state money. Gov. Pete Wilson in September 1991 had a conversion bill, AB 2248, awaiting his signature.[4]

Connecticut. Starting with a project in the Groton area, Connecticut has long had a a regional economic-diversification interest. In 1991 Rep. Luby's HBN 6391 became state law, creating a Defense Diversification Office in the state's Department of Economic Development and setting aside $10 million in bond authorization for diversification projects. A Legislative Committee on Business Opportunity, Defense Diversification, and Industrial Policy has been formed, led by former Sen. Tom Sullivan. Connecticut Innovations, Inc. is a quasi-public agency formed to help finance local development. A promising labor-management group has been formed at the Textron-Lycoming plant at Stratford.[5]

Maine. The Peace Economy Project has received favorable press attention. This may have encouraged Gov. John R. McKernan, Jr. in July 1990 to form a Task Force on Defense Realignment and the Maine Economy. The Task Force's report in 1991 recommended establishing conversion committees in all defense-dependent industries and communities, initiating a statewide planning process, appointing a citizens' advisory board, and providing state funding for these initiatives. Nearly 50 Maine communities have adopted a resolution to urge Congress to shift its priorities from military to domestic needs. Interesting local initiatives are emerging from the Bath-Brunswick Conversion Task Force and the Southern Maine Regional Planning Commission.[6]

Massachusetts. On his last day as governor, former Gov. Michael Dukakis signed into law the Massachusetts Economic Diversification Program, which calls for a broad-based advisory board to monitor state diversification efforts with technical support from state agencies. The bill was introduced by Rep. David Cohen (D-Newton), who is considering introducing an additional bill. The Department of Employment Training is under mandate to study the size of defense industries in the state's economy. The state's Industry Action Program has a good record in helping industries develop strategic plans for coping with economic restructuring. The Industrial Services Program backs up the state's initiatives with financing, training, and marketing programs. Pittsfield continues to be a significant focus of interest.[7]

New York. Gov. Mario Cuomo formed a business-labor Defense Advisory Panel and the State of New York Industrial Cooperation Council which, in conjunction with the National Electronic Industries Association, studied the likely impact of defense cuts. The state's report on diversification relied heavily on two earlier Long Island studies. The state budget included a tiny $150,000 for a pilot project on diversification in the state, and the line was eliminated by the legislature. Most of the conversion energy in the state is coming from Long Island-based groups (OEA is partly funding a study of Long Island's diversification potential), along with the new Albany-based Economic Conversion Coalition of the Capital Region.[8]

Ohio. Gov. Richard F. Celeste's office organized a useful January 1990 conference to acquaint small- and mid-sized contractors with commercial opportunities; it focused on encouragement of small businesses to generate new jobs.[9] The state also has in place a plan to prevent plant closures. Celeste's Republican successor since January 1991, Gov. George Voinovich, is reportedly continuing his predecessor's initiatives, but is not introducing any new ones.

Rhode Island. The state has begun a major study of the impact of defense cuts on its economy with funding provided jointly by OEA and the state.

Texas. The state's legislators are determined to preserve the defense industry that saved the state during the mid-1980s oil price slide. Gov. Ann Richards has formed a statewide Task Force on Economic Transition, which was meeting monthly in mid-1991 to develop both short- and long-term conversion strategies. The Texas Populist Alliance met in September 1991 with conversion as one of its key goals. Approximately 500,000 jobs are tied to defense in Dallas/Ft. Worth.[10]

Virginia. As in other states, state action began with the formation of a citizens' group, the Virginia Task Force on Economic Conversion. It supported a legislative initiative, passed in March 1991 – a Joint Resolution creating a Joint Subcommittee of legislators, plus advisers to be selected by the governor, to study economic conversion and other economic-development issues. The subcommittee is holding meetings around the state during the fall of 1991. Their mission is to "study the measures necessary to assure Virginia's economic recovery."

Washington. This state has a model law and a model community base behind it. It is reviewed in more detail later in this chapter.

Local Conversion Strategy

Based on past experience with local economic-development initiatives generally, the two key elements needed for successful local action are:

- *a core of community leadership,* and
- *a consensus-building long-range plan* that involves a broad spectrum of interests in a set of goals and related actions.

Lead the Way to a Plan

Communities that planned ahead for replacing jobs and lost businesses have been able to overcome adverse effects more rapidly than others. "The key to successful local recovery is strong private sector involvement and effective local leadership," says John Lynch.[11]

The need for a plan means that defense-dependent communities need either to read some of the substantial literature on local strategic planning or to find someone who has done so already. The need to plan means also the need to pay attention to external factors that will affect the local economy, including the vagaries of the U.S. defense budget. If part of a terminated weapons system is manufactured in the community, leaders should be aware that some form of adjustment may be required.

Early warning can make a big difference in a smooth transition, because the community, company management, and workers can begin the process of thinking about alternative economic activities. Generally, if a program is terminated at the top, it will take at least 18 months before work ceases at the factory level. Employees of defense plants should also look for more subtle signs of plant closure: calls for early retirement; reluctance on the part of managers to modernize plant equipment; reduction of maintenance budgets; institution of a "no hiring" policy; depletion of inventories; acceleration of the production line even as production is shifted to other locations and local output declines; or adoption of harsher labor policies.[12]

When word is received of an impending plant closing, resentment is likely to arise among employees and the communities in which they live and shop. Getting past these hard feelings is important for creating an effective organization for the transition, and according to Lynch, "...the creation of a single, effective, local recovery organization represents the most important step a community can take."[13] To assist specific workers as production winds down, a committee of labor and management chaired by a nonpartisan outside community leader is a good model. An accessible job center or placement program is often very useful when layoffs start to occur, to teach job search skills and advise on training programs under the Job Training Partnership Act (JTPA, administered by the Department of Labor, as described at more length in Chapter 6) and other government programs.

Create or Use an Economic-Development Program

The first step is to create an economic-development task force if one does not already exist. If one already exists, attempt to use it for conversion purposes. The most common organizational forms of such groups are:[14]

1. Public Sector Organizations, which consist of officials appointed by a local government;
2. Quasi-Public Organizations, which often take the form of nonprofit corporations that combine efforts of the business and public sectors;

3. Private Sector Groups, or community/business consortiums that often focus on specific projects (e.g., downtown revitalization, local impact studies, or political organization) and sometimes are given grants by local governments; and

4. Regional Councils, which often serve to focus the resources of multiple communities in less urbanized areas.

The focus of an economic-development task force should be to formulate a strategic plan, not only for coping with cuts, but also to plan for economic development generally. Economic-development research often points to community-wide strategic planning as a positive factor in giving focus and energy to community response to change.[15]

The essence of strategic planning is building consensus. For that reason, it is commonly linked to public-private partnership, as in the "Choices for Pennsylvanians" plan initiated by Richard Thornburgh when he was Governor of Pennsylvania.[16] Some private institutions may act as quasi-public bodies — as the South Shore Bank in Chicago did in providing assistance to a part of Chicago that was lacking in capital.

Strategic planning at the local level is nothing new. Boston had a highly organized plan that started in World War I.[17] After World War II, faced with the decline of traditional industries in the Boston area, an informal strategic planning process led by the Federal Reserve Bank of Boston paved the way for the growth of knowledge industries around Route 128.

An economic-development task force will commonly recommend creation of a local economic development office, if one does not already exist, to keep an eye on the long-term viability of the local economy and key businesses. If a business could be diversified or a plant retooled at a reasonable cost, a lot of strife would be avoided and union memberships would be kept intact. To encourage thinking about alternative uses for physical facilities and workers, planning commissions or city councils can offer small grants, tax breaks, or other incentives. For example, members of the International Brotherhood of Electrical Workers Local 2047 are trying to convince management to use energy-efficient technologies in manufacturing new lines of commercial goods at Unisys plants in the Twin Cities (MN) area. Barring some kind of conversion, many workers at this plant will probably be laid off and forced to seek new work.[18]

Encourage Economic-Diversification Potential

A task force seeking to diversify its community can:

- *Offer diversification incentives* to defense contractors to encourage them to look into commercial markets (funding for such projects may also come from the state level).

- *Encourage growth industries* to take root in their communities through use of aggressive marketing and "incubator" programs that can include tax abatements, government and university advice, subsidies, and community improvements.

Some programs seek to bring investment to an area, such as the Michigan Strategic Fund and the Lancaster Economic Development Corporation. The latter brought a strong and important marketing strategy to Los Angeles County's Antelope Valley, when shut-downs of the B-1B production terminated 6,200 jobs. The Lancaster Economic Development Corporation managed to attract four new plant activities that brought in 925 new jobs,[19] and NASA's shuttle replacement called back another 1,000 or so employees. Job growth does not always mean the development of a strong and durable economic base. A "fly-by-night" type of business seldom improves a community's standard of living or helps adjustment to plant closures.[20]

Often investment attraction simply requires keeping industrial brokers and utilities (which sometimes informally serve the broker function) up to date on improvements in the business climate. The city of Mentor, OH had a reputation for red tape and strict zoning policies long after it had changed its practices to make life easier for small businesses.[21]

Provide Education and Training

Education is one of the best long-term investments of any community. A well-educated work-force is a big advantage in attracting new industry. Continuing education and vocational training programs have the fastest payoff because the knowledge that is transferred is put to work immediately in the economy.

A model program that combines education initiatives with the possible efforts mentioned above is the comprehensive and decentralized Ben Franklin Partnership Fund, which brings together higher education institutions and small businesses in Pennsylvania's "Advanced Technology Centers," such as the computer science center of East Stroudsburg University.[22] Other good state programs have been developed by Massachusetts, Michigan, New Jersey, and Ohio.

Education and training are usually essential to any successful economic transition. Approximately 80 percent of workers in the year 2000 will have entered the workforce before 1985, and technological advances will require workers in many occupations to switch jobs several times during their working lives. Displaced defense workers (both the highly skilled and the less skilled) can be retrained for changing job opportunities. In addition to programs instituted at the local level, the previously mentioned Federal JTPA facilitates employment-generation programs at a metropolitan or multi-community level.

Assist Local Companies and Their Employees

Working to keep businesses in the community is an essential strategy given that, in general, existing businesses create 88 percent of new jobs. In the 1980s, large U.S. companies were mostly "downsizing," and net new U.S. jobs came entirely from the growth of small- and medium-sized businesses.[23] Several strategies are effective for helping local small businesses grow. Many cities have created "one-stop" centers for dealing with the array of business problems. Small-business "incubator" programs (described above) should be designed to assist existing businesses as well as attract new ones. Economic-development agencies can also provide financial and management assistance for small businesses and help cut through red tape to comply with local regulations or obtain city services.

Sometimes a community may want to intervene to help a struggling company keep its plant open through hard times. An example is the Armstrong Tire Co. plant in Hanford, CA, the last tire factory in the state. When the parent company announced it was closing the plant, the state put together a package that consisted of a substantial training contract to improve efficiency at the plant, an agreement with the union and managers to reduce salaries, and negotiated lower energy rates and various other concessions from Armstrong's suppliers. As a result the plant became viable again and remained open. Another example is the Chrysler/Jeep agreement that kept the Toledo, OH plant open during an economic recession.[24]

Government intervention is usually accompanied by inducements that have one or more of the following objectives: internal restructuring, cost cutting, management or marketing changes, development of new product lines, plant renovation, or changes in ownership or capital structure.[25] Other forms of company assistance include subsidy of technology transfer (whereby the local, state or Federal government defrays the cost of acquiring new techology) and assistance in entering new export markets. An innovative example is the nation's first publicly sponsored export trading company, XPORT, established by the Port Authority of New York and New Jersey.

At the risk of sounding ungrateful for the important work of economic-development officials, we should note for the record that the most important thing a city or state can do to encourage small businesses is to provide a decent level of services without a crushing burden of business taxes.[26]

Model State and Local Programs

Likely substantial defense cuts in FY 1992 and subsequent years' defense spending will require serious adjustment efforts by defense-dependent industries and communities. Localities cannot afford to wait for state action. To indicate the kind of effort that pays off, we describe a model state program in Washington, a model regional program in St. Louis (MO) and a model local program in San Diego.

A Model State Program: Washington

We have reviewed above eight statewide conversion initiatives. Of these, the best model is Washington because it was the first with the most and it therefore has more experience with actually carrying out the process as opposed to simply passing a law. Its achievements reflect the fact that it probably has the most active and sophisticated statewide conversion lobby in the nation (see Chapter 8 for more details on the state).

With bipartisan support in both houses, the Washington State Legislature on March 12, 1990 passed a law (SHB 2706, "Relating to the Promotion of Economic Diversification for Defense-Dependent Industries and Communities")[27] that would help contractors cope with cuts. It was quickly signed into law by the Governor. The main problem with the legislation is that it appropriated only $200,000 for the program – but that's $50,000 more than the amount Gov. Cuomo asked for and was refused.

The three key provisions of this bill are to:

1. *Create a task force* to identify communities reliant on Department of Defense spending and track shifts in Federal spending priorities.
2. *Assist communities* in utilizing state and Federal programs and in co-ordinating adjustment efforts.
3. *Create a statewide plan* for economic development by a panel representing local governments, business, non-government community interests and the military. A problem for many states in implementing such a plan is the fear that it will lead to new expenditures in a period when many states are facing serious budget deficits.

The law is being carried out by the Community Diversification Program within the State Department of Community Development (Paul Knox is the contact, 206-586-8973).

To carry out the first mandate, in September 1990 the state appointed a broad-based Community Diversification Advisory Committee, which met about every seven weeks. It prepared a work plan for one year and priorities for two years in carrying out the second and third mandates. The required statewide plan is called "The Diversification Plan for Washington State's Military-Dependent Communities and Businesses."

A Model Regional Program: St. Louis

Partly because of the magnitude of the area's problem, the St. Louis Economic Conversion Project and the broad-based St. Louis Economic Adjustment and Diversification Task Force that it helped organize in 1990, has been receiving a good deal of attention from the OEA, which participates in monthly regional planning meetings.

The St. Louis program is a model in showing (1) what can be done without new state laws or initiatives, (2) what can be done with Federal resources, (3) how different jurisdictions can cooperate in developing a plan for conversion, and (4) how a community organization can leverage its influence.

Besides working on a regional plan, the St. Louis group has sponsored such interesting activities as:

- Visits to agencies and groups interested in conversion in other areas facing similar problems in Connecticut, Maine (Bath), Massachusetts, and New York (Long Island).
- A forum featuring four small defense firms that have diversified.
- Entrepreneurship-training courses attended by more than 320 Mc-Donnell Douglas employees who expressed interest in starting businesses.[28]

A Model Local Program: San Diego

San Diego is a model program because it shows how a local group can carry its ideas to a public forum and become part of mainstream politics and decision-making.

The San Diego Economic Conversion Council in 1990 succeeded in persuading the City Council to form an Economic Conversion Subcommittee with the mission of preparing plans for the "orderly and smooth" transition of the region to a "peace-based economy." The subcommittee worked with a broad-based Advisory Group, which held monthly Town Meetings to get public input and not incidentally build visibility and support.

The subcommittee's report is being incorporated in a new Economic Development Task Force that will be looking more broadly at the region's economic future. The Executive Director of the San Diego Economic Conversion Council was appointed to the Task Force, so that conversion ideas will not be lost; it may be reached at 619-278-3730. For more information on San Diego see the California profile in Chapter 8.[29]

Associations of States and Localities

The following lists groups that are likely to be good sources of information on detailed questions about how a state or locality can best adjust to defense cuts. Not all of them have active conversion-related programs, but all can be expected to take an interest in conversion during the 1990s. They include only organizations that are directly responsible to state and local officials.[30] National and regional organizations of citizens and other private entities are listed in Chapter 7, while state-level and substate groups are identified in Chapter 8. Unless otherwise indicated, the area code for all phone and fax numbers is 202.

In dealing with these organizations, remember that they are run by and for the benefit of state and local officials, yet they collect information that is extremely useful for individuals concerned about conversion issues.

The best way for an individual to get access to this information is often by making an investment in a group's publications. Most of these groups have publications that are designed for these officials but are extremely useful for individuals and civic groups. These publications may be a major source of a group's income. You will get a good initial reception by making your first call to the person who handles publications. Once you have a publication in hand that approximately addresses your needs, it will usually be a cinch for you to get any additional information you need by phone.

Regional Groups

Coneg, Conference of Northeastern Governors, Rm. 382, 444 North Capitol St. Washington, DC 20001; 624-8450; fax 783-2950. Anne Stubbs, Director.

Coalition of Northeast Municipalities, 20 Park Plaza, #603, Boston, MA 02116; 617-542-5444. Henry Bourgeos, Executive Director.

Northeast-Midwest Institute, 218 D Street, S.E., Washington, DC 20003; 544-5200. Dick Munson, Executive Director.

Southern Governors' Association, Rm. 240, 444 North Capitol St. Washington DC 20001; 624-5897; fax 624-7797. Candis Brown Penn, Executive Director.

The Sunbelt Institute, 600 Maryland Ave., S.W., Washington, DC 20024; 554-0201. Joseph W. Westphal, Executive Director.

Western Governors' Association, 444 North Capitol St. Washington DC 20001; 624-5402. Richard Bechtel, Director.

Western States Foundation, 444 North Capitol St. Washington DC 20001; 624-8485. Richard Acocozza, Director.

National Groups

Council of State Governments, Iron Works Pike, P.O. Box 11910, Lexington, KY 40578; 606-252-2291. Carl W. Stenberg, Executive Director. Several of its divisions, especially the Northeast Division based in New York City, are taking an active interest in economic adjustment.

International City Management Association, 1120 G Street, N.W., Washington, DC 20005; 626-4600. William H. Hansell, Jr., Executive Director.

National Association of Towns and Townships, 1522 K Street, N.W., Suite 730, Washington, DC 20005. 737-5200. Jeffrey H. Schiff, Executive Director.

National Conference of State Legislatures, 1050 17th Street, Suite 2100, Denver, CO 80265. 303-623-7800. Earl S. Mackey, Executive Director.

National Council for Urban Economic Development, 1730 K Street, N.W., Suite 1009, Washington, DC 20006. 223-4735. Jeffrey A. Finkle, Executive Director. Published John Lynch's important book of examples of community adjustment to economic dislocation, *Plant Closures and Community Recovery* (1990).

National Governors' Association, Hall of the States, 444 North Capitol Street, Washington, DC 20001. 624-5300. Raymond C. Scheppach, Executive Director. In November 1991, under a grant from the Economic Development Administration and with assistance from the OEA, sponsored a workshop in Chicago entitled "Economic Conversion: State Policy and Program Options;" the NGA is also preparing a "Governors' Guide to Economic Conversion" under the grant.

National League of Cities, 1301 Pennsylvania Avenue, N.W., Washington, DC 20004. 626-3000. Alan Beals, Executive Director. The National League of Cities has historically been home to smaller cities as well as the large ones. At its 1989 Atlanta Congress, delegates discussed the impact of defense cuts on American cities and passed a Federal Budget Priorities resolution that addressed the possibilities for expanding public services.

U.S. Conference of Mayors, 1620 Eye Street, N.W., Washington, DC 20006. 293-7330. J. Thomas Cochran, Executive Director. The USCM represents primarily the largest cities. At their 1987 annual meeting, the mayors commissioned a study of the potential dividend from conversion for urban social needs. In January 1990 they passed an "Economic Conversion and Peace Dividend" Resolution, which urged redirecting defense priorities to a peace economy, and (2) assisting defense-dependent communities and workers by providing grants to local governments most affected by defense cuts.

Notes

1. This chapter benefitted from our having received an advance copy of Janet Stone, *Conversion Organizer's Update* (Mountain View, CA: Center for Economic Conversion, October 1991). Besides the assistance of state and local organizations listed at the end of the chapter, we were also helped in 1990 by Brad Johnson, Washington representative of New York State, 202-638-1311 and Maryland Assemblyman Paul Pinsky, 301-772-1287. Full listings of contacts within each state are provided in Chapter 8.

2. See Congressional Budget Office, *The Economic and Budget Outlook: Fiscal Years 1991-1995*, 1990 Annual Report, Figure III-2, "Defense Budget Authority and Outlays" p. 63. The years cited are for changes in authorizations. Actual outlays lag changes in authority, usually by a year or so.

3. Department of Defense, Office of Economic Adjustment, *25 Years of Civilian Reuse: Summary of Completed Military Base Economic Adjustment Projects, 1961-1986* (Washington, May 1986), p. 3.

4. See Alan R. Gianini, "The California Economic Adjustment Program," Chapter 38 in John E. Lynch, ed., *Economic Adjustment and Conversion of Defense Industries* (Boulder: Westview Press, 1987), pp. 104-105. Eugene Chollick and Rosy Nimroody, "Economic Consequences of Peace: Regional Responses to Defense Cuts," *Research Report* (New York, N.Y.: Council on Economic Priorities), October 1989. Lynch, former Associate Director of OEA, believes California has one of the two best plant closure intervention programs in the nation, along with Massachusetts; but some union leaders

express reservations about the program's effectiveness. Conversion bill: Stone, *op. cit.*, p. 2.

5. Connecticut's diversification approach was the model for Federal legislation (HR 2852) introduced by Rep. Sam Gejdenson (D-CT); it had its impact on the 1990 Conversion Law ("Division D" of the 1990 Defense Authorization Bill).

6. Susie Schweppe heads the Peace Economy Project, 207-781-3947. Stone, *op. cit.*, pp. 3-5.

7. Information in part from Stone, *op. cit.*, pp. 5-6. Also: State of Massachusetts, *Adjusting to Changes in Defense Spending: A Report to the Legislature*, pp. x-xi. John E. Lynch, ed., *Plant Closures and Community Recovery* (Washington, DC: National Council on Urban Economic Development, 1990), Chapter 39.

8. The Electronics Industry Association is at 2000 I St. N.W., Washington, D.C., 202-457-7900. The New York Industrial Cooperation Council is led by Lee Smith, Executive Director, 1515 Broadway, 52nd Floor, New York, NY 10036; 212-930-0111.

9. Tim Miller, "State Braces for Impact of Military Spending Cuts on Economy," *The Dayton Daily News*, December 11, 1989, p. 1.

10. Dave Montgomery, "Texas Legislators Ready for Defense Budget War," *Ft. Worth Star-Telegram*, January 21, 1990, p. 1. Stone, *op. cit.*, p. 11.

11. Lynch, "Conclusion: Dealing with Major Plant Closures," in Lynch, ed., *op. cit.* (1987), p. 243. Stanley Lundine comes to a similar conclusion in "The Jamestown Experience," in Betty G. Lall, ed., *Economic Dislocation and Job Loss* (New York: Cornell University, New York State School of Industrial and Labor Relations, 1985), pp. 146-151.

12. Lynch, "Military Base Civilian Reuse Experience," in Lynch, ed., *op. cit.* (1987), pp. 81-90.

13. Lynch, "Composite Plant Recovery Recovery Approach," in Lynch, ed., *op. cit.* (1990), p. 189. See also Miles Friedman and Deborah Culbertson, "State-Local Economic Development Roles," Chapter 40 in *ibid.*, pp. 109-112.

14. See Lynch, "Composite Plant Closure Recovery Approach," in Lynch, ed., *op. cit.* (1990), p. 190.

15. John Tepper Marlin, *The Wealth of Cities* (New York: Council on Municipal Performance, 1974; pp. 22-29.

16. Richard Thornburgh, "States Connect Jobs and Amenities," *National Civic Review*, 77:1 (January-February 1988), p. 4.

17. "Surprise: Strategic Planning!" *National Civic Review*, 76:1 (January-February 1987), p. 31.

18. Mel Duncan, "Reversing the Current," *Plowshare*, Summer 1989, p. 1. Unisys has announced plans to work on one of the ideas proposed by the IBEW Committee, but at a facility in another state. Stone, *op. cit.*, p. 7.

19. Fred Trueblood, Phillip D. Wyman, Vern Lawson Jr., and Pete Eskis, "Organizing Industry Manpower Programs: Lancaster and Palmdale, California," from Lynch, ed., *op. cit.* (1990), p. 33. A more detailed model was created by the Groton Task Force on Diversification.

20. Marlin, *op. cit.*, p. 29. The essentials of a model strategic plan for economic development have not changed.

21. Robert Ady, "Normal Industrial Plant Redevelopment Process," in Lynch, ed., *op. cit.* (1987), pp. 137-154.

22. Walter H. Plosila, "State-University Technology Applications programs," Chapter 42 in Lynch, ed., *op. cit.* (1990), p. 116.

23. John Tepper Marlin, *Cities of Opportunity* (New York: MasterMedia, 1988), p. 27.

24. Alan R. Gianini, "Saving the Plant—Armstrong Tire: Hanford, California," Chapter 15 in Lynch, ed., *op. cit.* (1990), p. 48. Toledo example from the Office of the Governor of Ohio, December 1990.

25. Lynch, "Military Base...," *loc. cit.*

26. The size of government economic-development offices correlates more with economic distress than with prosperity. See Marlin, *op. cit.* (1974), p. 30.

27. For more on the law, contact Washington State SANE/Freeze, 5516 Roosevelt Way, NE, Seattle, WA 98105. 206-527-8050. See also Stone, *op. cit.*, p.

28. Interview with Mary Ann McGivern, St. Louis Economic Conversion Project, 314-726-6406, and Stone, *op. cit.*, pp. 7-8.

29. Stone, *op. cit.*, p. 2.

30. A fuller description of such organizations is provided at the end of the Directories section of *The Municipal Year Book* published annually by the International City Management Association, Washington, DC.

6

The Federal Role

"In the United States those in authority often accept high unemployment with an air of resignation, as if it stemmed from acts of nature rather than acts of man. This is an attitude conducive to paralysis."

—Princeton Professor Alan Blinder.[1]

This chapter reviews the Federal response to defense-cut-related unemployment, the Federal role in conversion, 1990 legislation, and possible future laws. It concludes with an agency-by-agency review of current Federal involvement.

National Industrial Policy?

Some of our advisers have urged us to open up this chapter to a discusssion of the need for a major Federal role in establishing a national industrial/economic policy for the nation. Proponents of such a role point to the successes of Japanese and European industrial policies. They argue that without Federal leadership in this area, substantial private capital will not be transferred to civilian activities and large companies will simply downsize drastically instead of converting.

The argument is that defense contractors could with proper incentives switch to another government-sponsored activity as they did in response to energy-crisis programs under the Carter Administration.

Following this line of thinking, as part of its conversion effort the Federal Government would initiate new development programs in education, energy, transportation, and other areas. These programs would give large defense contractors the incentive to convert by undertaking large-scale, urgently needed physical and social infrastructure ventures. The Federal programs could be structured so that after an appropriate transitional period of, say, five years, the companies would be on their own to compete in world markets. Federal assistance would be in the form of support for research and development, tax incentives, and low-cost capital during the investment year.[2]

These ideas are indeed interesting and the need for U.S. domestic investment in infrastructure is unquestionable. Therefore we put before the reader a call to put the conversion discussion that follows in a larger framework that Federal programs might pursue. But the ideas are both controversial and complex. They deserve a separate investigation rather than speculative exploration as an adjunct to the subject of this book, which is conversion.

The Federal Response to Unemployment

For years the Department of Defense has taken a strong interest in the employability of its uniformed personnel after discharge and has in-house training and outplacement programs that by all reports do a good job or preparing people for civilian jobs.

Similarly, as we have seen in Chapter 1, since 1961 the Department of Defense has played a useful role in helping communities adjust to defense cuts through the planning, information, and coordinating roles of its Office of Economic Adjustment (OEA). But OEA's primary role has historically been in base-closure situations and its ability to help with defense-contractor cuts is constrained both by law and by funding both of OEA and the Federal and state agencies with which it works.

The Case for a Federal Response Now

States and localities affected by defense cuts or other industrial retrenchments need not resign themselves to a long period of higher unemployment. The Swedish labor-market policies of the mid-1980s — a combination of job-training, subsidies, and unemployment services — are credited with achieving a 1988 unemployment figure of only 1.9 percent as inflation stayed in line with the OECD average. If these policies can work for an entire country, they should be able to work, with Federal help, for states and localities struggling to deal with defense-related joblessness.

Federal programs are essential in 1992 and future years because:

- The likely defense cuts are larger, at least in dollar terms, than after the Korean or Vietnam Wars. They loom even larger compared to the high expectations that communities and companies had in an era of a growing Department of Defense budget.[3]
- As we noted in the Introduction, whereas the post-World War II cuts were described as "reconversion" because most defense contractors had shifted from making civilian products to assisting in the war effort, today the cuts are more serious because they erode a permanent defense-contracting establishment.

- A disproportionate share of the adjustment burden is being borne by the relatively few areas that have the bulk of the defense contracts at risk, including: St. Louis, MO; the Phoenix area; central Long Island, NY; and Orange County, CA.
- Several of the most affected states are too strapped financially to take on substantial adjustment programs.

The main available Federal strategies are to provide:

- advice to affected communities on planning for reuse of military facilities and retraining of employees,
- planning grants,
- incentives such as tax deductions and loan guarantees to private-sector institutions to encourage job expansion in affected communities,
- pension-law incentives to facilitate early retirement of defense-contractor employees, and
- offsetting Federal spending on civilian projects, or extended unemployment benefits, in affected areas.

Costs and Benefits of Unemployment

The Congressional Budget Office estimates that a 1 percent increase in the average projected unemployment rate for the period 1990-1995 would mean a loss of $277 billion in Federal revenues over six years and an increase in the deficit of $364 billion over the same period. As a rule of thumb in the 1960s (Okun's Law), GNP dropped 2.5 percent for each 1 percent increase in the unemployment rate, a multiplier of 2.5.[4] If this rule applies in the 1990s, as the Congressional Budget Office in 1990 suggested it does, it means a 1 percent rise in unemployment would mean an additional 1.3 million unemployed people.[5]

If defense spending (in FY 1990 dollars) were to be cut from $300 billion to $175 billion within ten years, a $12.5-billion-a-year reduction, it would mean *an average decline of about 6 percent a year and an average reduction of 362,000 defense jobs per year.* Of the layoffs, typically 14 percent, or approximately 51,000 workers, would be taken care of by attrition (retirement or other voluntary separation including immediate re-employment).[6] Given the maturity of the aerospace industry and the related potential for early retirement, as many as half of laid-off employees might take early retirement *if* their pensions were fully vested, a condition that may be difficult to meet in some cases without amending Federal pension laws.

Historical data indicate that if 14 percent are taken care of by attrition, two-thirds of the remaining 312,000 laid-off workers would be re-employed by the end of the fourth month.[7] The net increase in unemployment after four months would be 104,000 workers, which represents a 0.08 percent increase in the unemployment rate and a corresponding $11 billion (0.2 percent) reduction in GNP. As these reductions occur annually, the effects will be cumulative.

The loss in GNP would be accompanied by a loss in tax revenues, as the unemployed workers' tax contributions fall significantly, and there would be an increase in welfare payments, notably unemployment-benefits compensation (discussed next).

To ameliorate the negative effects of layoffs, we recommend that job retraining and placement programs be implemented and that unemployment compensation be extended, in part to function as an incentive for laid-off workers to enroll in retraining, education and outplacement programs (as now occurs in some states, such as Massachusetts). This should have the effect of speeding up the transition and the growth of civilian employers in affected areas.

The benefits of unemployment relate to keeping down the cost of labor to employers, encouraging entrepreneurship (enterprise is weakest in cities with high labor costs).[8] Areas with high unemployment are often attractive locations for employers seeking to cut their per-unit costs. *But it is highly important that these employer advantages are quickly advertised and new employers successfully attracted*, not only because delays prolong the costs of unemployment but because work skills and morale deteriorate with prolonged unemployment and good workers leave town.

Cost and Benefits of Unemployment Compensation

The Unemployment Compensation system provides short-term (usually 26-week) income assistance to unemployed workers, using a state-operated system supported by Federal tax incentives. The system's framework was created by the Federal Unemployment Tax Act of 1939 and Titles III, IX, and XII of the Social Security Act.[9]

Unemployment compensation benefits in the first half of FY 1990 averaged $155 per week.[10] For defense workers, who are likely to have higher-than-average incomes, the average is likely to be higher, $160 per week or possibly more.

Unemployment compensation is paid out for an average of 13.5 weeks per compensated worker.[11] Defense workers are likely to be laid off in large numbers all at once, making it difficult for the local economy to absorb them. It is therefore likely that they will be collecting unemployment compensation for significantly more than the average period. A lowball estimate of unemployment compensation per defense-worker beneficiary is $160 x 15 weeks, or $2,400. So *layoffs of 100,000 defense workers a year would mean unemployment compensation outlays of $240 million a year.*[12]

The system not only benefits the affected workers by bridging the period between jobs; it also benefits the rest of the local economy. For instance, a Tucson area study showed that, on average, every $48,000 (in 1990 dollars) in unemployment insurance created one new local job.[13]

The Cost and Benefits of Job Training

Federal agencies have been deeply involved in economic-adjustment issues over the past decade, but the only source of leadership appears to be in the Pentagon. Other agencies that should play a larger role in adjustment are the Economic Development Administration (EDA, in the Department of Commerce), the Department of Labor, and the Small Business Administration (SBA).

The primary program that permits Federal involvement in advance of military cuts is the Title IX (of the Public Works and Economic Development Act) program of the EDA. It is designed to help communities plan for recovery from an economic downturn. This money has been appropriated by Congress despite the fact that the Reagan and Bush Administrations had "zeroed out" the agency.

The Department of Labor administers Title III of the Job Training Partnership Act (JTPA), which was the Reagan Administration's replacement for the Comprehensive Employment and Training Act (CETA) starting in FY 1984. CETA provided an average of about $6 billion a year between FY 1975 and FY 1983, and had the additional purpose of helping local governments provide services.

In line with Reagan-era cuts in domestic programs, JTPA was substantially less well funded than the pre-Reagan CETA program; states and localities seeking to address an economic adjustment problem suffered a drop in Federal assistance. With only $500 million in FY 1990, JTPA Title III was not in 1990 adequately funded to take care of traditional training needs of displaced defense workers. A question is whether the training programs are adequate for highly skilled and older defense workers.[14] Generally, the most economically valuable and rapidly repaid governmental investments in education are in adult and vocational programs, so that job training programs are easy to recommend.

Costs and Benefits of Small-Business Programs

It is not enough to train employees without making an effort to encourage the creation of new jobs. Most jobs come from the creation and growth of small businesses. To foster this process, SBA makes loans and guarantees to small businesses. Such assistance is especially important in communities affected by defense cuts. SBA programs relevant to economic adjustment fall into three categories: (1) The 7(a) loans or 90-percent loan guarantees to commercial banks, which in turn make loans to small businesses, (2) 100-percent loan guarantees to development companies, which make loans to small businesses, and (3) Economic Impact Disaster Loans, a small program of loans made directly to small businesses affected by economic downturns.[15]

Although SBA has no funds earmarked for conversion, it has funds that could be used to assist entrepreneurs in communities facing defense cuts. The benefits of SBA intervention are to speed up the creation of new employers.

Often the lessons that are learned by participants in small-business startups make them better employees or entrepreneurs.

For example, SBA's Small Business Investment Company program helps venture-capital companies make loans to small businesses. The launching of the Minute Maid orange juice company is one of its success stories.

Legislative Achievements in 1990

Since 1963, a conversion bill originally introduced by Sen. George McGovern has been kept alive by peace groups and most recently by Rep. Ted Weiss (D-NY). It was considered too anti-military (with mandatory company-based advance planning for conversion) to be palatable to the companies and communities heavily involved in defense work, and alternative bills were introduced in 1986 by Reps. Sam Gejdenson (D-CT) and Nick Mavroules (D-MA).[16] A 1989 effort to get the proponents to agree to a common bill was spearheaded by former House Speaker Jim Wright but moved slowly and died with his departure from the Congress. When Rep. Mary Rose Oakar (D-OH) held hearings on a new conversion bill in the summer of 1989, it had little support.

By the end of 1989, prospects for conversion legislation were bleak. Witnesses before the House Armed Services Committee minimized the need for Federal legislation, dismissing the economic significance of what was seen as a minor downward shift, over many years, of a defense budget that was taking a decreasing share of GNP.

Enter Majority Leader Gephardt

At the beginning of 1990, House Majority Leader Richard Gephardt started to pick up the mantle put down by former Speaker Jim Wright. He called on the Joint Economic Committee to start the process of legislative hearings by holding hearings on conversion legislation in March 1990 (CEP led the witness list).

He also called together all the legislators involved in promoting conversion legislation and encouraged them to work together again on a common bill.

CEP's 1990 Recommendations

CEP in its March 1990 testimony urged that a new law include the following four features:

1. *Target Assistance to Most Affected Areas.* The law should provide for targeting aid to the most severely affected areas. This could be achieved as follows:

- planning assistance to the most affected states and localities could be linked to the Vulnerability Index so that more funds would go to the more vulnerable states — for example, the top 25 might qualify;

- program implementation assistance, including extension of worker benefits, could be distributed to states and localities using the Defense Dislocation Index so that more funds would go to the most dislocated states – the top 20 might qualify.

2. *Provide Training Incentives.* The law's motivation to action should come from incentives, not regulation. This relationship should exist between the Federal agencies and the states and localities; it should also be encouraged between the states and the localities. For example, communities and companies in severely affected areas should be rewarded for instituting planning and training programs with Federal planning and training grants that encourage companies and communities to follow through with placement services.

3. *Extend Benefits for Laid-Off Defense Workers.* CEP urged extension of unemployment compensation (under Title IV, as an Economic Readjustment Allowance) by 26 weeks beyond the existing 26 weeks under the Federal Unemployment Tax Act.[17] The job cuts are likely to be concentrated in a few hard-hit communities. The unemployed workers themselves should be the bill's first priority. CEP urged that the bill provide for 26 additional weeks of unemployment compensation for laid-off defense workers in severely affected communities. The total 52-week coverage would provide time for a worker to relocate if necessary. If, as we calculated above, the cost of unemployment compensation for defense workers for the *first* 26 weeks (average of 14 weeks) is likely to be about $2,400 per laid-off worker, then a fund to cover a *second* 26-week increment would be substantially lower, as more workers by that time would have found new jobs – i.e. under $1,000 per laid-off worker and substantially less than that if the program was restricted to severely affected communities.

4. *Use Existing Federal Programs.* Link conversion aid to existing Federal programs such as EDA's Title IX, JTPA Title III, SBA, and Eximbank.[18]

The 1990 Conversion Law

Conversion legislation (HR 3999) introduced by Rep. Oakar began to pick up the support of the House leadership during the March-June 1990 period. Hearings were held in both the Armed Services and Banking Committees in June and July 1990. By the fall of 1990 the bill had a great deal of support. HR 3999 was designed to provide economic adjustment support to affected workers, companies, and communities by supporting the following Federal programs: a voluntary program for community and defense-contractor planning; unemployment compensation extensions (e.g., for workers being retrained), and use of such existing programs as OEA, JTPA's Title III, EDA's Title IX, Eximbank loan guarantees, and SBA's 7(a), Section 504, and Small Business Investment Company loan guarantees, small business loans, and Small Business Innovative Research grants.

"The Defense Economic Adjustment, Diversification, Conversion, and Stabilization Act of 1990" was originally drafted by Rep. Oakar as a compromise bill, then went to the House Armed Services Committee and finally appeared as Division D in the FY 1991 Defense Authorization Bill, adopted in September 1990, and the Defense Appropriation Bill the following month. The 1990 Conversion Law (called "Division D" by Washington insiders) incorporates three of the above four principles that CEP urged: targeting aid, creating incentives for participation, and using existing Federal programs. The fourth principle, extending jobless benefits, was adopted for all workers in the 1991 Congress and was signed into law, but President Bush has refused to provide the needed additional funds for the program.

The law continues oversight of the economic-adjustment function in the President's Committee, but made it statutory, as CEP had urged, and gave it three functions (1) Coordinating Federal agency assistance, (2) Serving as a national clearinghouse for economic adjustment efforts at all levels of government, and (3) Reporting annually to the President and Congress describing available programs and allocation of funds, specifying the number of communities, business, and workers affected by defense cuts and assisted by the Federal Government.

Funding for OEA was nearly doubled to the level CEP recommended, i.e. $7 million. As in the past, OEA was empowered to make direct grants to eligible communities for assistance to eligible companies or affected workers.

Targeting of aid was linked to the impact of cuts on communities, companies, and workers. To be eligible for Federal assistance:

- *Communities* must be facing a loss of 2,500 jobs in an urban area, or 1,000 jobs in a rural area, or 1 percent of the total civilian workforce in any area.
- *Companies* must have a prime defense contract of $5 million or more or a subcontract of $500,000 or more, and they must face the loss of 25 percent or more of their sales or production, or 80 percent or more of their employees in any division or plant.
- *Workers* must be at least 100 in number at a single defense facility and they must be otherwise eligible for assistance under Section 325 of the JTPA.

Additional funding of $50 million was allocated to EDA for its Title IX infrastructure assistance. This money is ordinarily provided to communities for fixing up former defense properties for commercial or industrial use. The law provides that in exceptional circumstances EDA funds can be used to assist eligible communities, companies, and workers directly.

Finally, additional funding of $150 million was allocated to the Department of Labor for the JTPA Title III program.

No specific allocation was made to the Eximbank or to the SBA, but the President was instructed to explore and report on the potential for using these two agencies to help with economic adjustment to defense cuts.

No specific regulations are being promulgated to implement the 1990 Conversion Law, although the Department of Labor in September 1991 produced an application form for Title III funds.

We encourage the Department of Labor to develop an educational program for defense scientists and engineers, to give them the cost accounting, marketing, and entrepreneurial skills to put their abilities to work in the civilian sector.

Needs for Further Legislation

Federal programs beyond those already passed in the 1990 Conversion Law are needed (1) to *minimize community opposition to reduced defense work that might derail progress toward peace by alarming the Soviets and other military powers*, (2) to *reduce the burden on employees* of conversion, and (3) to ensure that *sound strategic considerations* govern our transition to a post-Cold War world.

The major missing elements in the 1990 Conversion Law are the lack of support for small businesses and a longer period for unemployment compensation. Both issues are being pursued in the 1991 Congress, with a proposed small business fund for laid-off defense workers and a general extension by 20 weeks on unemployment compensation. President Bush refused to fund the general extension of unemployment compensation. The case for extending benefits for defense workers is strong for defense-related workers because they are often highly specialized and are laid off *en masse*.

The impact of cuts on the career military will be serious. Many who have planned a career in military service will have to reevaluate their plans. Several bills to provide separation benefits for mustered-out military personnel introduced by Reps. Jim Slattery (D-KS), Beverly B. Byron (D-MD), and Sens. William Cohen (R-ME) and John McCain (R-AZ).[19] The Slattery bill provides extended unemployment compensation (from 13 to 26 weeks), health benefits, job training, and relocation services to involuntarily released service-members.[20] The Byron bill provides for an array of benefits including separation pay, medical transition assistance, extended unemployment compensation, an Office of Military Personnel Readjustment Assistance, transition counseling, job fairs, job certification, employment preference in the Department of Defense and extended use of commissary and exchange privileges.

Provision for maintenance of health benefits would also be helpful. Existing laws protect the rights of workers to health insurance programs provided the laid-off worker keeps up payment of the insurance premium; but such payments are beyond the reach of some laid-off workers.

More broadly, the 1990 Conversion Law does not provide any overall guidance to the military on the conversion process. Sen. Sam Nunn's mid-1990 proposals for linking laid-off defense workers to environmental missions might bear a second look in the future.

Executive Branch Contacts

The following Federal agencies have a role in the conversion process. Unless the area code is provided, all phone and fax numbers are in area code 202.

Arms Control and Disarmament Agency, Defense Programs and Analysis Division, 320 21st St., N.W., Room 4953, Washington, DC 20451; Daniel Gallik, 647-1300.

Department of Agriculture, Farmers Home Administration (FHA), 14th & Independence Ave, S.W., S. Agricultural Bldg., Room 5022, Washington, DC 20250; Michael Wilkinson, 447-2564. The FHA makes business loans in rural areas.

Department of Commerce, 14th St. between Constitution Ave. & E St., NW, Washington, DC 20230. Secretary: Robert A. Mosbacher, 377-2113.

Economic Development Administration (EDA), Assistant Secretary L. Joyce Hampers, 377-4067, 377-3081. Director, EDA Office of Economic Adjustment, Room 7327; David McIlivin, 377-2659. EDA administers Title IX funds, which help distressed communities with infrastructure planning and financing.

Technology Administration, Assistant Secretary for Technology Administration: Debra Wince-Smith. Conversion could include shifting Defense Advanced Research Projects Agency funds to a civilian equivalent, probably under the Commerce aegis, as urged by the Office of Technology Assessment and Sens. Riegle, Glenn, Kennedy, and Sasser.[21]

Department of Defense, The Pentagon, Washington, DC 20301. Secretary: Dick Cheney 703-695-5261. Assistant Secretary for Force Management and Personnel, 3E764, Pentagon, Christopher Jehn, 703-695-5254.

Office of Economic Adjustment (OEA), Director, Pentagon, Room 4C767, Washington, DC 20301-4000, Robert Rauner, 703-697-8652, 703-697-9155, fax 703-697-3021. Deputy Director, OEA, 400 Army Navy Drive, Arlington, VA 22284, Paul Dempsey, 695-1800. OEA plays a central role in Federal aid to communities facing defense cuts. It reports to the President's [Interagency] Economic Adjustment Committee (EAC; see Executive Office of the President). The OEA conducts planning under Section 2391 (it may make planning grants directly to communities but is forbidden from engaging in civilian implementation programs) and spent $32 million (1990 $) on planning during the 1961-1989 period.

Department of Education, Federal Office Building 6, 400 Maryland Avenue, S.W., Washington, DC 20202. Deputy Under Secretary for Management, 400 Maryland Ave, S.W., Room 3181, Washington, DC 20202, Thomas

Anfinson, 732-5470. The Department administers school-impact assistance for 1-2 years beyond closure of bases, under Section 3e of PL 81-874.

Department of Health and Human Services (HHS), Deputy Under Secretary for Policy & Administration, Hubert H. Humphrey Building, Washington, DC 20201; Hon. Ann Agnew, 245-3400. HHS administers health-care programs, including regulation of health benefits for laid-off workers.

Department of Housing and Urban Development, 451 7th St., SW, Washington, DC 20410. Secretary: Jack Kemp, 755-6417. Under Secretary, Room 10100; Carl Covitz, 755-7123. HUD sometimes supports local conversion efforts.

Department of Labor, Asst. Secretary, Employment & Training Administration, 200 Constitution Ave., N.W., Washington, DC 20210; Hon. Roberts T. Jones, 523-6050 and 523-4000. Administrator, Office of Worker Based Learning, 200 Constitution Ave, NW, Room N4469, Washington, DC 20213; James Van Erden, 535-0540. Office of Worker Retraining & Adjustment, 200 Constitution Ave., N.W., Room N4703, Washington, DC 20213; Doug Holl, 535-0305. Labor administers Title III of the Job Training Partnership Act (JTPA), which provides funds to states and localities for retraining and placement of dislocated workers. Labor also administers unemployment programs (the U.S. Treasury administers the Federal Unemployment Tax).

Department of the Interior, Economic Adjustment Administrator, 18th & C St., N.W., Room 4340, Washington, DC 20240; Andrew Adams, 343-5521. Interior can provide some funds from its Land and Water Conservation Fund (cleaning up polluted bases after closure is a major conversion challenge).

Department of Transportation, Assistant Secretary for Administration, 400 7th St., S.W., Room 10314, Washington, DC 20590; Hon. John Seymour, 366-2332. DoT administers the Transportation Trust Fund, from which funds could be used (through the Federal Aviation Agency) for aviation planning. Sen. Adams has suggested increasing the size of this Fund.

Environmental Protection Agency (EPA), Waterside West Building, 401 M St., S.W., Washington, DC 20460. Administrator: William K. Reilly; 382-4700. EPA has supported economic-adjustment programs in the past. Sen. Nunn in June 1990 urged the military to consider undertaking environmental projects as a means of civilian deployment of unneeded military resources.

Executive Office of the President ("White House"). Besides the three entities listed below, the White House is responsible for setting the tone for macroeconomic policy; it can influence the decisions and effectiveness of, for example, the Federal Reserve System's monetary policies.

Council of Economic Advisors, Old Executive Office Building, Room 328, Washington, DC 20500; Carole Kitti, 395-5012.

Office of Management and Budget, Deputy Associate Director, Special Studies, National Security & International Affairs, 726 Jackson Place, N.W., NEOB, Room 10007, Washington, DC 20503; Daniel Taft, 395-3285.

President's [Interagency] Economic Adjustment Committee (EAC) operated at the convenience of the President until the 1990 Conversion Law made it a statutory body. The committee will be chaired, on an annually rotating basis, by the Secretaries of Defense, Commerce, and Labor. Besides these three agencies, the EAC includes representatives from OMB, HUD, Agriculture, Education, Interior, Justice, Transportation, Health and Human Services, EPA, and SBA.

Eximbank, Lafayette Building, 811 Vermont Ave., N.W., Washington, DC 20571; 566-8144. President: John D. Macomber. Makes loan guarantees to support non-weapon (in recent years) exports, with special emphasis on lending to small and medium-sized businesses in defense-impacted communities.

General Services Administration, Assistant Commissioner for Real Estate Policy, 18th & F Sts., N.W., Room 4236, Washington, DC 20405, John Neale, 535-7084.

Office of Personnel Management, Deputy Assoc. Director for Career Entry & Employees Development, 1900 E St., N.W., Room 6F08, Washington, DC 20415; Len Klein, 632-6005.

Small Business Administration (SBA), Assoc. Administrator for Procurement 1441 L St., N.W., Washington, DC 20416: Monika Harrison, 653-6635. Director, Office of Procurement Policy and Liaison; Gene Van Arsdale, 632-6101. SBA makes loans and loan guarantees directly to small businesses and to lenders to and investors in them — for example, it makes Section 504 loan guarantees to certified development companies, which make loans to small businesses. Authority for Economic Impact Disaster Loans has expired. SBA will require more funds for 7(a) and Section 504, 40 percent loan guarantees (to be funded through the Federal Finance Bank). Another valuable resource is the Small Business Innovative Research grant program, which could help laid-off engineers.

Congressional Contacts

The House of Representatives Zip Code is 20515 and the Senate's is 20510. the Area Code for both is 202. Key elected officials are italicized in their main listing.

House Appropriations, Defense, Don Richbourg, 225-2847.

House Armed Services, Rep. Les *Aspin* (D-WI), Chairman; 2336 RHOB, 225-3031. Kim Wincup 225-4151. Aspin and Rep. Nick *Mavroules* (D-MA, Northern Boston suburbs) played a key role in passing the 1990 Conversion Law; Mavroules' assistant for conversion is Margaret Sullivan, 2432 Rayburn; 225-8020.

House Banking, Finance & Urban Affairs, Economic Stabilization subcommittee: Rep. Mary Rose *Oakar* (D-OH, Cleveland) chaired the Subcommittee on Economic Stabilization in 1990 and played an important role in getting the 1990 Conversion Law passed. Herb Spira, 2231 Rayburn; 225-5871. William Cunningham 226-7515

House Majority Leader. Majority Leader Dick *Gephardt* (D-MO, St. Louis), 1432 Longworth; 225-2671. With substantial concern about economic adjustment in his own hometown of St. Louis, Gephardt showed strong interest in remedial Federal legislation and played a central role in passage of the 1990 Conversion Law. Gephardt in 1990 assembled an important working group on this task composed of himself and Reps. Aspin, Gejdenson, Mavroules, Oakar, Weiss. His key adviser on the issue is Dan Nelson, in the Office of the Majority Leader, 225-0100.

House: *Other Interested Representatives.* The following are among those who showed some interest in the 1990 Conversion Law:

- *Clinger*, Rep. William F. (R-PA): Ed Feddeman, 2251 Rayburn; 226-3220.
- *Gejdenson*, Rep. Sam (D-CT, Groton, New London area, home of the Electric Boat Company): Maggie Bierwirth, 1410 Longworth; 225-2076. Introduced an economic adjustment bill and helped cement the coalition that got through the 1990 Conversion Law.
- *Green*, Rep. Bill (R-NY). 1110 Longworth; 225-2436.
- *Leach,* Rep. Jim (R-IA): Patricia Koch, 1514 Longworth; 225-6576.
- *Oberstar*, Rep. James L. (DFL-MN): Caroline Gabel, 2251 Rayburn; 225-9161. Interested in infrastructure improvement in the United States as a benefit of military cutbacks.
- *Spratt*, Rep. John M., Jr. (D-SC): Robert DeGrasse.
- *Weiss*, Rep. Ted (D-NY, Manhattan, Bronx): 2467 Rayburn; 225-5635. Nathaniel Moss, 252 Seventh Ave., New York, NY 10001. 212-620-3970. Representing Manhattan's Upper West Side, Weiss has for years carried forward a bill that embodies the narrow concept of conversion, i.e., mandatory company and community advance planning. His bill laid the groundwork for passage of the 1990 Conversion Law, though this law did not go as far as Weiss favored.

Joint Economic Committee, headed by Sen. Paul *Sarbanes* and Rep. Lee *Hamilton*. Richard Kaufman, Counsel 224-224-5171, fax 224-0240. The Committee was the first to hold hearings on conversion in 1990. They were chaired by Rep. Hamilton.

Senate Appropriations: Defense subcommittee, Francis Sullivan 224-7254.

Senate Armed Services. Sen. Sam *Nunn* (D-GA), Chairman. Other majority members are: Sens. Exon, Levin, Kennedy, Bingaman, Dixon, Glenn, Gore, Wirth, Shelby, and Byrd. Contact: Arnold L. Punaro, Staff Director, 224-3871, 222 SROB; Dick Combs specializes in conversion.

Senate Governmental Affairs, Leonard Weiss 224-4751.

Senate Majority Leader. Sen. George J. *Mitchell* (D-ME). Staff: Scott Harris, 176 Russell; 224-4344. Sen. Mitchell created a Task Force on the U.S. Economy in the 1990s. Don *Riegle* (D-MI) heads this Task Force. Other members are Sens. Adams, Bentsen, Bingaman, Boren, Conrad, Exon,

Hollings, Kennedy, Levin, Nunn, Pell, and Shelby. Sen. Claiborne *Pell* (D-RI) introduced an economic-adjustment bill in the Senate in 1990.

Notes

1. Alan S. Blinder, "The Challenge of High Unemployment," *American Economic Review*, May 1988, p. 2.

2. We are grateful to Peter H. Rose for pointing out the relevance of these issues to the Federal conversion role, and for providing some of the language we have used.

3. "Welfare and Work," *The Economist*, November 26, 1988, p. 20. 3. The Department of Defense projected a *9 percent real increase in spending* ("direct defense purchases and pay") between 1987 and 1992, from $236.2 billion to $258.3 billion in 1987 dollars. The Defense Economic Impact Modeling System (DEIMS) projections of May 21, 1987 of industry and regional impacts were based on this assumption. See Department of Defense, Directorate for Information, Operations and Reports, *Projected Defense Purchases: Detail by Industry and State: Calendar Years 1987 through 1992*, 1987.

4. On Okun's Law: The rule of thumb is cited by the Congressional Budget Office (CBO), *1990 Annual Report*, p. 56. The law is named after Arthur Okun, Chairman of the Council of Economic Advisers in the 1960s. On CBO prediction: *The Economic and Budget Outlook: Fiscal Years 1991-1995*, A Report to the Senate and House Committees on the Budget, January 1990, p. 55.

5. Lewis Franklin, Vice President, Space and Defense Sector, TRW, has two questions about the applicability of the multiplier to a high-tech defense-contractor community: (1) the economic multiplier should be higher than the 2.5 used in Chapter 4, because of the high labor component and the long string of indirect and induced labor-intensive suppliers and service vendors, but on the other hand (2) the larger number of two-income families in the 1990s, and the large number of employees near retirement (or early retirement) in the mature aerospace industry may offset and ameliorate the otherwise serious impact of defense-contractor cuts. The two factors work in opposite directions and might neutralize each other's effects. The civilian labor force averaged 118 million in 1986, 120 million in 1987, 122 million in 1988, and 124 million in 1989, a simple arithmetic progression adding 2 million persons a year. Extending this progression means 128 million in 1991, 130 million in 1992, and so forth. If jobs dropped by 1 percent, 1.3 million people would be newly out of work; but see text for attrition data and re-employment prospects. See Bureau of Labor Statistics, U.S. Labor Department, "U.S. Labor Force, Employment and Unemployment," cited in *The World Almanac, 1990*, p. 97.

6. In 1987 the attrition figure was 14 percent, the difference between the figure for "separations" in conditions of mass layoffs and the figure for "initial claimants for unemployment insurance." See Bureau of Labor Statistics, U.S. Department of Labor, *Permanent Mass Layoffs and Plant Closings, 1987*, Bulletin 2310, Table 3, p. 5. See the line for "Reason for Separation," 27,696 separations vs. 23,753 initial claimants. The overall attrition level is higher, 21.2 percent (406,887 separations vs. 319,343 initial claimants), but industry data from Table 2 on p. 4 suggest that attrition in the machinery, electrical, and transportation equipment industries is lower, 11.3 percent (111,744 separations vs. 99,069 initial claimants). In 1988 the attrition figure for the three industry categories was lower, 7.8 percent, but the overall attrition rate was higher, 22.4 percent, so that the 1987 figure seems to be a fair estimate for defense workers. See Bureau of Labor Statistics, U.S. Department of Labor, "BLS Reports on Mass Layoffs in 1988," press release for August 1, 1989, Tables 1 and 2.

7. That is, 14 weeks, which is the average duration of unemployment, though 21 percent of those who apply for unemployment compensation are still unemployed at the end of the 26-week period of coverage. In January-March 1987 in 29 states, 78,911 initial claimants for unemployment insurance came in at one end of the process while 18,421 "exhaustees" exited 26 weeks later in July-September, i.e. 23.3 percent of initial claimants exhausted their 26 weeks of unemployment compensation. See Bureau of Labor Statistics, *Permanent Mass Layoffs...*, *op. cit.*, Table 11, p. 13 and Table 36, p. 35. Similarly, in April-June 1987 the initial claimants numbered 89,884 and six months later the exhaustees numbered 16,870, 18.8 percent of the original claimants. See *ibid.*, Table 20, p. 21 and Table 45, p. 43. Based on this admittedly small sample, the average exhaustion rate is 21 percent.

8. John Tepper Marlin, *Cities of Opportunity* (New York: MasterMedia, 1988), p. 40.

9. State laws determine individual eligibility, benefit amount, benefit duration, and disqualification provisions, within broad Federal guidelines. For a state's employers to qualify for up to a 5.4 percent tax credit on the FUTA tax liability, state unemployment compensation laws must cover certain types of employment. States collect the 6.2 percent gross tax unemployment insurance taxes from employers and pay them to the U.S. Treasury, which maintains separate state accounts and makes funds available to states for benefit payments. Employers pay a net FUTA tax rate of 0.8 percent on the first $7,000 of an employee's wages; they collect this money in turn from employees. Celinda M. Franco, "How the Unemployment Compensation System Works," (Washington, DC: CRS Report, Congressional Research Service, November 5, 1987, updated May 22, 1989), p. 1.

10. *Loc. cit.*

11. FY 1989 data from Cory Oltman at the Congressional Budget Office, 202-226-2820; and Bob Hale, Assistant Director of the CBO, 202-226-2900; fax 202-226-2963.

12. Average U.S. unemployment compensation for the first two quarters of FY 1990 was $155/week, and average duration is 13 weeks. Because defense workers are likely to have higher incomes and be laid off in groups, we used $160/week in our projections, and a 15-week duration. All numbers and information from the CBO.

13. The Tucson study suggests that each $20,000 of unemployment insurance in 1976 created one job—$1 million in unemployment compensation created work for 50 people. Source: unidentified paper, pp. 17-18, sent to us by John Robinson, ETA, U.S. Department of Labor, 200 Constitution Avenue, N.W., Washington, DC 20210; 202-523-6194, fax 202-523-7312. We updated the $20,000 figure to 1990 using the Bureau of Labor Statistics Consumer Price Index series, which shows 53.8 in 1976 and 118.3 in 1988. The index was extrapolated to 128.3 in 1990. The series appears in the *World Almanac 1990*, p. 88.

14. Specialized training programs targeted to scientists and engineers, to assist them in adjusting to the cost control and marketing requirements of civilian work, may well go beyond the scope of existing Title III training programs. This is a current concern of the Committee for Economic Development. Another issue is the jobs that workers are being trained for—the once-touted need for keypunchers, for example, has been diminished by the new generation of optical-scanning equipment. The Department of Labor training programs have also been criticized for not working well for older employees.

15. Lawrence R. Rosenbaum, Comptroller, SBA, 202-653-6349. Greg Walter, Chief of Credit Programs, Budget Office, SBA.

16. John Tepper Marlin, "At Last: Economic Adjustment?" *CEP Research Report*, June 1989, p. 3.

17. See Economic Stabilization Subcommittee, House Banking Committee, "Summary of H.R. 3999, The Economic Adjustment, Diversification, Conversion and Stabilization Act of 1990," June 12, 1990, p. 4.

18. CEP's full testimony before the Joint Economic Committee in March 1990 was published as: John Tepper Marlin, *Written Testimony Presented to the Joint Economic Committee* (New York: CEP, 1990); a briefer version was made orally. CEP provided written and oral testimony later in the year before Mary Rose Oakar's subcommittee of the House Banking Committee, and presented written testimony to the House Armed Services Committee.

19. The Cohen bill extends to enlisted personnel the separation benefits that are already available to commissioned and warrant officers. The McCain bill is a comprehensive package of benefits designed by a coalition of military retirees at the request of Senator McCain. See Sergeant Major C. A. McKinney, USMC (Ret.), and Col. Paul W. Arcari, USAF (Ret.), *Statement* before the Subcommittee on Manpower and Personnel, Senate Committee on Armed Services, June 20, 1990, pp. 4-5. A good summary of existing and requested transitional programs is provided by the Assistant Secretary of Defense, Christopher Jehn, in his *Statement* to this subcommittee, June 20, 1990.

20. *Statement* of Rep. Jim Slattery before the Subcommittee on Military Personnel and Compensation, House Armed Services Committee, June 26, 1990, p. 1.

21. The proposal for CARPA is a major interest of Prof. Kosta Tsipis of M.I.T. See also Eduardo Lchica, "Panel Urges Civilian Technology Agency to Help U.S. Manufacturers Regain Edge," *The Wall Street Journal*, March 1, 1990. Dr. Peter B. Maggs, 209 Law Building, 504 East Pennsylvania Avenue, Champaign, IL 61820, 217-333-6711. He believes "R&D is inherently elitist," because of need for peer review to ensure quality; this he says is difficult for democratic politics to handle. He is also studying the legality of government support of R&D projects that benefit shareholders.

7

Groups Promoting Conversion

Some would make conversion a special subset of economic-development problems. States and localities must cope with all kinds of economic disruptions, including the business cycle; conversion is considered just another of these disruptions. To the state and local economic-development professionals referenced in Chapter 5, that is perhaps all that conversion amounts to.

But for those concerned about a peaceful world, conversion is the other side of the disarmament coin. Peace is not just the absence of war, any more than health is just the absence of sickness. An intellectual appreciation of peace and the issues relating to economic adjustment and conversion is not enough. Conversion is a way to ensure that global gains for peace and personal freedom are sustained, a way to act on President Eisenhower's 1960 Farewell Address warning to U.S. voters not to "let the weight of this combination [the military-industrial complex] endanger our liberties or democratic processes."

This chapter is about the private-sector organizations that overlap peace and economic issues. We focus on national groups that look beyond arms control, have conversion as an explicit goal, and have substantive programmatic activity in the area. We have sought to err on the side of inclusiveness.

Four key constituencies work on behalf of conversion:

1. *Peace groups* are aware of conversion's importance as a way of hastening and sealing the move from the Cold War to a peacetime economy.
2. *Workers* laid off by military contractors and the *communities* they live in have an interest in conversion to reduce the burdens of unemployment and reduced income. Some key unions are listed at the end of this chapter.
3. *Entrepreneurs in the economic-development field and educators* are interested in helping to open up the potential for spending more on domestic infrastructure, raising the nation's quality of life and economic growth. Local-government economic-development organizations are listed in Chapter 5. Officials are listed state-by-state in Chapter 8.

4. *Privatizers and venture capitalists* are interested in conversion as a way to move resources from less productive government control to more productive private control. These investors often use vehicles such as the organizations in this chapter and Chapter 5 to generate information and initiate contacts.

Conversion Activities

The needed steps to promote conversion are:

- At the *company and union level*, devote attention to a move to civilian production.
- At the *Federal and state level*, develop programs to assist economic adjustment in affected plants and communities.
- At the *community level*, mobilize other constituencies but especially labor and the local power structure; with other groups, develop a vision of peaceful production, then gear up an educational program to spread this vision, describing success stories and how they worked; institutionalize the planning process by centralizing and making accessible technical expertise and models for change in an information clearinghouse; get resources for doing political work and include a national legislative component.[1]

Organizations involved in conversion issues do so in through the following kinds of activities:

Conferences

Conversion conferences are an opportunity for academics, community leaders, or officials to exchange information and compare strategies. Here are a few examples:

The Center for Economic Conversion, based in Mountain View, CA, holds an annual strategy retreat for community-based organizations interested in conversion. The 1990 retreat was on Block Island, N.Y.; 1991's was in Austin, TX. Their purpose is to seek ways to involve workers and the community in conversion.

The Council on Economic Priorities initiated a U.S.-Soviet conference on conversion in Boston in September 1990 and sponsored one in Moscow in 1991.

The U.N. sponsored an international conference on conversion in Moscow in August 1990, and is continuing with programs in Beijing in 1991 and Dortmund, Germany in 1992.

The Hofstra University Institute for Business Research sponsored a conference on conversion on Long Island in 1989.

Stanford in mid-1991 sponsored a one-day conference on converting the Soviet aviation industry.

Environmental Linkage

Two issues that have been among the hottest topics in recent years, the defense budget and the health of our environment, are being brought together in light of the defense cuts. Such groups as the National Toxics Campaign Fund are working to take advantage of the cuts to reduce hazardous activities that affect the environment. The U.S. military has been marked as one of the greatest contributors to toxic waste generation. Toxic chemicals and other debris are often littered across military bases and leak from nuclear weapons production plants. The cost of their clarnup runs into billions of dollars. The closing of many of these bases will mean the closing of major contributors to environmental pollution, unidentified until recently because of secrecy and exemption from EPA and other environmental regulatory bodies. If these military facilities are to be converted into civilian facilities, however, the necessary clean-up will still be very costly, perhaps prohibitively so. The National Toxics Campaign Fund is producing a report examining the full extent of environmental problems resulting from the military, and it is encouraging the public to put pressure on military facilities in their area to clean up the toxic waste sites and other environmental hazards on the bases. The cuts in the defense budget are also important for individuals and groups concerned with the environment because some of the funds that had previously gone for military personnel or production could be transferred to useful Federal efforts to clean up the environment.

Information Collection and Dissemination

Many organizations are working to provide information and education about the theory and practice of economic conversion to individuals and interest groups. Groups hold forums and distribute pamphlets and attempt to get word to members of Congress. The Center for Defense Information is composed largely of military retirees who research alternative uses for military spending. The Center for Economic Conversion has been focusing on conversion for 15 years and is a good source of information about current U.S. (and occasionally foreign) conversion projects, especially where a local activist group is involved; it does an annual resource update that has appeared in 1989 and 1990 and will appear twice in 1991. The Council on Economic Priorities is focused more broadly on national security and conversion policy; each year 2-3 monthly CEP Research Reports are addressed to conversion in the U.S. and Soviet Union. The National Commission for Economic Diversion and Disarmament produces a useful newsletter on conversion.

Investor Information

As the seriousness of the economic adjustment needs has become clearer, increasing numbers of investment banking, venture capital, and privatization groups have focused on economic adjustment and conversion projects in the United States (as well as in the Soviet Union and Eastern Europe). The Lockheed takeover battle in 1989-90 derived from the drop in the company's stock price to the point where the total market value of the company's shares was less than the value of its California real estate.[2] The Interfaith Center for Corporate Responsibility follows corporate involvement in arms manufacture and sales and encourages conversion. Prescott Bush (the President's brother) is co-chairman of the previously mentioned Privatization Council, which has a strong interest in infrastructure projects and includes many members with expertise and contacts applicable to infrastructure project development; it sponsors conferences on urban infrastructure and on military base conversions. Several socially responsible mutual funds have banded together and meet as the Social Investment Forum. The Urban Land Institute, also based in Washington, has a long-standing program to bring together experts to assist localities with planning for land use and reuse.[3]

Organizing and Lobbying

Some conversion organizing is an outgrowth, in light of budget cuts, of peace lobbying, such as that of chapters associated with SANE/Freeze, the Council for a Livable World, and Jobs with Peace. Other organizing is more specifically motivated by the desire to see conversion occur, for example by the previously mentioned Center for Economic Conversion and the National Commission for Economic Conversion and Disarmament, which are working to increase awareness of conversion issues at the grass-roots level.

The major political success of recent years in the national conversion arena was the passage of the 1990 Conversion Law ("Division D"). But in 1991 the places to watch most carefully are scattered throughout the country, in Olympia and Seattle, WA; in Sacramento and San Diego, CA; in St. Louis, MO and Hartford, CT. In periods of major shifts of thinking about policy in America, the way has historically often been led by states and localities. We may be in one of those periods in relation to our thinking about national and global security, and students of conversion have something to contribute to this discussion.

Placement

Some groups, such as High Technology Professionals for Peace, are working directly to transfer workers to jobs outside of military-related work.

Research

Universities both sponsor research and provide a vehicle for educating the public about conversion. Research is being undertaken by many organizations to determine how to make a most effective and smooth economic adjustment. Key researchers on conversion at universities in the U.S., most of whom also teach in the area, are at Augusta College (Jurgen Brauer), Carnegie Mellon (Judyth Twigg), Columbia University (Seymour Melman, retired), Harvard (Ashton Carter), Hofstra (John Ullman), M.I.T. (Steve Meyer), New York University (Wassily Leontief), SUNY Binghamton (Manas Chatterji, management), Temple University (Fyodor Kushnirsky), UCLA Center for International and Strategic Studies (Michael Intriligator), University of Pennsylvania (Lawrence Klein), University of Illinois (Peter Maggs), University of Texas (Lloyd Dumas, economics). A comprehensive review of scholarship in the area would have to delve into a number of disciplines and would be a research project of its own.[4] Besides educating their own students, at some universities institutes seek to educate the outside community. See below for information on what many individual groups are actually doing.

The non-university think tanks most involved in research activities on U.S. conversion in the 1980s — as measured by cumulative output of conversion-related publications that are discussed at conferences and cited by other scholars — are the Council on Economic Priorities, Employment Research Associates (Lansing, MI), and the National Commission for Economic Conversion and Disarmament (Washington, DC).

Groups with Conversion Programs

A major thrust of most national groups is to lobby for Federal programs. The groups with programs for U.S. conversion as of September 1991 are listed below.

An **(A)** means the group is listed in the August 1990 ACCESS Resource Brief as being especially concerned with U.S. conversion. A **(B)** identifies the group as one in the ACCESS computer database in January 1991 identified as "focusing on economic conversion."

Some national groups that primarily assist state and local governments have been listed at the end of Chapter 5 — organizations oriented toward the state-municipal function of economic development will be found there. Federal agencies and legislators are listed at the end of Chapter 6. Groups focused on the conversion or economic development of a single state or community are under the appropriate community heading in each state in Chapter 8.[5]

Many of the following are helpful to local groups, which are doing some of the most difficult and time-consuming work. The local level is where the actual adjustments are taking place. Local groups, identified in Chapter 8 and in the Center for Economic Conversion's *Conversion Organizers Update*, deserve great credit for their perseverance and progress.

ACCESS: A Security Information Service, 1730 M Street, N.W., #605, Washington, DC 20036; 202-785-6630; fax 202-223-2737. Mary Lord is Executive Director; the Director of Publications and Research is Ronald J. Bee. Its summary on conversion is called "From Guns to Butter?: USA & USSR," *Resource Brief*, IV:3, August 1990.

Aerospace Engineers/Workers for Social Responsibility, P.O. Box 21471, Los Angeles, CA 90021. 213-641-8929. This organization includes employees of military contractors and promotes conversion.

AFL-CIO, 815 16th Street, N.W., Washington, DC 20006. Adopted a resolution in February 1990 calling on Congress to enact conversion legislation that provides planning at the national and local level.

American Friends Service Committee, National Office, 1501 Cherry Street, Philadelphia, PA 19102. 215-241-7000, fax 215-864-0104; in New York, 212-598-0964. Asia Bennett is Executive Secretary. Has launched a citizens campaign for writing and petitioning congressional members on various issues including transformation to a peace economy. Publishes newspaper, *Quaker Service Bulletin*, edited by Diane Sandor. Also, *Friends Committee on National Legislation*, 245 Second Street, N.E., Washington, DC 20002. 202-547-6000. Joseph Volk, Executive Secretary. Publishes issue briefs on conversion.

American Public Health Association, Peace Caucus, 731 Santa Barbara Road, Berkeley, CA 94707. Rosalind Singer. Sponsored a meeting in Chicago on conversion in October 1989.

Americans for Democratic Action, 1511 K Street, N.W., #941, Washington, DC 20005. 202-638-6447; fax 202-638-2962. Amy Isaacs, National Director. Pursues progressive goals, such as conversion, at all levels of government. **(B)**

Arms Control Research Center of the Center for Peace and Progressive Politics, 942 Market Street, #709, San Francisco, CA 94102. 415-397-1452. Saul Bloom. Has launched a national effort to focus on nuclear waste at military facilities; this will loom large in the base-conversion process.

Business Executives for National Security, 21 Dupont Circle, N.W., Suite 401, Washington, DC 20036. 202-737-1090, fax 202-737-1079. Stanley Weiss, President; Kevin Pedraja, Policy Associate. Business leaders involved in research and legislation on national-security issues. Concerned with conversion and conducted an interesting community dialog on this subject in Connecticut. **(A)**

Cato Institute, 224 Second Street, S.E., Washington, DC 20003. 202-546-0200, fax 202-546-0728. Edward H. Crane, III, Executive Director. Has prepared a proposal for using the peace dividend to reduce taxes and become strategically independent; free-market approach to conversion. **(A)**

Center for Economic Conversion, 222C View Street, Mountain View, CA 94041. 415-968-8798. Michael Closson, Executive Director; Jim Wake and Janet Stone. Formerly the Mid-Peninsula Conversion Project. Does an excellent job of monitoring conversion developments and helping local and grass-roots groups function more effectively. Provides information, consulting, and assistance nationwide on base closings or "realignments." It works with military-dependent communities to help them develop strategies for diversifying their economies. **(A,B)**

Center for Interregional Conversion, 30 Irving Place, 9th Floor, New York, NY 10003. 212-995-9270, fax 212-420-0988. John Tepper Marlin, President. Gordon Feller, Director, West Coast Office, 415-491-4233, fax 415-492-1414. Created to help communities seeking to convert, learn from others that have already faced the challenge effectively; publishes working papers on economic conversion.

Center for Strategic and International Studies, 1800 K Street, N.W., #400, Washington, DC 20006. 202-887-0200, fax 202-775-3199. David M. Abshire, Chancellor. Interested in conversion, also protecting the defense-industrial base.

Center for the Study of American Business, Washington University, Campus Box 1208, 1 Brookings Drive, St. Louis, MO 83130. 314-889-5662. Murray Weidenbaum wrote a book entitled *Beyond the Cold War*, telling how to reconcile a reduced defense budget with a healthy economy (free-market approach). **(A)**

Committee for National Security, 1601 Connecticut Avenue, N.W., #302, Washington, DC 20009. 202-745-2450; fax 202-387-6298. John Parachini, Director. Executive Council includes Amb. Paul Warnke, Lawrence Korb, Hon. William Colby. In 1990 merged with, and became a division of, the Council on Economic Priorities and at that time made conversion one of its goals.

Computer Professionals for Social Responsibility, 18 Center St., #102, Cambridge, MA 02139. 617-497-7440, fax 617-864-5164. Gary Chapman. Is behind the *Twenty-First Century Project*, seeks to develop a new national agenda for science and technology, to redirect them to peaceful ends, for grassroots activists and policymakers.

Council on Economic Priorities, 30 Irving Place, 9th Floor, New York, NY 10003. 212-420-1133; fax 212-420-0988. Alice Tepper Marlin, Executive Director. Conversion staff: Eugene Chollick, Betty Lall, and John Tepper Marlin. Seeks local outreach through research, conferences, publications, and public speaking by its staff and directors. One of the groups with the longest history of work on conversion, it publishes 2-3 *Research Reports* a year on the subject plus occasional studies. CEP's U.S.-Soviet project brought together researchers in Moscow in 1990 to discuss conversion issues, followed up with the report *Soviet Conversion 1991*. **(A,B)**

Defense Budget Project, 777 North Capitol St., N.E., #710, Washington, DC 20002. 202-408-1517; fax 202-408-1526. Gordon Adams, Director. Operates under the aegis of the Center on Budget and Policy Priorities. Has estimated the employment impact of defense cuts. Coordinates a task force estimating the impact of defense cuts. **(A)**

Economic Strategy Institute, 1100 Connecticut Ave., N.W., #1300, Washington, DC 20036. 202-728-0993, fax 202-728-0998. Kevin Kearns. Project to examine how conversion can improve U.S. competitiveness. **(A)**

Economists Against the Arms Race, P.O. Box 20365, New York, NY 10025. 212-663-3852 (same number for fax). Nobel laureates Lawrence Klein and Kenneth Arrow are co-chairs. Robert Schwartz, Treasurer. ECAAR was established in December 1988 by economists across the country. It has sponsored many panel discussions on conversion, including a two-day conference at Notre Dame University, from which papers have been collected and edited by Jurgen Brauer (Augusta College, 404-737-1560, fax 404-737-1773) and Manas Chatterji (SUNY Binghamton, 607-777-2182, fax 607-777-4422) for publication in 1992 by NYU Press as *Economic Issues of Disarmament.* **(B)**

Employment Research Associates, 115 W. Allegan Street, #810, Lansing, MI 48933. 517-485-7655. Marion Anderson, Director. Studies and consults on the economic and employment impact of defense spending on individual states, and seeks to bring the data to local groups. Presented a report on U.S. adjustment to defense cuts resulting from the INF Treaty to the International Labor Organization. **(A,B)**

Families USA Foundation, 1334 G St., N.W., #300, Washington, DC 20005; 202-628-3030. Sponsored a report on the likely impact of defense cuts on businesses, communities, regions, and workers, outlining special needs that must be addressed in conversion efforts: for example, providing extra job search assistance for women, minorities, and older workers.

Friends Committee on National Legislation, 245 Second Street, N.E., Washington, DC 20002; 202-547-6000. Joseph Volk, Executive Secretary. Publishes issue briefs on economic conversion.

Global Communities, 1601 Conn. Ave., N.W., Washington, DC 20009; 202-234-9382. Its newsletter covers conversion. Project of the Institute for Policy Studies. Michael Shuman, Ona Ashton.

High Technology Professionals for Peace, 639 Massachusetts Ave., Room 316, Cambridge, MA 02139. 617-497-0605. Helps professionals find employment outside of military-related work.

Institute for Peace and International Security, 91 Harvey St., Cambridge, MA 02140-1718. 617-547-3338. Everett Mendelsohn, Paul Walker. Campaigned for the creation of a Joint Congressional Committee to address redirecting military and budget priorities. Created the Committee on Economic Security, focusing on conversion.

Interfaith Center on Corporate Responsibility, 475 Riverside Drive, Room 566, New York, NY 10115. 212-870-2936. Timothy H. Smith, Executive Director; Valerie Heinonen. This respected group has the attention of many U.S. churches and other corporate monitors. Its goals include world peace and conversion. It has filed proxy resolutions on conversion with such companies as Motorola, Northrop, Textron, Unisys, and United Technologies.

International Association of Machinists and Aerospace Workers, 1300 Connecticut Ave., N.W., Washington, DC 20036. 202-857-5200. Actively involved in conversion issues. Holds that military spending does not increase employment, i.e., that the same amount of money spent on construction, education, or transportation would create even more jobs. The IAM's annual meeting in 1990 included a panel on conversion.

Jobs with Peace, 76 Summer Street, Boston, MA 02110. 617-338-5783. Jill Nelson, Executive Director; George Pillsbury, Mary Westropp. Believes that the number of military-related jobs lost as a result of the defense cuts would be more than offset by new jobs in construction and related industries. Involved in efforts to convert Philadelphia's largest naval yard to build bridge spans and other products. In Minnesota it helped create a state task force to provide funding for conversion projects. Has successfully passed referendums on the issue of economic conversion in San Francisco, Detroit, Boston, and other cities. The Field Development Fund is supporting and training local chapters to campaign for the need to shift Federal spending priorities from the military to social and environmental concerns.

National Center for Policy Alternatives, 2000 Florida Ave., N.W., Washington, DC 20009. Washington, DC 20009. 202-387-6030. Surveying existing and proposed state-level conversion programs for the transition from military to civilian-based economies.

National Commission for Economic Conversion and Disarmament (ECD), 1801 18th St. NW Suite 9, Washington, DC 20009. 202-462-0091; fax 202-232-7087. Columbia Professor Emeritus Seymour Melman, Chair. Greg Bischak, Executive Director. The Commission was established in 1988. It reports on the economic impact of conversion and disarmament with periodic substantive papers. ECD publishes *The New Economy* five times a year; it provides timely updates of conversion and disarmament issues. **(A,B)**

National Priorities Project, 377 Hills South, University of Massachusetts, Amherst, MA 01003. 413-545-2038. Greg Speeter. Working with SANE/-Freeze and other groups on adjustment and conversion issues in California, Connecticut, Illinois, Maine, Massachusetts, New Jersey, Ohio, and Tennessee.

National Toxics Campaign Fund, National Office, 1168 Commonwealth Ave., Boston, MA 02134. 617-232-0327. Gary Cohen, Executive Director. National Toxics Campaign Fund's Military Toxics Network, NTC Fund, 2802 East Madison, Suite 177, Seattle, WA 98112. 206-328-5257. Dyan Oldenburg. A grassroots organization addressing environmental concerns relating to defense cuts. Campaigning for creation of an "Environmental Security Fund" to shift funding to the clean-up of the thousands of toxic waste sites created on military bases. Also supports creation of a "Worker Superfund" to compensate workers who lose their jobs as a result of shifting to an environmentally sound peacetime economy.

New York State School of Industrial and Labor Relations of Cornell University, New York, NY and Ithaca, NY. Organized a national conference to launch assistance programs that will help defense contractors convert to non-military production.

Operation Real Security, 2076 E. Alameda Drive, Tempe, AZ 85282. 602-921-090, fax 602-829-1489. Jim Driscoll, National Co-Director. Working to mobilize local peace groups around the country for local activities, media programs, and lobbying. Provides information and mini-grants to local action groups.

Oil, Chemical, and Atomic Workers, Legislative Office, 1126 16th Street, N.W., #411, Washington, DC 20036; 202-223-5770. Tony Mazzocchi, President. This union has taken strong stands for peaceful reuse of defense dollars.

Peace Dividend Network, contact through Social Policy, 25 West 43rd St., Room 620, New York, NY 10036. 212-642-2929. Frank Riessman, Director. Works toward using the money saved from military-budget cuts for human needs and rebuilding America. Calls for a rapid conversion to a peace economy and a reordering of national priorities. Its Peace Economy newsletter is free and well-edited (by Stanley Moses).

Professional Organizations for Nuclear Arms Control and Conversion to a Peace Society, 3624 Market St., #508, Philadelphia, PA 19105. 215-898-6304. Lois H. Young-Tulin, Executive Director. Supports seven professional groups on conversion-related issues. **(B)**

Real Security Education Project, 1601 Connecticut Ave., N.W., Washington, DC 20009. 202-234-9382. Barbara Wien, Director. Spin-off from the Institute for Policy Studies. Training programs for grass-roots leaders throughout the U.S. on the impact of the military on local communities.

SANE/Freeze Campaign for Global Security, 1819 H Street, N.W., Suite 640, Washington, DC 20006. 202-862-9740, fax 202-862-9762. Monica Green, Executive Director; Ira Schorr; Mark Harrison. Co-sponsored a "Directors' Summit" in June 1990 to discuss national budget priorities and conversion strategies. Has strong (and strongly independent) chapters in Washington State, Anchorage, Baltimore, and Illinois. Over 100 of its chapters are involved in the Peace Economy Campaign. **(B)**

Sister Cities International, 120 South Payne St., Alexandria, VA 22314. 703-836-3535, fax 703-836-4815. Richard G. Neuheisel, President. Sponsored a conference for several dozen U.S.-Soviet sister cities, September 1991 in Cincinnati. Many of the Soviet cities that had a significant defense-production capacity were actively interested in help for their conversion efforts.

Stanford Center for International Security and Arms Control, Stanford University, 320 Galvez St., Stanford, CA 94395. 415-723-2186, fax 415-723-0089. David Bernstein, Assistant to the Directors. Conducting studies of what they call the "restructuring" of regional economies.

Trade Union Committee for the Transfer Amendment & Economic Conversion. Contact through Labor Research Association, 80 E. 11th St., New York, NY

10003. 212-473-1042. Coalition of labor locals dealing with conversion issues.

Tri-State Conference on Steel, 300 Saline Street, Pittsburgh, PA 15207. A 1989 conference of a broad spectrum of groups monitoring conversion.

Unitarian/Universalist Peace Network, 5808 Greene St., Philadelphia, PA 19144. 215-843-2890. Stephanie Nichols. The Unitarian/Universalist annual meetings regularly include panels and resolutions on conversion issues.

United Auto, Aerospace & Agricultural Implement Workers (UAW), 8000 East Jefferson Ave., Detroit, MI 48214. 313-926-5000. Delegates adopted a resolution calling for military cuts and conversion legislation. The union is concerned with saving workers and providing job and income security for workers in defense-related industries. The UAW is supporting Federal legislation for a conversion program that should include a national conversion committee with representatives from labor, industry and government, worksite alternative use planning committees, and community-based planning committees. They also support mandatory advance notification of defense cancellations to allow time to develop conversion plans, and a trust fund to pay wages of defense workers through the period of job search and training.

United Electrical Workers, 1141 K Street, N.W., #1005, Washington, DC 20005. 202-737-3072. Bob Kingsley.

Women's Action for Nuclear Disarmament, 691 Massachusetts Ave., Arlington, MA 02174. 617-643-6740. Marjorie Smith, Executive Director. Helen Caldicott, founder. Aims to empower women to shape U.S. policies toward peaceful goals.

Women Strike for Peace, 105 Second St., N.E., Washington, DC 20002. 202-543-2660. Organizes demonstrations, lobbies Congress, and organizes special projects to make women aware of defense spending.

Worldwatch Institute, 1776 Massachusetts Ave., N.W., Washington, DC 20036; 202-452-1999; fax 202-296-7365. Lester R. Brown, President; Michael Renner. Has written about U.S. conversion in the context of world-wide conversion.

Notes

1. The community-group steps are from *Proceedings: Nationa Strategy Retreat on Economic Conversion*, Block Island, June 11-13 (Mountain View, CA: Center for Economic Conversion, 1990).

2. See Stephen Kindel, "La-La Land: What Does Harold Simmons See in Lockheed that Wall Street Doesn't?" *Financial World*, March 20, 1990, p. 30, or Richard W. Stevenson, "Why Lockheed Is Under Siege," *The New York Times*, March 13, 1990, pp. D1, D8.

3. For example, in April 1990 it convened such a group in Chicago to advise on reuse of the Chanute Air Force Base. Tom Black is Director of Research, Urban Land Institute (ULI), 1090 Vermont Ave., N.W., 300 Washington, DC 20005, 202-289-8500, direct line

202-289-3345. Black also serves as the ULI's liaison with the Privatization Council, the executive director of which is Jenny Hefferon, 1101 Connecticut Ave, N.W., #700, Washington, DC 20036, 202-857-1142.

4. See Betty G. Lall and Lyn Fine, *Peace Studies in Graduate Education Reference Guide* (New York: New York University, 1988). A New York Metropolitan Peace Studies Consortium Project, New York University, SEHNAP, Studies in Intercultural Education, 635 East Building, New York, NY 10003. 212-998-5492.

5. Sources for the following information include Access *Resource Brief* IV:3 (August 1990) and an Access computer search in January 1991; Elizabeth Bernstein, Robert Elias, Randall Forsberg, Matthew Goodman, Deborah Mapes, Peter M. Steven, *Peace Resource Book: A Comprehensive Guide to Issues, Groups, and Literature* (Cambridge, MA: Ballinger Publishing Co., for the Institute for Defense and Disarmament Studies, 1986); the Center for Economic Conversion, *Conversion Organizers' Update* (Mountain View, CA: CEC, 1989, 1990, and 1991); and phone-call followups.

8

State Conversion Profiles

If by this point you have come to share our appetite for the details of U.S. conversion, you have before you a banquet of economic data and legislative developments, corporate actions and community initiatives in every state. For each state we describe the economic challenges and how governments, companies and citizens private actors are attempting to meet them. The information is as current as we could humanly make it in October 1991.

To collect data for these profiles, we first sent letters to every state and every relevant county or locality in 1989, asking about their plans for moving to less dependence on military spending. We then wrote up profiles for each state and sent them in 1991 for review to the governor of every state and the mayor of every listed city, advising them also of the availability of Federal assistance for conversion. We also sent questionnaires to defense contractors, asking how they expected to be affected by defense budget cuts and what, if anything, they were doing about it.

The resulting profiles that follow are all organized the same way to make them easy to use. They start with a data page and then include 1-6 text pages, depending on the amount of defense spending and civic activity in the state.

Data Page

The first page for each state profile collects together key data on military expenditures in the state and related benchmarks. Unless otherwise noted, all data are as of FY 1990 and all rankings are out of 52 (50 states plus DC and Puerto Rico). On each data page are found six sets of data: (1) Benchmarks with Icons, (2) Other Benchmarks, (3) Contractor Trends, (4) Top Five Contractors, (5) Top Ten Defense-Dependent Sites, and (6) a Map of Defense-Dependent Locations.

Benchmarks

The six icons at the top of each data page are all designed to provide a general picture of the likely impact on a state of defense cuts. The states (50 states plus DC and Puerto Rico) are divided into three groups of 17 or 18 depending on whether they are *relatively affected by defense cuts a great deal, moderately, or very little.* The number on which each icon is based is provided in the box with the "Benchmarks" heading; it is next to the correspondingly lettered benchmark. An explanation of each icon follows:

Icon A: $. The $ icon shows the total amount of defense spending in the state. This total is the sum of the next two icons, i.e., the total Department of Defense payroll in the state and the total prime-contract spending in the state. A large plus sign (+) underneath means it's in the top third of states; a middle-sized plus sign means it's in the second third; a minus sign (-) means it's in the bottom third. California ranks No. 1 on this measure with $35.9 billion in FY 1990, and gets a large " + ". Alabama, first of the profiles to follow, ranks 18th with $3.8 billion, and just barely makes it into the medium-sized + group.

Icon B: Soldier. The Soldier icon shows the total Department of Defense payroll in the state. This payroll includes both uniformed and civilian workers on the bases, but not defense-contractor personnel, the number of whom is not known exactly. This icon uses the same symbols as the previous one – two plus signs and a minus sign. California again ranks No. 1 and gets a large " + ". Alabama ranks No. 13 and gets the same.

Icon C: Factory. The Factory icon shows the total amount of prime contracts in the state. It uses the same two symbols as the previous two icons. Again, California is No. 1 and Alabama makes it into the top third, ranking 16th out of 52.

Icon D: Chart. The Chart icon shows the overall trend in prime contracts. If the arrow is horizontal it means little change relative to other states. If the arrow points up, it means the state is increasing its share of prime contracts. If it points down, it means it is reducing its share of prime contracts. California's arrow is horizontal even though the change in its prime-contract income is down 18 percent over four years; the state's ranking as No. 24 on prime-contract change means that it is in the middle range of cuts relative to other states. Alabama's arrow points up because it has increased its share of prime contracts between FY 1987 and FY 1990.

Icon E: VI. The VI (Vulnerability Index) is described in Chapter 4. This index is derived by adding the unemployment rate (for the year ending April 1991) to the defense-dependence ratio. The VI measures the *a priori* likelihood of economic damage from defense cuts, without knowing anything about the size of the cuts. Two exclamation marks means the state is very vulnerable. Alabama and California both get two exclamation marks. One exclamation mark is for the middle range of states, and a "-" indicates the least vulnerable states.

Icon F: DDI. The DDI (Defense Dislocation Index) shows the likely economic impact of coming defense cuts. As described in Chapter 4, it is the product of the Vulnerability Index and the ratio of likely cuts to total defense spending. The figure for likely cuts is derived from 1990 announcements about

Department of Defense cuts, plus late-1990 Congressional budget plans for weapon systems, applied to the locations where the weapons are made. A large pair of scissors means large cuts are coming relative to the defense dollars in the state; a small pair of scissors means the cuts won't be so severe; and a pair of fingers giving the all clear sign means the cuts will not cause much dislocation for the state as a whole (localities may still need to worry). *This is the best predictive measure on the page.*

Other Benchmarks. On the right-hand side of the box with the Benchmark data are six additional benchmarks. The first is the total number of defense-dependent jobs are in the state; this number appears as Table 4.1 and is explained in Chapter 4. The second is the change in defense-dependent jobs between FY 1989 and FY 1990. California lost 8 percent of its defense-dependent jobs during this year and ranks 20th out of 52. Alabama's defense-dependent jobs grew 17 percent during the year, so it ranks 46th out of 52 (remember, the higher the rank, the greater the economic vulnerability). The third number is the average of the 12 monthly unemployment rates for the year ending April 1991; it eliminates seasonal swings in unemployment and is a good current measure of 1991 unemployment. The fourth number is the change in unemployment between 1989 and 1991. The fifth number is per capita income for each state, current as of April 1991, provided by the Bureau of Economic Analysis of the Department of Commerce, except for Puerto Rico, which was estimated. The final number is the state's population in 1990, also current as of April 1991 and from the Bureau of Economic Analysis.

Other Data

Other data on the first page besides the benchmarks are:

Contract Trends. The four black bars on every data page show the trend in prime-contract revenues for each year, FY1987 through FY 1990. At a glance the prime-contract trend for each state can be visualized. The numbers have been adjusted for inflation, so a flat series of bars would mean that prime-contract revenues are in fact growing each year by the inflation rate. In the case of Alabama total prime-contract revenues dipped in the two middle years but were slightly higher in FY 1990 than they were in FY 1987.

Top Five Contractors. Immediately underneath the four black bars are the five top prime contractors in the state, with the amount of revenues they received from the Department of Defense in FY 1990. These contractors are often discussed in the text. They need not be weapons producers; they may supply fuel or even food.

Top Ten Sites. The large box at the bottom of the data page is packed with information. It lists the ten sites that received the most money from the Department of Defense in FY 1990. In parentheses after the name of the site (which may be a city or a base) is the rank of defense income out of 501 sites nationwide (10 sites each in the 50 states plus the District of Columbia as one site; we did not include Puerto Rico in these computations). In the next column is the name of the Congressional District in which the site is located, the name of the Member of Congress who represents the district, and the political party of this person. The next column shows the rank of the site in the previous year, FY 1989. In the next column is the total Department of Defense revenues accruing to the site (both payroll and contracts), followed by two columns that show the payroll and the prime-contract totals separately. Finally in the last column is the number of Department of Defense employees at each site. From this information one could calculate the average cost per Department of Defense employee at each site, or the change in rank between 1989 and 1990. Three caveats: The prime contracts that are listed are only those valued over $25,000, so the figures exclude about 10 percent of contract spending. Next, note that the national rankings of sites start with the 10 top sites in each state; this means, for example, the eleventh largest site in California, which is not listed, could conceivably be ranked as high as 52nd. Finally, be aware that total spending figures shown here do not include Department of Energy spending on nuclear weapons.

Map of Defense-Dependent Locations. A map is provided for each state showing military and defense-contractor locations in the state. These maps are slightly modified and reduced in size from the Department of Defense *Atlas*, FY 1990.

Text Pages

After the initial data page for each state, the remaining pages of each profile provide textual material on the status of conversion.

Overall Economy. Each profile starts with a brief review of the state's economy. The stronger the state's economy, the easier a job it will have absorbing laid-off defense workers. This section explains the state unemployment rate and trend.

Defense and the Economy. This section relates the military budget in each state to its overall economy, and thereby helps explain the defense-dependence side of the Vulnerability Index. State contacts are provided in notes at the end of this section, for followup and updating.

State Legislative Initiatives. New conversion-related legislation is described in states where relevant. Some state legislatures, like California and Washington, have passed some interesting laws or resolutions in 1990-91.

Community Surveys. Finally we look in detail at the effects of defense cuts and steps toward conversion in all the main affected communities, both bases and companies, with full information on the work of local groups with conversion interests.

Alabama

A	B	C	D	E	F
$				VI	DDI
+	✚	✚	↑	‼	✂

Benchmarks	No.	Rank	Benchmarks	No.	Rank
A. Total DoD $	$3.8 bil.	18	Def.-Dependent Jobs ('000), 90	192	17
B. Personnel Payroll	$1.9 bil.	13	Change in Def.-Dep. Jobs, '89-'90	+17.1%	46
C. Prime Contracts (PC)	$1.9 bil.	16	Unemployment Rate, '90-'91	7.3%	13
D. PC Change, FY '87-'90	+5.0%	44	Unemp. Rate Change, '89-'91	+0.4%	35
E. Vulnerability Index	12.3	9	Per Capita Income	$14,826	45
F. Defense Disloc. Index	0.89	25	Population ('000)	4,041	22

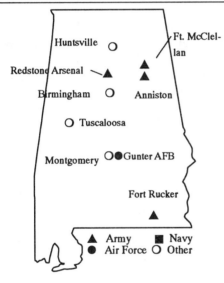

Army ▲   Navy ■
Air Force ●   Other ○

Prime Contract Trends, FY'87-'90
(Constant FY '92 $Billions)

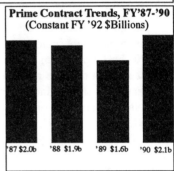

'87 $2.0b   '88 $1.9b   '89 $1.6b   '90 $2.1b

Top 5 Contractors	$Millions
Teledyne	$230.9
Boeing	219.9
General Electric	171.5
Dyncorp	86.1
Nichols Research	64.2

Top 10 $ Sites[a]	Congressional Dist., Representative	1989 Rank	Total DoD$[c]	Payroll[c]	Prime Contracts[c]	Per-sonnel[d]
1-Huntsville (23)	5-Cramer, d	42	$1,175.1	$119.6	$1,055.5	2.1
2-Fort Rucker (69)	2-Dikinson, r	97	512.6	343.6	169.0	12.0
3-Redstone Ars'l. (107)	5-Cramer, d	93	370.2	292.7	77.5	11.8
4-Montgomery (116)	2-Dikinson, r	136	343.8	262.7	81.0	1.3
5-Mobile (190)	1-Callahan, r	244	184.2	61.5	122.6	1.2
6-Ft. McClellan (197)	3-Browder, d	154	175.6	145.8	29.9	5.6
7-Anniston (239)	3-Browder, d	174	125.0	56.3	68.7	1.4
8-Gunter AFB (276)	2-Callahan, r	283	93.2	67.6	25.7	2.3
9-Birmingham (312)	(6,7)[b]	277	65.8	49.6	16.1	0.9
10-Tuscaloosa (315)	7-Harris, d	348	60.4	15.5	44.9	--

[a] Rating in parentheses is out of 511 sites, the top ten in each state and PR, plus D.C.
[b] Multidistrict r-Rep. d-Dem. [c] $Millions (may not add due to rounding) [d] Thousands

Alabama

Alabama's real state product for 1990 was up a modest 1.8 percent over 1989. The state's unemployment rate is high, ranking 13th, but its change in unemployment a relatively benign 35th (employment declined only slightly more than the labor force). The state's economy is heavily dependent on the manufacturing and construction sectors, which account for almost 29 percent of real state product. These sectors are sensitive to interest rates, which declined through the first half of the decade, hit a low in 1986, and then climbed part of the way back again. The economy is becoming more diversified as the trade, finance, and insurance sectors grow.

Defense and the Economy

The government/military sector of the economy accounted for 24 percent of total employment in northern Alabama in 1987, up from 23 percent in 1980. In 1990 the Department of Defense spent $3.8 billion in Alabama, the 18th highest state in defense revenues. High defense dependence and unemployment make the state vulnerable to cuts in base personnel.[1]

Total Department of Defense prime-contract awards to Alabama firms were $1.9 billion in 1990; most was earmarked for missile and space development. Two Alabama sites are in the top 100 in the nation.[2]

Community Surveys

Military dollars in Alabama are concentrated in the northern part of the state; contract dollars are concentrated in the Huntsville and Birmingham areas.

Anniston. Local residents rallied to save Fort McClellan, a 46,000-acre military installation north of town, when the Department of Defense announced in April 1991 that it wanted to close the base. About 14,500 civilian jobs were considered to be at stake. The Base Closure Commission ultimately decided to spare the fort—partly because Alabama legislators were able to play on the importance of the base's unique chemical-warfare training center in the wake of the Gulf War. McClellan remains vulnerable to future cuts, but will benefit from the movement to it of ground-communications maintenance work previously done from the Sacramento Army Depot. The local Chamber of Commerce is implementing a diversification program.[3]

Childersburg. The Alabama Ammunition Plant, inactive since 1954, was slated for closure by the 1989 Armey Bill. The site is on the EPA's National Priorities List because of contamination, including the presence of asbestos. By Federal law, re-use cannot occur until cleanup is complete.[4]

Huntsville. Huntsville may benefit from being an important R&D locale. The worst scenario forecast by locals has expenditures dropping by 3 to 6 percent, though the Chamber of Commerce predicts increases in expenditures and personnel. The city, along with the nearby Redstone Arsenal, is the largest recipient of Federal defense money in Alabama. The scaleback of the Arsenal, employer of 8,900 civilians and 2,800 military personnel, is due to be completed by 1992. Aerospace and electronics are the largest local industries and most important sources of community income; the defense-related sectors of the economy employed 32,500 in 1989[5]

Talledega. Congress decided to close the Coosa River Annex (essentially inoperative for several years) when it passed its first base-closure bill in 1989. The government expects to profit from sale of the land, but first it faces the tough task of cleaning up hazardous-waste contamination (including asbestos and PCBs) at the site.[6]

Notes

1. Chris Paul and Niles Schoening, *Joint UAH/TVA Economic Forecast for North Alabama 1987-1992*, March 1989, p. 4. *Atlas/Data Abstract for the United States and Selected Areas, Fiscal 1990*, Department of Defense, prepared by Washington Headquarters Services, Directorate for Information, Operations and Reports, p. 13.

2. *Loc. cit.* Contacts: (1) Governor's Office, William C. Armistead, Special Assistant to the Governor, State Capitol, Montgomery, AL 36130; 205-242-7155. (2) Alabama Development Office, Fred Braswell, 11 South Union, Montgomery, AL 36130; 205-263-0048. (3) Economic Planning, Don Hines, Chief, 3465 Norman Bridge Road, Montgomery, AL 36105; 205-242-8672. (4) Alabama Department of Industrial Relations, John Allen, 649 Monroe St., Montgomery, AL 36130; 205-242-5386. (5) Huntsville Mayor's Office, Mayor Steve Hettinger, P.O. Box 308, Huntsville, AL 35804; 205-532-7304.

3. "Pentagon's Proposals: Base Closures, Reductions," *USA Today*, January 30, 1990, p. 8. "Fort McClellan saved," *Birmingham Post-Herald*, July 2, 1991, p. 4. *Base Closure and Realignment Report*, Department of Defense, April 1991, pp. 42-43.

4. *Base Realignments and Closures*, Report of the Defense Secretary's Commission, December 1988, p. 59.

5. Interview in June, 1990 with Gene Anderson, Vice-President of Governmental Affairs, Chamber of Commerce, Huntsville, AL, 205-535-2030. Niles Schoening and Juan Gonzales, *The Huntsville Economic Forecast 1989-1993*, December 1989, pp. 1-3.

6. *Base Realignments...*, *op. cit.*, p. 56.

Alaska

A	B	C	D	E	F
$	👷	🏭	📅	VI	DDI
−	+	−	→	‼	✌

Benchmarks	No.	Rank	Benchmarks	No.	Rank
A.Total DoD $	$1.3 bil.	36	Def.-Dependent Jobs ('000), '90	64	36
B. Personnel Payroll	$0.9 bil.	31	Change in Def.-Dep. Jobs, '89–'90	-11.1%	13
C. Prime Contracts (PC)	$0.4 bil.	38	Unemployment Rate, '90–'91	7%	18
D. PC Change, FY '87–'90	-20.5%	19	Unemp. Rate Change, '89–'91	-0.1%	40
E. Vulnerability Index	12.6	7	Per Capita Income	$21,761	7
F. Defense Disloc. Index	0.08	42	Population ('000)	550	51

Prime Contract Trends, FY'87-'90
(Constant FY '92 $Billions)

'87 $0.7b '88 $0.5b '89 $0.6b '90 $0.5b

Eielson AFB, Clear Ear. Warn.
N. Pole
▲ Ft. Wainwright
▲ Ft. Greely
Ft. Richardson
Adak
Elmendorf AFB
Anchorage
Shemya AFB

▲ Army ■ Navy
● Air Force ○ Other

Top 5 Contractors	$Millions
Mapco	$94.1
ITT	51.8
Piquniq	16.3
General Electric	16.3
Halliburton	15.3

Top 10 $ Sites[a]	Congressional Dist., Representative	1989 Rank	Total DoD$[c]	Payroll[c]	Prime Contracts[c]	Per-sonnel[d]
1-Elmend'f AFB (134)	1-Young,r	143	$300.4	$243.3	$57.1	7.8
2-Ft. Richardson (162)	"	167	229.3	202.0	27.3	5.1
3-Ft. Wainwright (220)	"	152	141.7	103.8	38.0	4.7
4-Eielson AFB (236)	"	238	129.7	111.3	18.5	4.0
5-Anchorage (253)	"	248	111.8	64.2	47.6	0.8
6-North Pole (281)	"	338	89.5	2.7	86.8	--
7-Clear MSLEW (313)	"	317	61.6	6.6	55.0	--
8-Adak Station (324)	"	321	53.6	50.0	3.6	2.2
9-Shemya AFB(380)	"	362	30.5	15.2	15.4	0.6
10-Ft. Greely (398)	"	--	24.5	19.5	5.0	0.9

[a]Rating in parentheses is out of 511 sites, the top ten in each state and PR, plus DC.
[b]Multidistrict r-Rep. d-Dem. [c]$Millions (may not add due to rounding) [d] Thousands

Alaska

Alaska's basic industries are petroleum, fishing, tourism, timber and mining. Only 1.4 percent of the land is owned by individuals, 13 percent by "native corporations," and the rest by Federal, state, and local governments. Approximately 85 percent of state revenues come from the petroleum industry, and the overall economy reflects oil-industry swings. Unemployment ranked 18th highest in the country in April 1991 and change in unemployment a relatively positive 40th (employment grew slightly faster than the labor force).

Defense and the Economy

An Alaskan economist says that "by the 1950s and 1960s Alaska had become primarily an 'exporter' of military defense." The discovery of oil at Prudhoe Bay altered this picture somewhat, but the military is still one of the leading industries; 13 percent of the state's output is related to defense. One in 26 people in Alaska is an active-duty military employee, which is the second highest ratio in the nation and gives Alaska the nation's seventh highest Vulnerability Index. Most of the money spent in the state is for support of the large military-personnel presence. The industries that receive the most Pentagon procurement dollars in Alaska are construction and petroleum, which together accounted for 73 percent of its 1989 prime contracts awards.[1]

Because no major weapon systems are produced in Alaska, the state will not be significantly affected by Pentagon prime contracting cuts. The overall military presence should increase, primarily as Alaska benefits from troop transferrals from closed bases in other states and in Europe. Alaska remains a key strategic location for troop reassignment because forces are easily deployable both to the Pacific (Tokyo is eight hours away) and to Europe (Frankfurt can be reached in eight hours by plane).[2]

Notes

1. George Rogers, quoted in Neal Fried and Greg Huff, "The Military and Alaska's Economy," *Alaska Economic Trends*, November, 1987, p. 6. Response to the Economic Adjustment Questionnaire of the Productive Peace Project, returned by Alaska's Department of Community and Regional Affairs, March 7, 1990. *Prime Contract Awards by Region and State, Fiscal Years 1989, 1988, 1987,* Department of Defense, Washington Headquarters Services, Directorate for Information, Operations and Reports, p. 19. Sold by the Superintendent of Documents, U.S. Government Printing Office, Washington, D.C. 20402. DTIC/NTIS identification number is DIOR/P06-89.

2. Contacts: (1) Alaska Department of Commerce, Larry Merculieff, c/o Governor's Office, Juneau, AK 99801. (2) Alaska Department of Labor, Jim Simpson, c/o Governor's Office, Juneau, AK 99801.

Arizona

A	B	C	D	E	F
$	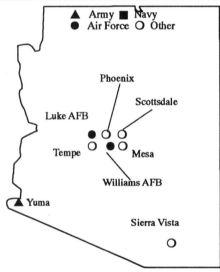			VI	DDI
✚	+	✚	↑	‼	✂

Benchmarks	No.	Rank	Benchmarks	No.	Rank
A.Total DoD $	$4.9bil.	15	Def.-Dependent Jobs ('000), '90	262	14
B. Personnel Payroll	$1.5 bil.	19	Change in Def.-Dep. Jobs, '89-'90	+9.6%	43
C. Prime Contracts (PC)	$3.4bil.	12	Unemployment Rate, '90-'91	4.5%	48
D.PC Change, FY '87-'90	-4.7%	39	Unemp. Rate Change, '89-'91	-0.7%	48
E. Vulnerability Index	12.2	10	Per Capita Income	$16,297	35
F. Defense Disloc. Index	8.23	3	Population ('000)	3,665	25

▲ Army ■ Navy
● Air Force ○ Other

Phoenix
Scottsdale
Luke AFB
Tempe
Mesa
Williams AFB
Yuma
Sierra Vista

Prime Contract Trends, FY'87-'90
(Constant FY '92 $Billions)

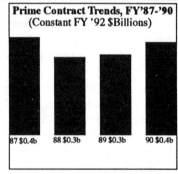

| 87 $0.4b | 88 $0.3b | 89 $0.3b | 90 $0.4b |

Top 5 Contractors	$Millions
McDonnell Douglas	$1,435.7
General Motors	860.9
Motorola	337.9
Allied Signal	157.2
McD. Doug./Bell Heli. JV	103.6

Top 10 $ Sites[a]	Congressional Dist., Representative	1989 Rank	Total DoD$[c]	Payroll[c]	Prime Contracts[c]	Per-sonnel[d]
1-Mesa (16)	1-Rhodes, r	41	$1,657.2	$51.4	$1,605.8	0.2
2-Tucson (30)	(2,5)[b]	25	1,024.5	127.2	897.3	1.1
3-Sierra Vista (103)	5-Kolbe, r	95	385.4	271.2	114.2	--
4-Scottsdale (111)	(1,4)[b]	124	355.7	19.3	336.4	--
5-Phoenix (136)	(1-4)[b]	153	288.6	141.1	147.5	1.3
6-Davis-Mo. AFB (180)	5-Kolbe, r	199	198.4	181.7	16.7	6.5
7-Luke AFB (183)	3-Stump, r	195	192.5	167.1	25.4	6.5
8-Yuma Prv. Grd.(194)	2-Vacant	182	176.7	130.2	46.4	5.1
9-Tempe (240)	1-Rhodes, r	180	121.9	16.3	105.6	0.1
10-Williams AFB (250)	1-Rhodes, r	233	114.7	77.9	36.8	2.4

[a]Rating in parentheses is out of 511 sites, the top ten in each state and PR, plus DC.
[b] Multidistrict r-Rep. d-Dem. [c]-$Millions (figures may not add due to rounding) [d]Thousands

Arizona

The Arizona economy is recovering from a period of sluggish growth in the 1980s, when the bottom fell out of the real estate market after years of speculation followed by the collapse of the local savings and loan industry. The strong performance of the services, retailing, transportation, and government sectors have offset these losses, and the general outlook for the state economy is good. Growth in real gross state product is expected to return to a healthy 2.5 percent rate in 1991. Arizona's unemployment and its change in unemployment ranked 48th (employment grew more than twice as fast as the labor force).

Defense and the Economy

The Pentagon's $4.9 billion spending in Arizona, mostly on contracts, represents a large 6.9 percent of gross state product. The state's low unemployment rate offsets the high defense dependence, but Arizona stands to lose an extremely large portion of its contracts, especially the Apache helicopter, the Phoenix missile programs and the Advanced Medium Range Air-to-Air Missile (AMRAAM). The five biggest locations of military personnel are also being closed or reduced.

Two of Arizona's top expenditure sites are in the top 100, compared to three in FY 1989. The combined receipts of this area, home to McDonnell Douglas and Motorola plants, is slightly higher than defense expenditures in Tucson. Airframe production and missile and space system development together accounted for 67 percent of all 1989 prime contracts.[1]

Community Surveys

One-third of Department of Defense procurement dollars in Arizona go to firms in the Scottsdale/Mesa/Tempe triangle.

Flagstaff. The Navajo Army Depot was recommended for closure by the Base Realignment and Closure Commission in 1988. The government expected to give the closed facility to the Arizona National Guard while transferring the ammunition installation located there to another base. Savings from the closure are expected to total $3.1 million annually.[2]

Litchfield Park. Luke Air Force Base was scheduled for cuts of 647 military and 20 civilian personnel by FY 1991.[3]

Mesa. Mesa is the home of the AH-64 Apache helicopter produced by McDonnell Douglas' McDonnell Helicopter Division, which is also working on projects other than the Apache. Loss of contracts to McDonnell Douglas resulted in July 1990 layoffs of some 400 workers from the Mesa plant. The Helicopter Division was placed on the Army's Contractor Alert List in July 1991 because of "systematic management problems."[4]

Nearby Williams Air Force Base, which pumps more than $130 million a year into the regional economy, could be eliminated by 1996. Williams was targeted because its airspace continues to be encroached on by nearby commercial development and its facilities are in the poorest condition of all the bases that the government considered for closing. Direct and indirect job loss will amount to 6,000 positions out of a total regional job pool of 1.2 million workers. Annual income loss will be $130 million out of a regional income of $33 billion. It will cost the Air Force $222 million to close the base, but it expects annual savings of $54.1 million subsequently. Williams is on the Environmental Protection Agency's National Priorities List because heavy metals are contaminating the soil and fuels and lubricants are in the ground water. Under Federal regulations, commercial re-use cannot begin until cleanup is complete.[5]

Phoenix. Cuts in the Phoenix and AMRAAM missile systems will greatly affect Hughes Aircraft in Phoenix.

Tempe. Motorola's OV-1D Aircraft Modification Program is located in this region. The Litton Corporation laid off approximately 300 employees in the first half of 1991. However, the city's diverse high-tech, information-processing base is expected to carry its economy through the cuts.[6]

Tucson. The Tucson area receives over one-quarter of Arizona's defense money. Hughes Aircraft is a prime contractor on the Maverick and Phoenix missiles (the Phoenix was cut by Secretary Cheney) and the AMRAAM. These three programs make up three-quarters of production at the site, the other main program being the TOW missile, which will probably survive cuts. Hughes, the largest defense contractor in Tucson, has cut nearly 4,000 jobs since 1986 with another 1,600 of the remaining 5,600 due to be eliminated by 1992. Regional employment is 325,000 jobs so while defense is important the economic base is diverse. Total employment has been expanding at a much slower rate than the rest of the state, indicating that it might be hard for the city to absorb workers laid off from defense-related industries; but fortunately, many companies are planning to move into the area, including a Lockheed aircraft-repair subsidiary. Davis-Monthan AFB, home of the 836th Air Division, was slated to be reduced by 346 military and 9 civilian positions.[7]

The Tucson Economic Conversion Council, PO Box 42108, Tucson, AZ 85733 (602-620-1241), headed by Rosalyn Boxer, has met with, among others, the Arizona AFL-CIO and Hughes Aircraft to discuss conversion, and is pursuing a pilot conversion project with Durodyne Inc., a small defense manufacturing company. Tucson Economic Conversion Committee, Robert Cook, P.O. Box 41144, Tucson, AZ 85717; 602-323-0242.

Notes

1. Contacts: (1) Governor's Office, Vada Manager, Press Secretary, State House, Phoenix, AZ 85007; 602-542-4331. (2) Arizona Department of Economic Security, Dan Anderson, 1717 West Jefferson, Phoenix, AZ 85007; 602-542-3871. (3) Arizona Department of Commerce, David Janofsky, Director, 1700 West Washington, Phoenix, AZ 85007; 602-542-5371.

2. *Base Realignments and Closures*, Report of the Defense Secretary's Commission, December 1988, p. 56.

3. "Pentagon's Proposals: Base Closures, Reductions," *USA Today*, January 30, 1990, p. 8.

4. Interview in March, 1990 with Wayne Balmer, Community Development Manager, Mesa, AZ; 602-644-2388. Richard W. Stevenson, "Aircraft Company to Cut 17,000 Jobs," *The New York Times*, July 17, 1990, p. D7. "McDonnell Helicopter Unit Gets Warning From Army," *Wall Street Journal*, July 16, 1991, p.9.

5. *Atlas/Data Abstract for the United States and Selected Areas Fiscal 1990*, Department of Defense, Directorate for Information, Operations and Reports, p. 17. *Base Closure and Realignment Report*, Department of Defense, April 1991, pp. 108-109. "Pollutants Plague Bases Set to Close," *USA Today*, July 5, 1991, p. 7.

6. Interview in March, 1990 with Jan Schaeffer, Economic Development Administration, Tempe, AZ; 602-350-8225.

7. Ralph Vartabedian, "High Price of War May End Up Costing Defense Firms Plenty," *The Los Angeles Times*, January 26, 1991, p. D3. Interview in March, 1990 with Marshall Vest, University of Arizona Economic and Business Research Center; 602-621-2155. "Pentagon's Proposals...," *loc. cit.*

Arkansas

	A	B	C	D	E	F
	$	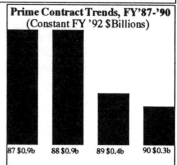			VI	DDI
	–	+	–	↓	!	✂

Benchmarks	No.	Rank	Benchmarks	No.	Rank
A. Total DoD $	$1.0bil.	37	Def.-Dependent Jobs ('000), '90	39	38
B. Personnel Payroll	$0.7 bil.	33	Change in Def.-Dep. Jobs, '89-'90	-11.4%	12
C. Prime Contracts (PC)	$0.3bil.	42	Unemployment Rate, '90-'91	7.5%	9
D. PC Change, FY '87-'90	-61.8%	1	Unemp. Rate Change, '89-'91	-0.4%	42
E. Vulnerability Index	9.6	25	Per Capita Income	$14,218	48
F. Defense Disloc. Index	2.55	12	Population	2,351	34

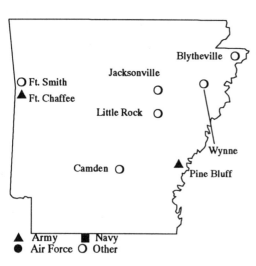

Prime Contract Trends, FY'87-'90
(Constant FY '92 $Billions)

87 $0.9b   88 $0.9b   89 $0.4b   90 $0.3b

▲ Army   ■ Navy
● Air Force   ○ Other

Top 5 Contractors	$Millions
Asea Brown Boveri	$33.8
General Dynamics	26.4
Munro	21.2
Tyson Foods	19.0
Willard Company	15.6

Top 10 $ Sites[a]	Congressional Dist., Representative	1989 Rank	Total DoD$[c]	Payroll[c]	Prime Contracts[c]	Per-sonnel[d]
1-Jacksonville (191)	2-Robinson,r	207	$182.2	$159.7	$22.5	--
2-Pine Bluff (266)	4-Anthony,d	261	104.4	46.4	57.9	1.6
3-Blytheville (275)	1-Alexander,d	276	93.3	82.4	10.9	--
4-Little Rock (315)	2-Vacant	315	63.5	51.8	11.7	1.3
5-Fort Smith (388)	3-Ham'rschmidt,r	408	27.4	14.0	13.3	0.3
6-Camden (390)	4-Anthony,d	300	26.9	2.6	24.3	0.0
7-N. Little Rock (399)	2-Vacant	--	23.8	23.4	0.3	0.1
8-Wynne (402)	1-Alexander,d	--	22.6	1.2	21.4	--
9-Fort Chaffee (416)	3-Vacant	402	18.9	7.7	11.2	0.6
10-East Camden (418)	4-Anthony,d	336	18.7	0	18.7	--

[a]Rating in parentheses is out of 511 sites, the top ten in each state and PR, plus DC.
[b]Multidistrict r-Rep. d-Dem. [c] $Millions (may not add due to rounding) [d]Thousands

Arkansas

The Arkansas economy is one of the weakest in the nation, with per capita income among the bottom five. The manufacturing and finance, insurance, and real estate industries comprised more than one-third of the gross state product. The state's unemployment rate ranked 9th highest and change in unemployment was a relatively favorable 42nd (the labor force declined more than employment decreased, for a net reduction in unemployment).[1]

Defense and the Economy

The Department of Defense spent less than a billion dollars in Arkansas in 1990, so that it ranked 37th in defense expenditure. But the state's high unemployment rate increases the vulnerability of its economy to cuts. Prime contracts in Arkansas likely to be cut or facing impending termination include the M-1 tank and F-15 fighter programs. The industries that receive the most Pentagon business in Arkansas are construction, missile/ammunition (General Dynamics Corp., Sequa Corp., Bei Electronics Inc.) and clothing (Munro & Co., Inc.). These three sectors account for 75 percent of total prime contracts awarded in the state in 1989.[2]

Community Surveys

Blytheville. Eaker Air Force Base appeared on the Base Commission's final list of recommended closures in July 1991. The Air Force has excess capacity of approximately six bases and Eaker ranks low on strategic location. The 3,191 personnel who will lose their jobs or be transferred out-of-state as a result of the base closing, represent nearly 9 percent of the 1990 military presence in Arkansas. Residents are attempting to create a movement to bring in private developers in case Eaker—home of the 97th Bombardment Wing— is shut down. Alternatively, they are proposing a dual basing plan whereby troops presently stationed overseas would have Eaker as a home base and be shipped abroad when a crisis arises. This is in line with the Federal government's objective to reduce the American military presence abroad.[3]

Fort Smith. Fort Chaffee was targeted for closing by the Base Closure and Realignment Commission in July 1991. The base's active military units will be transferred to Fort Polk in Louisiana but it will continue to maintain facilities for reserve units. The realignment could result in the loss of 6.1 percent of local jobs, but the continuation or expansion of oil and gas drilling activity at the base could mitigate the impact.[4]

Notes

1. *Statistical Abstract of the United States 1989*, Bureau of Census, U.S. Department of Commerce, pp. 429, 431, 433.

2. *DoD Prime Contracts Awards by Region and State, Fiscal Years 1989, 1988, 1987*, Department of Defense, Washington Headquarters Services, Directorate for Information, Operations and Reports, p. 21. Contacts: (1) Arkansas Industrial Development Commission, Mr. David Harrington, 1 Capitol Mall, Little Rock, AR 72201; 501-682-1121. (2) Economic Development. Mr. Phil Price, Senior Assistant, c/o Governor's Office, State Capitol, Little Rock, AR 72201. 501-682-2345.

3. *Atlas/Data Abstract for the United States and Selected Areas Fiscal 1989*, Department of Defense, Prepared by Washington Headquarters Services, Directorate for Information, Operations and Reports, p. 19. Maylon T. Rice, "Buck for Blytheville' Response Encouraging as Dollars Roll In," *Courier News*, March 18, 1990. "Alexander Wins Another Round on Dual Basing," *Jonesboro Sun*, July 13, 1990.

4. *Base Closure and Realignment Report*, Department of Defense, April 1991, pp. 38-39.

California

A	B	C	D	E	F
$				VI	DDI
+	+	+	→	!!	✂

Benchmarks	No.	Rank	Benchmarks	No.	Rank
A. Total DoD $	$35.9 bil.	1	Def.-Dependent Jobs ('000), '90	1,842	1
B. Personnel Payroll	$13.6 bil.	1	Change in Def.-Dep. Jobs, '89-'90	-8.2%	20
C. Prime Contracts (PC)	$22.3 bil.	1	Unemployment Rate, '90-'91	7.4%	10
D. PC Change, FY '87-'90	-18.1%	24	Unemp. Rate Change, '89-'91	+2.3	10
E. Vulnerability Index	11.3	17	Per Capita Income	$20,795	8
F. Defense Disloc. Index	2.98	.10	Population ('000)	29,760	1

▲ Army ■ Navy
● Air Force ○ Other

Sacramento

Sunnyvale

LOS ANGELES AREA:
Los Angeles, Long Beach,
El Segundo, Fullerton,
Azusa, Anaheim

■ Camp Pendleton

San Diego ■

Prime Contract Trends, FY'87-'90
(Constant FY '92 $Billions)

'87 $29.5b   '88 $27.4b   '89 $26.0b   '90 $24.2b

Top 5 Contractors	$ Millions
Lockheed	$2,464.3
GM-Hughes	2,143.2
McDonnell Douglas	1,787.6
Rockwell	1,523.6
Gencorp	1,132.2

Top 10 $ Sites[a]	Congressional Dist., Representative	1989 Rank	Total DoD$[c]	Payroll[c]	Prime Contracts[c]	Personnel[d]
1-San Diego (2)	(41,43-45)[b]	2	$4,819.9	$2,508.6	$2,311.3	48.2
2-Los Angeles (9)	(21,23-29,31-2,42)[b]	9	2,459.2	217.4	2,241.8	--
3-Sunnyvale (11)	12-Campbell, r	5	2,270.9	79.9	2,191.0	--
4-Long Beach (13)	(27,31,32,42)[b]	4	2,058.0	522.1	1,535.9	7.9
5-Sacramento (25)	(3,4)[b]	24	1,094.6	208.1	886.5	--
6-El Segundo (26)	27-Levine, d	26	1,067.0	74.4	992.6	--
7-Fullerton (38)	39-Dannemeyer, r	51	890.0	12.6	877.4	--
8-Azusa (39)	30-Martinez, d	--	857.8	2.2	855.6	--
9-Cp. Pendleton (41)	37-McCandless, r	36	826.6	671.8	154.8	21.6
10-Anaheim (55)	(38,39)[b]	37	686.1	23.2	662.9	--

[a]Rating in parentheses is out of 511 sites, the top ten in each state and PR, plus D C.
[b]Multidistrict r-Rep, d-Dem. [c]$Millions (figures may not add due to rounding) [d]Thousands

California

The most populous U.S. state with almost 29 million people, California's economy would rank among the top 10 in the world. The state's economy has prospered enormously during the last 30 years, with gross state product of $757 billion projected for 1991 by UCLA. The "60-Mile Circle" surrounding Los Angeles, with 5 percent of the state's total land area, accounts for nearly half of the state's population, non-farm employment, and personal income. The state's economy has a large supply of natural resources, strong agricultural and manufacturing sectors, and a powerful concentration of technological leadership. The services sector, especially tourism and entertainment, is also strong. But the recession has had its effect. Both unemployment and change in unemployment ranked 10th highest (the labor force grew six times faster than employment), a sign of trouble. Facing a budget shortfall of $7 billion over 18 months, Gov. Pete Wilson announced cuts in state programs at the start of 1991.[1]

Defense and the Economy

Almost one-fifth of U.S. defense prime-contract dollars are spent in California. The state is also home to over 75 military bases, 170,000 active-duty military personnel, and 130,000 additional civilians. Overall, the Federal Government spent $36 billion on defense in the state in 1990 (not including small contracts or subcontracts), directly employing at least 424,000 people and providing jobs for nearly one million people. But the jobs in the high-tech communications, missiles and space, and aerospace industries all declined in 1989 and 1990. California receives more defense dollars than any other state; thus it ranks high on both the Vulnerability Index and the Defense Dislocation Index. All top 10 sites in California in total expenditures rank in the top 100 nationally.[2]

Even though defense purchases are up by over 80 percent from the late 1970s, defense spending fell from over 14 percent of gross state product in the 1960s to about 8 percent in 1990. Approximately 53 percent of defense production is in prime contracts; the rest is subcontracting. In 1988 the Pentagon awarded over $6.8 billion worth of contracts for cargo planes, none in California, but almost $1.5 billion made it to California in subcontracts.[3]

Most large U.S. defense contractors have defense-related business in the state of California. The five largest defense firms in the state had $9.1 billion in contracts for FY 1990, more than 40 percent of all Pentagon contract dollars to the state. The top four contractors gave approximately $4 million in PAC contributions between 1979 and 1986.[4]

Procurement accounts for three-fifths of defense expenditures in California, or $23.1 billion. California ranked as one of the top five recipients in procurement for 17 of the 25 major procurement programs in FY 1989. California accounted for a fifth or more of total U.S. expenditures on four procurement programs: missile and space systems, weapons, combat vehicles, and ammunition.[5]

Research and Development constitutes almost 19 percent of total military expenditures in California. R&D contracts in the state for FY 1990 totaled close to $6.6 billion and accounted for over one-quarter of the total spent on R&D for the whole nation. These figures do not include many classified "black budget" contracts for SDI or other secret weapons. The state may have received another $1 billion or more for secret R&D.[6]

According to the Federation of American Scientists, the top six California contractors on the SDI project for the years 1983-1988 were Lockheed (in Sunnyvale, Palo Alto, Burbank), Hughes/GM)(El Segundo, Canoga Park, Goleta, Malibu, Fullerton, Anaheim, Los Angeles, Carlsbad, Torrance, Culver City), TRW (Redondo Beach, El Segundo, San Juan Capistrano), Rockwell International (Canoga Park, Seal Beach, Downey, Anaheim, Thousand Oaks), McDonnell Douglas (Huntington Beach), and Lawrence Livermore (Livermore). Together these firms account for one-third of U.S. spending on SDI research.[7]

Personnel accounted for about 38 percent of the defense money going to California in 1990, over $13 billion. Besides paying the 170,000 active uniformed personnel in the state, who received nearly $6 billion in employee pay, the military provides compensation to over 120,000 civilian employees and an equal number of reserve and National Guard troops.

State Legislative Initiatives

State employment officials in 1990 established the Aerospace Human Resources Network to provide free computerized job placement and training services for white-collar workers in the industry. The system, with which Rockwell Corp., General Dynamics, Hughes Aircraft, Lockheed, McDonnell Douglas, Northrop, and TRW agreed to cooperate, was geared toward helping laid-off workers return to work as soon as possible. It closed down in 1991 for lack of state funding (see under Manhattan Beach).

If layoffs are severe, the state could resurrect the Emergency Employment Act, putting unemployed engineers to work on civilian projects, and applying for JTPA's Title III funds. The state also has a number of job and financial assistance programs and educational programs in place to assist laid-off workers, including: (1) The Job Service Program, administered by the Employment Development Department (EDD),and the Employment Training Program, administered by the Employment Training Panel (ETP); (2) post-secondary vocational education and adult education; and (3) Unemployment insurance, which provides up to 26 weeks of cash grants with an additional 26 weeks offered to those who enroll in a Training Extension program.[10]

Commerce Department officials convinced Hughes Aircraft to remain in the town of Torrance by extending state education and job training aid to its employees. The Business Environmental Assistance Center was created to help companies make sense of complicated environmental laws. The California Supplier Improvement Program was created to improve the quality and reduce the costs of component parts supplied by defense subcontractors. The state planned to spend $7 million at the beginning of 1991 for these programs.[11]

State Sen. John Garamendi helped create the California Competitive Technology program in 1989 with $6 million in state funds to help move California's manufacturing sector back into high-growth commercial markets.[12] The program is a collaborative effort by researchers, manufacturers and venture capitalists to expand the private sector production in the state by converting defense industries to commercial manufacturing.

In April 1990, a delegation of 27 Democratic and seven Republican congressional representatives from California called for conversion planning. They asked that a California Economic Transition Project be coordinated by the University of California's Institute on Global Conflict and Cooperation, to be involved in information services, research, retraining programs, and conversion projects in areas targeted for cuts. Rep. George Miller (D-Martinez) said that while one estimate foresaw 200,000 defense-related jobs lost in California by 1995, the impact of cuts "need not be a detrimental impact on the vitality of the state or its residents." Miller held that many companies have already begun to diversify and that the state is much less defense-dependent than it was in the late 1960s. As of September 1991, Gov. Wilson had a conversion bill, AB 2248, on his desk awaiting signature. The bill, introduced by Assemblyman Farr, would create a base-closure advisory council.[13]

Community Surveys

In FY 1989, Los Angeles County received $11.7 billion in prime defense contracts and a large amount of direct defense money through four Navy bases and one Air Force base; it received over 45 percent of all defense money flowing into the state. Santa Clara County, which comprises much of Silicon Valley, procured the second most direct defense dollars in the state, nearly $3,000 per capita and 17 percent of the total spent on prime contracts in the state. Orange County received the third highest amount of defense dollars with 11 percent of the state total. Cumulatively, Los Angeles, Santa Clara, and Orange Counties received over 73 percent of all defense contract dollars in the state. Inyo County received the most per capita contract dollars, $3,810 per person.[8]

In May 1990, Northrop announced plans to cut at least 3,000 workers as $14.4 billion was slashed from the $75 billion B-2 budget. Seventy-five percent of Northrop's 41,000 employees are located in Southern California, so this area will be the hardest hit by the layoffs. Cuts by Lockheed Corp. and McDonnell Douglas are affecting workers in several locations. McDonnell Douglas announced in July 1990 that 17,000 workers will be laid off across the nation, 9,000 in Southern California. Because of cancellation of several combat-aircraft programs, such as the F-15 fighter, the company said it will offer services to help those who lose their jobs find new employment. General Dynamics announced plans to cut its workforce from 90,000 to 63,000 nationwide; some cuts will inevitably come in California.[9]

Adelanto. The 1989 Base Closure Act targeted the 5,350-acre George Air Force Base for closing by 1992. The base, which houses F-4G fighters, has an annual payroll of $93 million. Steps were immediately taken to dampen the impact of the military pullout; closure was estimated to result in loss of over 5,000 military and civilian jobs. The city is spending $1 million to promote the creation of High Desert International Airport on the site of the base. Formed by some nearby towns, the Victor Valley Economic Development Authority prefers a plan that would begin with a smaller domestic-travel airport that might expand with market forces. But the U.S. government may give part of George to the Federal Bureau of Prisons for a penitentiary. George AFB Task Force, chaired by San Bernardino County Supervisor Marsha Turoci for the 1st District, is preparing a comprehensive base re-use plan.[14]

Burbank. Lockheed announced in April 1990 that it would lay off about 1,800 employees in the city of Burbank as part of an effort to cut 2,750 from its aeronautical systems division. The company later announced plans to close much of its operation in Southern California, removing all aircraft operations from the city, displacing another 7-8,000 workers. Five thousand workers will remain at the company's Palmdale facility. In May 1990, Lockheed announced that it was moving the company headquarters from Burbank to Marietta, GA (home state of Senate Armed Services Committee Chairman Sam Nunn), resulting in the transfer of some 500 workers. Additional job losses are likely if more production functions are moved to Marietta.[15]

China Lake. The Naval Weapons Center will be realigned according to the Defense Department. The Pentagon estimates that 1,100 of 6,300 positions will be transferred or cut.[16]

Downey. The Combined Effects Munitions contract held by Aerojet may not be renewed, but no local anticipatory activity could be uncovered.[17]

El Segundo. Home of the Hughes Corp.'s M-1 tank, which is in danger of being cut. About 2,000 layoffs are scheduled at Hughes by the end of 1991, 1,600 from its Missile Systems Group and 300 from its Radar Systems Group. The city is not as diversified as it would like to be, and defense cuts will delay the recovery of the depressed housing market. Most initiatives to market the city have been taken by private developers.[18] The research and development branch of the Air Force is located at the Los Angeles Air Force Base in El Segundo. The base was targeted for closure in 1990, but was spared the ax after a report on the ramifications of closing the airport; an estimated 3,200 jobs were saved.[19]

Hawthorne. One of the several locations in the Los Angeles area most affected by the Northrop cutbacks, the aircraft division at Hawthorne was expected to lose some 1,350 jobs starting in 1990. The jobs are going to be eliminated through retirements, voluntary leaves, and layoffs.[20]

Huntington Beach. McDonnell Douglas is engaged in the Army Helicopter Improvement Program here. The city isn't too concerned about layoffs because Orange County is so diversified. Of the 17,000 layoffs announced by McDonnell Douglas in July 1990, 400 are to occur at the Space Systems division in Long Beach, and employees are beginning to feel concerned.[21]

Imperial. Salton Sea Test Base is an inactive facility in Southern California that was slated for clusure in 1988. But it has no personnel, so no jobs are at stake.[22]

Irvine. The city of Irvine was awarded a $70,800 grant in 1991 from the Defense Department for a one-year conversion plan called the Economic Development Demonstration Project (Margo Bowers, Coordinator, P.O. Box 19575, Irvine, CA 92713; 714-724-6253). One possibility for converted industry is work on components and services for advanced transit systems being planned for the Orange County area.

Livermore. The Lawrence Livermore National Laboratory (see Chapter 3) is engaged in about $750 million of military-related activities, 75 percent of its budget. Primarily a weapons laboratory, Livermore will be affected by the defense cuts, as Congress is sure to cut many aspects of the lab's budget. The Livermore management is doing very little about conversion planning, but staff members worry. Hugh Dewitt, a theoretical physicist at Livermore for over 33 years, says "the Livermore Lab is in a precarious position right now. It is not yet clear how deep the cuts will be. Right now the labs are in a kind of calm before the storm."[23]

Lompoc. The city of Lompoc, a community of 39,000 in the Lompoc Valley (pop. 55,000) located in northern Santa Barbara County, is seeking to cope with the government's plan for Vandenberg AFB to gain control over 54,000 acres of land. Some landowners are worried about it. A recent study found that the military contributes some $300 million a year to the regional economy. About half the jobs in Lompoc Valley depend directly or indirectly on the base.[24] Mayor J.D. Smith, City Hall, 100 Civic Center Plaza, P.O. Box 8001, Lompoc, CA 93438-8001; 805-736-1261, fax 805-736-5347.

Long Beach. This could be one of the hardest hit communities in the nation. The Base Closure Commission recommended the closing of the Naval Station and Naval Hospital in July 1991. The Long Beach Naval Shipyard (which was itself a closure target in 1991) will assume control of the station's functions. The Pentagon estimates about 30,000 jobs will be affected, about 0.5 percent of the area's labor force. The government plans to spend $109 million on the closure process but expects the resale value of the land to be $27 million and hopes to save $112 million annually on top of that. Long Beach was specifically targeted because it has high labor costs, is too small to act as a homeport for all ships in the Southern California region, and duplicates nearby San Diego's homeport.[25] Long Beach Economic Development, Gerald Miller, Manager, 230 Pine Avenue, Long Beach, CA 90802; 213-590-6097.

As if this weren't bad enough, McDonnell Douglas has kept up a drumbeat of layoff news. It announced in 1990 that it would eliminate 4,000 jobs from its Douglas Aircraft plant, the largest employer in Long Beach, as part of 17,000 layoffs nationwide. At the start of 1991, the company said it would eliminate an additional 5,600 jobs—some, inevitably, in Long Beach. Major cuts in the Air Force's C-17 transport program and other programs have created serious problems for the company, on top of problems in the transport division. While Douglas has a record backlog of orders for its MD-80/90 series of commercial jetliners, the MD-80 is not consistently profitable and its MD-11 wide-body jets were six months behind schedule. In March 1991, the company announced that it would seek a location outside of California for the construction of a $750-million assembly plant for its new commercial jets, the MD-12X. In April 1991 it announced it would drop another 1,000 workers. The company is shifting more of the production work on the C-17 to St. Louis, MO. However, harried local officials think they see light at the end of the tunnel, i.e., a stabilizing of Douglas' Long Beach employment at about 35,000.[26]

Los Angeles. The Naval Space Systems Activity will close and 29 civilian positions will be lost.[27] "The Los Angeles Initiative" is a strategic plan developed by a group of business, labor, government leaders of Southern California to reduce the negative impact of area defense cuts. It examines conversion possibilities for bases and shipyards to be closed. Los Angeles City Council Member Robert Farrell has introduced a resolution to establish a Defense Production Alternatives Commission.

Hughes Aircraft won an $837 million contract to build an air-defense system for Saudi Arabia. The company was awarded the deal by the Pentagon after Boeing, the original winner of the contract, failed to meet development deadlines. The contract, while not huge, should help the General Motors subsidiary minimize personnel cuts for the next few years.[28] The contract follows on the heels of the termination of the Army's FOG-M missile program which Hughes was working on with Boeing.

Lockheed's prospects are better than those of most other defense contractors despite cancellation in 1990 of a deal to build P-7A submarine-hunting aircraft for the Navy. Along with General Dynamics and Boeing, it is building the Air Force's new generation of fighter aircraft, the F-22s. As a result of the plane's performance in the Gulf Crisis, the U.S. Congress and the British government have expressed interest in buying more of Lockheed's F-117A fighter-bomber aircraft. Lockheed has also recently negotiated a $1 billion deal with Motorola to supply it with small satellites.[29]

Northrop Corporation is building the Pentagon's next generation of radar-evading missiles in the area. The Defense Department wants to buy 8,650 missiles at a cost of $15.1 billion. Northrop was awarded the development contract for the missiles in 1986.[30] The contract should help the firm stay afloat despite possible termination of its B-2 bomber program.

TRW eliminated 950 jobs from its Space and Defense Sector facility in Los Angeles in 1990, more than half resulting in layoffs and the remainder through attrition.

Since 1984, an annual study of the impacts of shifts in defense spending priorities has been required on the City Charter. To accomplish this, the Southern California Association of Governments sponsors a Jobs with Peace Task Force. Also an Aerospace Task Force, made up of governmental and industry leaders, has been organized by Los Angeles County's Economic Development Corporation. The City is also helping laid-off workers by sponsoring workshops and by working with Job Training Partnership Act recipient agencies. The City itself has received $613,000 from the Department of Labor to help retrain and place about 200 workers. It is hoped that the conversion effort can be structured by a coalition of eight Private Industry Councils in the area.

The Los Angeles City government has taken an active interest in conversion, for example by sponsoring research on electric car manufacturing. Contact Mayor Tom Bradley, Los Angeles City Hall, Los Angeles, CA 90012; 213-485-3311.

Manhattan Beach. The free computerized job-location and training center that opened here in 1990 to assist laid off white-collar aerospace workers was closed down in 1991 because the state terminated funding.[31]

Marin. Hamilton Army Air Field— an air support station for the San Francisco Presidio and an Army Reserve training center—was slated for closure under the Base Closure and Realignment Act of 1988. The field should be closed by 1995 and the Sixth Army Aviation Detachment will be relocated to Fort Carson in Colorado.[32] Environmental cleanup is necessary.

Menlo Park. Raychem Corp., an electronic components supplier, cut 900 jobs in 1990 and planned to restructure to concentrate on commercial business.[33]

Merced. Castle Air Force Base will be shut down. The 93rd Bombardment Wing will be inactivated and other units will be transferred to Fairchild AFB in Washington and KI Sawyer AFB in Michigan. The Pentagon projects a population loss of 16,000 and an annual income loss of $162 million to the local economy. Castle is on the EPA's National Priorities List (nitrates and pesticides contaminate ground water) so commercial use of the base will have to wait.[34]

Monterey. Fort Ord could lose more than two-thirds of its 16,000 troops over the next few years, as the 7th Infantry Division is transferred to Fort Lewis, WA. The Pentagon decided to close the base because it has low military value: many other bases are more strategically located and Ord's airfield is not capable of handling C-141 military aircraft, forcing the Army to use a nearby civilian airfield. The Defense Department expects to profit from the closure of the base, mostly from the sale of land worth $400 million, and hopes to save $70 million annually subsequently. The towns of Marina, Seaside, and Sand City are heavily dependent on Fort Ord, which contributes $1 billion to the local economy and provides about 5,000 local jobs for civilians. The annual payroll at the fort is around $610 million. Military families and retirees near the base number 92,866 —almost a quarter of the population of the county. The Monterey Peninsula Unified School District has already decided to close down five schools and lay off at least 140 teachers, costing the area over $7 million in Federal aid. Using the 28,000-acre oceanfront area for low-income housing and housing for the elderly and handicapped has been suggested, as has an oceanographic research center and an industrial park. The Navy has also expressed interest in acquiring some of the fort's housing units for its personnel. However, the base is on the EPA's National Priorities List due, inter alia, to the contamination of ground water. Under Federal law, civilian use cannot take place until the area has been cleaned. Water decontamination can take 30 or more years.[35]

Newport Beach. Ford Aerospace, which won contracts to manufacture the guidance system for the Chaparral missile here, was sold in July 1990 to New York-based Loral in partnership with the investment firm of Shearson Lehman. The new firm is called Loral Aeronutronic.

Orange County. Alliance for Survival, 200 N. Main Street, #M-2, Santa Ana, CA 92701 (714-547-6282), headed by Marion Pack, it grew out of Huntington Beach and was set up to ask city and county officials to work on identifying which areas of the county will be affected by military cuts, and to plan for economic diversification.

Palmdale. The Northrop plant in this town in Los Angeles County seeks to gain from the layoffs at the Hawthorne and Pico Rivera plants in the coming year. Northrop spokesmen say that production of the center fuselage section of the B-2 bomber will be transferred from Pico Rivera to Palmdale, and the Palmdale facility will grow from 2,200 to 3,000 employees.[36] Palmdale is also home to a Lockheed plant, and will be affected by Lockheed's 7,000 layoffs in California as the headquarters move to Georgia.

Pico Rivera. The Southern California town outside of Los Angeles is home to Northrop's B-2 bomber plant. Northrop announced in July 1990 that it will lay off about 1,400 workers from the plant, as part of the company's plan to make 3,000 workers redundant.

Point Mugu. The Pacific Missile Test Center will be realigned it was announced in April 1991. Its separate technical command will be eliminated. Along with the Naval Weapons Center at China Lake, CA, it will serve as the head of the Naval Air Warfare Center Weapons Division. The consolidation will cost 820 positions.[37]

Pomona. General Dynamics announced in August 1990 that it would consolidate its two Southern California facilities in Pomona and Rancho Cucamonga, to result in the loss of 1,500 to 2,000 jobs by the end of 1991. The Pomona division, which produces Standard and Sparrow missiles and Phalanx Close-in Weapons Systems, and the Valley Systems in Rancho Cucamonga, which builds Stinger and Rolling Airframe missiles, will be combined into the Air Defense Systems Division. The company announced that it would provide career counseling and placement assistance for the laid-off workers.[38] Pomona City Manager's Office, Mr. Julio Fuentes, City Manager, Pomona, CA 91766.

Redondo Beach. According to news reports, TRW announced in November 1990 it would cut 200-300 jobs in 1991 from the Redondo Beach facility of its Space and Defense Sector, in addition to 1,600 jobs already eliminated nationally from this sector in 1990.

Riverside. The 1989 Base Closure and Realignment Act mandated the reorganization of March Air Force Base. Under the Act all 184 Headquarters Air Force Audit Agencies, originally located at Norton AFB in San Bernardino, were to be moved to March AFB in Riverside. However, due to the planned reorganization of the Auditor General's Office, only 139 of the Audit Agencies will now be moved to March.[39]

Rosamond. Yet another Southern California military facility to be affected by cuts in the defense budget, Edwards Air Force Base will have to cut over 400 of its nearly 6,000 employees. The cuts will likely come through attrition or early retirement.[40]

Sacramento. Mather Air Force Base is slated for closure by September 1993. The base has 5,000 employees and a $150 million payroll. The Sacramento Area Commission on Mather Conversion (SACOM-C), on which both Mayor Anne Rudin and Congressman Robert T. Matsui (D-CA) serve, has drafted a report for re-use alternatives for Mather. SACOM-C's report has been submitted to the Sacramento County Board of Supervisors for consideration. The re-use proposal calls for commercial development that complements Mather's aviation functions—perhaps aircraft maintenance, air cargo, or general aviation support facilities. SACOM-C wants to maintain Reserve and National Guard space at Mather, as well as medical facilities for military retirees. Air base housing may be used to alleviate the affordable-housing crunch in the county and recreational facilities are recommended for retention for community use. Environmental cleanup will be necessary. The Sacramento Employment and Training Agency is busy getting involved in assisting workers in job training and job placement. It has obtained $200,000 through the Economic Dislocated Workers Adjustment Assistance Act, which is part of the federal Job Training Partnership Act , and plans to seek additional funds.

McClellan AFB, the third largest site of personnel in the state with 15,400 employees, plans to shed 800 to 1,700 civilian jobs during the next few years.

The Sacramento Army Depot was also slated for closure on the July 1991 list of the Base Closure and Realignment Commission. The Army wants to consolidate its functions by moving the depot's ground communications maintenance work to sites in Pennsylvania, Texas, and Alabama. Sacramento officials urged that the depot's functions be merged with the storage facility at nearby McClellan Air Force Base, but this plan was rejected by the Base Commission. Hazardous waste cleanup will be required, including ground water and asbestos remedial action, as the depot is on the EPA's National Priorities List, but the government eventually plans to save $56 million annually by the closure. A reserve component will remain at the base, but the Pentagon still expects the closure to eliminate 0.8 percent of Sacramento jobs.[41] Sacramento SANE/Freeze, P.O. Box 60860, Sacramento, CA 95860 (916-448-7158), headed by Steve Wirtz, led a coalition of local groups to monitor the Base Closure and Realignment Commission's work.

San Bernardino. Norton Air Force Base, which employs 5,000 military and 3,700 civilian personnel, was one of the 86 bases approved for closure in early 1989. Lockheed Corp. wants to turn the facility into an aircraft maintenance facility for Boeing 747s. They have leased one of the four huge hangars and plan to acquire the rest by 1994. Lockheed hopes to keep costs down in an expensive business environment by hiring from the experienced aerospace labor pool that could be dislocated by other cuts in the defense budget.[42] The conversion process may not continue on its smooth path however. Toxins have been found under the hangar floors that might slow the leasing process being supervised by the Inland Valley Development Agency (IVDA), the body in charge of Norton's conversion. Moreover, two communities, Redlands and Highland, that have not joined IVDA are mounting a legal challenge to its supervisory authority.

The Norton Economic Expansion Committee is chaired by Mayor Evelyn Wilcox of the City of San Bernardino and 5th District Supervisor Robert L. Hammock of the County of San Bernardino. The group is preparing a comprehensive reuse plan for recommended uses of base property and a "Concept Plan" to serve as the groundwork for future planning efforts.

San Diego. The area is highly vulnerable to base closings. The Integrated Combat Systems Test Facility and Naval Electronic Systems Engineering Center have appeared on potential base closure or realignment lists. The Marine Recruiting Depot and the Naval Training Center, which train 63,000 military personnel annually, were considered for closure but remained off the Base Commission's final recommendation list.[43] Defense Secretary Dick Cheney has stated that he would like to move 20 ships stationed at the San Diego homeport. The city's 53,000 military and civilian defense employees add up to the biggest concentration of defense-related workers in the country. In 1990 2,600 were laid off and in for 1991 1,500 more layoffs were predicted.[44]

General Dynamics, the largest defense contractor in the area, decided in the spring of 1991 that it would eliminate 27,000 positions in its 90,000-member national labor force over the following four years. The company—86 percent of whose business is military contracts—has been suffering from the scaleback of Pentagon spending, including the cancellation of the Navy's A-12 fighter jet program which the company had already been contracted to build.[45]

The Institute for Effective Action, 5380 El Cajon Blvd., San Diego, CA 92115 (619-582-3990) is headed by Donald Cohen. It drafted a "Dollar for Dollar Act" that cuts made in military spending from American cities should be returned to those cities, dollar for dollar. The San Diego City Council and the California State Legislature have both endorsed the campaign and are urging Congress to adopt such an act. The money that would be cut from the cities would instead be spent on such needs as job training and placement, crime and drug prevention. For 10 years the cuts in military spending in a county would be placed in an Economic Security Fund for that county. The Dollar for Dollar Act also calls for a National Economic Security Fund that would receive money originally to be spent overseas. City Council Member Bob Filner and State Assembly Member Delaine Eastin are the major proponents of the act.

The San Diego City Council passed a "dollar for dollar" resolution on April 23, 1990 and (at the urging the San Diego Economic Conversion Council, described next), created a three-person Economic Conversion Subcommittee to hold hearings and prepare plans for economic transition for the city. Conversion plans call for assistance to laid-off workers, steps to diversify the economy, and cooperation with industries located in the area to preserve and increase job opportunities.The subcommittee worked with a broad-based Advisory Group, held monthly Town Meetings, and delivered a report in July 1991. The City Council has submitted the report to a new Economic Development Task Force that includes representation from conversion proponents.[46]

The San Diego Economic Conversion Council (SDECC), 405 West Washington Street, Suite 143, San Diego, CA 92103 (619-278-3730), is headed by Marcia Boruta. Formed in 1985, it focused in 1990-91 on shifting Federal spending priorities, diversification of local economies, and converting companies. The group works with local elected officials, and in 1991 was organizing a Congressional Task Force on Economic Conversion with Rep. Jim Bates. SDECC is working on coalition-building and a Town Meeting effort, which is supported by the National Steel and Shipbuilding union.[47]

San Francisco. The proposed closing of the Presidio Army base in San Francisco was met with efforts by California Representatives Barbara Boxer and Nancy Pelosi, both liberal Democrats, to reverse the decision. They succeeded in reaching a compromise whereby an Army hospital and some reserve activities would be spared. While 3,000 jobs at the base were in danger of being lost, many felt that there were advantages for the community in closing the Presidio. The 1,500 acres of the base have been added to the Golden Gate National Recreation Area; many of the base's facilities and buildings could be put to public and civilian use. The Arms Control Research Center, 942 Market Street, San Francisco, CA 94102 (415-397-1452), headed by Saul Bloom, sponsored a conference on the Presidio in 1989.[48]

The Base Commission targeted the Treasure Island Naval Station's Hunters Point Annex for closing but the Naval Station itself was spared. The decision to close the Annex is a revision of the 1989 Base Closure Act which mandated only its realignment. Approximately 60 civilian positions will be eliminated. Since the site is on the Environmental Protection Agency's National Priorities List, commercial re-use cannot proceed until benzene and PCBs in the ground water is cleaned up.[49]

San Jose. Jim Tucker, a staff expert from the San Jose Chamber of Commerce, stated that "defense work could easily be as high as 15 percent of [San

Jose's] manufacturing output." FMC, makers of the Bradley Fighting Vehicle, announced in May 1990 that it would have to start laying off some of its 4,500 workers.[50]

Santa Barbara County. The 100,000-acre Vandenberg Air Force Base in Santa Barbara County, in the midst of declines in aerospace contract expenditures, is trying to extend its perimeter to encompass some 54,000 additional acres. It is believed that the government will spend some $110 million to purchase the rights to the land, while buying the land outright could cost millions more. The military claims that this is to keep the land for agricultural purposes.

Peace Resource Center of Santa Barbara, 331 N. Milpas Street, Suite F, Santa Barbara, CA 93103 (805-965-8583), Greg Cross. Worked on a successful effort to persuade the Area Planning Council of Santa Barbara to plan for conversion in the county. Santa Barbara Area Planning Council, 222 East Anapamu St., Santa Barbara, CA 93101 (805-568-2546). Michael Powers. Released economic conversion study for Santa Barbara. Santa Barbara County Association of Governments, Michael G. Powers, Deputy Director-Planning, 222 East Anapamu St., Suite 11, Santa Barbara, CA 93101; 805-568-2546.

Santa Clara. The Defense Advanced Research Projects Agency (DARPA) announced that it was investing $4 million in Gazelle Microcircuits here to help keep critical technology on American soil (instead of losing it to Japan). The company is one of the few American firms that makes gallium arsenide for semiconductors. DARPA, in exchange for the investment, has the choice of 12 percent of the company's stock or royalties from its returns. Jerry Crowley, Gazelle Chief Executive, informed DARPA officials of his financial problems and of the interest of Japanese venture-capital firms in his company, and within a month the company received the funds.[51] Santa Clara County has lost thousands of electronics jobs over the last two years.

Santa Monica. Voters to End the Arms Race, 1431 Ocean Avenue, Suite B, Santa Monica, CA 90401, Mariette Vandermolen. With other groups was organizing a statewide 1990 initiative to create a state conversion commission and reallocate resources for human and environmental needs.

Sunnyvale/Mountain View. Both the towns of Sunnyvale and Mountain View in the Bay Area are officially home to Moffett Field Naval Air Station. The base, which costs some $25 million annually to operate, is likely to close. The Navy estimates that the closure will cost 12,200 jobs, but local officials are not nearly so sanguine. They argue that the closing of the base will force the Lockheed Missiles and Space Company, which uses the airport, to move some of its operations elswhere and take a portion of its 21,000 jobs with it. The Moffett Field Commmittee is lobbying to keep the air station open because of its importance to the Silicon Valley hi-tech economy. If salvation is not possible, it supports operation of the base by NASA as a research facility and use by defense contractors. One problem though is that the station is on the EPA's National Priorities List (cleanup has already started).[52]

Center for Economic Conversion, 222 C View Street, Mountain View, CA 94041, 415-968-8798; Michael Closson, Executive Director, Jim Wake, Janet Stone. This 16-year-old organization headed by an energetic former Stanford University dean has conducted a California-wide study on conversion and spends about one-fifth of its time on its home state. CEC was originally formed as the Mid-Peninsula Conversion Project in the 1970s. The group has national outreach and is listed in Chapter 7. Sunnyvale Office of the City Manager/City Council, Karen Dairs, P.O. Box 3707, Sunnyvale, CA 94086-3707.

Tustin. The Marine Corps Air Station, the city's largest employer, will close. The departure of 3,500 Marines could mean the loss of millions in income.[53] Economic consequences could be mitigated if, as seems likely, some base housing is retained to meet the needs of Marine families at the Air Station in nearby El Toro. Local officials, however, welcome the opportunity to diversify economically by creating new commercial, industrial, and residential development at the base. Private uses give every indication of being extremely profitable as Orange County is rapidly expanding. However, environmental cleanup at the station will be necessary before commercial use can proceed. Office of the City Manager, Tustin, William A. Huston, City Manager, 15222 Del Amo Avenue, Tustin, CA 92680; 714-544-8890.

Vallejo. Since FY 1990, Mare Island Naval Shipyard employment has declined from 9,000 to 6,000 civilians. The workforce is expected to remain stable for the near future at 11,000 military and civilian employees. The Vallejo Naval Electronic Systems Engineering Center, the source of employment for 300, was recommended for closure by the Base Commission. Its functions will shift to Point Loma and it will close by 1995. Vallejo Economic Development Department, Craig Whittom, 555 Santa Clara St., Vallejo, CA 94590; 707-648-4444.

Notes

1. *Portrait for Progress: The Economy of Los Angeles County and the Sixty-Mile Circle Region*, Los Angeles City Economic Development Office, July 1988, pp. 3, 8. The ranking is based on 1985 gross product figures.

2. *Atlas/Data Abstract for the United States and Selected Areas Fiscal 1989*, Department of Defense, Prepared by Washington Headquarters Services, Directorate for Information, Operations and Reports, p. 21. *Impact of Federal Expenditures on the State of California* (Sacramento Commission on State Finance, Fall 1989), *pp. 1-3.*

3. "Cargo Plane Subcontractors," *California Military Monitor*, August, 1988, p. 2.

4. California Military Monitor, August, 1988, based on *Top Guns: A Common Cause Guide to Defense Contractor Lobbying*, by Philip J. Simon, Common Cause, 2030 M Street, NW, Washington, DC 20036, 1987.

5. *Prime Contract Awards by Region and State, Fiscal Years 1989, 1988, 1987*, Department of Defense, Washington Headquarters Services, Directorate for Information, Operations and Reports, pp. 7, 69.

6. Eugene Chollick, "FY '89 Top 100 Defense Contractors: Beyond The Cold War," *Research Report*, Council on Economic Priorities, May 1990, p. 3.

7. Printed in "Top 25 SDI (Star Wars) Contractors in California 1983-88,"*California Military Monitor*, August 1988, p. 5. FAS is at 307 Massachusetts Avenue, NE, Washington, DC 20002, 202-546-3300. CMM is published by the Pacific Studies Center, 222B View St., Mountain View, CA 94041; 415-969-1545.

8. *Defense Spending in the 1990s: Impact on California* (Sacramento: Commission on State Finance, Summer 1990), p. 22. Statistics are compiled by Data Resources, Inc. Contract dollars per county exclude certain classified contracts and contract awards under $25,000.

9. Brian Perry, "Cuts in Stealth Bomber Program to Force 3,000 Layoffs at Northrop," *The Washington Times*, May 17, 1990, p. C-1. Ralph Vartabedian, "Northrop Will Lay Off 1,400 at B-2 Facility," The Los Angeles Times, July 10, 1990, p. D2. Richard W. Stevenson, "Aircraft Company to Cut 17,000 Jobs," *The New York Times*, July 17, 1990, p. A1.

10. *Defense Spending...*, pp.49-58.

11. Debra Polsky, "California Government Takes Measures To Keep Defense Contractors In State," *Defense News*, January 21, 1991, p. 29.

12. David Evans and Thom Shanker, "States Try to Ease Blow of Defense Spending Cuts," *The Chicago Tribune*, February 27, 1990.

13. Paul Houston, "Study of Effect of Defense Cuts in State Asked," *The Los Angeles Times*, April 5, 1990, p. D2. Conversion bill: Janet Stone, *Conversion Organizers Update*, Center for Economic Conversion, October 1991 (advance copy), pp. 2-3. Contacts: (1) Gov. Pete Wilson, State Capitol, Sacramento, CA 95814; 916-445-2841. (2) California Department of Commerce, Office of Economic Research, C. Lance Barnett, Chief Economist, Susan Takeda, 801 K Street, #1700, Sacramento, CA 95814; 916-324-5853. (3) Economic Analysis and Development Program, Southern California Association of Governments, 818 W. 7th Street, 12th Floor, Los Angeles, CA 90017; 213-236-1800. (4) Sacramento City Hall, Anne Rudin, Mayor, City Hall, Rm. 205, 915 I St., Sacramento, CA 95814-2672; 916-449-5300.

14. Testimony given by Lauren Wasserman, Project Coordinator for Air Force Base Reuse for San Bernardino County, to California Assembly Committee on Economic Development and New Technologies, March 13, 1989. Michael Lev, "As Air Base Dies, Town Fights Over Its Afterlife," *The New York Times*, April 12, 1991.

15. Sandra Sugawara, "Aerospace Industry In a Spin," *The Washington Post*, April 28, 1990, p. D-10. Breakdown of the 2,750 mentioned in the article was obtained by phone on May 3, 1990. Interview in May, 1990, with Don Nakamoto of IAM District Lodge 727, 2600 W. Victory Blvd., Burbank, CA 91505; 818-845-7401. Maria Saporta, "Lockheed's Shot In The Arm," The Atlanta Constitution, May 10, 1990, p. 12.

16. *Base Closure and Realignment Report*, Department of Defense, April 1991, p. 74.

17. Interviews in January with Bruce Devine, Southern California Association of Governments (SCAG), 213-236-7800; and the City of Downey, in Los Angeles County, 213-869-7331, 213-773-1383. Some regional networking by affected companies seems under way through the Aerospace Task Force and the Los Angeles Aerospace and Defense Special Interest Group (LA-ADSIG) of the Association of Private Industry Councils (APIC).

18. Interview in March, 1990 with Lynn Harris, Director of Development Services, El Segundo, CA, 213-322-4670.

19. "The Painful Reordering of National Priorities,"*The Los Angeles Times,* April 16, 1991, p. B4.

20. Vartabedian, *loc. cit.*

21. Interview in March 1990 with Richard Barnard, Deputy City Administrator, City of Huntington Beach, 714-536-5511. Jonathan Weber, "Many Workers Fear the 'Worst Is Yet to Come,'" *The Los Angeles Times,* July 17, 1990, p. D1.

22. *Defense Spending...,* p. 41.

23. "In Search of a New Formula," interview with Hugh Dewitt conducted by Peter Holtzclaw, *Plowshare Press,* Summer 1990, p. 3.

24. E.A. Torriero, "Rockets vs. Cowboys: Air Force Goes After Ranches in Turf War," *Mercury News,* February 7, 1990, back page. Letter to John Tepper Marlin from Mayor Smith, July 29, 1991. King Patrick Leonard is Planning Director for the City of Lompoc.

25. *Base Closure and Realignment Report, op. cit.,* pp. 60-61.

26. "McDonnell Has Loss and Cuts Payout," *The New York Times,* February 6, 1991, p. D5. Stevenson, "Grim Contractors Ready for Cutbacks on Arms," *The Los Angeles Times,* April 27, 1990. Stevenson, "Battling the Lethargy at Douglas," *The New York Times,* July 22, 1990, sec. 3, p. 1. Bettina Boxall, "Little Fear of Flight," *The Los Angeles Times,* March 13, 1991, p. B1.

27. "Military Bases: Look of Future," *USA Today,* July 1, 1991, p. 8A.

28. Stevenson, "Hughes Awarded Contract For Saudi Military System," *The New York Times,* July 4, 1991, p. D3.

29. Stevenson, "Lockheed Sees Fortunes Improve," *The New York Times,* July 12, 1991, p. D6.

30. Stevenson, "Pentagon Unveils A Stealth Missile," *The New York Times,* June 8, 1991, p. A8.

31. Opening: Laura Suomisto, "Free Jobs Center Opens," Santa Monica Daily, March 15, 1990, p. B5; workers were described as "optimistic" about it. The Center was closed in 1991, according to Alan Coy, Human Resources, TRW, interviewed in September 1991.

32. *Defense Spending...,* p. 41.

33. Pete Carey, "Valley Defense Firms Seek New Directions," *San Jose Mercury News,* May 7, 1990, p. 1.

34. *Base Closure and Realignment Report, op. cit.,* pp. 94-95.

35. *Ibid.,* pp. 43-44. Ann W. O'Neill, "Planners Envision Rosy Future For Fort Ord," *San Jose Mercury News,* January 26, 1990, p. 12A. Miles Corwin, "Impending Closure of Ft. Ord Draws Numerous Pet Projects," *Los Angeles Times,* August 25, 1991, p.3. Robert W. Stewart, "Legislators Seek to Save Ft. Ord, Long Beach Base," *The Los Angeles Times,* May 22, 1991, p. 3. Paul Hoversten, "Some Military Bases Will Never Be Cleaned Up," *USA Today,* July 5, 1991, p. 7.

36. Vartabedian, *loc. cit.*

37. *Base Closure and Realignment Report., op. cit.,* p. 74.

38. "General Dynamics Plans Layoffs," *The New York Times,* August 7, 1990, p. D3.

39. *Base Closure and Realignment Report., op. cit.,* p. 113.

40. Adrianne Goodman, "Budget: Proposed Cuts Imperil Jobs at 3 Bases," *The Los Angeles Times,* January 30, 1990, p. 10.

41. *Base Closure and Realignment Report., op. cit.,* pp. 44-45.

42. Vartabedian, "Lockheed Proposes to Convert Norton Base to Civilian Use," *The Los Angeles Times*, Jan. 9, 1990, p. D1.

43. Melissa Healy, "State Wins, Loses on Base Closings," *The Los Angeles Times,* July 1, 1991, p. 1.

44. *Defense Spending...*, p. 39. *San Diego Base Conversion News*, March/April 1991.

45. Richard W. Stevenson, "Dynamics Set to Trim 27,000 Jobs," *The New York Times*, May 2, 1991, p. D1-D2.

46. "San Diego: A City in Search of the Peace Dividend," *Municipal Foreign Policy,* Summer 1990, p. 19. *San Diego Economic Conversion News,* December 1990. Stone, *op. cit.,* p. 2.

47. Marcia Boruta, San Diego Economic Conversion Council, *Proceedings: National Strategy Retreat on Economic Conversion,* Block Island, June 11-13, 1990 (Mountain View, CA: Center for Economic Conversion, 1990), p. 1.

48. Jane Gross, "Base Closings Seen as Opportunity Inside Problem," *The New York Times,* January 31, 1990, p. 13. Center for Economic Conversion, "Opportunity Knocks," *Base Conversion News,* Summer 1990, p. 2.

49. *Base Closure and Realignment Report*. April 1991, pp. 59-60.

50. Evans and Shanker, *loc. cit..* Pete Carey, "Valley Defense Firms Seek New Directions," *San Jose Mercury News,* May 7, 1990, p. 1A.

51. Harris Collingwood, "In Business This Week: Seed Money From the Pentagon," *Business Week,* April 23, 1990, p. 40.

52. Nick Anderson, "Moffett's Two Hometowns Predict Base Won't Close," *San Jose Mercury News,* January 27, 1990, p. 5B. Guy Gugliotta, "Lawmaker Takes Base Closings in Stride," *The Washington Post,* April 22, 1991, p. 7. "Pollutants Plague Bases Set to Close," *USA Today*, July 5, 1991, p. 7.

53. *Base Closure and Realignment., op. cit.,* pp. 68-69.

Colorado

A	B	C	D	E	F
$				VI	DDI
+	+	+	↑	!!	✂

Benchmarks	No.	Rank	Benchmarks	No.	Rank
A. Total DoD $	$5.1bil.	13	Def.-Dependent Jobs ('000), '90	272	13
B. Personnel Payroll	$1.8bil.	15	Change in Def.-Dep. Jobs, '89-'90	+1.9%	37
C. Prime Contracts (PC)	$3.3bil.	13	Unemployment Rate, '90-'91	5.4%	39
D. PC Change, FY '87-'90	+9.0%	46	Unemp. Rate Change, '89-'91	-1.2%	51
E. Vulnerability Index	12.0	14	Per Capita Income	$18,794	17
F. Defense Disloc. Index	1.74	.16	Population ('000)	3,294	26

Boulder O

Denver OO Aurora

Englewood O

O Littleton

Colorado Springs O

Ft. Carson ▲

▲ Pueblo

▲ Army ■ Navy
● Air Force O Other

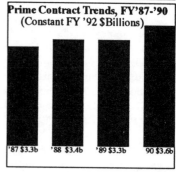

Prime Contract Trends, FY'87-'90
(Constant FY '92 $Billions)

'87 $3.3b　'88 $3.4b　'89 $3.3b　90 $3.6b

Top 5 Contractors	$Millions
Martin Marietta	$2,156.6
Litton	209.1
IBM	137.7
Ford	113.4
Flightsafety Int'l	41.0

Top 10 $ Sites[a]	Congressional Dist., Representative	1989 Rank	Total DoD$[c]	Payroll[c]	Prime Contracts[c]	Per-sonnel[d]
1-Denver (8)	(1,6)[b]	11	$2,506.1	$288.0	$2,218.1	1.0
2-Col'do Springs (35)	5-Hefley, r	45	911.5	351.5	560.1	1.0
3-Fort Carson (86)	"	67	453.8	401.8	52.0	13.3
4-Aurora (143)	6-Schaefer, r	128	273.9	236.2	37.7	4.4
5-Air Force Acad. (186)	5-Hefley, r	191	187.6	150.8	36.8	8.7
6-Boulder (200)	2-Skaggs, d	211	172.3	9.1	163.2	--
7-Englewood (233)	"	--	46.2	7.0	39.2	--
8-Lakewood (335)	6-Schaefer, r	344	45.5	8.7	36.8	--
9-Littleton (340)	(5,6)[b]	319	43.7	11.0	32.7	--
10-Pueblo (353)	3-Campbell, d	356	39.8	29.2	10.6	0.7

[a]Rating in parentheses is out of 511 sites, the top ten in each state and PR, plus DC.
[b]Multidistrict r-Rep, d-Dem. [c]$Millions (figures may not add due to rounding) [d]Thousands

Colorado

Colorado rebounded from a recession in the mid-1980s to outperform the nation in most measures of economic performance. The state has a lower inflation rate (4.4 percent in 1990) and a higher personal-income growth rate (6.1 percent in 1990) than the nation as a whole, although it lags in job creation (1.9 versus 2.2 percent in 1990). Services, retail trade, and communications are the fastest-growing business sectors. An expanding semiconductor industry is also boosting the state economy. The state economy, which has a significant agricultural sector, is also susceptible to droughts. The state's unemployment rate ranked 39th and its change in unemployment ranked 51st (the number of employed persons increased more than the labor force). State economists are looking to the future with cautious optimism.[1]

Defense and the Economy

The state economy benefited greatly from the Reagan defense buildup, as defense-industry growth partly offset a recession in other sectors. Defense expenditures account for 9.5 percent of state personal income, well above the national average of 5.0 percent. Colorado has 122,460 military and defense-related employees, approximately 8.2 percent of total employment. But even before President Bush decided to take unilateral action to reduce the U.S. nuclear stockpile in September 1991, forecasters were predicting that defense spending will no longer be a major source of its growth in the 1990s.[2]

A breakdown of Department of Defense expenditures in Colorado encourages analysts to hope that state procurement contracts will not be severely slashed. Of every defense dollar spent in the state, 69 cents goes toward research and development contracts, which tend to be the most stable during budget cuts. The state is among the top recipients of SDI research contracts, receiving over $1 billion annually for the project. Recent Department of Defense decisions to cut the SDI budget are therefore of concern to Colorado and have already caused Martin Marietta to lay off workers.[3]

State Legislative Initiatives

House Joint Resolution 1019 would have created an economic adjustment commission. It passed the legislature but was vetoed by the Governor. However, at the start of 1991, the Colorado Office of State Planning and Budgeting, charged with the task of studying the impact of military cuts on the state by the Federal Budget Task Force, constructed a list of possible legislative initiatives that would ease the move to a more diversified and civilian-based economy.[4]

Community Surveys

Colorado's dependence on defense spending is most acute in the Colorado Springs and Metro-Denver areas. In Colorado Springs, military-related projects account for 26 percent of regional employment. About one-quarter of the military personnel in Colorado is located in the Denver area. These two regions are likely to experience slow growth as Department of Defense dollars become more scarce.

Arapahoe County. The Bennett Army National Guard Facility, which has no personnel assigned to it, will close. Environmental cleanup is necessary; the facility has underground storage tanks.[5]

Colorado Springs. One out of five workers in Colorado Springs is employed on a military base—45,000 out of a total workforce of 220,000. Fort Carson is home to the U.S. Army's 4th Mechanized Division and to nearly half of all military personnel in the state. One of the fort's three brigades was deactivated in the wave of the defense cuts in December 1989, forcing reassignment of more than 3,000 soldiers and affecting more than 9,200 family members. In addition to the several thousand personnel who were transferred to other units, thousands of pieces of machinery, weapons, ammunition, and other supplies were shipped to other locations. The Air Force Academy has announced plans to cut the number of admitted cadets by 30 percent. The area stands to gain, however, from the movement of 6th Army Headquarters from the San Francisco Presidio to the fort. There are also plans to relocate the 1,000-member 10th Special Forces Group (the"Green Berets") to the base by 1992.[6]

Martin Marietta announced plans to cut 230 Colorado Springs jobs. An additional 100 company positions at nearby Falcon Air Force Base will be eliminated due to cuts in SDI funding. As a result, Marietta's subcontractors plan to let go of 130 employees. Consolidation at the Air Force Space Command Center will cause the trimming of 400 facility jobs during the next three years.[7]

Denver. The city of Denver receives close to 45 percent of the total Department of Defense money spent in the state. Lowry Air Force Base—one of the largest training centers in the country and employer of 5,750 military and 5,800 civilian employees—was earmarked by the Base Closure Commission for closure by September 1994. Two large base facilities, the Air Reserve Personnel Center and the Defense Finance and Accounting Service Denver Center, which employ 500 military and 3,000 civilian workers, will continue to operate. In his 1992 budget, President Bush proposed cutting 119 military and 145 civilian positions at the base.[8]

The Astronautics Group of Martin Marietta located in Denver is concerned with the defense cuts. Joe Lehman, its director of business development, says the company is actively seeking new business, both civilian and military. A major possibility for conversion is using the company's technology for commercial space equipment or environmental cleanup equipment. Of the company's 13,500 employees, 1,000 retired or were laid off in 1990 and 1,000 more are expected to either retire or be laid off in 1991.[9]

Pueblo. The Army Depot Activity was targeted in the 1989 Base Closure Act. Ammunition warehouse facilities will be closed by 1995 and 600 civilian jobs will go. However, the depot was chosen as the site of a $6.3 million facility for the destruction of intermediate range missiles, as mandated by a U.S.-Soviet arms accord.[10]

Rocky Flats. A plutonium-processing weapons plant managed by the Department of Energy employs 6,000 workers to produce plutonium triggers for nuclear warheads. The DOE decided in February 1991 to close the plant and relocate its operations over a period of from 10 to 15 years.[11]

Notes

1. Colorado Economic Perspective. Office of State Planning and Budgeting. December 20, 1990, p. 12, 14. *Colorado Economic Chronicle*, May 1, 1989, p. 2.

2. *Impact of the Defense Industry on the Colorado Economy*, prepared by the Office of State Planning and Budgeting at the request of The Federal Budget Task Force. February 1991, p. 7. *Colorado Economic Chronicle*, op. cit., p. 5.

3. *Impact of the Defense...*, *op. cit.*, pp. 5, 9.

4. Contacts: (1) Colorado Springs Mayor's Office, Robert M. Isaac, Mayor, P.O. Box 1575, Colorado Springs, CO 80901; 719-578-6600). (2) Mayor's Office of Economic Development, Jon Bowman, 216 16th St., Suite 1000, Denver, CO 80202; 303-572-4600. (3) Office of State Planning and Budgeting, Manlio Huacuja, Chief Economist, 111 State Capitol Building, Denver, CO 80203; 303-866-3310. (4) Colorado Coalition for the Prevention of Nuclear War, Hugh Catherwood, 1738 Wynkoop, Suite 302, Denver, CO 80202; 303-297-2809. Publishes *Conversion News*, a quarterly newsletter, addressing issues of both nuclear arms and testing reduction and economic conversion. Members of the coalition include: Rocky Flats Project, Colorado Council of Churches, Colorado Peace Council, Gray Panthers, Physicians for Social Responsibility, SANE/Freeze, and Women's Action for Nuclear Disarmament. (5) David Hite, Legislative Council, Rm. 029, State Capitol Building, Denver, CO 80203; 303-866-3521.

5. *Base Realignments and Closures.*, Report of the Defense Secretary's Commission, December 1988, p. 80.

6. Henry Dubroff, "Economic Conversion in Colorado," *The Denver Post*, reprinted in Colorado Coalition for the Prevention of Nuclear War, *Conversion News*, Summer 1990, p. 1. Evans and Shanker, "Death of 2nd Brigade Touches Many Lives," *Chicago Tribune*, February 28, 1990, p. 1. *Impact of the Defense Industry...*, p. 32.

7. *Colorado Economic..*, *op. cit.*, p. 22.

8. *Ibid.*, p. 15.

9. Cynthia Tew Thekan, "Martin Marietta Moves With Nation," *Conversion News*, Summer 1990, insert. *Impact of the Defense Industry...*, p. 31.

10. *Loc. cit.*

11. *Loc. cit.*

Connecticut

A	B	C	D	E	F
$	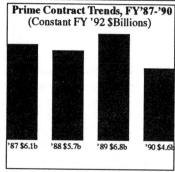			VI	DDI
+	−	+	→	!	✂

Benchmarks	No.	Rank	Benchmarks	No.	Rank
A. Total DoD $	$4.9bil.	14	Def.-Dependent Jobs ('000), '90	287	11
B. Personnel Payroll	$0.6bil.	35	Change in Def.-Dep. Jobs, '89-'90	-31.3%	2
C. Prime Contracts (PC)	$4.3bil.	10	Unemployment Rate, '90-'91	5.2%	42
D. PC Change, FY'87-'90	-24.1%	23	Unemp. Rate Change, '89-'91	+2.1	11
E. Vulnerability Index	10.4	20	Per Capita Income	$25,358	1
F. Defense Disloc. Index	2.21	14	Population ('000)	3,287	27

▲ Army ■ Navy
● Air Force ○ Other

Prime Contract Trends, FY'87-'90
(Constant FY '92 $Billions)

'87 $6.1b   '88 $5.7b   '89 $6.8b   '90 $4.6b

Top 5 Contractors	$Millions
United Technologies	$1,976.9
General Dynamics	1,130.1
Textron	470.1
Kaman	116.5
Analysis & Technology	47.3

Top 10 $ Sites[a]	Congressional Dist., Representative	1989 Rank	Total DoD$[c]	Payroll[c]	Prime Contracts[c]	Per- sonnel[d]
1-Groton (18)	2-Gejdenson, d	6	$1,421.4	$283.7	$1,137.8	7.3
2-Stratford (28)	3-Delauro, d	19	1,048.4	14.9	1,033.5	0.4
3-E. Hartford (50)	1-Kennelly, d	29	742.1	11.9	730.3	0.4
4-Stratford A.E.P. (85)	3-Delauro, d	170	461.7	0	461.7	--
5-New London (202)	2-Gejdenson, d	216	169.8	112.8	57.0	1.9
6-Bloomfield (251)	1-Kennelly, d	289	114.3	2.3	112.0	--
7-Windsor Locks (264)	6-Johnson, r	281	105.5	13.2	92.3	0.3
8-Danbury (306)	5-Franks, r	333	70.6	2.9	67.7	--
9-Norwalk (310)	4-Shays, r	222	68.5	4.0	64.5	--
10-Bridgeport (314)	"	--	63.7	4.2	59.5	--

[a]Rating in parentheses is out of 511 sites, the top ten in each state and PR, plus DC.
[b]Multidistrict r-Rep, d-Dem. [c]$Millions (figures may not add due to rounding) [d]Thousands

Connecticut

The Connecticut Gross State Product grew by an average of almost 10 percent a year during the 1980s. Despite a very high level of manufacturing employment compared to total state employment (Connecticut is the ninth most dependent state in the nation),[1] Connecticut possesses a diversified economy. Of special importance is the insurance industry, a high-value exportable service product. Connecticut, especially Hartford, prides itself on being the insurance capital of the world. But the boom in the commercial real-estate sector during the 1980s which led to great prosperity for the city of Hartford came to an abrupt end across the Northeast at the end of the decade, and the Connecticut capital in 1990 was facing many financial hardships that add up to a fiscal crisis. The state unemployment rate ranked only 42nd highest but its change in unemployment ranked 11th (employment shrank much faster than the labor force).

Defense and the Economy

Direct and indirect Department of Defense spending in Connecticut (including in-state spending by defense personnel and contractors) was estimated at $12.6 billion in 1989. Even as the first round of cuts were taking effect in 1990, defense spending and companies accounted for 8.7 percent of Connecticut's State Gross Product and about 8 percent of the state's workforce.[2]

The high percentage of prime contracts in total Department of Defense spending in the state (87 percent in 1990) makes the state more likely to experience supply cutbacks. Connecticut's ranking among states in defense-contract awards declined during the 1980s; ranking fourth in FY 1979, it fell to tenth place in FY 1989.[3]

One company that prepared for the inevitable downside to the Reagan buildup is Kaman Corp. of Bloomfield. In the 1970s Kaman adjusted to the post-Vietnam slump in contracts in part by applying vibration technology developed for attack helicopters to the manufacture of electric guitars. The diversification this time around has been more conventional—the company has picked up subcontracts from GE and Boeing to build engines and wing-frames for commercial aircraft. According to Kaman Aerospace's president, Walter Kozlow, "One of our priorities was to stabilize employment. So we got very interested in the commercial sector."[4] At the height of the Reagan buildup the company derived no more than 5 percent of its sales from commercial contracts. Now the figure is 25 to 30 percent.

According to Rep. Sam Gejdenson (D-CT), "It's not like when the woolen mills closed. These are not workers with skills from the past. These people have skills at the high end of the technology scale. They are welders. They are electricians and they are among the best in the world. They should be in demand in any decent economy." For a decade already Connecticut has had a statewide task force concerned with diversification of its economy away from dependence on defense contracts.[5]

State Legislative Initiatives

It's hard to keep up with all the Connecticut initiatives. A diversification project in Groton led to a statewide study of diversification needs initiated by the state legislature. The State Task Force on Manufacturing (chaired by then State Sen. Tom Sullivan of Guilford) met in October 1989 and in early 1990 recommended diversifying Connecticut's economy. Kevin Bean and later Kevin Cassidy chaired a subcommittee of the Task Force that lobbied unsuccessfully in 1990 for more sectoral strategic state planning, i.e., helping small companies to form work cooperatives to generate new products, along the lines of successful programs in Germany and Italy.[6]

Former Rep. Joel Gardis (D-Colbrook) in 1991 advocated local property tax credits for companies that invest in new machinery and funding of defense contractors' feasibility studies for alternative projects. His bill did not become law,[7] but it turns out a 1990 law gave those powers to the state.

In 1991, conversion activists did get a diversification law passed, HBN 6391, introduced by Rep. Tom Luby (D-Meriden), 32 Westfield Road, Meriden CT 06450, 203-235-2568. It set aside $10 million in bond authorization for diversification projects and established a Defense Diversification Office inside the Connecticut Department of Economic Development.

The legislature also created the Legislative Commission on Business Opportunity, Defense Diversification, and Industrial Policy, headed by former Sen. Tom Sullivan. Meanwhile conversion advocates have been working with the Department of Labor on a broader 1992 bill.[8]

Community Surveys

Connecticut has just one major military installation, the New London submarine base. It employs over 80 percent of the military personnel in the state.

Groton and Stratford account for nearly $3 billion of the $4.9 defense-contract spending in the state. General Dynamics' Electric Boat Division in Groton, Pratt & Whitney (a subsidiary of Hartford-based United Technologies) in East Hartford, Sikorsky Aircraft in Stratford (also owned by United Technologies), and Textron-Lycoming of Stratford (a subsidiary of the Providence-based Textron Inc.) are the largest contractors.

East Hartford. Pratt & Whitney produces jet engines and has about $12 billion worth on order from the Department of Defense. In April 1991, the company won the right to supply engines for the Air Force's new ATF jet fighters. But, production is not expected to start until 1997. Of the company's revenues, 35 percent come from military contracts. The company has been trying to shift more of its business toward commercial aircraft. It has a $20 billion backlog in passenger-jet engine orders, but they are spread out over a ten-year period, which decreases their potential to offset the full near-term impact of military cuts. Having eliminated over 2,600 jobs in 1988 and 1989, in August 1990 the company announced it would eliminate some 4,000 jobs by 1993 from its facilities in Connecticut, Maine, Georgia and, in particular, Florida. By February 1991, executives, citing a deteriorating financial position, announced that layoffs had to take place at a faster rate, starting with as many as 1,500 job cuts (4 percent of the work force) starting in March and occurring within months, mostly in East Hartford and 70 percent in Connecticut, primarily through attrition. An encouraging development for Pratt is its opening of a large spare-parts inventory-control facility, an intelligent effort to turn maintenance of its aging engines into a more significant profit center as prospects dim for production of more advanced weapons.[9]

Groton. A council member is involved with regional and statewide diversification efforts, but Groton's finance officer said in 1990 he and his fellow officers have had little involvement. General Dynamics' Electric Boat Division in Groton expects to be occupied for years with a 16-submarine backlog. The Trident program, for which it does work, may be terminated. At the start of 1991, the company landed a $614.7 million contract with the Navy to build the second Seawolf fast-attack submarine, for which Connecticut legislators in Congress are given great credit. But the award is being disputed in Federal court, the company trimmed 1,000 jobs during 1990-91, and it may cut 11,000 more of its 22,000 jobs by 1995 as other Navy contracts dry up or suffer cuts.

Due to transfers and decommissions at a nearby Navy submarine base, the number of military personnel in the area should fall from 14,000 to 10,000 by the mid-1990s.[10]

Hartford/Rocky Hill. Connecticut SANE/Freeze, 55 Van Dyke Avenue, Hartford, CT 16106. 203-522-7661. Patricia (Pat) Wass. Created an Economic Conversion Task Force in 1981. The group has in 1990-91 been doing much of its work with labor unions and it held a conversion workshop in March 1990, co-sponsored by unions, which helped initiate a Connecticut Town Meeting in Hartford in May 1990. SANE/Freeze has successfully lobbied on the state level for the conversion legislation, HBN 6391, that provided $1 million for a state-level defense diversification office and $10 million in bonding, in addition to $10 million bonding already budgeted for a quasi-public agency, Connecticut Innovations, Inc.

Both of these significant state economic-development programs are located in a suburb of Hartford, Rocky Hill. The Office of Defense Diversification of the Department of Economic Development is directed by Martha (Marty) Hunt, 203-258-4219.

Next door is Connecticut Innovations, Inc., which David C. Driver serves as Executive Director (203-258-4305), which in 1990-1991 was jointly working with the Department of Economic Development to draw up a list of defense contractors, their products, and the value of their business to help develop strategies for diversification, and to hire a diversification coordinator. CII in 1991 put together a financing package for Reidville Tool & Manufacturing, a Waterbury-based manufacturer of hydraulic motors for submarines; the package was approved by the CII board but the company decided to have it financed privately.[11]

Montville/Uncasville. UNC Naval Products, makers of nuclear reactors to power submarines, underwent its first round of massive layoffs in the first half of 1990, announcing that it would be forced to lay off all 950 employees from the plant near New London over the next two years. The first layoffs occurred in the winter of 1989, as 117 employees were cut from UNC when the Navy said it would no longer purchase nuclear propulsion systems for its SSN-688 Los Angeles-class submarines from UNC. The company is currently suffering from a decision by the Department of Energy to consolidate all future marine reactor work with Babcock & Wilcox in Lynchburg, VA. UNC is also phasing out its aerospace division in the town. Many UNC employees live in the surrounding towns of New London, Norwich, Bozrah, and Ledyard.[12]

In May and June 1990, workers of UNC held meetings called Save Our State (SOS). The company is not so concerned with keeping the defense contracts, so long as the jobs remain intact. Both SOS and the management of UNC testified before the House Subcommittee on Economic Stabilization on June 12, 1990 in favor of conversion legislation. R. Bruce Andrews, President of UNC, suggested that the government give contracting preference to companies that relocate in designated labor surplus areas. SOS testimony, however, insists that any legislation must help companies in their established communities, and not encourage them to relocate.[13]

New Haven. The New Haven Peace Commission, Thomas Holahan, 769 Whitney Avenue, New Haven, CT 06511. 203-782-9332. The group succeeded in placing on the November 1989 ballot a referendum which stated that military spending should be cut, and that the peace dividend should be spent in U.S. cities for social services. It passed with 83 percent in favor, including Mayor Biagio Dilieto.[14]

New London. The Naval Underwater Systems Center Detachment will be realigned. The restructuring, which could start as early as October 1991 and would continue for five years, will involve the transfer of 800 to 1,100 of 1,495 positions to Newport, R.I.[15]

Norwalk. Norden Systems, military radar manufacturer, laid off 500 employees between 1989 and 1990.

Stratford. The Naugatuck Valley region includes Sikorsky and Textron-Lycoming and their many smaller subcontractors. Stratford is home to Textron-Lycoming, which makes gas-turbine engines for the OV-1D Aircraft Modification Program and makes for the Army's M-1 tank on a subcontract from General Dynamics. With the termination of the M-1 contract in 1992, the company faced possibly laying off as many as 1,350 workers, but the contracts have been stretched out to 1994. Lycoming will be supplying 400 engines for battle tanks being sold to Saudi Arabia under a contract approved in 1991 by the U.S. government. The $120 million dollar deal will provide income between 1993 and 1996. Expansion into foreign markets, subject to U.S. government approval, is viewed as providing an income base for avoiding major layoffs for several years. Top prospects are Egypt, Great Britain, Sweden, Pakistan, and South Yemen.[16]

Military contracts for Sikorsky helicopters declined from 165 to 120 between 1987 and 1990. But at the start of 1991, the company won work on the Army's $34 billion project to build LHX light helicopters. The contract will allow the helicopter manufacturer, which laid off approximately 900 employees in 1990, to stabilize its workforce at 10,500. An increase in its international business will continue to help Sikorsky to offset some of the decline in U.S. military contracts.[17]

The Town of Stratford is properly worried about layoffs at the two contracting giants and the inability of subcontractors to obtain other work. Fortunately for the town, the private, nonprofit Naugatuck Valley Project and UAW's Local 1010 have joined together in a model joint, voluntary process on an informal level to involve management, union, religious, and other community leaders in brainstorming new product alternatives that could offset losses in tank-engine contracts. They have formed an "optimum use committee" that is looking at use of and markets for gas-turbine engines for small- and medium-scale electric-power production using non-fossil fuels.[18]

West Hartford. Chandler Evans, a missile actuator and engine fuel pump concern, laid off 100 workers between 1989 and 1990.

Notes

1. *1990-1991 Economic Report of the Governor* (Hartford: State of Connecticut, Dept. of Economic Development, 1991), p. 3.

2. Sandra Sugawara, "High and Dry in a Time of Peace," *The Washington Post*, June 3, 1990, p. H4.

3. *1990-1991 Economic Report...*, *loc. cit.*

4. Robert Weisman, "Kaman Wins in Decline of Defense," *Hartford Courant*, December 23, 1989, pp. D1, 15.

5. "State Should Survive Military Cuts," *Hartford Courant*, January 28, 1990. Rep. Gejdenson's specialist on defense-related issues in Washington is Maggie Bierwirth; in his home district the specialist is Naomi Otterness. Connecticut's diversification committee was the original model for the Federal diversification bill (HR 2852) introduced by Rep. Gejdenson and folded into the successful Federal 1990 Conversion Law.

6. See Lloyd J. Dumas, "Economic Conversion: An Exchange," *Bulletin of the Atomic Scientists,* October 1986, pp. 45-50. The report, the *Annual Report of the Task Force on Manufacturing,* is available by calling the Connecticut State Legislature in Hartford and asking for the General Law Committee. Professor Kevin Cassidy is with the Politics Department, Fairfield University, Fairfield, CT 06430; 203-254-4000, ext. 2860. His predecessor, Kevin Bean, is active in Stratford with the Naugatuck Valley

Project. The sectoral strategic planning concept has been studied extensively by Richard Hatch at the New Jersey Institute of Technology.

7. Interview, May 1990, with Kevin Cassidy, whose addresses are listed in Notes 6 and 8.

8. For latest developments, contact Connecticut SANE/Freeze, 55 Van Dyke Ave., Hartford, CT 06106; Pat Wass, 203-522-7661. Janet Stone, *Conversion Organizers' Update* (Mountain View, CA: Center for Economic Conversion, October 1991; from advance copy). Ann Hoskins and Keith Cunningham, *Economic Initiatives* (Washington, DC: Center for Policy Alternatives, July 1991). Contacts: (1) Connecticut Department of Economic Development, Stephen Heintz, 865 Brook St., Rocky Hill, CT 06067; 203-258-4201. (2) Connecticut Department of Labor, Larry Fox, 211 Folley Brook Blvd., Wethersfield, CT 06109; 203-566-4388. (3) Governor's Office, Jon Sandberg, Press Secretary, State Capitol, Hartford, CT 06106; 203-566-4840. (4) Connecticut Economic Conversion Task Force, Kevin Cassidy, 245 Ellsworth St., Bridgeport, CT 06605; 203-254-4000. (5) New London Office of Development and Planning, Charlotte M. Schroeder, Assistant Director, Municipal Building, New London, CT 06320.

9. Andrew Julien, "Defense Contract Wins Said No Cure for Slump," *Hartford Courant,* May 5, 1991, p. 1. Jonathan P. Hicks, "4,000 Jobs Being Cut By Pratt & Whitney," *The New York Times,* August 3, 1990, p. D4; Hicks, "1,000 to 1,500 Job Cuts For Pratt & Whitney," *The New York Times,* February 20, 1991, p. D5; and Hicks, "United Technologies' Bumpy Ride," *The New York Times,* May 1, 1991, p. D1. Interview in March 1990 and in May 1990 with Mike Dayton, Town Planner, East Hartford, CT, 203-289-2781.

10. Interview in May 1990 with Anthony Timpano, Groton Finance Officer, 203-441-2110. Julien, *loc. cit.* Nick Ravo, "As Navy Shrinks, a Corner of Connecticut Founders," *The New York Times,* April 27, 1991, p. 28.

11. Interview with Kevin Bean, October 1991.

12. Pat Wass, Connecticut SANE/Freeze, *Proceedings: National Strategy Retreat on Economic Conversion, Block Island, June 11-13, 1990* (Mountain View, CA: Center for Economic Conversion, 1990), p. 1. Sugawara, *op. cit.,* pp. H1, H5. Nick Ravo, "The High Cost of Peace Jolts a Connecticut Factory Town," *The New York Times,* April 26, 1990, p. B1.

13. From *Prepared Statement of R. Bruce Andrews, President UNC Naval Products, Before the Subcommittee on Economic Stabilization of the House Banking, Finance and Urban Affairs Committee,* July 1990, p. 2.

14. Interview with Tom Holahan by David Adams in "Planning for Peace in New Haven," *Municipal Foreign Policy,* Summer 1990, p. 32.

15. Nick Ravo, "As Navy Shrinks...," *loc. cit.*

16. "Defense Industries Feeling...," *loc. cit.* Weisman, "Stratford Company to Make Tank Engines for Saudis," *Hartford Courant,* July 10, 1990, p. D1.

17. "Defense Industries Feeling...," *loc. cit.* Julien, *loc. cit.,* p. 1.

18. Naugatuck Valley Project, 47 Central Ave., Waterbury, CT 06702; Kevin Bean, Director, 203-574-2410, fax 203-574-3545. Interviews in May 1990 and October 1991. Interview in March, 1990 with Joseph Stavola, Director, Community Economic Development, Stratford, CT, 203-385-4000.

Delaware

A	B	C	D	E	F
$	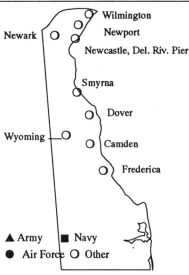			VI	DDI
–	–	–	↓	–	✌

Benchmarks	No.	Rank	Benchmarks	No.	Rank
A.Total DoD $	$0.3 bil.	47	Def.-Dependent Jobs ('000), '90	15	47
B. Personnel Payroll	$0.2 bil.	44	Change in Def.-Dep. Jobs, '89-'90	-25.0%	3
C. Prime Contracts (PC)	$0.1bil.	47	Unemployment Rate, '90-'91	7.4%	10
D. PC Change, FY '87-'90	-56.4%	2	Unem. Rate Change, '89-'91	4.4%	3
E. Vulnerability Index	8.1	37	Per Capita Income	$20,039	12
F. Defense Disloc. Index	0.10	40	Population('000)	666	47

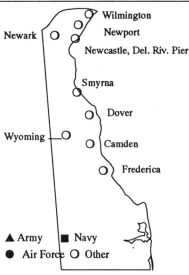

Wilmington
Newark
Newport
Newcastle, Del. Riv. Pier
Smyrna
Dover
Wyoming
Camden
Frederica

▲ Army   ■ Navy
● Air Force   ○ Other

Prime Contract Trends, FY'87-'90
(Constant FY '92 $Billions)

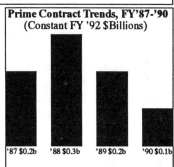

'87 $0.2b	'88 $0.3b	'89 $0.2b	'90 $0.1b

Top 5 Contractors	$Millions
Whitemarsh Investment	$11.4
Du Pont	9.2
Noramco	7.1
Caesar School District	5.6
J&K Distributors	4.9

Top 10 $ Sites[a]	Congressional Dist., Representative	1989 Rank	Total DoD$[c]	Payroll[c]	Prime Contracts[c]	Per-sonnel[d]
1-Dover (196)	1-Carper, d	204	$175.7	$158.6	$17.1	5.7
2-Wilmington (346)	"	396	40.5	6.5	34.1	.05
3-New Castle (430)	"	418	14.2	12.1	2.1	--
4-Newark (442)	"	436	11.1	3.9	7.2	.03
5-Camden (452)	"	452	8.8	3.1	5.6	--
6-Del. River Pier (454)	"	--	8.3	0	8.3	--
7-Frederica (460)	"	450	7.5	1.7	5.9	--
8-Smyrna (472)	"	--	5.5	1.7	3.8	--
9-Wyoming (475)	"	455	5.1	0.2	5.0	--
10-Newport (486)	"	--	4.3	4.2	.04	.07

[a]Rating in parentheses is out of 511 sites, the top ten in each state and PR, plus D.C.
[b]Multidistrict r-Rep, d-Dem. [c]$Millions (figures may not add due to rounding) [d]Thousands

Delaware

Its central geographic position has long given Delaware access to the entire East Coast market. In the early 1980s the state also began to develop into an important financial center. The construction and durable goods/manufacturing sectors are among the slowest growing parts of the economy (as they are nationally), while wholesale industry is expected to continue with strong growth. The sectors of the economy with the greatest net job growth continue to be services, retailing, finance, insurance and real estate.[1] Delaware's unemployment ranked 10th and its unemployment change 3rd (its labor force grew while employment decreased).

Defense and the Economy

The Department of Defense has a small economic presence in Delaware. In 1990 the entire state received from the Department of Defense less than a third of the amount awarded to the fifth largest contractor in California. Due to Delaware's low defense dependence, the state is one of the least vulnerable to defense cuts. The state petroleum industry, which received 3 percent of total Department of Defense fuel procurement, is the only industry with significant military contracts. One company, Texaco, Inc. of Delaware City, accounted for 98 percent of state defense petroleum business. Sen. William Roth of Delaware has sponsored a bill that would allow local communities to assume ownership of closed Federal bases for any purpose. The community, under the bill, would have to agree to retrain base workers, offer them severance pay, and share a percentage of its profit with the government for 25 years.[2]

Notes

1. *Delaware Economic Outlook,* University of Delaware Bureau of Economic and Business Research, Spring 1990, pp. 2-3, Purnell Hall, University of Delaware, Newark, DE 19716; 302-451-8401. Supplied by James Craig, Office of the Secretary, State of Delaware Department of Finance.

2. *Atlas/Data Abstract for the United States and Selected Areas Fiscal 1990,* Department of Defense, Washington Headquarters Services, Directorate for Information, Operations and Reports, p. 31. *Prime Contract Awards by Region and State, Fiscal Years 1989, 1988, 1987,* Department of Defense, Washington Headquarters Services, Directorate for Information, Operations and Reports, p. 25. *Atlas... 1990, op. cit.,* p. 31. "Communities Could Own Bases," *Delaware State News,* March 2, 1990. Contacts: (1) Budget Office, Michael Ferguson, Director, Thomas Collins Building, Dover, DE 19903; 302-739-4204. (2) Delaware Department of Labor, Jan E. Robinson, Secretary, Carvel State Building, Wilmington, DE 19801; 302-577-2710. (3) Delaware Development Office, Douglas M. Clendaniel, Director of Business Research, 99 Kings Highway, Dover, DE 19903; 302-736-4271. (4) Labor Market Information, State of Delaware, Jim McFadden, University Office Plaza, Newark, DE 19714; 302-368-6962.

Dist. of Columbia

A	B	C	D	E	F
$				VI	DDI
+	+	+	↑	!!	✌

Benchmarks	No.	Rank	Benchmarks	No.	Rank
A.Total DoD $	$2.8bil.	22	Def.-Dependent Jobs ('000)	155	20
B. Personnel Payroll	$1.1bil.	23	Change in Def.-Dep. Jobs, '89-'90	19.2%	48
C. Prime Contracts (PC)	$1.7bil.	20	Unemployment Rate, '90-'91	7.0%	18
D. PC Change, FY '87-'90	+19.8%	50	Unemp. Rate Change, '89-'91	1.8%	16
E. Vulnerability Index	14.6	3	Per Capita Income	$24,181	3
F. Defense Disloc. Index	0.09	41	Population ('000)	607	49

▲ Army
■ Navy
● Air Force
○ Other

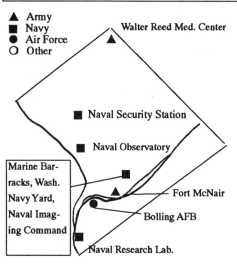

Walter Reed Med. Center ▲

■ Naval Security Station

■ Naval Observatory

Marine Barracks, Wash.
Navy Yard,
Naval Imaging Command

▲ Fort McNair

Bolling AFB

Naval Research Lab.

Prime Contract Trends, FY'87-'90
(Constant FY '92 $Billions)

'87 $1.5b | '88 $1.9b | '89 $1.4b | '90 $1.8b

Top 5 Contractors	$Millions
U.S. Dep't of Energy	$349.3
AT&T	302.4
CSX	225.5
Int'l Shipbuilding	140.5
Shore Management	42.9

Top 10 $ Sites[a]	Congressional Dist., Representative	1989 Rank	Total DoD$[c]	Payroll[c]	Prime Contracts[c]	Personnel[d]
1-Washington (4)	Fauntroy, d	8	$2,770.6	$1,076.7	$1,693.9	27.8
--	--	--	--	--	--	--
--	--	--	--	--	--	--
--	--	--	--	--	--	--
--	--	--	--	--	--	--
--	--	--	--	--	--	--
--	--	--	--	--	--	--
--	--	--	--	--	--	--
--	--	--	--	--	--	--
--	--	--	--	--	--	--

[a]Rating in parentheses is out of 511 sites, the top ten in each state and PR, plus DC.
[b]Multidistrict r-Rep, d-Dem. [c]$Millions (figures may not add due to rounding) [d]Thousands

District of Columbia

Washington, DC's economy is based primarily on the Federal payroll and secondarily on the payrolls of the lobbies that seek access to the government. The District has more than its share of economic problems, with the 18th highest unemployment rate of the 52 "states" (including Puerto Rico as well as DC) and the 16 highest change in unemployment (both the labor force and employed persons sharply declined, but employment declined more).

Defense and the Economy

The Department of Defense has always been a large component of the Federal payroll. Defense purchases represent an estimated 4.8 percent of the metropolitan $120 billion economy[1] and over 5 percent of the District's. Over 44,000 residents of the District are directly employed by the Department of Defense, making DC one of the largest and most concentrated sites of Department of Defense personnel. The special ties that Washington businesses have with the Department of Defense and its personnel contribute to the District's heavy defense dependence. The other, positive side of this equation is that the proximity of Department of Defense headquarters and top personnel ensures the District will not see the drastic cutbacks in contracts that characterize some communities. In 1990, services accounted for 37 percent of all prime contracts awarded to District businesses. It is unlikely the level of service contracting will be significantly reduced, but ship construction is most vulnerable.

Community Surveys

With the Department of Defense Building located right across the Potomac River in Roslyn, VA, the Department of Defense will always have a large presence in the metropolitan area.

The huge employee cutbacks announced by McDonnell Douglas in July 1990 will have some effect on the DC area, as 80 of the 17,000 layoffs will occur in McDonnell Douglas plants in McLean, Crystal City, and other program offices in the capital area.

The Naval Electronic Systems Security Engineering Center has also been targeted for cuts by the Department of Defense.[2]

Notes

1. Stephen Goldstein, "Pentagon Trimming May Hurt Area Less Than Non-Defense Cuts," *The Washington Times*, April 18, 1990, p. C3.

2. Sandra Sugawara, "McDonnell Douglas to Cut Jobs," *The Washington Post*, July 17, 1990, p. C1. "Bases Affected by Cutbacks," *The Washington Post*, April 13, 1991, p. 10. Contacts: (1) Office of Policy, Management, and Evaluation, Government of the District of Columbia, Enid Simmons, Acting Director, Washington, DC 20004-3001; 202-727-6330.

Florida

A	B	C	D	E	F
$				VI	DDI
+	+	+	→	!	✂

Benchmarks	No.	Rank	Benchmarks	No.	Rank
A. Total DoD $	$10.6 bil.	4	Def.-Dependent Jobs ('000), '90	459	6
B. Personnel Payroll	$5.7 bil.	4	Change in Def.-Dep. Jobs, '89-'91	+2.5%	38
C. Prime Contracts (PC)	$4.9 bil.	7	Unemployment Rate, '90-'91	6.6%	23
D. PC Change, FY '87-'90	-24.3%	22	Unemp. Rate Change, '89-'91	+1.5%	20
E. Vulnerability Index	10.5	18	Per Capita Income	$18,586	20
F. Defense Disloc. Index	0.78	27	Population ('000)	12,938	4

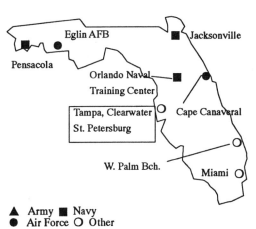

Army ▲ **Navy** ■
Air Force ● **Other** ○

Prime Contract Trends, FY'87-'90
(Constant FY '92 $Billions)

'87 $7.0b   '88 $6.2b   '89 $5.0b   '90 $5.3b

Top 5 Contractors	$Millions
Martin Marietta	$985.3
United Technologies	790.8
Olin	227.2
Honeywell	172.0
Harris	111.8

Top 10 $ Sites[a]	Congressional Dist., Representative	1989 Rank	Total DoD$[c]	Payroll[c]	Prime Contracts[c]	Per-sonnel[d]
1-Orlando (14)	11-Bacchus,d	16	$1,800.5	$480.3	$1,320.2	18.6
2-Jacksonville (19)	4-James,r	22	1,414.1	1,205.1	209.0	12.5
3-W. Palm Beach (42)	(12,14)[b]	78	825.3	21.1	804.2	--
4-Pensacola (53)	11-Bacchus,d	55	694.7	633.3	61.4	17.0
5-Eglin AFB (73)	"	82	501.1	373.7	127.4	13.5
6-Tampa (74)	7-Gibbons,d	86	499.0	302.3	196.6	--
7-St. Petersburg (109)	8-Young,r	177	362.3	48.9	313.4	--
8-Cape Canaveral (131)	11-Bacchus,d	145	305.5	15.2	290.3	--
9-Clearwater (163)	(8,9)[b]	179	224.7	20.5	204.2	--
10-Miami (189)	(17-19)[b]	--	184.6	39.8	144.8	--

[a]Rating in parentheses is out of 511 sites, the top ten in each state and PR, plus DC.
[b]Multidistrict r-Rep, d-Dem. [c]$Millions (figures may not add due to rounding) [d]Thousands

Florida

The Florida economy is likely to experience slowing growth in the coming years. Total personal income, non-farm employment and housing starts have all been improving in recent quarters, but at rates below earlier forecasts. Unemployment, especially in the construction sector, is expected to rise through 1991, but job expansion, at 3.6 percent in 1989-90 and 3.4 percent in 1990-91, was stronger than expected. Florida's unemployment rate ranked 23rd in April 1991 and its change in unemployment ranked 20th (the labor force grew faster than employment). The largest industries in Florida are health care ($29 billion) and tourism ($26 billion).[1]

Defense and the Economy

Direct defense spending in Florida in FY 1990 was $11 billion. With indirect and induced spending it is the state's third largest economic sector, employing 650,000 people in the state's defense-related industries. The bases alone spend $6 billion in the state directly. Fifty percent of all high-technology jobs created in Florida counties from 1980 to 1984 were a result of defense-supply contracts. The state's healthy and relatively diverse economy helps to lessen its overall vulnerability to defense cuts, but certain geographic areas are heavily dependent on Department of Defense spending.

The state industry that receives the most Department of Defense business is communication/electronic equipment. Florida firms received $5 billion in prime contracts in FY 1990, much of it for production of such high-tech equipment.[2] Florida's share of total Department of Defense expenditures has been steadily declining in recent years, but it will still be impacted by defense cuts in the Apache helicopter, the F-15 and F-14 fighters, and the Chapparal missile. Florida's location and industrial base should ensure it continues to receive a substanta; share of Department of Defense presence for the next decade.

State Legislative Initiatives

An economic conversion bill passed the House but failed in the Senate in 1990. There were plans to reintroduce the bill.[3]

Community Surveys

Eight counties accounted for 80 percent of all Federal defense contracts in FY 1988: Dade (Miami), Orange (Orlando), Palm Beach, Brevard, Pinellas (Tampa), Duval (Jacksonville), Volusia, and Okaloosa. Expenditures by the Navy are heavily concentrated in the Northern Panhandle area. Therefore, although the overall vulnerability index for the state is moderate, the economy of North Florida would be severely affected by cutbacks in Department of Defense spending.[4]

Homestead. The Air Force Base here—employer of 3,760 military and 1,040 civilian personnel—appeared on a Base Closure Commission hit list in 1991.[6] However the base is likely to remain open and will even expand if a 1991 House bill mandating the construction of a $30 million military hospital at the base passes the Senate.

Jacksonville. Action groups formed to protect the Naval Aviation Depot which was targeted for cuts in 1988 and 1991. The Depot employs 3,600 workers.[7] The city, which receives $1.36 billion annually from the Navy, is the Florida community most dependent on Federal defense spending.

Melbourne. A recent agreement between Grumman and Boeing to build highly sophisticated radar aircraft for the Army and the Air Force will mean business for Grumman's newly-built Melbourne facility. The Joint Surveillance Target Attack Radar plane (JSTAR) contract, for which Grumman would be the prime contractor, could be worth about $7 billion. Although it is not definite that Congress and the President will approve the program, Thomas Guarino, a Grumman vice president and overseer of the JSTAR program, says that despite the recent build-down in Europe the plane could be used for verification of peace treaties as well as more military functions.[8]

Orlando. This city receives the most defense dollars and personnel in the state. The Naval Training Center-Recruit Training Center and its affiliated Naval Hospital, the primary military installation in the city with 14,400 military personnel, 2,160 civilian employees, and 27,000 recruits, was recommended for shutdown by the Department of Defense in April 1991. Florida launched a $75,000 advertising campaign to save the facility, recommending that the Great Lakes Naval Training Center in Illinois or the San Diego Naval Training Center be closed instead. The Orlando facility remained off the Base Commission's July 1991 final list of recommended closures, (as did the Great Lakes and San Diego facilities) because experts testified that it would take 20-100 years to recoup the $400 million cost of closing Orlando. Harris Corporation said it would be cutting back its personnel by 500 to increase the profitability of its semiconductor business.[9]

Panama City. The Naval Coastal Systems Center will be realigned with the Combat Weapons Systems R&D Division also in Panama City. There will be some transfer of functions to bases in Rhode Island and Virginia. A total of 285 jobs will be eliminated or transferred.[10]

Pensacola. The Naval Station was targeted for realignment but now seems likely to remain intact. The installation's 6,100 civilian and 7,500 military jobs would be affected if realignment does occur.

Stuart. The OV-1D Aircraft Modification Program of Grumman Aerospace is located in Stuart. This, Grumman's Florida facility, could be used to retrofit older F-14s if funding became available. Both the state and county have been less concerned with the downside of the economy than with managing growth.[11]

Sunrise. James Burke, Jr., director of industry marketing, simulation and training of Encore Computer Corp., feels that the company's marketing and sales activity will increase as a result of the cuts in defense spending. Trends in the simulation and training systems business that Encore is involved in, according to Burke, tend to run contrary to trends in defense spending, and thus should increase in upcoming years.[12]

Tampa/Florida Panhandle. MacDill Air Force Base was recommended for realignment by Secretary Cheney in 1988. MacDill employs 6,460 military and 974 civilian personnel and was scheduled for realignment in 1991. The government plans to move the 56th Tactical Fighter Wing and all F-16 jets to Luke AFB in Arizona while keeping administrative functions at MacDill, requiring a reduction of 3,185 jobs at MacDill. Locals fear that loss of air base functions will eventually lead to the complete shutdown of a facility that is a major resource for 100,000 to 250,000 military retirees and their dependents.[5] Tampa Department of Planning, Bill Brooks, Planning Research Analyst; 813-227-7176.

West Palm Beach. The Naval Weapons Reserve Plant—a storage facility for aircraft parts—was among the military installations recommended for closure or realignment in 1988.

Notes

1. "Memorandum on U.S. and Florida Economic Estimating Conferences," Executive Office of the Governor of Florida, January 25, 1990. Florida Growth Management and Planning Policy Unit, *Department of Defense, Florida's Economic Transition: Ensuring Productivity and Economic Gains*, p. 2.

2. *Prime Contract Awards by Region and State, Fiscal Years 1989, 1988, 1987*, Department of Defense, Washington Headquarters Services, Directorate for Information, Operations and Reports, p. 27.

3. *Conversion Organizers' Update*, Center for Economic Conversion, August 1990, p. 4. Contacts: (1) Governor's Office, Gov. Lawton Chiles, The Capitol, Tallahassee, FL 32399-0001; Blair Kruger, Senior Analyst; 904-487-2814. (2) Florida Coalition for Peace & Justice, Bruce Gagnon or Beth Hollenbeck, P.O. Box 2486, Orlando, FL 32802; 407-422-3479. (3) Florida Department of Economic Development, Pat Propst, 501-B Collins Bldg., Tallahassee, FL 32301; 904-488-6300. (4) Florida Labor & Employment Security, Linda Lee Frazier, 2574 Seagate Drive, Suite 203, Tallahassee, FL 32399-0674; 904-488-1048.

4. Lynda C. Davis, Director of the Florida Washington Office, quoted by Susan P. Respess, "States Don't Know Where Military Cuts Will Hit," *Florida Times Union*, April 9, 1990. *Atlas/Data Abstract for the United States and Selected Areas Fiscal 1989*, Department of Defense, Washington Headquarters Services, Directorate for Information, Operations and Reports, pp.34-35

5. Susan P. Respess, "States Don't Know Where Military Cuts Will Hit," *Florida Times Union*, April 9, 1990, p. B1. "Bases Affected by Cutbacks," *The Washington Post,*

April 13, 1991, p. 10. Jeff Testerman, "Partial Closing a Partial Victory For Some," *St. Petersburg Times*, July 1, 1991, pp. 1, 10.

6. *Atlas/Data Abstract for the United States and Selected Areas Fiscal 1990,* Department of Defense, Washington Headquarters Services, Directorate for Information, Operations and Reports, p. 35.

7. Respess, *loc. cit.*, p. B-1.

8. James Bernstein, "Grumman, Boeing Reach Settlement," *Newsday*, June 22, 1990, p. 47.

9. B. Drummond Ayres, Jr., "As Bases Are Closed, Some Towns Transform Setback Into Advantage," *The New York Times*, April 13, 1991, p. 8. Mitchell Locin, "Push is on to Save Great Lakes Base," *The Chicago Tribune*, June 6, 1991, p. II-1. Mitchell Locin, "Panel Rejects Plan to Expand Great Lakes Naval Center," *The Chicago Tribune*, July 1, 1991, p. 5. "Harris to Reorganize Semiconductor Line, *Defense News*, February 11, 1991, p. 35.

10. *Base Closure and Realignment Report*, Department of Defense, April 1991, p. 81.

11. Interview in March, 1990 with Dave Brangaccio, Budget and Finance Director, Martin County, FL, 407-288-5518.

12. James Burke, Jr., Encore Computer Corp., from a survey by Myron Struck, Defense Electronics, 1990 M Street, NW, Suite 500, Washington, DC 20036, 202-659-0308.

Georgia

A	B	C	D	E	F
$	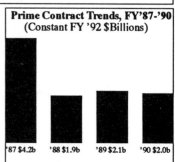			VI	DDI
+	+	+	↓	!	✂

Benchmarks	No.	Rank	Benchmarks	No.	Rank
A.Total DoD $	$4.9bil.	16	Def.-Dependent Jobs ('000), '90	238	16
B. Personnel Payroll	$3.1bil.	5	Change in Def.-Dep. Jobs, '89-'91	-12.2%	11
C. Prime Contracts (PC)	$1.8bil.	17	Unemployment Rate, '90-'91	5.2%	42
D. PC Change, FY '87-'90	-53.6%	3	Unemp. Rate Change, '89-'91	-0.4%	42
E. Vulnerability Index	9.4	27	Per Capita Income	$16,944	31
F. Defense Disloc. Index	0.34	33	Population ('000)	6,478	11

▲ Army ■ Navy
● Air Force ○ Other

Marietta
○ ○ Duluth
Atlanta
m
Ft. Gordon ▲
○ La Grange
Savannah
● Robins AFB
▲ Ft. Benning
▲ Ft. Stewart
Kings Bay ■

Prime Contract Trends, FY'87-'90
(Constant FY '92 $Billions)

'87 $4.2b '88 $1.9b '89 $2.1b '90 $2.0b

Top 5 Contractors	$ Millions
Lockheed	$688.0
General Motors	214.6
Rockwell	153.9
Georgia Tech Research	43.8
Johnson Controls	39.3

Top 10 $ Sites[a]	Congressional Dist., Representative	1989 Rank	Total DoD$[c]	Payroll[c]	Prime Contracts[c]	Per-sonnel[d]
1-Marietta (45)	7-Darden, d	50	$780.1	$90.0	$690.1	1.8
2-Robins AFB (61)	8-Rowland, d	60	613.7	543.7	69.9	18.7
3-Atlanta (81)	(4-6),[b]	92	470.0	287.4	182.6	--
4-Ft. Benning (83)	3-Ray, d	57	468.2	405.2	63.0	22.5
5-Ft. Gordon (126)	10-Barnard, d	80	316.8	244.6	72.2	10.0
6-La Grange (167)	3--Ray, d	--	217.5	1.9	215.6	--
7-Ft. Stewart (185)	1-Thomas, d	76	190.4	153.4	37.0	6.6
8-Duluth (212)	9-Jenkins, d	259	154.5	2.9	151.6	--
9-Savannah (224)	1-Thomas, d	101	138.5	106.4	32.1	--
10-Kings Bay (233)	8-Rowland, d	202	131.4	131.0	0.3	3.7

[a]Rating in parentheses is out of 511 sites, the top ten in each state and PR, plus DC.
[b]Multidistrict r-Rep, d-Dem. [c]$Millions (figures may not add due to rounding) [d]Thousands

Georgia

The Georgia economy, along with that of the rest of the Southeast, experienced an economic boom during most of the 1980s. The services sector, particularly business and health services, is one of the largest and fastest growing. Retail trade remains another key element, employing around 20 percent of total non-agricultural employment. The strongest manufacturing industry, not surprising for a southeastern state, is textiles, although it did not grow as fast as the rest of the economy in the 1980s.[1] The state's 1990-91 unemployment rate and its change compared to two years earlier ranked a low and healthy 42nd (employment grew faster than the labor force).

Defense and the Economy

Sen. Sam Nunn (D-GA), Chairman of the Senate Committee on Armed Services, is viewed by some as both awesomely influential and a protector of Georgia's military pork barrel. His position is credited with Lockheed's moving its aeronautical headquarters to Marietta. But Sen. Nunn has not spared his own state from its share of cuts. Based on published Department of Defense data, our national ranking of every major base site in Georgia dropped between FY 1989 and FY 1990, and prime contracts dropped by over half between FY 1987 and FY 1990, the third largest decline in the country (see data page).

Georgia received $4.9 billion from the Department of Defense in FY 1990, representing 2.3 percent of total U.S. defense spending. A large portion of the Department of Defense money spent in Georgia is for personnel payroll, $3.1 billion, the fifth highest state. The state defense industry received nearly $2 billion in prime contracts in 1990 and employs over 37,000 workers. This dependence is partially offset by the state's low unemployment rate and overall healthy economy.[2]

The F-15 jet fighter program is being phased out and the impact on the state will be substantial. Lockheed's plant in Marietta is hoping to increase its Department of Defense business in the coming years. But a relatively low percentage of cuts to overall prime contracts may be accompanied by significant personnel cuts from proposed base closures in coming years. Aircraft construction accounts for more than one-third of defense expenditures in Georgia. In 1989, Lockheed Corp., the largest single recipient of Department of Defense funds in the state, received $545 million just for airframe work. The Department of Defense spends $261 million in Georgia for construction and equipment, but the Senate Armed Services Committee has recommended that construction expenditure on Georgia bases drop dramatically in FY 1992 by over 50 percent to $69.4 million. State firms receive 5.6 percent of all U.S. defense spending on textiles and clothing.[3]

Community Surveys

The spending of defense money in the state is unusually evenly distributed geographically throughout the state and also among the four components, i.e., defense industry and the three armed services.

Atlanta. Based upon an idea of former Mayor Andrew Young, Atlanta has sought ex-GI's to teach in the inner cities. The city offers veterans a scholarship to return to school and then teach. It provides schools with more male role models, as well as offering veterans the opportunity to continue their education.[4]

Clayton County. Department of Defense officials announced that Fort Gillem, which employs more than 2,300 civilians, will be "warm-based" by the end of 1991. Sen. Nunn and Fort administrators have asked the Department of Defense to clarify what it means by warm basing, which local officials fear is a euphemism for cold storage.[5]

Columbus. Fort Benning, the largest location of personnel in the state with 17,750 military and 4,780 civilian employees, will gain 1,036 personnel as troop reductions in Europe proceed.[6]

Kingsland. Camden county officials, with the congressional support of Sen. Nunn, were pressing the Navy to continue annual payments referred to as "community impact assistance." The FY 1991 defense budget was the first in eight years not to provide such funds, which are earmarked for mitigating the potentially disruptive effect of new bases on local communities.

Marietta. In July 1990, Lockheed announced that it was moving the headquarters of its Aeronautical Systems Co. from Southern California to the Marietta plant. Lockheed's move from California to Georgia was seen by some as an attempt to hold Sen. Nunn's feet to the fire, because Marietta's economy will be more dependent than ever on the success of Lockheed's Aeronautical Systems Co. But Lockheed's move to Marietta makes business sense because it will reportedly reduce divisional overhead by $50 million and should greatly improve efficiency. If Lockheed wins contracts it expects to, employment at the Marietta facility should increase from 8,800 in 1990 to between 12,000 and 15,000 in a few years.[7]

Valdosta. The Base Closure and Realignment Commission considered the Moody Air Force Base, home of the 347th Tactical Fighter Wing, for closure but decided against it. Thus 730 civilian jobs and $98 million a year for the local economy were saved.[8]

Warner-Robins. Robins Air Force Base, the second largest site of funds and personnel in the state, lost approximately 400 civilian employees and 150 military personnel in the 1989-1990 period. The Department of Defense plans to spend $30 million on new base construction in preparation for the housing of JSTAR radar planes at Robins.[9]

Notes

1. *Georgia Labor Market Trends*, Georgia Department of Labor, p. 3.

2. *Atlas/Data Abstract for the United States and Selected Areas Fiscal 1990*, Department of Defense, Washington Headquarters Services, Directorate for Information, Operations and Reports, 37. *Georgia Labor Market Trends, op. cit.*, p. 4. "Georgia & Military Austerity," *Waycross Journal-Herald*, January 16, 1990.

3. Maria Saporta, "Lockheed Could Beef Up Ga. Operation," *Atlanta Constitution*, May 8, 1990, p. 1. Mike Christensen, "Georgia Losing Military Dollars," *Atlanta Constitution*, July 13, 1991, p.1. *Prime Contract Awards by Region and State, Fiscal Years 1989, 1988, 1987*, Department of Defense, Washington Headquarters Services, Directorate for Information, Operations and Reports, p. 28. Contacts: (1) Governor's Office, Susan Kahn, Special Assistant to the Governor, State Capitol, Atlanta, GA 30334; 404-656-6870. (2) Georgia Department of Labor, Joe Tanner, 148 International Blvd., Atlanta, GA 30303; 404-656-3011. (3) Industry & Trade, State of Georgia, George Berry, Commissioner, P.O. Box 1776, Atlantà, GA 30301; 404-656-3556.

4. "Military Skills," *Dallas Morning News*, June 25, 1990, p. 12.

5. "Military Budget Plan Could Virtually Close Fort Gillem," *Atlanta Constitution*, January 30, 1990, p. D-1.

6. Christensen, *loc. cit.*

7. Maria Saporta, "Lockheed's Shot in the Arm," *Atlanta Constitution*, May 10, 1990.

8. Christensen, *loc. cit.*

9. *Atlas...*, *op. cit.*, p. 37 . Christensen, *loc. cit.*

Hawaii

A	B	C	D	E	F
$		📷🔨	▦	VI	DDI
+	✚	–	→	!	✌

Benchmarks	No.	Rank	Benchmarks	No.	Rank
A. Total DoD $	$2.5 bil.	24	Def.-Dependent Jobs ('000), '90	116	26
B. Personnel Payroll	$2.0 bil.	12	Change in Def.-Dep. Jobs, '89-'91	-8.7%	19
C. Prime Contracts (PC)	$0.5 bil.	35	Unemployment Rate, '90-'91	2.3%	52
D. PC Change, FY '87-'90	-0.2%	40	Unemp. Rate Change, '89-'91	-0.4%	42
E. Vulnerability Index	11.6	15	Per Capita Income	$20,254	11
F. Defense Disloc. Index	0.04	47	Population ('000)	1,108	42

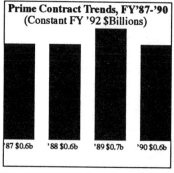

Prime Contract Trends, FY'87-'90
(Constant FY '92 $Billions)

'87 $0.6b — '88 $0.6b — '89 $0.7b — '90 $0.6b

Pearl Harbor, Schofield Barracks, Hickam AFB, Honolulu, Kaneohe, Barbers Point, Wahiawa, Wheeler AFB, Aiea, Camp H.M. Smith

▲ Army ■ Navy
● Air Force ○ Other

Top 5 Contractors	$ Millions
Broken Hill Proprietary	$59.1
GTE	53.4
Fedrick/Nova Joint Venture	28.8
Computer Sciences	28.7
Hawaiian Electric	16.2

Top 10 $ Sites[a]	Congressional Dist., Representative	1989 Rank	Total DoD$[c]	Payroll[c]	Prime Contracts[c]	Pensonnel[d]
1-Pearl Harbor (48)	1-Abercrombie, d	49	$764.0	$702.7	$61.3	17.5
2-Schofield (117)	2-Mink, d	84	337.1	307.6	29.5	14.7
3-Hickam AFB (144)	1-Abercrombie, d	146	272.9	225.0	47.9	7.7
4-Honolulu (145)	(1,2)[b]	100	272.6	129.8	142.8	2.0
5-Kaneohe (178)	2-Mink, d	156	199.8	189.9	9.8	5.3
6-Barbers Point (204)	"	253	168.2	108.6	59.5	1.9
7-Wahiawa (341)	"	328	43.5	42.0	1.5	--
8-Wheeler AFB (357)	(1,2)[b]	331	38.3	34.3	4.0	1.3
9-Aiea (360)	1-Abercrombie, d	--	36.9	34.7	2.2	--
10-Cp. H. Smith (369)	"	359	33.8	30.8	2.9	--

[a]Rating in parentheses is out of 511 sites, the top ten in each state and PR, plus DC.
[b]Multidistrict r-Rep, d-Dem. [c]$Millions (figures may not add due to rounding) [d]Thousands

Hawaii

The Hawaii economy is reliant on the health of the visitor industry which is estimated by state economists to account directly and indirectly for over 40 percent of the state's gross state product of $28 billion in 1990. The once dominant sugar and pineapple industries together represent less than 5 percent of the economy. Continued gradual decline in these industries is expected, being replaced by growth in more contemporary crops such as macadamia nuts. The state has a relatively high per capita income and its unemployment rate of 2.3 percent was the lowest of all the states at the start of 1991. The state has shown strong economic growth in the 1988-91 period. Its already low unemployment actually declined; though both the labor force and employment grew rapidly, job growth outpaced labor-force growth.

Defense and the Economy

Hawaii's key strategic location makes it an important part of the military payroll. The state received $2.5 billion from the Department of Defense in 1990, and approximately 20,200 civilian jobs are directly tied to military base activity. Military personnel and their dependents represent almost 12 percent of the state population, and have substantial consumer impact on local business. The Department of Defense also has large contracts for local purchase of fuel, needed to traverse the thousands of miles from Pearl Harbor to Asian ports, and hundreds of smaller contracts for repair and maintenance of base facilities. The Department of Defense annually spends in the state about $0.9 billion in civilian pay and $0.5 billion in purchase of local goods and services.[1] Most procurement spending in Hawaii is in the form of service contracts for the state's immense military payroll. Since the state is expected to gain personnel from realignments, the level of service contracting is not likely to be drastically reduced. The state's Vulnerability Index is high, but its Defense Dislocation Index is very low.

State Legislative Initiatives

Hawaii has been taking cautious steps toward making the state less vulnerable to defense cuts. In 1989, a resolution calling for research into the potential civilian industrial uses of Pearl Harbor Naval Shipyard was discussed in a legislative committee but failed to reach the legislature floor. Democratic Party Conventions in 1988 and 1990 adopted resolutions calling for the development of a state strategy to deal with military cutbacks that could hit Hawaii in the future.[2]

Community Surveys

Military personnel and their paychecks are heavily concentrated on Hawaii's largest island, Oahu, which is home to Kaneohe Bay Marine Air

Station, Schofield Barracks, Hickam Air Force Base, and Pearl Harbor Naval Base. Pearl Harbor alone employs almost half of the total civilian military personnel in Hawaii.[3]

Honolulu. The Base Closure Commission in 1988 sought the closure of Kapalama Military Reservation Phase III, a warehouse, maintenance, and administrative facility. Personnel could be relocated to nearby Schofield Barracks. The possible existence of PCBs or asbestos will require environmental cleanup or containment programs.[4]

Kaneohe. In 1988 the Department of Defense announced that the Naval Ocean Systems Center Detachment would be realigned. Its functions were to be consolidated with those at a San Diego facility. A net loss of 15 positions was expected. In 1991, the Base Commission considered closing the facility.[5]

Notes

1. *Federal Activities in Hawaii*, State Department of Business and Economic Development, September 1989, p. 9. Spending figures have been updated.

2. *Conversion Organizers' Update* (Mountain View, CA: Center for Economic Conversion, August 1990), p. 4. Contacts: (1) Hawaii Department of Business, Economic Development & Tourism, Murray E. Towill, Kamamalu Building, 250 South King St., Honolulu, HI 96804. (2) Hawaii Department of Labor Statistics, Frederick Pang, 830 Punchbowl St., Honolulu, HI 96813; 808-548-7639.

3. *Federal Activities in Hawaii, loc. cit.*

4. *Base Realignments and Closures.*, Report of the Defense Secretary's Commission, December 1988, pp. 62-63.

5. "Bases Affected by Cutbacks," *The Washington Post,* April 13, 1991, p. 10. *Base Closure and Realignment Report*, Department of Defense, April 1991, p. 78.

Idaho

A	B	C	D	E	F
$				VI	DDI
–	–	–	↓	–	✌

Benchmarks	No.	Rank	Benchmarks	No.	Rank
A. Total DoD $	$0.3bil.	48	Def.-Dependent Jobs ('000), '90	11	50
B. Personnel Payroll	$0.3bil.	43	Change in Def.-Dep. Jobs, '89-'91	-21.4%	5
C. Prime Contracts (PC)	$.04bil.	51	Unemployment Rate, '90-'91	6.6%	23
D. PC Change, FY '87-'90	-49.2%	4	Unemp. Rate Change, '89-'91	+1.6%	19
E. Vulnerability Index	7.9	39	Per Capita Income	$15,160	41
F. Defense Disloc. Index	0.00	49	Population ('000)	1,007	43

▲ Army ■ Navy ● Air Force ○ Other

Coeur D'Alene
Moscow
Lewiston
Idaho Falls
Blackfoot
Caldwell
Boise
Nampa
Pocatello
Mountain Home AFB

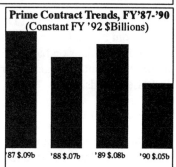

Prime Contract Trends, FY'87-'90
(Constant FY '92 $Billions)

'87 $.09b	'88 $.07b	'89 $.08b	'90 $.05b

Top 5 Contractors	$ Millions
Morgen & Oswood	$6.0
Basic American	3.5
Scientech	3.4
Heinz	2.9
Empire Airlines	2.8

Top 10 $ Sites[a]	Congressional Dist., Representative	1989 Rank	Total DoD$[c]	Payroll[c]	Prime Contracts[c]	Per- sonnel[d]
1-Mtn. Hm. AFB (268)	1-LaRocco, d	265	$101.5	$89.1	$12.4	3.8
2-Boise (321)	"	314	55.6	49.6	6.1	0.9
3-Idaho Falls (358)	2-Stallings, d	355	37.2	33.0	4.1	1.2
4-Moscow (443)	1-LaRocco, d	--	10.6	3.5	7.1	.04
5-Blackfoot (474)	2-Stallings, d	391	5.2	1.4	3.8	--
6-Coeur d'Alene (479)	1-LaRocco, d	480	4.8	4.7	.04	--
7-Pocatello (485)	2-Stallings, d	475	4.4	4.7	0.3	.03
8-Lewiston (487)	1-LaRocco, d	--	4.3	3.0	1.2	.01
9-Nampa (490)	"	--	4.0	3.7	0.3	--
10-Caldwell (492)	"	482	3.9	3.8	.03	--

[a]Rating in parentheses is out of 511 sites, the top ten in each state and PR, plus DC.

[b]Multidistrict r-Rep, d-Dem. [c]$Millions (figures may not add due to rounding) [d]Thousands

Idaho

After a relatively weak performance in the first half of the 1980s, the Idaho economy began to grow at a stronger rate than the nation in 1988. Strong recoveries by the machinery, mining and lumber sectors, along with more moderate growth in the agricultural and construction industries, are the driving forces behind Idaho's economic comeback.[1] Idaho's unemployment ranked 23rd and its change in unemployment ranked 19th (unemployment increased because rapid labor force growth overshadowed a modest gain in employment).

Defense and the Economy

The state ranks 48th on Department of Defense spending and is also near the bottom of the Defense Dislocation Index. Defense employs slightly more than 1,000 civilians on bases. The state has very little defense-related industry; its procurement contracts represent just 0.1 percent of total Department of Defense awards.[2]

Community Surveys

Outside of Mountain Home Air Force Base, which is central to the economy of southwest Idaho, defense spending has a secondary role in the state economy.

Mountain Home. Mountain Home Air Force Base purchases from local businesses in southwest Idaho represent 20 percent of Department of Defense procurement in the state. Most of this procurement is in the service sector of Elmore and Ada counties. As a result of the 1989 Base Closure Act, one F-111A squadron was retired in June 1990 and another in June 1991. In April 1991, the base was targeted for further realignment. Mountain Home will lose some units but gain others. State officials are working with the Department of Defense's Office of Economic Adjustment, which has awarded a diversification grant to help Elmore and Ada Counties adjust to the military cutback.[3]

Notes

1. *Idaho Economic Forecast*, July 1989, p. 13.

2. *Prime Contract Awards by Region and State, Fiscal Years 1989, 1988, 1987*, Department of Defense, Washington Headquarters Services, Directorate for Information, Operations and Reports, p. 29. Contact: Elmore County Impact Steering Committee, David A. Jett, Special Assistant, Office of the Governor, 390 East 2nd North St., Mountain Home, Idaho 83647; 208-587-2968.

3. Neil Meyer and Roger Coupal, "Impact of Transferring F-4s to the Mountain Home Air Force Base on the Economy of Elmore and Ada Counties," *Idaho Economic Forecast, op. cit.*, p. 37. *Base Closure and Realignment Report*, Department of Defense, April 1991, pp. 114-115.

Illinois

A	B	C	D	E	F
$	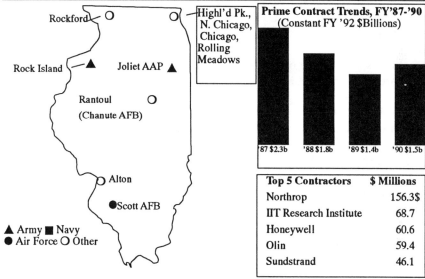			VI	DDI
+	✚	+	↓	−	✂

Benchmarks	No.	Rank	Benchmarks	No.	Rank
A. Total DoD $	$3.2bil.	19	Def.-Dependent Jobs ('000), '90	166	19
B. Personnel Payroll	$1.9bil.	14	Change in Def.-Dep. Jobs, '89-'91	+0.6%	36
C. Prime Contracts (PC)	$1.3bil.	24	Unemployment Rate, '90-'91	6.5%	25
D. PC Change, FY '87-'90	-37.4%	8	Unemp. Rate Change, '89-'91	+0.8%	29
E. Vulnerability Index	7.5	43	Per Capita Income	$20,303	10
F. Defense Disloc. Index	1.91	15	Population ('000)	11,431	6

Rockford

Highl'd Pk., N. Chicago, Chicago, Rolling Meadows

Rock Island

Joliet AAP ▲

Rantoul
(Chanute AFB)

Alton

●Scott AFB

▲ Army ■ Navy
● Air Force ○ Other

Prime Contract Trends, FY'87-'90
(Constant FY '92 $Billions)

'87 $2.3b   '88 $1.8b   '89 $1.4b   '90 $1.5b

Top 5 Contractors	$ Millions
Northrop	156.3$
IIT Research Institute	68.7
Honeywell	60.6
Olin	59.4
Sundstrand	46.1

Top 10 $ Sites[a]	Congressional Dist., Representative	1989 Rank	Total DoD$[c]	Payroll[c]	Prime Contracts[c]	Per-sonnel[d]
1-N. Chicago (87)	(10,12)[b]	88	$452.3	$418.6	$33.7	--
2-Scott AFB (99)	21-Costello, d	115	391.4	354.1	37.3	10.1
3-Rock Island (122)	17-Evans, d	142	323.2	273.3	50.0	8.2
4-Chicago (138)	(1-3,5-9,11)[b]	138	285.8	91.0	194.8	2.0
5-Rolling Mdws. (209)	(10,12)[b]	290	161.5	2.2	159.3	--
6-Rantoul (234)	15-Madigan, r	231	130.7	106.6	24.1	--
7-Highland Park (255)	10-Porter, r	255	108.7	91.6	17.1	--
8-Joliet AAP (302)	(4,15)[b]	288	74.8	0	74.8	--
9-Rockford (313)	16-Cox, d	273	65.4	8.0	57.4	--
10-Alton (316)	21-Costello, d	--	59.4	2.6	56.8	--

[a]Rating in parentheses is out of 511 sites, the top ten in each state and PR, plus DC.
[b]Multidistrict r-Rep, d-Dem. [c]$Millions (figures may not add due to rounding) [d] Thousands

Illinois

Illinois' gross state product grew by an average of 3.8 percent a year during the 1980s, less than GNP average growth of 4.1 percent during the same period. Illinois' personal income was $20,303 in 1990, an increase of 7.6 percent on the previous year. Unemployment ranked 25th in the country (about average) at the start of 1991 and change in unemployment ranked a middling 29th (the labor force grew while employment declined slightly).

Defense and the Economy

Defense spending plays a relatively minor part in the Illinois economy. Illinois firms were awarded $1.3 million in prime contracts in FY 1990, just 1 percent of all defense contracts. In 1988, only four states received less in defense spending, although Illinois contributed the fourth highest amount of tax revenues.[1]

Illinois is therefore one of the few states in a position actually to increase its share of Department of Defense dollars in coming years; its high-tech equipment will be among the fastest-growing defense needs in the post-Cold War environment. The nation's smaller armed forces will need to rely increasingly on surveillance and verification, say defense experts, and Illinois' specialties in intelligence/surveillance equipment, as well as computer simulation systems, are compatible with these changing needs. Weapons programs in the state that are facing termination include the F-15 fighter and M-1 tank. Base closures and reductions will result in loss of more than 6,000 jobs in coming years.[2]

Community Surveys

Most contracting is in the north of the state near Chicago. Rep. John Porter (R-N. Chicago) represents the 10th Congressional District, which includes Highland Park and part of Rolling Meadows. Another major defense beneficiary is the 21st CD, which includes both Scott Air Force Base and Alton.

Chicago. A key resource is Illinois SANE/Freeze, Chicago Peace Conversion Commission, Bernice Bild, 17 N. State St., Suite 1132, Chicago, IL 60602; 312-372-7867. Chicago's situation was analyzed by Professors Wim Wiewel and Joseph Persky of Illinois University, utilizing data provided by the Peace Conversion Commission. Presented in December 1990, it concludes that Chicago is insufficiently defense-dependent (only 200 out of over 56,000 firms are defense, prime contractors) and sufficiently diverse economically not to have to worry about significant dislocation from defense cuts. However, it also recommends that the Department of Commerce prepare targeted materials to make the availability of its technical and financial resources widely known to smaller defense contractors in the city, especially the availability of Federal financing aid and information on other Federal programs.[3] The Department's

Business Services Division reports that it is following up these recommendations. The Peace Conversion Commission has also issued its own report.

Highland Park (N. Chicago). Fort Sheridan is slated to be closed by 1994, affecting 3,000 civilian and military jobs. A locally based commission, formed by Rep. John Porter (R-N. Chicago), has submitted a land-use plan to Secretary Cheney. The proposal calls for keeping some Army Reserve facilities as well as a military cemetary on the base and using the the rest of the land for educational and research activities and a national veterans cemetary (the Department of Veterans Affairs is seeking the land). The plan's success with Secretary Cheney may hinge on the Navy's efforts to acquire some of the base's housing. The Navy's goals would conflict with the commission's proposals.[4]

N. Chicago (Barrington). The Chicago suburb is home to Recon/Optical Inc., the largest supplier of intelligence-gathering cameras carried aboard jets. Because the impending cuts to defense spending should not weigh heavily on the high-tech industries, the 436-worker Recon/Optical plant should not be very affected by the cuts, as it has $110 million in back orders and business is expected to grow.[5]

N. Chicago (Great Lakes NTC). The Great Lakes Naval Training Center—the largest recruit training facility in the world—was at the center of political squabbling. In April 1991, residents were celebrating when Defense Secretary Dick Cheney announced his plan that the base get 15,500 more jobs due to the planned closure of a similar facility in Orlando, Florida. But about a month later it was announced that the Base Closure Commission was considering the advantages of closing Great Lakes Naval instead of the Orlando facility.[6] Neither base was on the Base Commission's final list of closures, so Great Lakes is likely to remain where it started—not headed for shutdown but not expanding either.

Rantoul. Officials of the City of Rantoul, Champaign County, and the State of Illinois have fought to save Chanute Air Force Base, which is slated for closure by 1993, but have also been pushing ahead with conversion plans. It was originally thought that closure of the base—employer of 6,000 military personnel, 1,100 Civil Service personnel, 800 civilian personnel, and 800 other personnel directly and approximately 1,000 additional people indirectly through contractors and food services—would be devastating to Rantoul's economy and school system. Fears have been partially allayed by a comprehensive conversion plan developed by the Chanute Re-Use Committee that calls for putting base facilities to educational and industrial uses: a language training institute, and an aircraft maintenance center and training center. Establishment of the latter facility will require the use of two base hangars and the modernization of two long-inactive runways. The base was among ten sites being considered in early 1991 by United Airlines for a maintenance facility. The town has offered the company concessions such as an exemption from state sales tax and an offer to buy additional land to extend the base's runways. A major problem facing re-use efforts is that it is unknown when or if the land will be put up for sale.

The Air Force must complete an environmental impact study and the land must first be offered to organizations for the homeless under the McKinney Act. No timetable for these procedures is in place.[7]

Rock Island. The Army Arsenal was targeted for realignment in 1991. Illinois legislators have announced that they will fight the move because a net of approximately 700 jobs will be lost.[8]

Notes

1. *Atlas/Data Abstract for the United States and Selected Areas FY 1990*, Department of Defense, Washington Headquarters Services, Directorate for Information, Operations and Reports, p. 43. Evans and Shanker, "Illinois May Get More From Defense Pie," *Chicago Tribune*, March 1, 1990, p. 6.

2. "Iraq May Help to Keep Warren Making Tanks," *Detroit News*, August 20, 1990, page B-1. Contacts: (1) Governor's Office, Thomas Skinner, Economic Development Assistant, c/o Governor's Office, State Capitol Building, Springfield, IL 62706; 312-814-6707. (2) Illinois Department of Commerce, Steve McClure, 620 E. Adams, Springfield, IL 62706; 217-782-3233. (3) Illinois Department of Employment Security, Sally Jackson, 555 S. Panfield St., Springfield, IL 62704; 217-785-5069. (4) Rantoul Mayor's Office, Mayor Katy B. Podagrosi, 333 S. Tanner St., Rantoul, IL 61866; 217-893-1661.

3. Christopher Hall, Joseph Persky, and Wim Wiewel, "Responding to Defense Cuts: The Case of Chicago," Paper Prepared for Meetings of Economists Against the Arms Race, Washington, DC, December 1990 (Chicago, IL: University of Illinois at Chicago, Photocopied Draft, 1990). Their presentation suggests the need for a manual for defense contractors (as well as economic development officials) on the availability of Federal and state support for conversion.

4. Robert Enstad, "Cheney Will Receive Ft. Sheridan Plan," *The Chicago Tribune*, June 24, 1991, p. II-3.

5. Evans and Shanker, p. 6.

6. Mitchell Locin, "Push Is On to Save Great Lakes Base," *The Chicago Tribune*, June 6, 1991, p. II-1.

7. Linda Eardley, "Fighting to Save Chanute Base," *St. Louis Post Dispatch*, August 27, 1989, p. 4B. *Base Conversion News* (Mountain View, CA: Center for Economic Conversion, Winter 1991), p. 6.

8. Mitchell Locin and Elaine S. Povich, "Pentagon's Proposal Could Bring 15,500 Jobs to Great Lakes," *The Chicago Tribune*, April 13, 1991, p. 1.

Indiana

A	B	C	D	E	F
$				VI	DDI
+	+	+	↓	−	✁

Benchmarks	No.	Rank	Benchmarks	No.	Rank
A.Total DoD $	$2.7bil.	23	Def.-Dependent Jobs ('000), '90	141	22
B. Personnel Payroll	$1.0bil.	27	Change in Def.-Dep. Jobs, '89-'91	-6.6%	24
C. Prime Contracts (PC)	$1.7bil.	19	Unemployment Rate, '90-'91	5.9%	31
D. PC Change, FY '87-'90	-31.6%	15	Unemp. Rate Change, '89-'91	+1.7%	17
E. Vulnerability Index	8.1	35	Per Capita Income	$16,864	32
F. Defense Disloc. Index	2.53	13	Population ('000)	5,544	14

South Bend — ○ ▲ Mishawaka

○— Garrett

Fort Wayne ○

● Grissom AFB

○ Indianapolis

○ Columbus

○ Crane

▲ Indiana AAP

Evansville
○

▲ Army ■ Navy
● Air Force ○ Other

Prime Contract Trends, FY'87-'90 (Constant FY '92 $Billions)

'87 $2.7b	'88 $1.8b	'89 $2.0b	'90 $1.8b

Top 5 Contractors	$ Millions
General Motors	$400.7
LTV	297.6
Philips	205.5
Imperial Chemical	79.2
Cummins	66.5

Top 10 $ Sites[a]	Congressional Dist., Representative	1989 Rank	Total DoD$[c]	Payroll[c]	Prime Contracts[c]	Pen-sonnel[d]
1-Indianapolis (29)	(2,6,10)[b]	32	$1,040.7	$450.2	$590.5	4.6
2-Mishawaka (140)	3-Hiler, r	236	284.1	1.7	282.4	--
3-Ft. Wayne (153)	4-Long, d	85	258.5	28.5	229.9	0.5
4-Crane (210)	8-McCloskey, d	223	159.1	157.8	1.2	4.9
5-South Bend (267)	3-Hiler, r	194	103.7	9.1	94.6	0.1
6-Grissom AFB (286)	5-Jontz, d	264	85.6	74.8	10.8	3.2
7-Indiana AAP (294)	9-Hamilton, d	293	79.2	0	79.2	--
8-Columbus (296)	(2,9)[b]	311	78.7	2.7	76.0	--
9-Garrett (307)	4-Long, d	--	70.5	0.2	70.3	--
10-Evansville (327)	8-McCloskey, d	347	50.8	10.5	40.4	--

[a]Rating in parentheses is out of 511 sites, the top ten in each state and PR, plus DC.
[b]Multidistrict r-Rep, d-Dem. [c]$Millions (figures may not add due to rounding) [d] Thousands

Indiana

In the second half of the 1980s, the Indiana economy grew at the same rate as the nation's. The statewide trend in the 1990s is away from reliance on durable goods manufacturing. The economy of the state's northwest is perhaps the least vulnerable to business cycles, while the Indianapolis area is the most vulnerable.[1] Indiana's unemployment rate ranked 31st at 5.9 percent and its unemployment change 17th (employment declined faster than the labor force).

Defense and the Economy

The $2.7 billion spent in the state in 1990 by the Department of Defense made it the 23rd highest recipient of defense funds, accounting for more than 5 percent of state revenue. The Department's prime targets for cuts in the state include the M-1 tank and the Chaparral missile, but proposed cuts as of mid-1991 represented a small fraction of the state's defense-contract dollars.

Community Surveys

The largest contractor in the state is General Motors (GM), which has two divisions under the name Allison based in Indianapolis. Almost a quarter of the prime contracts awarded to Indiana firms in 1990 were earmarked for production of vehicle components and vehicles. Other important defense-related industries include communications equipment, which accounts for about a quarter of Indiana prime contracts. ITT Aerospace Optical in Fort Wayne receives almost half of Indiana's electronic/communications-related contracts. State firms account for over 6 percent of total defense spending on aircraft engines, with Allied-Signal Inc.'s Bendix divisions in South Bend in the lead.[2]

Charlestown. The Army Ammunition Production Plant located here is scheduled to be closed in 1993.[3]

Crane. The Naval Weapons Support Center will be realigned with the nearby Combat and Weapon Systems Engineering and Industrial Base Division. Consolidation will eliminate 1,065 positions. However, a House bill calls for the establishment of a $10 million electronic-countermeasures systems center at the Naval Weapons facility.[4]

Indianapolis. The Army Helicopter Improvement Program and the M-1 tank, are projects of Allison Gas Turbine, a GM division that reports to GM Defense Operations in Los Angeles. The other GM division is Allison Transmission, whch reports to GM Automotive Components Groups in Detroit; it receives over $173 million just for defense-related transmission systems. Allison's large defense and commercial operations employ about 13,000 workers in a city employing 430,000.

The Naval Avionics Center will merge with the Naval Air Warfare Center Aircraft Division centered in Maryland. Realignment will eliminate 630 positions.[5] The Base Closure Commission announced in April 1991 that Fort

Benjamin Harrison, the largest location of military personnel in the state, may be closed. The closure will eliminate 1 percent of the jobs in the Indianapolis area, though new jobs may be created for the base's hazardous-waste cleanup.[6]

Madison. The 55,000-acre Jefferson Proving Ground, a 50-year-old ammunition testing facility, was slated for shutdown by 1995 by the Base Closure Act. The Jefferson Proving Ground Survival Committee is accusing the Department of Defense of underestimating the cost of cleaning the facility, which is contaminated with unexploded ordnance. Cleanup estimates range from $30 million to $5 billion. The Survival Committee wants legislation to allow the base to stay open on the grounds that it won't pay to close it and clean it up.[7]

Peru. The Base Closure Commission recommends the conversion of Grissom Air Force Base since it has poor bombing ranges and the cost of closure compares favorably with that of other air bases. Most of its military units will be retired or given to the 434th Air Reserve. The Air Force Reserve will create a containment area, maintain the property and aim to include civilian facilities. It will also maintain the airfield if local authorities decide against the construction of a commercial airport. About 5,200 of 101,000 area jobs will disappear.[8]

South Bend. AM General, a subsidiary of LTV Corp., is a manufacturer of jeeps and other vehicles for the military. The company is under contract to produce 33,000 more High Mobility Multipurpose Wheeled Vehicles (Hummvees) for the Department of Defense, but it has been marginally profitable in 1990. The company plans to sell a limited number of modified vehicles commercially beginning in the fall of 1991. The Hummvees, no-frills versions of the Range Rover, have obtained an enthusiastic reception from potential buyers as far away as Singapore.[9]

Notes

1. Morton Marcus, "The 1990 Indiana Outlook," *Indiana Business Review*, December, 1989.

2. *Atlas/Data Abstract for the United States and Selected Areas Fiscal 1990*, Department of Defense, Washington Headquarters Services, Directorate for Information, Operations and Reports, p. 45. *Prime Contract Awards by Region and State, Fiscal Years 1989, 1988, 1987*, Department of Defense, Washington Headquarters Services, Directorate for Information, Operations and Reports, p. 32.

3. "Pentagon's Proposals: Base Closures, Reductions," *USA Today*, January 30, 1990, p. 8.

4. *Base Closure and Realignment Report*, Department of Defense, April 1991, p. 82.

5. Interview in March 1990 with Ron Miller, Assistant Budget Officer, Indianapolis, IN, 317-236-2600. *Base Closure...*, *op. cit.*, p.74.

6. *Ibid.*, pp. 37-38.

7. *Base Conversion News* (Mountain View, CA: Center for Economic Conversion, Winter 1991), p. 6.

8. *Base Closure...*, *op. cit.*, pp. 97-99.

9. Lois Therrien, "What's $40,000, Weighs 5,000 Pounds and Comes in One Color?" *Business Week*, July 8 , 1991, p. 31

Iowa

	A	B	C	D	E	F
	$				VI	DDI
	−	−	−	→	−	✂

Benchmarks	No.	Rank	Benchmarks	No.	Rank
A.Total DoD $	$0.7bil.	43	Def.-Dependent Jobs ('000), '90	35	41
B. Personnel Payroll	$0.2bil.	49	Change in Def.-Dep. Jobs, '89-'91	+12.9%	44
C. Prime Contracts (PC)	$0.5bil.	36	Unemployment Rate, '90-'91	4.7%	45
D. PC Change, FY '87-'90	-25.9%	20	Unemp. Rate Change, '89-'91	+0.6%	32
E. Vulnerability Index	5.7	51	Per Capita Income	$17,244	27
F. Defense Disloc. Index	0.45	31	Population ('000)	2,777	31

▲ Army ■ Navy
● Air Force ○ Other

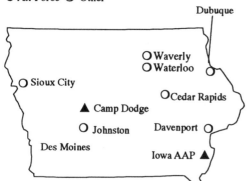

Dubuque

○ Waverly
○ Waterloo
○ Sioux City
○ Cedar Rapids
▲ Camp Dodge
○ Johnston   Davenport ○
Des Moines
Iowa AAP ▲

Prime Contract Trends, FY'87-'90
(Constant FY '92 $Billions)

'87 $0.7b   '88 $0.7b   '89 $0.5b   '90 $0.5b

Top 5 Contractors	$ Millions
Rockwell	$230.9
Duchossois Enterprises	91.0
De Mason	35.0
Pirelli	23.3
John Deere	14.2

Top 10 $ Sites[a]	Congressional Dist., Representative	1989 Rank	Total DoD$[c]	Payroll[c]	Prime Contracts[c]	Pen-sonnel[d]
1-Cedar Rapids (155)	2-Nussle, d	157	$254.6	$8.4	$246.2	0.1
2-Waterloo (272)	3-Nagle, d	392	97.1	4.6	92.5	.08
3-Des Moines (318)	4-Smith, d	346	56.6	26.2	30.4	0.4
4-Iowa AAP (362)	3-Nagle, d	303	36.7	0	36.7	--
5-Davenport (400)	1-Leach, r	393	23.5	4.6	18.9	.05
6-Dubuque (403)	2-Nussle, d	440	22.6	4.4	18.2	--
7-Sioux City (425)	6-Grandy, r	447	15.4	14.6	0.7	0.3
8-Johnston (447)	4-Smith, d	--	9.6	8.5	1.1	--
9-Waverly (450)	3-Nagle, d	416	9.2	0.1	9.1	--
10-Camp Dodge (459)	5-Lightfoot, r	453	7.6	7.3	0.3	0.3

[a]Rating in parentheses is out of 511 sites, the top ten in each state and PR, plus DC.
[b]Multidistrict r-Rep, d-Dem. [c]$Millions (figures may not add due to rounding) [d]Thousands

Iowa

Most forecasts predict slow growth for the Iowa economy in the early 1990s. Personal income is expected to rise along with the national rate, but employment growth should level off. The manufacturing sector is experiencing slight growth, but still shows signs of relative weakness. The service-producing sector, on the other hand, is expected to become one of the strongest pillars of the economy.[1] Iowa's unemployment ranked a healthy 45th and its change in unemployment 32nd (the labor force grew and employment declined slightly).

Defense and the Economy

The $687 million the Department of Defense spends in the state is not negligible, especially for private contractors, but it is not a dominant part of the economy. Iowa is in the bottom fifth of all states in receiving Department of Defense dollars, and procurement contracts are down from 1987.[2] Combined with Iowa's low unemployment rate, the small defense presence puts the state in an excellent position to endure cuts.

Iowa's most significant defense work is research and development, 15 percent of the total. Since these contracts are vulnerable to cutbacks, the downward trend in defense prime contracts will probably continue.

Community Surveys

The industry with the most defense business in 1990 was electronics and communications. Most, $231 million, went to one company—Rockwell International, based in Cedar Rapids.[3]

Des Moines. The Base Closure Act of 1989 targeted Fort Des Moines for partial closure. The fort, which is on the National Register of Historic Places, may require cleanup of pesticides.[4]

Notes

1. *The Iowa Economic Forecast,* The Institute for Economic Research at the University of Iowa, March 1990, pp. 2-4.

2. *Atlas/Data Abstract for the United States and Selected Areas Fiscal 1990,* Department of Defense, Washington Headquarters Services, Directorate for Information, Operations and Reports, p. 47.

3. *Prime Contract Awards by Region and State, Fiscal Years 1989, 1988, 1987,* Department of Defense, Washington Headquarters Services, Directorate for Information, Operations and Reports, p. 33. *Atlas..., op. cit.,* 1990, p. 47. Contacts: (1) Governor's Office, Allan Thomas, Executive Assistant, State Capitol, Des Moines, IA 50319; 515-281-6750. (2) Iowa Economic Development, Richard Timmerman, 200 E. Grand Avenue, Des Moines, IA 50319. (3) Iowa Employment Services, Steve Smith, 1000 E. Grand Ave., Des Moines, IA 50319; 515-281-8181.

4. *Base Realignments and Closures,* December 1988, Report of the Defense Secretary's Commission, pp. 80-81.

Kansas

A	B	C	D	E	F
$	👷	🏭	📅	VI	DDI
+	+	+	↓	!	☮

Benchmarks	No.	Rank	Benchmarks	No.	Rank
A. Total DoD $	$1.9bil.	31	Def.-Dependent Jobs ('000), '90	96	31
B. Personnel Payroll	$1.0bil.	26	Change in Def.-Dep. Jobs, '89–'91	-10.3%	14
C. Prime Contracts (PC)	$0.9bil.	28	Unemployment Rate, '90–'91	4.7%	45
D. PC Change, FY '87-'90	-33.3%	14	Unemp. Rate Change, '89–'91	+1.0%	26
E. Vulnerability Index	8.2	33	Per Capita Income	$17,986	22
F. Defense Disloc. Index	0.06	45	Population ('000)	2,478	33

Prime Contract Trends, FY'87-'90
(Constant FY '92 $Billions)

'87 $1.5b '88 $1.1b '89 $1.1b '90 $1.0b

Map labels:
Ft. Leavenworth
Topeka
Ft. Riley ▲ ○
Sunfl. AAP ▲○
Wichita ○ Overl'd Pk. ○
McConnell ●
Liberal ○ AFB
Kansas AAP ▲

▲ Army ■ Navy
● Air Force ○ Other

Top 5 Contractors	$ Millions
Boeing	$340.7
McDonnell Douglas	150.7
Hercules	54.3
Raytheon	53.8
Day & Zimmermann	32.1

Top 10 $ Sites[a]	Congressional Dist., Representative	1989 Rank	Total DoD$[c]	Payroll[c]	Prime Contracts[c]	Per-sonnel[d]
1-Wichita (56)	4-Glickman, d	58	$655.9	$31.6	$624.3	0.3
2-Ft. Riley (93)	2-Slattery, d	69	432.8	392.8	40.0	15.7
3-Ft. Leavenw'th (179)	2-Slattery, d	168	199.7	150.6	49.1	6.0
4-McConn'l AFB (241)	4-Glickman, d	260	121.5	109.9	11.6	4.2
5-Sunflower AAP (322)	3-Meyers, r	334	55.5	0	55.5	--
6-Liberal (343)	1-Roberts, r	415	41.9	0.6	41.3	--
7-Overland Park (368)	3-Meyers, r	330	33.8	27.0	6.8	0.1
8-Kansas AAP (376)	"	--	32.1	0	32.1	--
9-Leavenworth (385)	2-Slattery, d	376	28.9	17.5	11.4	--
10-Topeka (392)	"	390	26.6	21.7	4.9	0.3

[a]Rating in parentheses is out of 511 sites, the top ten in each state and PR, plus DC.
[b]Multidistrict r-Rep, d-Dem. [c]$Millions (figures may not add due to rounding) [d]Thousands

Kansas

The Kansas economy, recently hurt by a drought and major strikes, grew at a rate below the national level for most of the 1980s and is expected to continue along that path. The services, government and durable goods manufacturing sectors experienced impressive growth and job expansion, while the mining and construction sectors declined. The gross state product, aided by a 9.6 percent gain in the service sector, increased 5.4 percent in 1990.[1] The unemployment rate ranked 45th and change in unemployment 26th (the labor force increased faster than employment).

Defense and the Economy

Most of the FY 1990 defense money spent in Kansas was earmarked for the state's relatively large military payroll, with less than $1 billion in the form of prime contract awards. The only program that Defense Secretary Dick Cheney has proposed reducing in Kansas is F-14 fighter production. The state receives 1.5 percent of Department of Defense procurement dollars and accounts for over 6 percent of total defense aircraft procurement.[2]

Community Surveys

Though two Army Ammunition Plants in the state are in danger of being closed by 1994, the Department of Defense has not slated Kansas for major cuts. The military spent $1.9 billion in the state in FY 1990, of which approximately $656 million went to the Wichita area.

A statewide activist group in Topeka issued a report stating that Kansas could save money from military-budget cuts, money which could go to education, social services, the environment, and roads and highways. It is available from Kansas National Priorities Project, 4330 NE Indian Creek Road, Topeka, KS 66617; 913-286-0456; Bill Beachy, Executive Director.

De Sota. The Sunflower Army Ammunition Production Plant is scheduled to be closed by FY 1994.[3]

Parsons. The Army Ammunition Plant run by Day & Zimmerman is scheduled to be closed by FY 1993.[4]

Riley. Riley's military-related problems are different from those of almost all other communities cited in this chapter: the military is not cutting back, but is trying to expand. The army, based to the southwest at Fort Riley, wants to add 82,000 acres of neighboring farmland, which disturbs some residents of this 700-person town.[5]

Wichita. Many analysts feel that Wichita's unusually diverse economy, with growing service and health care sectors, may be in a good position to absorb the impacts of defense cuts. Boeing in particular may be able to get significant commercial contracts to make up for any loss in military spending. Boeing considers production of the KC-135—a 30-year-old refueling plane—to be a mainstay of its Wichita plant. Approximately 1,500 of the plant's 23,000 workers are involved in the $1.9 billion KC-135 contract. Although Boeing officials have announced that the cutbacks in the KC-135 would not result in layoffs, Sen. Robert Dole (R-KS) has fought hard to save the tanker from cancellation.[6]

Notes

1. *The State of Kansas Economy 1989-1990*, Kansas Department of Commerce, p. 2.

2. *Atlas/Data Abstract for the United States and Selected Areas Fiscal 1990*, Department of Defense, by Washington Headquarters Services, Directorate for Information, Operations and Reports, p. 69. *Prime Contract Awards by Region and State, Fiscal Years 1989, 1988, 1987*, Department of Defense, Washington Headquarters Services, Directorate for Information, Operations and Reports, p. 34. Contacts: (1) Governor's Office, Dennis Taylor, Chief of Staff, State Capitol, Topeka, KS 66612; 913-296-3232. (2) Ray Siehndel, Secretary of Human Resources, State of Kansas, 401 S. Topeka, Topeka, KS 66612; 913-296-7474. (3) Kansas Department of Commerce, Harland Priddle, 400 W. 8th, Topeka, KS 66612; 913-296-3480.

3. "Pentagon's Proposals: Base Closures, Reductions," *USA Today*, January 30, 1990, p. 8.

4. *Loc. cit.*

5. James Coates, "Army Puts Squeeze on Small Towns," *The Chicago Tribune,* April 29, 1990, p. 21.

6. Robert Hershey, "Easing Business Cycles: the Wichita Experience," *The New York Times,* Dec. 14, 1989, p. D-11. Alissa Rubin, "Defense Fable Has a Kansas Twang," *The Wichita Eagle*, May 5, 1990.

Kentucky

A	B	C	D	E	F
$	👷	🏭	📅	VI	DDI
+	+	−	→	!	✂

Benchmarks	No.	Rank	Benchmarks	No.	Rank
A.Total DoD $	$1.6bil.	32	Def. Dependent Jobs ('000), '90	88	32
B. Personnel Payroll	$1.2bil.	21	Change in Def.-Dep. Jobs, '89-'91	-6.4%	26
C. Prime Contracts (PC)	$0.4bil.	39	Unemployment Rate, '90-'91	7.3%	13
D. PC Change, FY '87-'90	-14.4%	28	Unemp. Rate Change, '89-'91	+0.8%	29
E. Vulnerability Index	8.5	31	Per Capita Income	$14,929	44
F. Defense Disloc. Index	1.26	21	Population ('000)	3,685	24

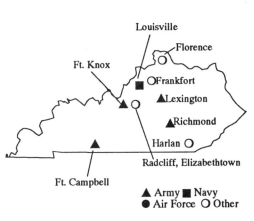

Louisville
Florence
Ft. Knox
Frankfort
Lexington
Richmond
Harlan
Radcliff, Elizabethtown
Ft. Campbell

▲ Army ■ Navy
● Air Force ○ Other

Prime Contract Trends, FY'87-'90
(Constant FY '92 $Billions)

'87 $0.6b	'88 $0.5b	'89 $0.4b	'90 $0.5b

Top 5 Contractors	$ Millions
E Systems	$133.3
Keco Industries	33.2
Freeway Truck Sales	17.9
U.S. Dep't Justice	17.7
Grasseto & Incisa USA	12.2

Top 10 $ Sites[a]	Congressional Dist., Representative	1989 Rank	Total DoD$[c]	Payroll[c]	Prime Contracts[c]	Personnel[d]
1-Ft. Campbell (78)	1-Hubbard, d	53	$488.0	$452.8	$35.2	20.4
2-Ft. Knox (112)	2-Natcher, d	59	349.5	278.2	71.3	15.9
3-Lexington (168)	6-Hopkins, r	305	217.0	55.7	161.3	1.2
4-Louisville (176)	3-Mazzoli, d	183	203.1	150.2	52.8	4.4
5-Florence (367)	4-Bunning, r	371	34.8	1.3	33.5	--
6-Richmond (404)	6-Hopkins, r	397	21.9	21.3	0.6	0.5
7-Radcliff (411)	2-Natcher, d	404	20.4	20.3	0.1	--
8-Frankfort (417)	6-Hopkins, r	407	18.7	18.5	0.2	0.3
9-Elizabethtown (434)	2-Natcher	428	13.5	12.9	0.6	--
10-Harlan (439)	5-Rogers, r	--	12.4	0.2	12.2	--

[a]*Rating in parentheses is out of 511 sites, the top ten in each state and PR, plus DC.*
[b]*Multidistrict r-Rep, d-Dem.* [c]*$Millions (figures may not add due to rounding)* [d]*Thousands*

Kentucky

The Kentucky economy experienced a strong recovery between 1982 and 1988, bouncing back from a severe recession suffered in the early 1980s. Although the state outpaced the nation's employment growth in the second half of the 1980s, the effects of the recession are still felt in Kentucky pocketbooks. The state's April 1991 unemployment rate ranked 13th highest in country and its change in unemployment 29th highest (labor force growth outstripped employment growth). Kentucky's economy is dependent on the manufacturing sectors, which led both the recession of 1979-83 and the recovery of 1983-88, while the services-producing sector has shown limited growth. The post-industrial economy over the next century, according to the University of Kentucky's Center for Business & Economic Research, will have more emphasis on high-tech, services-producing industries than on manufacturing.[1]

A portent for the future is the basing of the United Parcel Service's national distribution center in Louisville. Companies interested in rapid distribution of their products, such as medical supply companies, are following UPS to Louisville.

Defense and the Economy

Only 20 "states" received fewer Department of Defense dollars than Kentucky's $1.6 billion in 1990. Despite this relatively low amount, Kentucky's high unemployment rate and current economic base make it quite vulnerable to cutbacks. In this light, the good news for the state is that the Department of Defense has not proposed significant spending cutbacks here. The procurement contracts most common in the state, including fuel and construction, will remain important to the changing defense needs of the country. Although personnel cuts slated for state bases are certainly weighty, they represent only a moderate dent in Kentucky's large military payroll.

Although Kentucky firms receive only 0.3 percent of total Department of Defense procurement programs, they obtain nearly one-fourth of defense spending for non-petroleum fuel. This makes Kentucky the most important site of defense procurement for non-petroleum fuel. Louisville Gas & Electric alone receives over $10 million.

Community Surveys

Most defense spending is concentrated in the Louisville/Frankfort/Lexington triangle, which encompasses Fort Knox. Local officials expect this area to be the hardest hit by cuts. Two bases in the area, and another one just over the

Ohio River in Indiana, are scheduled for closure or cutback according to Defense Secretary Dick Cheney's proposals.[2]

Lexington. The Bluegrass Army Depot is being closed. Thirty-seven military and 1,131 civilian jobs will be lost.

Louisville. The Louisville Naval Ordnance Station was among the bases recommended for closure by Secretary Cheney. The station employs about 2,350 civilians, many of whom have been there for over 30 years.[3] As of early 1991 Louisville Airport was one of the finalists in the United Air Lines competition to find a new location for an aircraft maintenance facility; the Naval Ordnance Station could serve such a function. Most recently, the Base Closure Commission has recommended that the station be realigned. The station would continue to be a major operating site but slightly fewer than 300 positions would be lost.

Fort Knox has 12,000 permanently assigned military personnel and 5,760 soldiers from the 194th Armored Brigade. President Bush has proposed to cut 3,000 soldiers from the 194th and about one-fourth of the permanently assigned personnel. Fort Knox also houses the Armor and Engineer Board, which the Army has provisionally decided to move to Fort Hood, Texas, resulting in a further loss of 168 military and 125 civilian personnel. Troops currently in Europe could be reassigned to Fort Knox, depending on U.S.-Soviet conventional-arms accords and initiatives.[4]

Notes

1. Lawrence Lynch, "The Kentucky Economy: A Performance Assessment," *Kentucky 1989 Annual Economic Report*, Center for Business & Economic Research at the University of Kentucky, p.10.

2. *Prime Contract Awards by Region and State, Fiscal Years 1989, 1988, 1987*, Department of Defense, Washington Headquarters Services, Directorate for Information, Operations and Reports, p. 35. "Louisville Area to be Hit Hard by Defense Cuts," *Harlan Daily Enterprise*, January 30, 1990. Contacts: (1) Governor's Office, David Lovelace, Administrative Assistant, State Capitol, Frankfort, KY 40601; 502-564-2611. (2) Cabinet of Human Resources, State of Kentucky, Edward Blackwell, 275 E. Main Street, Frankfort, KY 40601; 502-564-7976. (3) Kentucky Budget Office, Merl Hackbart, Budget Director, Capitol Annex, Frankfort, KY 40601; 502-564-7300. (4) Kentucky Department of Economic Development, Gene Royalty, Capitol Plaza Tower, Frankfort, KY 40601; 502-564-7670. (5) Louisville Office of the Mayor, Jerry E. Abramson, Mayor, 601 W. Jefferson St., Louisville, KY 40202-2728; 502-625-3061.

3. "Louisville Area...," *loc. cit.*

4. Greg Kocher, "Fort Knox's Role Changing," *Elizabethtown News Enterprise*, March 14, 1990, p. 1.

Louisiana

A	B	C	D	E	F
$				VI	DDI
+	+	+	→	!	✂

Benchmarks	No.	Rank	Benchmarks	No.	Rank
A.Total DoD $	$2.8bil.	21	Def.-Dependent Jobs ('000), '90	149	21
B. Personnel Payroll	$1.2bil.	20	Change in Def.-Dep. Jobs, '89-'91	-5.1%	29
C. Prime Contracts (PC)	$1.6bil.	21	Unemployment Rate, '90-'91	6.3%	26
D. PC Change, FY '87-'90	-13.1%	30	Unemp. Rate Change, '89-'91	-2.3%	52
E. Vulnerability Index	9.5	26	Per Capita Income	$14,931	46
F. Defense Disloc. Index	0.93	24	Population ('000)	4,220	21

O Bossier City
O ▲Louisiana AAP
Shreveport
● England AFB
▲ Ft. Polk
O Baton Rouge
OLake Charles
N. Orleans
▲ Army ■ Navy
● Air Force O Other
Lockport Harvey

Prime Contract Trends, FY'87-'90
(Constant FY '92 $Billions)

'87 $2.0b	'88 $1.7b	'89 $1.9b	'90 $1.8b

Top 5 Contractors	$ Millions
Avondale Industries	$468.8
Textron	214.6
Bollinger Shipyard	166.8
Thiokol	126.3
Exxon	107.7

Top 10 $ Sites[a]	Congressional Dist., Representative	1989 Rank	Total DoD$[c]	Payroll[c]	Prime Contracts[c]	Per-sonnel[d]
1-New Orleans (44)	(1,2)[b]	33	$815.6	$175.6	$640.0	5.3
2-Ft. Polk (114)	4-McCrery, r	77	347.2	331.3	16.0	15.0
3-Bossier City (161)	"	163	240.7	221.4	19.3	--
4-Lockport (205)	3-Tauzin, d	--	166.9	0.2	166.8	--
5-Baton Rouge (219)	(6,8)[b]	245	142.1	18.0	124.1	0.1
6-Lake Charles (221)	7-Hayes, d	230	139.8	13.1	126.7	.09
7-Louisiana AAP (222)	4-McCrery, r	267	138.8	0	138.8	--
8-Shreveport (263)	"	219	105.9	28.7	77.1	0.2
9-England AFB (283)	8-Holloway, r	275	86.2	79.7	6.5	3.5
10-Harvey (303)	(1,3)[b]	--	74.8	3.9	70.9	--

[a]Rating in parentheses is out of 511 sites, the top ten in each state and PR, plus DC.
[b]Multidistrict r-Rep, d-Dem. [c]$Millions (figures may not add due to rounding) [d]Thousands

Louisiana

The decade of the 1980s was a tough one for the Louisiana economy, particularly in rural areas, as the recession created massive unemployment and resulted in a population decline in the middle of the decade. The real per capita income actually fell in five of the years from 1981-1988.[1] The Louisiana Department of Economic Development expects a gradual upturn in the economy, particularly in industrial investment and manufacturing. The apparel, chemical, and paper industries have all been on the rise in recent years. Finance/banking/real estate is the sector that will be the greatest drag to the state economy. Projections for 1991 see growth of less than 1 percent in real per capita income. The state's unemployment rate ranked a moderate 26th in April 1991 and its change in unemployment came 52nd as the most favorable in the country (employment increased while the labor force contracted slightly).

Defense and the Economy

The Department of Defense spent over $2.8 billion in Louisiana in 1990.[2] The state receives 5.4 percent of its total revenue from the Department of Defense, a significant, but not overwhelming figure. Secretary Cheney proposed the cancellation of an M-1 missile contract in Louisiana. Other recommendations from outside the Department of Defense call for cutting back much more spending in Louisiana. William Kaufmann's 1990 plan involves the cancellation of a LSD-41 Variant (an attack landing vehicle) program worth over $183 million in prime contracts to the state.

State Legislative Iniatives

The Governor's Commission on Military Affairs was created in the summer of 1990. Its creation was partially motivated by Louisiana's eagerness to be the new location for the military's Southern Command Post now that the Department of Defense has decided to move its location from Panama to the U.S. The state has begun dealing with the impact of defense cuts. It is helping workers who were laid off when a defense contractor's plane repair facility closed; it is also looking into commercial uses for the closed plant.[3]

Community Surveys

Most of the money Louisiana firms received from the Department of Defense in 1990 was for ship construction. Only four states received more defense shipbuilding business than Louisiana. In New Orleans, Avondale industries alone received $469 million in FY 1990 for construction of cargo and tanker vessels. The Department of Defense's demand for such bulk ships tends to be relatively stable even as defense needs change, since cargo and tanker ships also have significant civilian use potential. Another important defense-related industry in Louisiana is non-petroleum fuel, which also will continue to have a steady demand in both the military and civilian sectors.[4]

Alexandria. England Air Force Base will close. One squadron will move to McChord AFB in Washington and another to Eglin AFB in Florida; all other units will be retired. The decision to eliminate England AFB rested on its weather and limited airspace disadvantages. Regional impact will be severe: 5,700 of 60,000 local jobs could be lost and annual regional income of $1.5 billion could decline by $97 million.[5]

Lake Charles. The Naval Station was targeted for closure by the Base Commission in 1988. The station has approximately 100 employees

Leesville. Realignment of Fort Polk calls for the transfer of the 5th Infantry Division to Fort Hood, TX and the movement of the Joint Readiness Training Center from Fort Chaffee, AR to Polk. The Army hopes to save $23 million annually by the concentration of divisions in Texas. However, the smaller force in Leesville may result in 25 percent fewer jobs.[6] On the other hand, more than 2,000 troops coming back from Europe might be transferred to Polk.

New Orleans. The Military Ocean Terminal was slated for closure in 1988. Inadequate piers limited the terminal's future usefulness. Environmental cleanup may be necessary.

Shreveport. Sen. J. Bennett Johnston (D-LA) managed to restore $238 million in funding for a new "RDX" ammunition plant in the city. More than $300 million was spent on the plant in 1988 and 1989. The facility is built to make TNT compounds that are currently manufactured in Kingston, TN. However, there is no guarantee that the new plant will go into operation even if it is completed. One plan calls for mothballing it pending "wartime need."[7]

Notes

1. Loren C. Scott and James A. Richardson, *The Louisiana Economic Outlook: 1990 and 1991*, The Louisiana Bankers Association, October 1989.

2. *Atlas/Data Abstract for the United States and Selcted Areas Fiscal 1990*, Department of Defense, by Washington Headquarters Services, Directorate for Information, Operations and Reports, p. 53.

3. *Status of State Economic Conversion Activity*, March 28, 1991, compiled by the National Governors' Association, p. 2. Contacts: (1) Louisiana Department of Economic Development, Nadia L. Goodman, Director Policy and Planning, P.O. Box 94185, Baton Rouge, LA 70804; 504-342-5359. (2) Louisiana Office of Labor Secretary, Phyllis Mouton, P.O. Box 94094, Baton Rouge, LA 70804-9094; 504-342-3111.

4. *Atlas...*, *loc. cit.* Also: *Prime Contract Awards by Region and State, Fiscal Years 1987, 1988, 1989*, Department of Defense, Washington Headquarters Services, Directorate for Information, Operations and Reports, p. 69.

5. *Base Closure and Realignment Report*, Department of Defense. April 1991, pp. 96-97.

6. *Ibid.*, pp. 46-47.

7. Dan Morgan, "Of Swords, Plowshares and ...Pork," *The Washington Post*, May 2, 1990, p. 21.

Maine

A	B	C	D	E	F
$	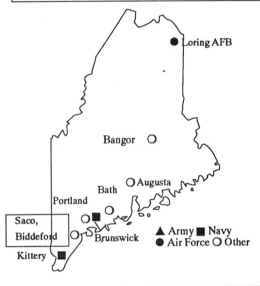			VI	DDI
+	+	+	→	!!	✂

Benchmarks	No.	Rank	Benchmarks	No.	Rank
A. Total DoD $	$1.5bil.	34	Def.-Dependent Jobs ('000), '90	79	33
B. Personnel Payroll	$0.7bil.	34	Change in Def.-Dep. Jobs, '89-'91	+58.0%	51
C. Prime Contracts (PC)	$0.8bil.	30	Unemployment Rate, '90-'91	8.5%	4
D. PC Change, FY '87-'90	-8.6%	36	Unemp. Rate Change, '89-'91	+3.9%	4
E. Vulnerability Index	12.4	8	Per Capita Income	$17,200	29
F. Defense Disloc. Index	1.42	19	Population ('000)	1,228	39

Prime Contract Trends, FY'87-'90
(Constant FY '92 $Billions)

'87 $1.0b '88 $0.6b '89 $0.4b '90 $0.9b

Top 5 Contractors	$ Millions
Bath Holding	$733.9
Duchossois	41.7
Fiber Materials	8.8
Maine Public Service	3.4
Asea Brown Boveri	3.2

▲ Army ■ Navy
● Air Force ○ Other

Top 10 $ Sites[a]	Congressional Dist., Representative	1989 Rank	Total DoD$[c]	Payroll[c]	Prime Contracts[c]	Per-sonnel[d]
1-Bath (49)	1-Andrews,d	161	$755.4	$23.9	$731.5	0.4
2-Kittery (151)	"	149	259.2	256.5	2.6	8.1
3-Brunswick (271)	"	272	97.9	97.3	0.6	--
4-Loring AFB (273)	2-Snowe,r	247	97.0	81.5	15.4	3.6
5-Saco (339)	1-Andrews,d	343	44.1	2.2	41.9	--
6-Bangor (381)	2-Snowe,r	406	30.5	23.9	6.6	0.7
7-Portland (426)	1-Andrews,d	375	15.2	8.4	6.9	--
8-Biddeford (445)	"	441	10.1	1.2	8.9	--
9-Augusta (453)	"	--	8.6	8.1	0.6	0.2
10-Brunswick NAS (467)	"	272	6.3	0.0	6.3	1.6

[a]Rating in parentheses is out of 511 sites, the top ten in each state and PR, plus DC.
[b]Multidistrict r-Rep, d-Dem. [c]$Millions (figures may not add due to rounding) [d]Thousands

Maine

Like the rest of the Northeast, Maine was hard hit by a recession in 1990-1991. State workers have been laid off and budget cuts of 15 percent were projected for some state departments. Unemployment and change in unemployment ranked 4th highest in the nation (labor force growth has been outpacing employment growth. The state possesses a diverse manufacturing base (which includes a large lumber industry), but manufacturing employment remained stagnant from 1982-1988. The construction, finance, and retail trade sectors of the economy have been growing fast.

Defense and the Economy

Maine calls itself "vacationland," because its largest single industry is tourism. If it went to its second largest source of revenue, it would have to refer to itself as "defenseland." For every two dollars generated by the tourism industry, the state economy relies on one dollar from the Department of Defense. According to the Maine Peace Mission, the $1.5 billion that the Department of Defense spends in the state (34th highest of the 52 "states" including DC and Puerto Rico) amounts to 8 percent of the state's gross state product. One out of 11 people in the state, or 9 percent of the workforce, is dependent on defense spending. The Department of Defense spends $640 million in payroll alone in a state in which only six employers have payrolls of over 1,000 workers. This acute defense dependence makes Maine vulnerable to defense cutbacks. The cuts in prime contracts to Maine firms proposed by Defense Secretary Dick Cheney are relatively minor, but the state stands to lose a significant number of uniformed personnel.

State Legislative Initiatives

A major organizing force in the state is the Maine Peace Economy Project, run by Susie Schweppe (pronounced SHWEPPY), 50 Thornhurst Road, Falmouth, ME 04105; 207-781-3947. In July 1990, under pressure from the high-visibility Project, Gov. John R. McKernan, Jr. established the Governor's Task Force on Defense Realignment and the Maine Economy, aimed at anticipating defense cuts. The Task Force received a grant of $150,000 in early 1991 to write up a proposal for state conversion programs, and is due to produce a report at the end of 1991. The Project recommended at a June hearing of the Task Force that it call for (1) establishing conversion committees in every defense-dependent community, (2) undertaking a statewide conversion-planning process, and (3) appointing a citizens' advisory board.

About 50 Maine towns and cities have adopted the Project's "Reinvest in Hometown America" resolution, which calls on Congress and the President to endorse conversion. The state legislature is scheduled to consider the resolution in 1991.[1]

The Project has also been working with Local 6 of the International Association of Machinists and Aerospace Workers to develop a labor skills bank. It is active in Bath and commissioned *A Shift in Federal Spending: What the Peace Dividend Can Mean to Maine, 1990* from Employment Research Associates.

Community Surveys

The ultimate impact of the defense cuts on Maine's economy depends on the status of the building and repairing industry of Navy ships after the full scope of defense cuts has been decided in 1991 and 1992. In addition, the status of the Tomahawk missile is significant as all ships built in Maine carry the Tomahawk. Although an Air Guard station in Bangor is scheduled for personnel reductions, the Air Force, which employed 64 percent of total active duty personnel in Maine in 1989, will remain a large economic presence in the state.[2]

Alfred. Alfred is the county seat of York County, the southernmost county in Maine. Many York County residents are dependent on the Port of Portsmouth, the Portsmouth Naval Shipyard, and the Pease Air Force Base, all of them across the state line in New Hampshire. The KEYS Coalition has been formed to bring together interested groups in York County to support strategic planning about the future of the southern Maine economy. For this purpose the Southern Maine Regional Planning Commission has applied for a planning grant to the Office of Economic Adjustment in the Department of Defense. David R. Adjutant is administrator of York County, York County Courthouse, Alfred, ME; 207-324-1571.[3]

Bath. Bath Iron Works, with 11,500 blue- and white-collar workers on the payroll, builds Aegis cruisers and destroyers for the Navy, brings in $734 million in defense contracts and has a $250 million annual state payroll. The facility produces ships exclusively for military use, and, despite a vigorous effort to obtain commercial contracts, is not building or planning to build a single ocean-going merchant ship. The company announced it would eliminate 2,400 jobs by 1993. The Bath Iron Works CEO, Duane (Buzz) Fitzgerald, is extremely open to conversion ideas. The dissenting voice in upper management resigned in September 1991.

The Maine Peace Economy Project helped set up the area's Economic Conversion Task Force in 1991 to promote economic diversification in the very defense-dependent region which hosts Bath Iron Works and Brunswick Naval Air Station. Social service groups and governments are represented on the Task Force along with defense contractors and other businesses. The Task Force is chaired by David Gleason of Coldwell Banker/Gleason Realty (207-725-8522) and set its goals as providing community support for the base and developing contingency re-use plans. In mid-1991 it was focusing on making use of land not being used by the Navy, for example by setting up a science and technology center or a recycling center.[4]

Limestone. The appearance of Loring Air Force Base–home to B-52 bombers–on the Base Closure Commission's recommended closures list in July 1991 shocked local residents, who have successfully fought attempts to close the base over the last 20 years. The Department of Defense picked Loring for elimination because of its limited tank utility and limited access to bombing ranges. Residents have formed the Save Loring Committee, which argues that closure would devastate Aroostook County since one-in-six jobs and 25 percent of regional income depend on the base. Members of Maine's congressional delegation have vowed to fight for Loring based on the role it played in the Gulf War and its importance to Limestone. The base appears on the EPA's National Priorities List because contamination by solvents and other toxics threaten the local water supply. Under Federal regulations, commercial re-use of the facility must wait until cleanup is complete.[5]

Saco. Saco Defense employs 750-800 out of total population of 17,000, and the town is also near the Portsmouth Naval Shipyard. The defense cuts could mean a possible 25 percent reduction in Saco Defense if the MK-19 Grenade Launcher is cut, making development officials concerned, but the planning is only in the talking stage.[6]

Notes

1. Janet Stone, *Conversion Organizers' Update* (Mountain View, CA: Center for Economic Conversion, October 1991, advance copy), pp. 3-4. Contacts: (1) Governor's Office, Harriet Dawson, Special Assistant, State House, Augusta, ME 04333; 207-289-3531. (2) Maine Department of Economic Development, Lynn Wachtel, Commissioner, SHS #59, Augusta, ME 04333; 207-289-2656. (3) Maine Department of Labor, Alice Kirkpatrick, SHS #54, Augusta, ME 04333; 207-289-3788. (4) Governor's Task Force on Defense Realignment and the Maine Economy, State Planning Office, Richard Silkman, Director of Planning, and Stephen J. Adams, State Economist, State House, Augusta, ME 04333; 207-289-3261.

2. William Kennedy, –Tremors at Maine Defense Sites," The Christian Science Monitor, December 19, 1989, p. 6. Peace Economy Project, "National Priorities are a Local Issue," *Peace Talk*, Summer 1990, p. 5.

3. Stone, *op. cit.*, p. 5.

4. *Ibid.*, pp. 4-5. Susie Schweppe, "Pinching the Pentagon," *Plowshares Press,* Spring 1990, p. 8. Kennedy, *loc. cit.*, p. 6. Besides Gleason, another active member of the Task Force is Wanda Plumer, Brunswick Chamber of Commerce, 207-725-8797.

5. *Base Closure and Realignment Report. Department of Defense.* April 1991, pp. 99-100. Denise Goodman, "Loring AFB in Maine also slated for closure," *The Boston Globe*, April 13, 1991, p. 51.

6. Interview in March, 1990 with Larry Mitchell, City Administrator, Saco, ME, 207-284-4831.

Maryland

A	B	C	D	E	F
$	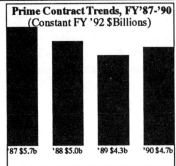			VI	DDI
+	+	+	→	‼	✂

Benchmarks	No.	Rank	Benchmarks	No.	Rank
A. Total DoD $	$7.2bil.	7	Def.-Dependent Jobs ('000), '90	396	8
B. Personnel Payroll	$2.8bil.	8	Change in Def.-Dep. Jobs, '89-'91	+4.8%	41
C. Prime Contracts (PC)	$4.4bil.	9	Unemployment Rate, '90-'91	5.6%	37
D. PC Change, FY '87-'90	-17.1%	25	Unemp. Rate Change, '89-'91	+2.0%	13
E. Vulnerability Index	12.2	11	Per Capita Income	$21,864	6
F. Defense Disloc. Index	3.52	9	Population ('000)	4,781	19

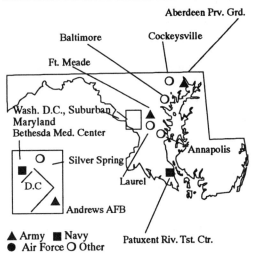

Aberdeen Prv. Grd.
Baltimore
Cockeysville
Ft. Meade
Wash. D.C., Suburban
Maryland
Bethesda Med. Center
Silver Spring
Annapolis
D.C
Laurel
Andrews AFB
▲ Army ■ Navy
● Air Force ○ Other
Patuxent Riv. Tst. Ctr.

Prime Contract Trends, FY '87-'90
(Constant FY '92 $Billions)

'87 $5.7b	'88 $5.0b	'89 $4.3b	'90 $4.7b

Top 5 Contractors	$ Millions
Westinghouse	$1,284.3
Johns Hopkins Univ.	374.8
Allied Signal	198.1
Martin Marietta	186.5
IBM	179.4

Top 10 $ Sites[a]	Congressional Dist., Representative	1989 Rank	Total DoD$[c]	Payroll[c]	Prime Contracts[c]	Personnel[d]
1-Baltimore (22)	(3,7)[b]	38	$1,199.4	$83.5	$1,115.9	2.1
2-Bethesda (76)	8-	72	494.0	233.8	260.2	7.0
3-Aberdeen (92)	1-Gilchrest, d	74	435.6	308.9	126.7	11.6
4-Laurel (98)	5-Hoyer, d	112	393.2	13.0	380.3	--
5-Andrews AFB (115)	4-McMillen, d	120	345.4	297.1	48.2	9.2
6-Annapolis (119)	"	121	333.4	202.8	130.6	8.7
7-Patuxent River (123)	1-Gilchrest, r	140	322.9	204.6	118.4	6.2
8-Cockeysville (124)	2-	--	322.2	4.3	317.8	--
9-Ft. Meade (141)	5-Hoyer, d	110	279.9	251.2	28.7	9.3
10-Silver Spring (146)	8-	126	269.9	23.2	246.7	--

[a]Rating in parentheses is out of 511 sites, the top ten in each state and PR, plus DC.
[b]Multidistrict r-Rep, d-Dem. [c]$Millions (figures may not add due to rounding) [d]Thousands

Maryland

Maryland is an extremely productive state, one of eight to receive the top Triple-A bond rating. Its largest manufacturing sector is printing and publishing, employing 14 percent of all manufacturing workers. The unemployment rate in Maryland ranked 37th highest and its change in unemployment 13th (the labor force grew while employment declined slightly). Its per capita income in 1990 of $21,864 was 6th highest and its median household income in 1989 of $35,185 was 3rd highest.[1]

Defense and the Economy

Although defense-contract awards to Maryland decreased in the latter half of the 1980s, Department of Defense revenues still represent a high 6.8 percent of the gross state product. Maryland is home to 27 defense-related Federal facilities, which employ 43,000 civilian personnel and 37,500 military personnel.[2]

Maryland ranks high in both the Vulnerability Index (11th) and Defense Dislocation Index (9th). Maryland subcontractors are extensively involved in 20 weapons systems scheduled for cuts, including the F-14 and F-15 fighter-jet programs.[3]

A study by the state's Department of Economic and Employment Development (DEED, Robert N. Schoeplein, Director, Office of Research, 217 East Redwood Street, 11th Floor, Baltimore, MD 21202; 301-333-6497) contends that Maryland firms are relatively well placed to absorb cuts, because the high-tech electronics industries are unlikely to experience sharp declines in demand. DEED considers it important to offer retraining and to make every effort to ensure continued availability of skilled workers, especially engineers and scientists. The report urges state action to assist small contractors, subcontractors, and suppliers because "most [are] vulnerable to cuts... [and] do not have strategic plans to alleviate their defense dependency." It noted that many major contractors are beginning to diversify.[4]

DEED teamed up with the Governor's office to assess the impact of a shrinking defense budget on the state. Among their preliminary recommendations are: (1) Design state procurement programs for high-technology items and encourage defense contractors to diversify; (2) Encourage major contractors to set up entrepreneurial ventures as a diversification strategy, funding numerous small, high-tech start-ups that need capital; (3) Lobby Congress for easing of restrictions on high-tech exports; and (4) Initiate training programs for prime and subcontractors in areas such as advanced production and computer languages.[5]

State Legislative and Executive Initiatives

Legislation in 1990 to establish a Maryland Task Force on Economic Conversion was defeated. In the 1991 session, HB 544 would have required the state government to target state needs with the "peace dividend." It died in committee.[6]

DEED has published *The Defense Industry and the Maryland Economy*, an excellent study that explains the state's defense involvement and offers recommendations for defense-oriented companies, especially small contractors and subcontractors. All states with high defense dependence should conduct a study like this one.

Community Surveys

DEED fears regional economies such as Harford, Charles, and St. Mary's counties could be affected, but labor reductions by major contractors are in "labor-critical areas" and the workers will be likely to find new work soon. The state is vulnerable to personnel reductions at the bases but if all the 1991 decisions of the Base Closure and Realignment Commission are adhered to, the southern half of the state could gain in personnel on a net basis.

Aberdeen Proving Ground. The Base Closure Commission in 1988 recommended closure of the Nike Site here and adding army researchg functions previously located in Virginia and Massachusetts. About 65 positions would be eliminated 294 added. Aberdeen is an EPA Superfund sight because of contamination by mustard gas and other chemicals. Local residents are worried that the Army is foot-dragging in its efforts at cleanup.[7]

Adelphi. The Department of Defense wants to realign the Harry Diamond Laboratories as part of its effort to streamline Army laboratories nation-wide. The Department expects the move will result in 0.1 percent more jobs in Adelphi.[8]

Annapolis. The David Taylor Research Center Detachment will be realigned. The government's plans call for the elimination or transfer (to Philadelphia or Carderock, MD) of 655 out of 973 jobs.[9]

Baltimore. On the defense-contract side, during the 1989-90 period, AAI Corp., developer and manufacturer of a variety of military systems, eliminated 1,000 jobs at its Baltimore County operations in Cockeysville, north of the city. Westinghouse Electric Corp., located near Baltimore's Friendship International Airport, was relatively unscathed by the cuts, but reduced its workforce by 500 in during the 1988-90 period and in 1991 its future depended on the need for its Airborne Self-Protection Jammer for fighter planes. In February 1991 Westinghouse laid off 1,200 people after Defense Secretary Dick Cheney cancelled the A-12 attack jet. The Metalcraft Corp. will be hurt by cuts in the Apache helicopter program.

On the military-base side, Fort Meade, the second largest location of personnel in the state, was targeted for cuts in 1988.

At the U.S. Conference of Mayors, Mayor Kurt Schmoke of Baltimore successfully called for the formation of an Urban Economic Policy Committee and in May 1990 he chaired its first meeting, calling on the Federal Government to use the funds freed up from the defense budget to help meet human and social needs. The Office of the Mayor (Erica Lindsay, 100 N. Holliday Street, Balti-more, MD 21202) published its annual report of the Baltimore City Develop-ment Commission on the impact of military spending in November 1990.

Baltimore Jobs with Peace (Katherine "Sissy" Corr, 100 S. Washington Street, Baltimore, MD 21231, 301-342-7404) helped create the Economic Conversion Committee of the Baltimore City Development Commission (Dick Ullrich, 301-366-1324), which met with the entire Maryland Congressional Delegation in early 1991 to lobby for a Peace Dividend and national conversion legislation. Led by Jobs with Peace, with the endorsement of Mayor Schmoke and the U.S. Conference of Mayors, more than 80 local organizations were working on a "Save Our Cities" march to Washington scheduled for October 12, 1991.[10]

Camp Springs. About 900 jobs at Andrews Air Force Base, near Camp Springs and Marlow Heights, MD south of Washington, DC are being termi-nated as the Air Force Systems Command Headquarters moves to Ohio in late 1991. Employees are being given the option of relocating to Ohio.[11]

Frederick. Fort Detrick was one of the few winners in the 1989 Base Closure Act, which called for the construction of an Army research institute at the base. The Department of Defense now wants to cancel that construction project and, additionally, disestablish the Biomedical Research Development Lab. There is a potential employment loss of 0.8 percent to the region.[12]

Hunt Valley. AAI Corp. has announced it is laying off 225 workers because of defense-contract cuts.[13]

Indian Head. The Naval Ordnance Station will be realigned by a merger with the Industrial Base Division in Crane, IN. As many as 610 positions could be lost. Maryland lawmakers hope to save this research facility and two others (in Silver Spring and St. Inigoes) by arguing that the Department of Defense should not evaluate research labs in the base-closure process. They argue that since Congress already established a commission on the future of military research, the Department of Defense does not have jurisdiction to terminate them.[14]

Middle River. Martin Marietta, the huge defense corporation based in Bethesda, has eliminated some 1,300 jobs at its Middle River complex since mid-1989.[15] The cancellation of the Sea-Lance missile program is significant to the Middle River facility.

Salisbury. Five hundred jobs could be lost by the phasing out of the F-14 program. Similar situations could occur at Glen Arm and Towson.[16]

Silver Spring. The Naval Surface Warfare Center Detachment, White Oak, a research center dealing with explosives, warheads, and mines, will be realigned. It is slated to lose about 1,250 of 1,800 jobs; most will be transferred to the Detachment's mother organization in Dahlgren, VA.[17]

Towson. The Mark XV Identification Friend or Foe System at the Allied-Signal Aerospace Co. is in danger of being cancelled in future budget cuts, which could result in the laying off of many workers from the facility in Towson. The company has said it would have to lay off 225 workers if the $4.5 billion project is cancelled.[18] The production of Apache helicopters at the Towson Allied-Signal facility is being cut.

Notes

1. *The Maryland Economy 1989*, Maryland Department of Economic and Employment Development, pp. 3-5. Helga Weschke, Joel Lee, Teresa Moore, Pradeep Ganguly, and Susan Sanabria, *The Defense Industry and the Maryland Economy*, Maryland Department of Economic and Employment Development, April 1990, p. 7.

2. Sandra Sugawara, "Defense Contract Awards Fall in Va., Md., and D.C.," *The Washington Post*, February 24, 1990, p. D-12. Richard Tapscott, "Study: Maryland Can Endure Defense Cuts," *The Washington Post*, April 24, 1990, p. D1.

3. Kent Jenkins, Jr., "Despite 1,500 Job Cuts, Region Gains Under Base Plan," *The Washington Post*, July 2, 1991, p. 4.

4. Tapscott, *Loc. cit.*, and Weschke et al., *op. cit.*, pp. ii-iii.

5. Weschke et al., *op. cit.*, pp. 8-12.

6. Contacts: (1) Governor's Office, Teresa Moore, Assistant to the Governor, State House, Annapolis, MD 21404; 301-974-3004. (2) Business Development, State of Maryland, James Pfeiffer, Director, 217 E. Redwood St., 10th Floor, Baltimore, MD 21202; 301-333-6985. (3) Labor Market Analysis, State of Maryland, Pat Arnold, 11 N. Eutaw St., Baltimore, MD 21201; 301-333-5000. (4) Maryland Department of Economic and Employment Development, Helga Weschke, 217 East Redwood Street, Baltimore, MD 21202; 301-333-6947. (5) Development Commission, William Burke, Chair, City of Baltimore, Room 250, City Hall, Baltimore, MD 21202.

7. *Base Closure and Realignment Report*, Department of Defense, April 1991, pp. 49-50. Samuel Goldreich, "Residents Doubtful of Plans to Clean Site at Proving Ground," *The Baltimore Sun*, July 26, 1991, p. B8.

8. *Base Closure...*, *loc. cit.*

9. *Ibid.*, p. 81.

10. Ted Shelsby, "AAI Lays Off About 225 Employees," *The Baltimore Sun*, April 6, 1990, p. 1B; Shelsby, "Maryland Defense Contracts Down 9.4 Percent in 1989," *The Baltimore Sun*, March 27, 1990, p. 13. Anne Swardson, "Westinghouse Plan Aids Laid-Off Workers in Maryland," *The Washington Post*, February 7, 1991, p. E1. Janet Stone, *Conversion Organizers Update* (Mountain View, CA: Center for Economic Conversion, October 1991, advance copy), p. 5.

11. Lisa Leff, "Andrews Due to Lose 900 Jobs," *The Washington Post*, January 11, 1991, p. C1.

12. *Base Closure...*, *op. cit.*, pp. 51-52.

13. Tapscott, *op. cit.*, p. D-1.

14. *Base Closure...*, *op. cit.*, p. 82. "Many Jobs Threatened by Proposed Spending Cuts at Navy Research Labs," *The Baltimore Sun*, June 9, 1991, p. 10B.

15. Shelsby, "Maryland Defense Contracts...," *loc. cit.*

16. Ted Shelsby, "Defense Contractors in Maryland Only Grazed in Budget War," *The Baltimore Sun*, December 10, 1989, p. 1-C.

17. Stacey Evers, "What's Behind Quiet Facade Could Blow Your Mind," *The Baltimore Sun*, May 6, 1991, p. C-3.

18. Tapscott, *loc. cit.*

Massachusetts

A	B	C	D	E	F
$				VI	DDI
✚	+	✚	➡	‼	✂

Benchmarks	No.	Rank	Benchmarks	No.	Rank
A.Total DoD $	$9.1bil.	5	Def.-Dependent Jobs ('000), '90	551	4
B. Personnel Payroll	$0.9bil.	28	Change in Def.-Dep. Jobs, '89-'91	-9.8%	16
C. Prime Contracts (PC)	$8.2bil.	3	Unemployment Rate, '90-'91	8.3%	5
D. PC Change, FY '87-'90	-15.4%	26	Unemp. Rate Change, '89-'91	+4.6%	1
E. Vulnerability Index	13.2	5	Per Capita Income	$22,642	4
F. Defense Disloc. Index	4.42	7	Population ('000)	6,016	13

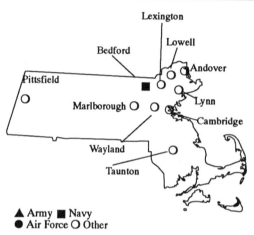

Lexington, Lowell, Bedford, Andover, Pittsfield, Marlborough, Lynn, Cambridge, Wayland, Taunton

▲ Army ■ Navy
● Air Force ○ Other

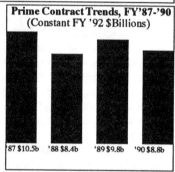

Prime Contract Trends, FY'87-'90
(Constant FY '92 $Billions)

'87 $10.5b '88 $8.4b '89 $9.8b '90 $8.8b

Top 5 Contractors	$ Millions
Raytheon	$3,026.5
General Electric	1,407.1
GTE	1,052.4
MIT	460.1
Mitre	407.4

Top 10 $ Sites[a]	Congressional Dist., Representative	1989 Rank	Total DoD$[c]	Payroll[c]	Prime Contracts[c]	Per-sonnel[d]
1-Taunton (36)	9-Moakley, d	14	$909.8	$2.9	$906.9	--
2-Lynn (40)	6-Mavroules, d	46	848.8	8.8	840.0	--
3-Wayland (46)	5-Atkins, d	113	775.3	1.5	773.8	--
4-Bedford (51)	"	56	738.1	0	738.1	--
5-Andover (63)	"	31	601.2	3.5	597.7	--
6-Lexington (81)	7-Markey, d	94	474.7	0	474.7	--
7-Pittsfield (89)	1-Vacant	75	445.9	7.4	438.5	--
8-Lowell (97)	5--Atkins, d	89	415.4	4.0	411.4	--
9-Marlborough (101)	3-Early, d	--	387.3	1.9	385.4	--
10-Cambridge (133)	8-Kennedy, d	135	304.4	7.3	297.1	--

[a]Rating in parentheses is out of 511 sites, the top ten in each state and PR, plus DC.
[b]Multidistrict r-Rep, d-Dem. [c]$Millions (figures may not add due to rounding) [d]Thousands

Massachusetts

The "Massachusetts Miracle," the cornerstone of former Gov. Michael Dukakis' ill-fated 1988 Presidential campaign, stemmed from growth of defense contractors in the state. As one shrewd observer explained, "The three reasons for the the state's growth were: (1) M, (2) I, and (3) T." As with the rest of the Northeast, Massachusetts has been hard hit by the recession of 1990 and 1991. The state's unemployment rate ranks 5th and its change in unemployment is the highest in the country (the labor force shrank but employment declined faster). On the other hand, as Allen L. Sinai, executive vice president and chief economist of the Boston Company, points out, "The times feel bad because times have been so good." He predicts that the state economy in the first half of the 1990s should perform no worse than that of the nation.[1]

Defense and the Economy

Only four states received more defense money than the $9.1 billion spent in Massachusetts in 1990. The state's vulnerability to defense cuts is compounded by its weak economy. The state is home to many firms that rely on research funds for SDI, a target for major cuts. Most of the $8.2 billion in prime contracts awarded to Massachusetts goes to high-tech industries, i.e., radio and television communications, electron tubes, aircraft, guided missiles and space equipment, engineering and scientific instruments, measuring and testing equipment, and optical instruments. These seven industries employ about 81,000 people, 3 percent of Massachusetts' private employment, with three firms accounting for 60 percent of the total defense employment. Massachusetts firms receive almost $3 billion a year for missiles and space systems, 14 percent of U.S. procurement for such programs. The state receives another $3 billion for electronics and communications equipment, which should remain a basic defense need in the 1990s.

Of the 11,000 workers involved in defense-related aircraft-engine production, most are employed by General Electric, which also produces commercial products. These defense workers are expected to face the least trouble shifting to commercial work if their jobs are cut. Those involved in missile production, however, are expected to have a much tougher time adjusting, as are many in the television/radio sectors heavily dependent on SDI funding.

State Legislative and Executive Initiatives

The State Legislature appointed the Massachusetts Joint Commission on Federal Base Conversion, which sponsored the Secondary Employment Impact of the 1973 Military Base Closings in Massachusetts, a study done by the

Commonwealth of Massachusetts in May 1974 that was a rare on-site study of base closures.

In August 1990, Gov. Dukakis sponsored a daylong meeting of the Conference of Northeast Governors to discuss economic conversion, and spent a good portion of the day at the meeting. On the day before he left office, the Governor signed into law the Massachusetts Economic Diversification Program, S 1864 introduced by Rep. David Cohen, which creates an advisory board to monitor and help implement economic diversification efforts. Although no funds were appropriated directly, the state will provide technical, financial and training resources to assist conversion. Massachusetts SANE/Freeze (Shelagh Foreman, 11 Garden St., Cambridge, MA 02138; 617-354-2169) aims to reinforce this program.

The Industrial Services Program is a quasi-public agency created in 1984 to address manufacturing job loss. ISP helps companies improve their planning, marketing, production management and financial position as a means of improving their competitiveness. Consulting and high-risk loans and equity investments from a state-funded capital pool are provided to businesses. Worker Assistance Centers are established and funded by ISP throughout the state in the event of major plant closings or layoffs. The ISP backs up the state's initiatives with financing, training, and marketing programs. Industry Action Projects, funded partly by the state Executive Office of Labor, seeks to foster industrial revitalization and economic transition. HBN 6178 extended the ISP by setting up an Economic Diversification Committee within it, which offers financial and technical aid to companies deriving more than 25 percent of their income from prime defense contracts or subcontracts. Delegate Turkington introduced HBN 5975 in 1990 to establish an Economic Conversion Commission. The bill was unsuccessful but was reintroduced for the November 1991 ballot.[2]

Community Surveys

Defense-related employment is heavily concentrated in four areas: Metro (Boston) South/West, Southern Essex, Lower Merrimack Valley, and Metro North. Four towns in Metro South/West (Bedford, Wayland, Needham, and Lexington) received $2 billion in prime contracts, representing 30 percent of all procurement spending in the state. Another vulnerable community is Lowell, where Raytheon Corp. makes the Phoenix missile, which Defense Secretary Dick Cheney wants to cut by over $100 million. Raytheon eliminated 800 jobs in several facilities in the state within the first three months of 1991.[3]

Ayer. The largest location of defense personnel in the state, Fort Devens, a major training facility that supports 50,000 Army Reservists and National Guard members, stood to gain personnel by the passage of the 1989 Base Closure Act, but has since been targeted for closure by the Base Commission. It is estimated that 3.5 percent of area jobs will be lost. Although Ayer has been discussed as the prime site for another Boston-area airport, several problems confront re-use plans. A final choice of airport will not be made for another two years and actual development may not take place for another 20. Furthermore, since Devens is on the EPA's National Priorities List, Federal regulations forbid re-use until pollution cleanup is complete. The Department of Defense's plans to maintain a Reserve facility with a firing range, besides having little potential to contribute significantly to regional income, could also interfere with re-use plans. Finally, redevelopment may be difficult because four communities (Ayer, Shirley, Harvard, and Lancaster) have jurisdiction over Devens' territory. Ayer has so far approved a project that would construct a mall on the base and plans to create a task force to deal with redevelopment.[4]

Boston. The Center for Applied Technology (9 Park Street, Boston, MA 02108. 617-727-7430; Frank Emspak, Project Director) is a program of the Massachusetts Centers of Excellence Corporation, funded jointly by the state and industry. It provides technical assistance on planning and implementing change in production technology to small and medium-sized businesses. The Center for Applied Technology requires that workers be involved in the planning and implementation of any changes, and the costs are shared by CAT and the companies. The center is also engaged in research projects for technology development and transfer.

Cambridge. Massachusetts SANE/Freeze (456 Massachusetts Avenue, Cambridge, MA 02139; 617-491-7809; Sheilagh Foreman) promotes the state Economic Diversification Act (H3693), which has obtained 10,000 signatures and has over 30 co-sponsors.

Cape Cod. A landmark agreement for the cleanup of hazardous wastes, which could be a model for other base decontamination proposals, at the 22,000-acre Massachusetts Military Reservation was signed between the EPA and the Department of Defense in July 1991. The agreement calls for neutralizing or removing millions of gallons of fuel, cleaning solvents, and carcinogens that were spilled or buried at the base and that contaminated the drinking water of nearby Falmouth back in 1978 and forced the Department of Defense to provide an alternative water source for the community. Under the agreement, the cleanup process should take ten years.[5]

Lexington. Raytheon, which employs about 77,000 workers, is based in this suburb of Boston, and has other in-state facilities in Lowell, Marlborough, Sudbury, Waltham, and Wayland. In July 1990, the $40-million Milstar communications-satellite system was cut by the Senate Armed Services Committee. Raytheon produces the ground terminals for the system, and the move is believed to put some 1,000 jobs in the state at risk,[6] not counting subcontractors. Massachusetts politicians, with Rep. Joseph P. Kennedy 2d (D-MA-8) among the most vocal, have urged the Defense Department to purchase the same Raytheon consoles for new systems, saving some of the jobs.

Raytheon and Massachusetts Congressional representatives were successful in saving two Raytheon projects in danger of being cut in 1990. The Hawk surface-to-air missile program was cancelled by the Army, jeopardizing 3,400 jobs, but Reps. Silvio Conte (R-MA-1), Joseph Moakley (D-MA-9), and Nicholas Mavroules (D-MA-6) revived the program. After the Italian government walked away from financing the joint Italian-U.S. Patriot Missile program between Raytheon and an Italian company, those same members of congress helped keep the project alive. When the Patriot was found effective against the relatively slow-moving Soviet-made Scud missile, Raytheon's stock rose as foreign governments like Saudi Arabia, Turkey, and Britain got in line after the Department of Defense for more of the missiles. The Patriot accounted for 15 percent of Raytheon's revenues in 1989. Ever since the mid-1960s, Raytheon has undertaken a serious campaign to reduce its dependence on the military. Its strategy of diversification through the process of acquisition has resulted in very little transference of workers from defense to non-defense related work.[7]

Lowell. The Maverick and Phoenix missiles are produced by Raytheon in Lowell. The Phoenix missile program has been cut by the Department of Defense. Although the Maverick missile was also scheduled for termination, the Department of Defense revived it when it ordered new missiles to replace those used in the Gulf. The city sees defense cuts coming sooner or later, and has also been feeling the impact of the slowdown of the high-tech industry (Digital has facilities in the Greater Lowell area and Wang is based in Lowell). The city feels that it has enough economic diversity to weather the storm but will look for state and Federal aid.[8]

Lynn. General Electric produces F-14D jet engines in Lynn; with the termination of the plane made by Grumman, the engine contract will also end. GE announced in 1990 it would eliminate 1,500 jobs by the end of 1992 (to be distributed between the plant at Lynn and its Evendale aircraft engine division in Cincinnati, OH). A sophisticated worker-retraining center was set up at the Lynn plant, funded by GE and the state. According to its managers, it has had an excellent track record for placing employees in situations roughly comparable in pay and job sophistication to what they had at GE.[9]

Newton. John Hughes, president of the Numerix Division of Mercury Computer Systems in Newton, has said that the company is moving to prepare for cuts in defense spending. Mercury is seeking to expand into non-defense-related business while concentrating on those Department of Defense projects which seem to be relatively safe. The company is fairly confident that money will still come to the areas of research and development, anti-submarine warfare, and intelligence and surveillance.[10]

Watertown. The Army Materiel Testing Lab employs several hundred civilians and was targeted for realignment by the Department of Defense in 1988. Its functions were to be divided up among the Detroit Arsenal, MI, the Picatinny Arsenal, NJ, and Fort Belvoir, VA. In 1991, the Base Commission, as a revision of that plan, decided to transfer the Lab's units to Aberdeen Proving Ground, MD. The revision will be implemented, if at all, after January 1992 since the Base Commission is awaiting a report by another Congressional task force on military lab realignments.

Weymouth. The South Weymouth Naval Air Station was on a Department of Defense list of military bases that may be closed. The base employs 450 military and 200 civilian personnel, and infuses around $30 million a year into the local economy. Local politicians and businessmen launched a huge campaign to pressure the Federal Government not to close the station.[12]

Williamstown (Berkshire County). SANE/Freeze (Berkshire County Chapter, P.O. Box 271, Williamstown, MA 01267; 413-458-4436; Pamela Gilchrist) held a conference on diversification in Pittsfield, which helped lead to the successful application to the state by Berkshire County, which is a large slice off the western end of the state, for a grant to develop an economic-diversification plan. The Massachusetts Office of Communities and Development awarded the county a $44,000 grant for its regional planning agency to develop the plan, first of its kind in the state. The largest employer in the county is General Electric's Defense Systems Division in Pittsfield. It has been laying off 500-800 workers per year and further layoffs are expected. No retraining facilities (despite support for such facilities by Federal plant-closing and conversion laws) exist in the area.

Notes

1. Lawrence Goodrich, "Problems, Yes; Crisis, No," *The Christian Science Monitor,* October 13, 1989, p. 7.

2. John E. Lynch, ed., *Plant Closures and Community Recovery* (Washington, D.C.: National Council on Urban Economic Development, 1990), Chapter 39. Anne Hoskins and Keith Cunningham, *Economic Initiatives,* published by the Center for Policy Alternatives, July 1991, p. 13. Contacts: (1) Division of Planning and Development, City of Lowell, Michael G. Demaras, Public Information Officer, John F. Kennedy Civic Center, Lowell, MA 01852; 508-970-4252. (2) Economic Development, State of Massachusetts, Thomas E. Hubbard, Director, State House, Boston, MA 02133; 617-727-1130. (3) Employment and Training, State of Massachusetts, James French, Hurley Building, Boston, MA 02114; 617-727-6100. (4) Massachusetts Office of Economic Affairs, Alden Raine, State House, Room 109, Boston, MA 02133; 617-727-1130.

3. *Employment Trends in Defense Oriented Industries,* Division of Employment Security, 1987, p. v. "Raytheon Lays Off 171 More Workers," *The Boston Globe,* March 9, 1991.

4. *Base Closure and Realignment Report,* Department of Defense, April 1991, pp. 39-40. James S. Robbins, "Close My Town's Army Base," *The New York Times,* April 25, 1991. Chris Black, "Redeveloping Ft. Devens expected to be difficult," *The Boston Globe,* July 2, 1991, pp. 1, 6.

5. Jeff McLaughlin, "US Agrees to Plan for Cape Base Cleanup," *The Boston Globe,* July 18, 1991, p. 23.

6. Michael Frisby and Joshua Cooper Ramo, "Raytheon Project Cut From Budget," *The Boston Globe,* July 18, 1990, p. 25.

7. *Loc. cit.* Rick Wartzman, Bruce Ingersoll, and Gary Putka, "By Performing in Gulf, Exotic Weapons Help Manufacturers as Well," *The Wall Street Journal*, January 21, 1991, pp. A1, A8. Philip Shenon, "Incoming Iraqi Missile Destroyed Over Saudi Base," *The New York Times*, January 19, 1991, p. A8. *Adjusting to Changes in Defense Spending: A Report to the Legislature*, Department of Employment and Training, State of Massachusetts, November 1989, p. 14.

8. Interview in March 1990 with Reginald Ouellette, Economic and Industrial Development Administration, Lowell, 508-970-4040. Also, in July 1991, contact with Michael G. Demaras, Public Information Officer, Division of Planning and Development, Lowell.

9. John McGuire and Joseph Shea, co-directors, Lynn Workers Assistance Center, Testimony before the U.S. House of Representatives, House Banking Committee, Subcommittee on Economic Stabilization, Hearings, *Economic Diversification and Worker Dislocation in Defense Dependent Communities*, June 13, 1989. "GE Aircraft and Engines Will Cut 1,500 Jobs," *The New York Times*, August 17, 1990.

10. John Hughes, Mercury Computer Systems, from a survey conducted by Myron Struck, Defense Electronics.

10. Gloria Negri, "Politicians Say They Will Fight for Weymouth Base," *The Boston Globe*, January 30, 1990, p. 13.

Michigan

A	B	C	D	E	F
$				VI	DDI
+	+	+	↓	!	✂

Benchmarks	No.	Rank	Benchmarks	No.	Rank
A.Total DoD $	$2.2bil.	27	Def.-Dependent Jobs ('000), '90	116	26
B. Personnel Payroll	$0.8bil.	32	Change in Def.-Dep. Jobs, '89-'91	-1.7%	32
C. Prime Contracts (PC)	$1.4bil.	23	Unemployment Rate, '90-'91	9.7%	2
D. PC Change, FY '87-'90	-34.4%	11	Unemp. Rate Change, '89-'91	+3.5%	6
E. Vulnerability Index	9.3	28	Per Capita Income	$18,346	21
F. Defense Disloc. Index	2.68	11	Population ('000)	9,295	8

▲ Army ■ Navy
● Air Force ○ Other

Sawyer AFB

Wurtsmirth AFB

Grand Rapids

Troy, Warren, Sterling Hgts., Detroit

Selfridge

Battle Crk.

A. Arb.

Prime Contract Trends, FY'87-'90
(Constant FY '92 $Billions)

'87 $2.2b	'88 $1.5b	'89 $1.4b	'90 $1.5b

Top 5 Contractors	$ Millions
General Dynamics	$553.4
Smiths Industries	60.7
Oldenburg Group	27.1
Textron	26.7
A.V. Technology	25.8

Top 10 $ Sites[a]	Congressional Dist., Representative	1989 Rank	Total DoD$[c]	Payroll[c]	Prime Contracts[c]	Per-sonnel[d]
1-Sterling Hts. (70)	14-Hurtel, d	159	$505.8	$3.6	$502.1	--
2-Warren (172)	(12,14)[b]	150	212.3	141.4	70.9	5.3
3-Troy (260)	14-Hurtel, d	--	106.9	1.6	105.3	--
4-Grand Rapids (265)	5-Henry ,r	196	104.7	11.8	92.9	--
5-Sawyer AFB (270)	11-Davis, r	263	98.0	84.3	13.7	3.7
6-Wurtsm'th AFB (278)	"	268	91.5	78.3	13.2	3.5
7-Battle Creek (290)	3-Wolpe, d	292	83.9	66.0	17.9	2.0
8-Selfridge (292)	12-Bonior, d	291	82.1	66.7	15.4	1.3
9-Detroit (298)	(1,13,14,17)[b]	280	77.4	51.1	26.3	1.6
10-Ann Arbor (329)	2-Pursell, r	--	48.8	6.1	42.7	--

[a]Rating in parentheses is out of 511 sites, the top ten in each state and PR, plus DC.
[b]Multidistrict r-Rep, d-Dem. [c]$Millions (figures may not add due to rounding) [d]Thousands

Michigan

The largest and most important industrial sector in the Michigan economy is still the auto industry. But its importance, along with the entire manufacturing sector, has been steadily declining in the 1970s and 1980s. Manufacturing employment, which accounted for 32 percent of the total state wage and salary employment in 1976, is expected to be down to 24 percent by 1995. The service sector of the economy is the fastest growing, and is expected to be the prime engine of state economic growth in the 1990s. The state's unemployment rate ranked 2nd highest in April 1991 and its change in unemployment 6th highest (the labor force grew slightly and employment suffered a sharp decline).[1]

Defense and the Economy

Only a few installations are left from the World War II days when Michigan proudly earned the title "the arsenal of democracy," but the military still has a large presence here. Defense spending in Michigan reached a high in 1985 at the peak of the Reagan buildup, but by 1990 its share had fallen to about 1 percent of the total defense budget and was still dropping.[2] The state is affected by the obsolescence of heavy-armor combat vehicles in which its industries have specialized. Some also speculate that Michigan is hit hard by cuts because of sparse Congressional representation (only three representatives) on key appropriations committees. Since it has a high unemployment rate, the Michigan economy is vulnerable to defense cuts.

The Department of Defense announced it will station rail-based MX missiles in the state, which could translate into significant business for local construction firms. To help small businesses secure defense contracts, the state has established a "local procurement outreach" program, which has apparently brought the state over $1 billion in defense business.[3]

Community Surveys

Nearly two-thirds of defense money comes to Michigan for defense contracts and the largest contractor by far is General Dynamics, which makes the M-1 tank. The General Dynamics Land Systems Division has an address in Warren, a suburb to the north of Detroit, but is listed by the Department of Defense by some quirk under Sterling Heights, one city north of Warren.

Chippewa County. Although not directly affected by 1990s defense cuts, Chippewa County is figuratively on the map for its successful conversion of the Kincheloe Air Force Base, near Sault Ste. Marie, in 1977. The closure meant 700 jobs were terminated and unemployment rate in the rural district soared to nearly 30 percent. The Chippewa County Economic Development Corporation converted the base into a combined-use complex, housing many industrial companies, businesses, public agencies, an airport, a prison converted from a dormitory, and housing on the base sold to local families. This was a successful example of a base conversion.

Marquette. Sawyer Air Force Base was scheduled to lose up to 6 planes and 200 military personnel by mid-1991, although the cuts are not expected to continue. There is much concern among local politicians, however, that the loss of personnel will mean a $2 million loss to the 50-mile-wide community radius. Sawyer is estimated to pump as much as $145 million yearly into the area.[4]

Muskegon County. Losses in Teledyne Continental Motors tank and diesel engine contracts could be partially offset by a possible future contract to produce a new generation of military trucks.

Oakland County. Proposed Air Force plans to cut cruise missile production by one-third may mean that the high-tech firms of Oakland County in south-eastern Michigan, such as Williams International, will be very adversely affected.[5]

Oscoda. Wurtsmith Air Force Base is scheduled to close. The Department of Defense's motivation rested on Wurtsmith's distance from low-altitude training routes and its poor refueling utility. The economic impact is likely to be severe since Wurtsmith is the region's largest single employer. The Department of Defense's conservative estimate is the loss of 4,500 of 915,000 local jobs. Local officials believe that some communities could lose one-third of their populations.[6]

Walled Lake. The defense role of Williams International Corp., which receives $90 million a year in Department of Defense contracts, may be reduced by arms- limitation agreements that restrict a type of cruise missile it produces.[7]

Warren. The Army's Tank-Automotive Command (TACOM), concerned with the maintenance and purchase of Army vehicles, faces a loss of 500 jobs. The layoffs were postponed in 1990 because of the Gulf War. TACOM supervises the Detroit Arsenal Tank Plant which is also vulnerable to an additional (reports indicate, though some double-counting may be occurring) 600 job cuts because its involvement in the building of the M-1 battle tank will diminish. The Detroit Arsenal Tank Plant will continue to produce spare parts for the tanks, but assembly operations end in 1991.[8]

As already mentioned, General Dynamics produces the M-1 tank at a plant in Warren. In July 1990, the Senate Armed Services Committee decided to stop purchasing new M-1s, but authorized a $149 million contract to upgrade earlier M-1 models. This, plus contracts with Egypt for 555 M1-A1 tanks and with Saudi Arabia for 465 M1-A2 tanks and for 235 more pending approval from Congress, should keep the General Dynamics plant in Warren going for some time, although employment will be lower. In 1991, General Dynamics announced that it would trim 27,000 positions from its 90,000-member national labor force over the 1991-1995 period with several hundred cuts in Warren occurring within months.

Cadillac Gauge Textron Inc. is a small subcontractor, also located in Warren, that produces the aiming system for the tank's gun. With major cuts in the M-1 program, Cadillac Gauge Textron estimates that it might have to lay off at least half of its 65 skilled engineers and hundreds of production workers.[9]

Notes

1. *Michigan Occupation/Industry Forecasts 1995*, Michigan Employment Security Commission, p. 16, p. 2.

2. *Atlas/Data Abstract for the U.S. and Selected Areas Fiscal 1990*, Department of Defense. Washington Headquarters Services, Directorate for Information, Operations and Reports, p. 63.

3. *Loc. cit.* Contacts: (1) Governor's Office, Mark Murray, Director-Business Research Office, State Capitol, Lansing, MI 48913; 517-373-4600. (2) Michigan Department of Commerce, Larry Meyer, 525 W. Ottawa, Lansing, MI 48913; 517-373-1820. (3) Michigan Department of Labor, Betty Howe, Director, 611 W. Ottawa, Box 30015, Lansing, MI 48913; 517-373-9600. (4) Michigan Employment Security Commission, Von Logan, Lansing, MI 48913.

4. Terri Hughes-Lazzell, "Sawyer AFB Would Lose 3 B52s, 135 Personnel Under Reductions," *Mining Journal*, January 30, 1990, p. 1.

5. *Loc. cit.*

6. *Base Closure and Realignment Report*, Department of Defense, April 1991, pp. 109-110. "Defending Wurtsmith SAC Base," *Detroit News*, April 4, 1991, p. 10.

7. Richard Willing, "Warren Tank Plant, Others Threatened," *Detroit News*, December 3, 1989, p. 19.

8. David Everett, "Local Base Stays Open," *The Detroit News*, April 13, 1991, p. 8. Caleb Baker, "Army to Keep Open Detroit Arsenal Tank Plant," *Defense News*, March 4, 1991, p. 7.

9. *Ibid.*, p. 1. Richard W. Stevenson, "Suppliers Brace for Arms Cuts," *The New York Times*, June 18, 1990, pp. D1-D2.

Minnesota

A	B	C	D	E	F
$	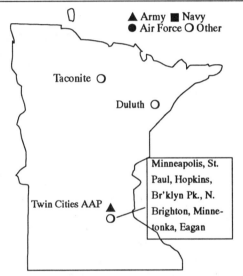			VI	DDI
+	−	+	↓	−	✂

Benchmarks	No.	Rank	Benchmarks	No.	Rank
A.Total DoD $	$2.1bil.	29	Def.-Dependent Jobs ('000), '90	118	25
B. Personnel Payroll	$0.4bil.	41	Change in Def.-Dep. Jobs, '89-'91	-5.6%	28
C. Prime Contracts (PC)	$1.7bil.	18	Unemployment Rate, '90-'91	5.0%	44
D. PC Change, FY '87-'90	-35.1%	10	Unemp. Rate Change, '89-'91	+0.1%	37
E. Vulnerability Index	7.1	47	Per Capita Income	$18,346	21
F. Defense Disloc. Index	1.25	22	Population ('000)	4,375	20

▲ Army ■ Navy
● Air Force ○ Other

Taconite ○

Duluth ○

Minneapolis, St.
Paul, Hopkins,
Br'klyn Pk., N.
Twin Cities AAP ▲ Brighton, Minne-
○ tonka, Eagan

Prime Contract Trends, FY'87-'90
(Constant FY '92 $Billions)

'87 $2.9b '88 $2.4b '89 $2.0b '90 $1.9b

Top 5 Contractors	$ Millions
Honeywell	$830.8
Unisys	231.2
FMC	201.7
Control Data	186.0
Grand Metropolitan	20.8

Top 10 $ Sites[a]	Congressional Dist., Representative	1989 Rank	Total DoD$[c]	Payroll[c]	Prime Contracts[c]	Per-sonnel[d]
1-Minneapolis (67)	5-Sabo, d	83	$568.8	$52.0	$516.7	1.1
2-St. Paul (120)	4-Venko, d	98	326.6	50.1	276.5	1.1
3-Hopkins (149)	3-Ramstad, r	139	263.3	2.9	260.4	--
4-Brooklyn Pk. (166)	6-Sikorski, d	173	223.3	1.6	221.7	--
5-New Brighton (201)	4-Venko, d	210	172.0	3.0	168.9	.07
6-Minnetonka (285)	3-Ramstad, r	284	85.8	0.8	85.0	--
7-Twin Cities (363)	4-Venko, d	302	36.5	0	36.5	--
8-Eagan (372)	3-Ramstad, r	--	33.4	31.7	1.6	.02
9-Duluth (375)	8-Oberstar, d	385	32.5	24.9	7.6	0.4
10-Taconite (393)	"	--	26.4	.01	26.4	--

[a]Rating in parentheses is out of 511 sites, the top ten in each state and PR, plus DC.
[b]Multidistrict r-Rep, d-Dem. [c]$Millions (figures may not add due to rounding) [d]Thousands

Minnesota

Since the early 1960s, the Minnesota economy has been expanding faster than the rest of the U.S. Although the state is not resistant to recession, the periods of growth between recessions have generally been among the most impressive in the nation. Minnesota's unemployment rate ranks a low 44th in the U.S. and its change in unemployment ranked 37th (the labor force and employment were both growing fast but labor force growth slightly outpaced employment). As with the rest of the nation, the Minnesota economy is moving steadily from a goods-producing manufacturing base to more of a services-producing base.[1]

Defense and the Economy

Defense revenues to Minnesota in 1990 were over $2 billion, most in the form of procurement contracts. As the data page shows clearly, Minnesota's prime contracts have been falling in value every year. Between 1987 and 1989, 29,000 defense jobs in the state were terminated, according to the Minnesota Task Force on Economic Conversion.

The Task Force also said that for every tax dollar the state sent to the Department of Defense in 1987, state firms received only 50 cents in prime contracts, so the average Minnesotan loses $418 yearly to the Department of Defense. Since contracts are concentrated in the relatively well off Twin Cities area, the per capita loss was more severe in the rural counties. The Task Force contended that defense procurement in the state represents a redistribution of wealth from the poorer rural areas to the cities.[2]

Minnesota has both a low defense dependence and a low unemployment rate, which explains its low Vulnerability Index ranking. Defense spending in the state, however, is likely to be cut significantly. Weapon systems made in part in the state that face termination are the Apache helicopter program, the M-1 tank, and the F-14 fighter. The industries hit hardest by proposed defense cuts will be the high-tech sectors, including ordnance, scientific equipment, and computers. Thousands of jobs will also be lost in retail, wholesale, services, and other industries.[3]

State Legislative Initiatives

The state Task Force on Economic Conversion was co-ordinated by Minnesota Jobs with Peace and made up of legislators, job and training officials, conversion groups, peace organizations, and labor representatives. It produced a study in 1989 on *Military Production and the Minnesota Economy*, examining the extent of state dependency on the military and the costs involved in economic conversion. The Task Force concluded that conversion could create an additional 9,200 jobs. The former Democratic Governor and all five Democratic Representatives from Minnesota supported the "alternative use" campaign at Unisys Corp.

The AFL-CIO supported a state bill requiring all contractors with $1 million or more in prime defense contracts to establish alternative-use committees with equal representation from management and labor and giving companies with alternative-use committees preferential treatment for state economic-development programs. But in the spring of 1990 contractors (Honeywell, Unisys, FMC, and Control Data) lobbied successfully to defeat this and other conversion bills before the state legislature.

The Task Force released a second report, *Forging a Peace Economy in Minnesota* in February 1991. Then in June 1991, much work in this field was called to halt when the new Republican Gov. Arne Carlson forbade any state officials from participating in the Task Force because conversion in her view was "not a priority."

Meanwhile representatives from Minnesota Jobs with Peace and the Minnesota Peace and Justice Coalition went on a "Peace Economy Tour," holding forums in each city and town on the peace economy.[4]

Community Surveys

The top eight sites out of the top ten in the state are all in the Minneapolis/Saint Paul metropolitan area. Honeywell has operations all over the state, but its major military-contract centers appear to be in Minneapolis (headquarters and military avionics), or its suburban areas of Brooklyn Park (armament systems) to the north, and Minnetonka (defense systems, precision weapons) to the southwest; the major exception is Hopkins, where Honeywell has its underseas systems division. The main contractor in Saint Paul is Unisys.

Duluth. The Duluth Air Force Base was one of the five bases to which the Air Force and the Office of Economic Adjustment of the Department of Defense took community officials as an example of conversion efforts on military bases. City Councilor Charles Noon of Portsmouth, NH, who went on the visit, was not altogether taken with what he saw; he said he thought what Duluth had done was an example of what not to do.

Minneapolis. Minnesota Jobs with Peace (1929 S. 5th Street, Minneapolis, MN 55454; 612-338-7955, headed by Janet Groat) survives as an active nonprofit focus of conversion interest, despite the withdrawal of state Executive Branch support for the Task Force.

Minnetonka. This Twin Cities bedroom community is concerned about Honeywell's plan to sell defense units, affecting some 4,000 employees.[5]

Saint Paul. Troubled Unisys Corp. in Saint Paul has been one of the central issues for people concerned with economic conversion in Minnesota. Mayor Jim Scheibel of Saint Paul and former Democratic Gov. Rudy Perpich joined Unisys employees in a protest calling on the company to develop a conversion plan. Alternative-use planning at Unisys has been conducted by International Brotherhood of Electrical Workers Local 2047 and Jobs with Peace, but the company (which has laid off 5,000 workers since 1986) has been slow to cooperate; it finally agreed to meet with members of the Alternative Use Committee in 1991, but problems arose over the labor composition within the new products committee. After a change of union leadership, the committee proposed 13 new products to replace declining defense contracts. Unisys decided to develop one of the technologies proposed by the committee, but at a plant out of state.[6]

Notes

1. *1990 Economic Report to the Governor*, prepared by the Minnesota Economic Resource Group.

2. *Atlas/Data Abstract for the U.S. and Selected Areas, Fiscal 1990*, Department of Defense, Washington Headquarters Services, Directorate for Information, Operations and Reports, p. 65. Wilbur Maki et al., *Military Production and the Minnesota Economy*, A Report for the Minnesota Task Force on Economic Conversion, May 1989.

3. *Ibid.*, p. 11.

4. Mel Duncan, Minnesota Jobs with Peace, *Proceedings: National Strategy Retreat on Economic Conversion, Block Island, June 11-13, 1990* (Mountain View, CA: Center for Economic Conversion, 1990), p. 2. Anne Hoskins and Keith Cunningham, *Economic Initiatives*, produced by the Center for Policy Alternatives, July 1991, p. 14. Janet Stone, *Conversion Organizers' Update* (Mountain View, CA: Center for Economic Conversion, October 1991, advance copy), pp. 6-7. Rep. Karen Clark, Minnesota Task Force on Economic Conversion, 612-296-0294. Contacts: (1) Department of Economic Development, Bob de la Vega, 150 E. Kellogg Blvd., Saint Paul, MN 55101; 612-296-3976. (2) Department of Jobs and Training, State of Minnesota, Ned Chottetanda, 390 N. Robert St., Saint Paul, MN 55155; 612-296-6546. (3) Economic Development, State of Minnesota, Lee Munnich, Commissioner, 150 E. Kellogg Blvd., Saint Paul, MN 55101; 612-296-8341. (4) Governor's Office, Tom Triplett, Commissioner of Finance, State Capitol, Saint Paul, MN 55155; 612-296-9271.

5. Interview in March, 1990 with Anne Perry, Director of Planning, City of Minnetonka, MI, 512-933-2511.

6. "Convert Now," *Municipal Foreign Policy*, Summer 1990, p. 8. *Conversion Organizers' Update* (Mountain View, CA: Center for Economic Conversion, February 1991), p. 7, and Stone, *op. cit.*, p. 7.

Mississippi

A	B	C	D	E	F
$	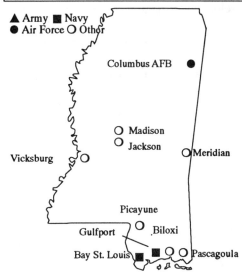			VI	DDI
+	+	+	➡	‼	✌

Benchmarks	No.	Rank	Benchmarks	No.	Rank
A.Total DoD $	$2,5bil.	25	Def.-Dependent Jobs ('000), '90	127	23
B. Personnel Payroll	$1.1bil.	24	Change in Def.-Dep. Jobs, '89-'91	+3.3%	40
C. Prime Contracts (PC)	$1.4bil.	22	Unemployment Rate, '90-'91	7.9%	7
D. PC Change, FY '87-'90	-12.8%	31	Unemp. Rate Change, '89-'91	+0.3%	36
E. Vulnerability Index	13.9	4	Per Capita Income	$12,735	51
F. Defense Disloc. Index	0.14	37	Population ('000)	2,573	32

▲ Army ■ Navy
● Air Force ○ Other

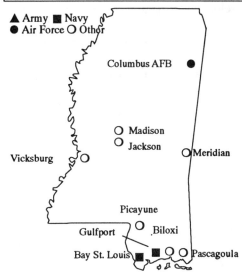

Columbus AFB ●

○ Madison
○ Jackson
Vicksburg ○
○ Meridian

Picayune
○ Biloxi
Gulfport
Bay St. Louis ■ ○ ○ Pascagoula

Prime Contract Trends, FY'87-'90
(Constant FY '92 $Billions)

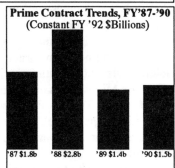

'87 $1.8b	'88 $2.8b	'89 $1.4b	'90 $1.5b

Top 5 Contractors	$ Millions
Litton Industries	$911.2
Raytheon	112.3
Avondale	72.7
Grumman	40.2
De Mason	31.4

Top 10 $ Sites[a]	Congressional Dist., Representative	1989 Rank	Total DoD$[c]	Payroll[c]	Prime Contracts[c]	Per-sonnel[d]
1-Pascagoula (32)	5-Taylor, d	52	$963.6	$37.1	$926.5	0.6
2-Biloxi (130)	"	129	307.1	266.7	40.4	--
3-Gulfport (171)	"	192	214.0	133.2	80.8	1.7
4-Vicksburg (214)	2-Espy, d	232	149.4	117.5	31.9	3.3
5-Bay St. Louis (256)	5-Taylor, d	313	108.1	63.0	45.1	1.6
6-Madison (289)	(2,3)[b]	327	84.8	1.3	83.5	--
7-Columbus AFB (291)	3-Montgomery, d	296	82.5	51.7	30.8	2.1
8-Meridian (295)	"	294	79.2	71.4	7.8	2.5
9-Jackson (300)	(3,4)[b]	279	76.9	30.9	46.0	0.5
10-Picayune (365)	5-Taylor, d	225	35.9	2.4	33.5	--

[a]Rating in parentheses is out of 511 sites, the top ten in each state and PR, plus DC.
[b]Multidistrict r-Rep, d-Dem. [c]$Millions (figures may not add due to rounding) [d] Thousands

Mississippi

Mississippi's unemployment rate of 7.9 percent ranks 7th highest. The state's unemployment rate increased slightly during the 1988-91 period (the increase in the labor force slightly exceeded the increase in employment).[1]

Defense and the Economy

The state has a high defense dependence; more than 8 percent of state revenue in 1989 came from the defense. The state as a whole will be moderately affected by defense-contract cuts. The prime contracts awarded to Mississippi firms are primarily for supply and service of ships, aircraft, and vehicles, less likely to be cut than research and development programs. Ammunition production and construction are also important defense-related industries in the state. Military expenditures and personnel are heavily concentrated on the Gulf Coast strip in the southeastern corner of the state. State officials are not worried about defense cuts, but reductions in the standing army could have adverse long-term effects on Mississippi's employment.[2]

Meridian. The Naval Air Station, a flight and technical training center with 3,000 military personnel, was targeted for closure but gained reprieve.

Pascagoula. The Navy's homeport was recommended for closure but did not appear on the Base Commission's final hitlist in 1991.

Picayune. The Mississippi Army Ammunition Plant, which had employed 1,400 people, in a county with a population of 25,000, was shut down in 1991. The Mississippi Congressional delegation is lobbying for the Army to turn the plant over to private users as a high-tech incubator. It is located in the Stennis Space Center area, the site of 16 Federal agencies.

Notes

1. *Population-Personal Income Data 1983-1988*, Labor Market Information Department, Mississippi Employment Security Commission, June, 1990, pp. 1, 8.

2. *Atlas/Data Abstract for the U.S. and Selected Areas Fiscal 1989*, Department of Defense, p. 67. Interview in January 1991 with John Waites, Office of the State of Mississippi, Washington, DC; 202-371-5746. Other contacts: Defense Subcommittee, House Appropriations Committee, 202-225-2847; Wayne Weidie, Office of Rep. Gene Taylor (D-MS), 1429 LHOB, Washington, DC, 202-225-5772; Army Materiel Command, 703-274-9836; Stennis Space Center, Bay St. Louis, 601-864-6161 or (after working hours) 601-688-3636. *Prime Contract Awards by Region and State, Fiscal Years 1989, 1988, 1987*, Department of Defense, p. 43. Contacts: (1) Mississippi Department of Economic Development, J. Mac Holladay, P.O. Box 849, Jackson, MS 39205; 601-359-3449. (2) Mississippi Department of Economic Development, Beneta Burt, 301 W. Pearl St., Jackson, MS 39203; 601-949-2234. (3) Missippi Employment Security, Linda Ross Aldy, Commissioner, P.O. Box 1699, Jackson, MS 39215-1699; 601-961-7401.

Missouri

A	B	C	D	E	F
$	🪖	🏭	📅	VI	DDI
✚	+	✚	➡	!!	✂

Benchmarks	No.	Rank	Benchmarks	No.	Rank
A.Total DoD $	$7.2bil.	8	Def.-Dependent Jobs ('000), '90	439	7
B. Personnel Payroll	$1.1bil.	22	Change in Def.-Dep. Jobs, '89-'91	-8.0%	21
C. Prime Contracts (PC)	$6.1bil.	6	Unemployment Rate, '90-'91	6.0%	30
D. PC Change, FY '87-'90	-9.0%	34	Unemp. Rate Change, '89-'91	+0.9%	27
E. Vulnerability Index	12.8	6	Per Capita Income	$17,497	24
F. Defense Disloc. Index	33.7	1	Population ('000)	5,117	15

▲ Army ■ Navy
● Air Force ○ Other

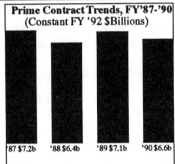

Prime Contract Trends, FY'87-'90
(Constant FY '92 $Billions)

'87 $7.2b   '88 $6.4b   '89 $7.1b   '90 $6.6b

Top 5 Contractors	$ Millions
McDonnell Douglas	$4,635.3
McDonnell/Gen Dyn. JV	555.0
Olin	170.3
Emerson	123.0
Light Heli. Turbine Eng.	49.1

Top 10 $ Sites[a]	Congressional Dist., Representative	1989 Rank	Total DoD$[c]	Payroll[c]	Prime Contracts[c]	Per-sonnel[d]
1-St. Louis (1)	(1,3)[b]	1	$5,616.0	$218.7	$5,397.3	12.0
2-Ft. Leon. Wood (128)	4-Skelton, d	81	307.9	257.7	50.2	12.5
3-Lake City (192)	"	155	181.5	0	181.5	--
4-Kansas City (213)	(5,6)[b]	197	150.6	73.1	77.5	2.6
5-Whiteman AFB (243)	4-Skelton, d	205	117.8	79.6	38.1	3.6
6-St. Charles (245)	(2,9)[b]	297	116.9	8.2	108.7	--
7-West Plains (328)	8-Emerson, r	364	49.4	2.1	47.2	--
8-Olivette (364)	(1,2)[b]	365	36.5	28.1	8.4	--
9-Springfield (384)	7-Hancock, r	--	29.0	26.9	2.2	0.2
10-Jefferson City (401)	(4,9)[b]	--	23.5	23.1	0.5	--

[a]Rating in parentheses is out of 511 sites, the top ten in each state and PR, plus DC.
[b]Multidistrict r-Rep, d-Dem. [c]$Millions (figures may not add due to rounding) [d]Thousands

Missouri

Missouri's gross state product grew about 8 percent a year during the 1980s, below the national average of 8.7 percent. The manufacturing, services and finance, insurance and real estate industries comprised more than one-half of Missouri's gross state product, with a total of more than $44 billion. Transportation and public utilities, retail trade and government also account for large sectors of the Missouri economy.[1] The state's unemployment rate of 6 percent is slightly higher than average. There was also an adverse unemployment change during the period 1988-1991 period (the labor force grew faster than employment).

Since the late 1970s, the number of very small and very large farms has grown at the expense of the number of middle-sized farms. About 7,000 farms went out of business during the 1980-1988 period, as the average value of farms per acre fell by more than 13.4 percent.[2]

Defense and the Economy

Missouri has the highest Defense Dislocation Index in the nation and the sixth highest Vulnerability Index.

McDonnell Douglas, General Dynamics, Emerson Electric, Olin Corp., and several other major defense contractors are based in Missouri. They in turn subcontract to a network of other St. Louis-area companies (including Ewing Technical Design, Earle M. Jorgenson Co., Tad Technical Services, and LPL Technical Services) who do about $100 million worth of business each year.[3]

Community Surveys

St. Louis gets the bulk of the state's defense money. More than 73,000 jobs are directly related to military spending in the St. Louis area. The largest component of this total is McDonnell Douglas, but it also includes other contractors such as General Dynamics (moving to Virinia) and Department of Defense agencies such as the Army Troop Support Command, the Aviation Support Command, and the Defense Mapping Agency.

Belton. The Department of Defense wants to close Richards-Gebaur Air Reserve Station, which the Air Force Reserve jointly operates with the Kansas City Department of Aviation and Transportation. Employment loss will be minimized by the realignment of the 442nd Tactical Fighter Wing to nearby Whiteman AFB, also in Missouri, but the job losses should still number 2,600. Annual savings could total $12.9 million after an implementation cost of $4 million.[4]

Fenton. Although it does not have a military plant, this community just to the southwest of St. Louis has a significant stake in the future of defense spending in the St. Louis area, because its residents need jobs. Already 4,500 people in the area have been laid off by the Chrysler Corporation when its Fenton-based LeBaron plant was closed in 1990-91.[5]

St. Louis. The city receives more money from the Department of Defense than any other in the U.S. and accounts for 78 percent of Missouri's total defense revenues. Defense, both in contracting and the military bases, is a significant factor in the regional economy of St. Louis. McDonnell Douglas Corp. before its 1990 cuts employed some 40,500 people in the St. Louis area, making it the area's largest employer, with one out of every 27 workers in the area on its annual payroll of $1.6 billion.[6] When it learned of the first round of defense cuts in 1990, the company announced some 4,500 layoffs from the St. Louis plant.

McDonnell Douglas is the largest U.S. defense contractor. The F-15 Eagle, the company's biggest money-maker, is facing termination (although the Gulf War generated new orders from Saudi Arabia), as are the F-15 Eagle, Navy A-12 jet, AV-8B and AH-64 Apache; the company is involved in four of the Department of Defense's five most expensive projects. The company is attempting to diversify into civilian aviation.

When the A-12 attack jet was definitively turned down by the Defense Department on January 7, 1991, McDonnell Douglas immediately announced the layoff of an additional 5,000 workers in a few days. The Department of Defense originally announced that it would try to give part of the $1.9 billion to McDonnell Douglas and its partner in the A-12 project, General Dynamics, which also until 1991 had its headquarters in St. Louis. However, those plans were shelved when it became apparent how financially strapped the two companies were and a loan guarantee plan of $1.3 billion in debt relief was extended to them. The company is also facing "potential[ly] serious cost problems" in several other programs. In April 1991, the Department of Defense announced it would award the Advanced Tactical Fighter contract to Lockheed; later in April, McDonnell Douglas announced another 500 layoffs in St. Louis; in May the company announced another 390 layoffs with more to follow.

Top executives in 1991 also announced huge layoffs to come at the St. Louis and other McDonnell Douglas plants, 17,000 personnel cuts across the nation, to trim their expenses by $700 million a year. Former McDonnell Douglas executive Dan Stanley, now an aide to Senate Minority Leader Robert Dole, states that the company was "struggling for its existence."[7]

General Dynamics, another major defense contractor which until 1991 was firmly based in St. Louis, is also vulnerable because its strength in Navy contracts makes it susceptible to heavy cuts in submarine programs. Although it will build the Navy's second Seawolf submarine and has a large order backlog, General Dynamics' subsidiary, Electric Boat, is planning several thousand layoffs (see under Groton, CT). The F-16 Falcon, and the Ohio and Michigan-based M-1 tank built by General Dynamics, are being phased out. The company is not diversifying, but "stresses flexibility of its arms in the new world environment."

The company announced in May 1991 that it would trim 27,000 jobs from its 90,000-strong national work force over the following four years as a result of defense cuts. It announced it would move its headquarters from St. Louis, MO to Fairfax Co., VA to be closer to its primary customer, the Department of Defense.[8]

Many smaller businesses in the area have also been forced to undergo major layoffs. The Belleville Shoe Manufacturing Co. announced it would lay off 203 of its 350 workers because of the decreasing Department of Defense demand for combat boots.[9]

Local economic-adjustment machinery alone does not appear adequate for coping with large-scale cuts; it must work in tandem with Federal efforts. Some local companies have taken in many of the laid-off McDonnell Douglas employees. The County Executive's office has taken the position that the peace dividend should not be consumed, but invested in education, infrastructure, and so forth, in building the kind of economy that could absorb highly paid aerospace engineers. Richard Gephardt (D-MO), House Majority Leader, has stated that Congress should adopt a "'Bill of Rights' for defense-dependent workers and communities." He played an important role in the passage of the 1990 Conversion Law (see Chapter 6) that provides $200 million in additional money for retraining of laid-off defense workers and rehabilitation of obsolete military facilities.[10]

The St. Louis County Executive Office under H.C. Milford was quick to deal with the massive layoffs at McDonnell Douglas, as it applied for and received $100,000 from the Office of Economic Adjustment of the Department of Defense (after several months during which disbursement of the money from the 1990 Conversion Law was held up). The County Executive's initiative also requested that St. Louis Community College's Metropolitan Re-Employment Project undertake a Worker Re-entry Plan in conjunction with McDonnell Douglas, which would entail retraining in growth industries. The Re-Entry Plan is successfully serving as a job information bank. Missouri has received $3.4 million from the U.S. Department of Labor (as well as "emergency" money from the Department) to retrain laid-off workers and $150,000 from the Department of Commerce for a study on economic conversion. Three ten-week Entrepreneurship Training Courses have been developed with funds provided by the Missouri Division of Job Development and Training, involving over 350 local employees.

The St. Louis Economic Conversion Project, headed by Mary Ann McGivern (438 N. Skinker, St. Louis, MO 63130; 314-726-6406), has been organizing the regional community to respond to defense cuts. The Project succeeded in getting passage of a number of shareholders' resolutions submitted to several of the large St. Louis-based contractors concerning the importance of conversion and the ethics of foreign arms sales and bidding on military contracts. It has won a subcontract to do the community-outreach component for the regional plan described in the next paragraph.[11]

The regional conversion plan (which we described as a model program in Chapter 7), under the name the St. Louis Economic Adjustment and Diversification Program, started in 1990. It is sponsored by the St. Louis County Executive, the St. Louis Regional Commerce and Growth Association, and St. Louis Mayor Vincent Schoemehl, Sr.[12]

The plan is in response to the layoffs at McDonnell Douglas and Chrysler, and includes certain counties in southwestern Illinois which border St. Louis County, in addition to the bordering counties within Missouri. The goals of the program are to retrain and re-employ the dislocated workers into growth industries, such as telecommunications and computers, diversifying and strengthening the St. Louis regional economy, and to coordinate the development and planning of such a program with local business, labor, government, job training, economic development, education, and research institutions. The plan is based on four basic components: (1) research; (2) job training; (3) business assistance; and (4) community outreach. Funding of the plan to the tune of $250,000 has been made available by the Office of Economic Adjustment of the Department of Defense and by the Economic Development Administration of the Department of Commerce. The funding has made possible a visit by St. Louis activists and officials to communities facing similar problems in Long Island, Massachusetts, and Maine. Also, among the training programs offered to laid-off workers is a course for would-be entrepreneurs, attended by 320 former McDonnell Douglas employees.[13]

The Defense Mapping Agency in St. Louis may be merged with another facility, saving possibly $23 million annually for the Department of Defense.

Whiteman. Though Whiteman Air Force Base is to be the home of the B-2, it received only $65 million of the requested $100 million in FY 1990, delaying the arrival of the Stealth until 1992. The B-2 will add an estimated 2,000 military personnel and 3,800 new jobs to the base, an overall population growth of 6,500 for the area by 1995.[14]

Notes

1. *Statistical Abstract of the U.S.*, 1989, Bureau of Census, U.S. Department of Commerce, pp. 429-431.

2. *State of the State 1986*, State of Missouri, p. 5. Made available by the Office of Social Economic Data Analysis, University Extension, University of Missouri-Lincoln University, 811 Clark Hall, Columbia, MO 65211; 314-882-7396. *Statistical Abstract...*, *op. cit.*, 1990, p. 639.

3. Adam Goodman and Christopher Carey, "Layoffs' Impact Spreads," *St. Louis Post-Dispatch*, June 24, 1990, p. 10. Contacts: (1) Department of Economic Development, Earl Cannon, Research Director, P.O. Box 720, Jefferson City, MO 65102; 314-751-3674. (2) Fenton Mayor's Office, Hassan Jadali, City Planner, 625 New Smizer Mill Road, Fenton, MO 63026; 314-343-2080. (3) McDonnell Douglas Corp, Barbara Anderson, Public Relations, St. Louis, MO; 314-233-2865. (4) Missouri Department of Commerce, Carl Koupal Jr., 301 W. High, Harry Truman Building, Jefferson City, MO 65102; 314-751-4770. (5) Missouri Department of Employment Security, Tom Righthouse, 321 E. Dunklin St., Jefferson City, MO 65102; 314-751-3215. (6) Office of Economic Adjustment, Joseph Cartwright, 4C767, Department of Defense, Department

of Defense, Washington, D.C. 20301; 703-697-3022, fax 202-697-3021; is working closely with St. Louis County on economic adjustment. (7) Office of Rep. Richard Gephardt, Bob Hoden or Mary Renick, 9959 Gravois Ave., St. Louis, MO 63123; 314-631-9959. (8) St. Louis County Economic Council, County Executive, Dennis Coleman, Executive Director, Clayton, MO 63105; 314-889-7663. (9) St. Louis County Executive, Dee Joyner, Chief of Staff, Clayton, MO 63105.

4. *Base Closure and Realignment Report*, April 1991, pp. 104-105.

5. Interview with Karen Brandon, St. Louis bureau, *Kansas City Star*, July 23, 1990; 314-726-5449; Fax 314-726-5370.

6. Adam Goodman, "McDonnell Plans Layoffs," *St. Louis Post-Dispatch*, June 21, 1990, p. 1.

7. Goodman and Carey, *op. cit.*, p. 1. Eric Schmitt, "Pentagon Scraps $57 Billion Order for Attack Plane," *The New York Times*, January 8, 1991, pp. A1, A9. Thomas C. Hayes, "Thoughts After Layoffs: Making Do and Moving," *The New York Times*, January 9, 1991, p. A12. Steven Pearlstein and Barton Gellman, "'Lockheed Wins Huge Jet Contract,'" *The Washington Post*, April 24, 1991, p. 1.

8. Andy Pasztor and Rick Wartzman, "As Defense Industry Shrinks, Suppliers Face Widely Varying Fates," *The Wall Street Journal*, p. A-7. Richard Stevenson, "Dynamics Set to Trim 27,000 Jobs," *The New York Times*, May 2, 1991, pp. D1, D2.

9. Goodman and Carey, *op. cit.*, p. 10.

10. Interview in March, 1990 with Dee Joyner, Chief of Staff, St. Louis County Executive, Clayton, MO 63105; 314-889-2016. Goodman, *op. cit.*, p. 9.

11. News release, St. Louis County Executive, H.C. Milford, June 21, 1990. Richard W, Stevenson, "So Far, St. Louis Shows It Has Been Able to Deal With the Pentagon Cuts," *The New York Times*, August 8, 1991, p. D11. *Conversion Organizers' Update*, February 1991, The Center for Economic Conversion, p. 8. John Tepper Marlin, "Who Is Hurt the Most by Defense Dept. Cuts," *The New York Times*, News of the Week in Review, September 8, 1991, p. 18.

12. Executive Summary, St. Louis Economic Adjustment and Diversification Program, released July 19, 1990. The program sponsors are: (1) St. Louis Regional Commerce and Growth Association, Bob Blanchard or Gary Broome, 100 South Fourth Street, #500, St. Louis, MO 63102; 314-231-5555 or 444-1170; (2) St. Louis County Executive, H.C. Milford, Clayton, MO 63105; 314-889-2021; and (3) Mayor Vincent Schoemehl, Sr., St. Louis, MO.

13. Janet Stone, *Conversion Organizers' Update* (Mountain View, CA: Center for Economic Conversion, October 1991, advance copy), pp. 7-8.

14. Jennifer Greer, "The Pain, Promise of Peace," *Kansas City Star*, December 10, 1989, p. 10N.

Montana

A	B	C	D	E	F
$				VI	DDI
–	–	–	↓	!	✌

Benchmarks	No.	Rank	Benchmarks	No.	Rank
A.Total DoD $	$0.3bil.	50	Def.-Dependent Jobs ('000), '90	12	49
B. Personnel Payroll	$0.2bil.	48	Change in Def.-Dep. Jobs, '89-'91	-7.7%	22
C. Prime Contracts (PC)	$.07bil.	44	Unemployment Rate, '90-'91	6.7%	22
D. PC Change, FY '87-'90	-33.8%	12	Unemp. Rate Change, '89-'91	+0.9%	27
E. Vulnerability Index	8.3	32	Per Capita Income	$15,110	42
F. Defense Disloc. Index	0.002	48	Population ('000)	799	45

▲ Army ■ Navy
● Air Force ○ Other

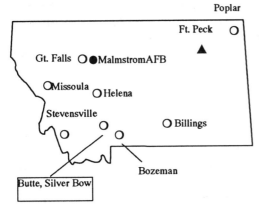

Prime Contract Trends, FY'87-'90
(Constant FY '92 $Billions)

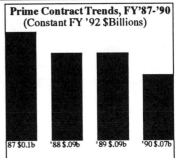

87 $0.1b	'88 $.09b	'89 $.09b	'90 $.07b

Top 5 Contractors	$ Millions
A&S Tribal Industries	$12.6
Montana Refining	11.2
Brinderson	5.6
Turner Engineering	3.7
Slish Ktnai Tribes	2.8

Top 10 $ Sites[a]	Congressional Dist., Representative	1989 Rank	Total DoD$[c]	Payroll[c]	Prime Contracts[c]	Per-sonnel[d]
1-Malmstrom (231)	2-Marlenee, r	228	$133.4	$106.6	$26.8	4.6
2-Great Falls (342)	"	351	42.5	31.2	11.3	0.4
3-Helena (431)	1-Williams, d	429	14.1	12.1	2.1	0.3
4-Poplar (437)	2-Marlenee, r	--	13.2	0.2	13.1	--
5-Billings (449)	"	448	9.3	8.9	0.5	.03
6-Missoula (471)	1-Williams, d	472	5.7	5.4	0.3	--
7-Bozeman (473)	"	478	5.2	4.3	0.9	.03
8-Ft. Peck (483)	2-Marlenee, r	--	4.5	1.0	3.5	.04
9-Stevensville (484)	1-Williams, d	459	4.4	0.7	3.7	--
10-Butte-S. Bow (491)	"	--	4.0	3.6	0.4	--

[a]Rating in parentheses is out of 511 sites, the top ten in each state and PR, plus DC.
[b]Multidistrict r-Rep, d-Dem. [c]$Millions (figures may not add due to rounding) [d]Thousands

Montana

The state did not experience the booming mid-1980s growth that many other parts of the country enjoyed. Agriculture, lumber, paper products and mining account for over 48 percent of the state's economic base. Montana's unemployment rate in 1991 was slightly higher than average. Its unemployment rate slightly increased during 1988-1991 (the increase in the labor force exceeded the increase in employment). Per capita income and non-farm labor income have been rising, but are still below the U.S. averages.[1]

Defense and the Economy

Only two states received less defense money than Montana in 1990. The only Department of Defense facility that is an important employer in the state is Malmstrom Air Force Base, which receives nearly 46 percent of the state's defense dollars. The construction and petroleum industries are the main defense-related prime contractors, taking over 56 percent of all 1989 Montana prime-contract dollars. The future of the battery of Minuteman missiles located in central Montana is uncertain. According to Defense Secretary Dick Cheney's recent proposals, the missiles will remain for a few more years, but with reduced funding. The long-term existence of the missiles, according to Maj. Gen. George Larson, is in serious jeopardy.[2]

Central Montana. Most missile sites in the state are in central Montana. Secretary Cheney's proposal to retire 450 Minuteman II missiles, saving $400 million yearly, was rejected by the Bush Administration. The nation's oldest, Montana's Minuteman missiles will most likely be retired by the end of the decade in favor of the Midgetman or MX.[3]

Great Falls. Though no cuts have been proposed in spending or personnel, 220 Malmstrom AFB personnel are taking advantage of the Air Force's early-release program, an acknowledgment of expectations of imminent cuts.[4]

Notes

1. Paul Polzin, *Montana Business Quarterly*, 28:1 (Spring 1990), p. 5.
2. *Atlas/Data Abstract for the U.S. and Selected Areas Fiscal 1990*, Department of Defense, p. 71. *Prime Contract Awards by Region and State, Fiscal Years 1989, 1988, 1987*, Department of Defense, p. 44. Alice Greenway, "Missiles Won't Go, But Funding Low," *Helena Independent Record*, January 30, 1990. Contacts: (1) Governor's Office, Donald Ramage, Administrative Assistant, Helena, MT 59260; 406-444-3111. (2) Montana Department of Commerce, Chuck Brook, 1424 9th Avenue, Helena, MT 59260; 406-444-3494. (3) Montana Department of Labor, Mike Micone, Lockey and Roberts, Helena, MT 59260; 406-444-3555.
3. "Cheney Plan to Junk Missiles Served No Strategic Purpose," Editorial, *Great Falls Tribune*, January 25, 1990.
4. Peter Johnson, "MAFB Gears for Budget Cuts With Early-Release Program," *Great Falls Tribune*, December 28, 1989.

Nebraska

A	B	C	D	E	F
$	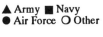			VI	DDI
–	–	–	→	–	✌

Benchmarks	No.	Rank	Benchmarks	No.	Rank
A. Total DoD $	$0.9bil.	39	Def.-Dependent Jobs ('000), '90	38	39
B. Personnel Payroll	$0.7bil.	36	Change in Def.-Dep. Jobs, '89-'91	-2.6%	30
C. Prime Contracts (PC)	$0.2bil.	43	Unemployment Rate, '90-'91	2.4%	51
D. PC Change, FY '87-'90	-15.3%	27	Unemp. Rate Change, '89-'91	-0.6%	47
E. Vulnerability Index	4.8	52	Per Capita Income	$17,221	28
F. Defense Disloc. Index	0	49	Population ('000)	1,578	37

▲ Army ■ Navy
● Air Force ○ Other

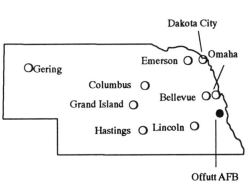

Prime Contract Trends, FY'87-'90
(Constant FY '92 $Billions)

'87 $0.3b   '88 $0.3b   '89 $0.2b   '90 $0.3b

Top 5 Contractors	$ Millions
Aksarben Foods	$30.2
Unisys	20.4
Harris	19.8
Sterling Software	16.7
Omega Group	11.9

Top 10 $ Sites[a]	Congressional Dist., Representative	1989 Rank	Total DoD$[c]	Payroll[c]	Prime Contracts[c]	Personnel[d]
1-Offutt AFB (71)	2-Hoagland, d	87	$505.6	$398.6	$106.9	13.8
2-Omaha (193)	"	200	178.1	111.8	66.3	2.1
3-Bellevue (314)	"	304	61.4	33.0	28.4	.02
4-Lincoln (336)	1-Bereuter, r	357	44.9	30.6	14.4	0.6
5-Emerson (451)	"	479	8.9	.08	8.8	--
6-Gering (476)	3-Barrett, r	--	5.1	0.7	4.4	--
7-Hastings (477)	"	486	4.9	3.1	1.8	.06
8-Dakota City (478)	1-Bereuter, r	485	4.9	0.1	4.8	--
9-Grand Island (499)	3-Barrett, r	--	2.8	2.4	0.4	--
10-Columbus (502)	"	--	2.5	1.3	1.2	--

[a]Rating in parentheses is out of 511 sites, the top ten in each state and PR, plus DC.
[b]Multidistrict r-Rep, d-Dem. [c]$Millions (figures may not add due to rounding) [d]Thousands

Nebraska

Almost 60,000 jobs were added during the second half of the 1980s, for an average growth of 2.9 percent, and in 1989 alone 23,000 jobs were added, making a growth rate of 3.3 percent for that year alone.[1] Nebraska ranked extremely well (second best) in the unemployment survey and there has been a slight decrease in the unemployment rate during the past two years (a large increase in employment slightly exceeded an equally big increase in the labor force). Much of Nebraska's economic future hinges upon Federal agriculture policy. "As agriculture goes, so goes Nebraska." The 1990 Farm Bill, pushed through by Nebraskan Clayton Yeutter, promoted market pricing to foster international demand for U.S. farm products. Compared to a year earlier, beef prices in January 1991 were up while wheat prices were down. This is good for Nebraska because beef is a major export; with its new meat packing plants, Nebraska may in 1990 have surpassed Kansas and Texas as the No. 1 beef producer.

Defense and the Economy

Total Department of Defense expenditures in Nebraska were only $886 million (less than some individual prime contracts in other states), and Offutt Air Force Base received 57 percent of the total Defense Department money; nearly 45 percent of the state's defense funds were solely for the payroll at the base. About three-fourths of defense expenditure in the state is for payroll. With the second lowest unemployment rate in the country and an extremely small defense presence, it is not surprising that Nebraska has the nation's lowest Vulnerability Index.[2]

Notes

1. James R. Schmidt, "Nebraska Economic Projections for 1990," *Business in Nebraska*, 45:544 (January, 1990), pp. 1, 3, 5.

2. Contacts: (1) Nebraska Department of Economic Development, Roger Christianson and Tom Doering, P.O. Box 94666, Lincoln, NE 68509; 402-471-3111. (2) Nebraska Labor Market Information, Wendell Olson, 350 South 16th St., Lincoln, NE 68509; 402-471-9000.

Nevada

A	B	C	D	E	F
$	🪖	🏭	▦	VI	DDI
–	–	–	↓	–	✂

Benchmarks	No.	Rank	Benchmarks	No.	Rank
A. Total DoD $	$0.7bil.	41	Def.-Dependent Jobs ('000), '90	27	44
B. Personnel Payroll	$0.5bil.	37	Change in Def.-Dep. Jobs, '89-'91	-12.9%	10
C. Prime Contracts (PC)	$0.2bil.	45	Unemployment Rate, '90-'91	5.9%	31
D. PC Change, FY '87-'90	-29.2%	17	Unemp. Rate Change, '89-'91	+1.1%	24
E. Vulnerability Index	7.7	41	Per Capita Income	$19,416	14
F. Defense Disloc. Index	0.84	26	Population ('000)	1,202	40

■ Fallon

○ Reno, Dayton, Sparks, Carson City

▲ Hawthorne

Mercury ○

Nellis AFB ●

▲ Army ■ Navy
● Air Force ○ Other

Las Vegas ○ Henderson

Prime Contract Trends, FY'87-'90
(Constant FY '92 $Billions)

'87 $0.3b | '88 $0.2b | '89 $0.3b | '90 $0.2b

Top 5 Contractors	$ Millions
Ford	$30.6
Day & Zimm./Basil JV	23.0
Worldcorp	18.4
Lockheed	11.5
Day & Zimmermann	10.5

Top 10 $ Sites[a]	Congressional Dist., Representative	1989 Rank	Total DoD$[c]	Payroll[c]	Prime Contracts[c]	Per-sonnel[d]
1-Nellis AFB (125)	2-Vucanovich, r	119	$318.4	$237.2	$81.1	9.2
2-Las Vegas (254)	(1,2)[b]	224	109.4	100.3	9.1	0.3
3-Fallon (320)	2-Vucanovich, r	286	55.8	33.9	21.9	1.2
4-Hawthorne(370)	"	398	33.5	0	33.5	0.1
5-Reno (374)	"	372	32.6	28.8	3.7	0.3
6-Henderson (407)	1-Bilbray, d	430	21.3	12.6	8.6	.02
7-Carson City (423)	2-Vucanovich, r	414	16.0	14.8	1.2	0.1
8-Sparks (429)	"	--	14.6	11.3	3.3	--
9-Dayton (455)	"	--	8.2	0.5	7.7	--
10-Mercury (470)	"	--	5.7	1.1	4.6	--

[a]Rating in parentheses is out of 511 sites, the top ten in each state and PR, plus DC.
[b]Multidistrict r-Rep, d-Dem. [c]$Millions (figures may not add due to rounding) [d]Thousands

Nevada

From 1984-1988, personal income growth in Nevada exceeded the national average. The cumulative average for those years was 9.77 percent for Nevada, compared to 7.36 percent for the nation.[1] Nevada ranked slightly better than average in its unemployment rate for April 1991 (the recent positive change in its unemployment rate reflected an increase in the labor force that slightly exceeded an increase in employment). Home to Las Vegas and Reno, Nevada's largest employment sector is hotels and gaming. Approximately 36,000 jobs were added in this sector alone during the 1980s, in comparison to approximately 27,000 total additional jobs in the mining, manufacturing and construction industries.

Defense and the Economy

Nevada is not very defense-dependent; its Vulnerability Index is ranked 41st among the states, and total Department of Defense spending in the state, at $722 million, is also 41st in the nation. Contract cuts and reduced SDI research could cut several hundred thousand dollars in defense dollars from Nevada.

Community Surveys

Carol Popoff, Assistant Director of Research for the University of Reno Business Research Institute, points out that because there is not much defense-oriented industry in Nevada, the greatest fear is in terms of personnel cuts. Almost 75 percent of defense expenditures in the state are in payroll outlays for the 18,137 civilian and military personnel.[2]

Las Vegas. The Department of Defense decided to cut 2,400 employees from Nellis Air Force Base and the research facility at Tonopah. The absolute numbers are not large relative to other states, but the cuts have a considerable impact on the small Nevada economy.

Notes

1. Thomas Cargill, "Forecasts of the Nevada Economy," September 25, 1989, pp. 3-5.

2. Interview with Carol Popoff in June 1990; 702-784-4864. Contacts: (1) Executive Chamber, State of Nevada, Gov. Bob Miller, Carson City, NV 89710; 702-687-5670. (2) Nevada Department of Economic Development, Andrew Grose, Director, c/o Governor's Office, Capitol Complex, Carson City, NV 87910; 702-687-4325. (3) Nevada Department of Employment Security, Jaine Hanna, Capitol Complex, Carson City, NV 89710; 702-885-4550.

New Hampshire

A	B	C	D	E	F
$	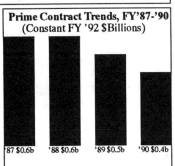			VI	DDI
–	–	–	→	!	✄

Benchmarks	No.	Rank	Benchmarks	No.	Rank
A. Total DoD $	$0.7bil.	44	Def.-Dependent Jobs ('000), '90	30	42
B. Personnel Payroll	$0.3bil.	45	Change in Def.-Dep. Jobs, '89-'91	-23.1%	4
C. Prime Contracts (PC)	$0.4bil.	40	Unemployment Rate, '90-'91	7.1%	16
D. PC Change, FY '87-'90	-25.0%	21	Unemp. Rate Change, '89-'91	+3.9%	4
E. Vulnerability Index	9.0	29	Per Capita Income	$20,789	9
F. Defense Disloc. Index	7.59	4	Population ('000)	1,109	41

▲ Army ■ Navy
● Air Force ○ Other

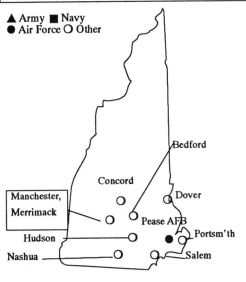

Prime Contract Trends, FY'87-'90
(Constant FY '92 $Billions)

'87 $0.6b   '88 $0.6b   '89 $0.5b   '90 $0.4b

Top 5 Contractors	$ Millions
Lockheed	168.5$
Sequa	31.9
Tricil Environmental	29.3
Sanders/Gen. Elec. JV	24.9
Sanders/AEL JV	20.9

Top 10 $ Sites[a]	Congressional Dist., Representative	1989 Rank	Total DoD$[c]	Payroll[c]	Prime Contracts[c]	Personnel[d]
1-Nashua (203)	2-Swett, d	169	$168.7	$14.9	$153.8	0.1
2-Pease AFB (259)	1-Zeliff ,r	254	107.6	89.3	18.2	2.4
3-Portsmouth (288)	"	306	84.9	32.7	52.2	0.5
4-Merrimack (323)	"	234	54.4	0	54.4	--
5-Hudson (344)	2-Swett, d	401	41.6	3.4	38.2	.01
6-Manchester (361)	1-Zeliff, r	377	36.7	7.4	29.3	0.1
7-Salem (446)	2-Swett, d	420	9.9	1.6	8.3	--
8-Dover (458)	1-Zeliff, r	--	7.8	6.5	1.3	--
9-Concord (463)	2-Swett, d	--	7.2	6.7	0.5	0.2
10-Bedford (466)	1-Zeliff, r	--	6.7	6.1	0.6	--

[a]Rating in parentheses is out of 511 sites, the top ten in each state and PR, plus DC.
[b]Multidistrict r-Rep, d-Dem. [c]$Millions (figures may not add due to rounding) [d]Thousands

New Hampshire

New Hampshire made the most of the economic boom in 1980s New England. The state experienced a remarkable jump in computer and other high-tech industries, and the number of firms located in the state expanded by 36 percent. This surge was partly due to the state's low wages, extremely low taxes, and business-oriented government. The services-producing sectors, particularly retail trade and finance, are the dominant components of the economy, accounting for more than half of total state employment. Important manufacturing industries include electronics and industrial machinery. New Hampshire, like its sister states in the Northeast, was hard hit by the recession of 1990-91. Its unemployment rate in April 1991 ranked 16th and its increase in unemployment between April 1989 and April 1991 ranked 4th (growth in the labor force greatly outpaced growth in employment).[1]

Defense and the Economy

The Department of Defense spends relatively little in New Hampshire. The $658 million the state received in 1990 was 9th from the bottom in state rankings. The defense payroll directly employs only 0.3 percent of the state's civilian labor force. Pease AFB, which accounted for about 15 percent of all defense spending in the state, was the first base closed under Defense Secretary Dick Cheney's plan. Approximately 2.6 percent of total state employment was dependent on the base, which also directly supports a quarter of the Portsmouth economy. The state also stands to lose several million dollars if M-1 tank and F-14 fighter contracts are terminated. These factors, combined with the worrisome unemployment and unemployment change rates, make the state rank high (4th highest) on the Defense Dislocation Index. However, New Hampshire firms will continue to do significant electronics and other necessary high-tech defense business; most of the 1990 prime contracts awarded to the state were related to communications and electronics.[2]

Community Surveys

The major focus of conversion advocates has been on Pease Air Force Base, but New Hampshire has considerable defense-contract dollars, mostly from the Lockheed's Electronics Systems Group and its subsidiary Sanders Associates in Nashua, NH; they and their joint ventures (JVs) account for three of the top five contractors in the state.

Concord. New Hampshire Action for Peace and Lasting Security, (P.O. Box 771, Concord, NH 03302; 603-228-0559, headed by Patricia Bass), organized peace dividend resolutions which were passed in 10 of 13 town meetings in March 1990. It lobbied for the State Senate to call on Gov. Judd Gregg to form a committee to study the impacts of defense cuts in New Hampshire and to help plan for conversion.

Portsmouth. Pease Air Force Base was the first of the 83 bases slated for closure or realignment that actually closed. As the touchdown site for George Bush's Air Force One on his Kennebunkport visits, and employer of 13,000, Pease was by far the largest base in New Hampshire. Estimated annual savings from closing Pease are expected to be $81.3 million.[3] Experts contend that Pease's location and existing capabilities make it ideal for civilian redevelopment. The progress of Pease's redevelopment will certainly be under the microscope as one of the first experiments of post-Cold War base conversion.

Officials from the Office of Economic Adjustment (OEA) and Air Force took officials from Portsmouth and from other affected communities to five bases that had undergone conversions (Lincoln, Duluth, Chippewa County, Bangor, and Rosewell) in July 1989, to observe a variety of reuse efforts.[4] Portsmouth City councilor Charles Noon went on the excursion, commenting that what he saw, in Duluth, MN showed communities what not to do.

The Pease Development Authority was founded by a joint effort of Portsmouth, the state, and the Air Force. The first thing it did was to hire San Francisco-based Bechtel to map out strategy. The Air Force contributed $572,000 for the air-related aspect of the study; OEA came up with a $150,000 grant to Portsmouth. Bechtel proposed a variety of uses for the base: an air freight facility, a passenger airport, creation of office spaces, and even an amusement park. Local residents are unhappy with the plan, which they say is not sufficiently sensitive to environmental concerns and lacked local input. A deliberate effort was made to separate Bechtel from local influence by the state-appointed Portsmouth Authority; officials of Portsmouth and nearby Newington, which shares jurisdiction over the base, had been arguing over re-use plans. Although local infighting has been dealt with, the Development Authority faces the difficult task of attracting investors. Negotiations have begun with a large German aircraft manufacturer, Deutsche Airbus.[5]

Notes

1. *1985-1988 Vital Signs, NH Economic and Social Indicators*, New Hampshire Department of Employment Security, December 1989. *Economic Conditions in New Hampshire*, New Hampshire Department of Employment Security, April 1990.

2. *Atlas/Data Abstract for the U.S. and Selected Areas Fiscal 1990*, Department of Defense, p. 77. Also *Economic Conditions in New Hampshire*, Civilian Labor Force Information, p. 1. Patrick Jonsson, "City Copes with Airbase Closing," *The Christian Science Monitor*, January 8, 1990, p. 8. *Prime Contract Awards by Region and State, Fiscal Years 1989, 1988, 1987*, Department of Defense, p. 47.

3. *Loc. cit.*

4. From a letter to the Council on Economic Priorities from John Lynch, July 1990.

5. *Loc. cit.* "Surveying the Landscape," *Base Conversion News*, Spring 1991, p. 4. Charles A. Radin, "Mustered out, Pease Looks to Succeed in Civvies," *The Boston Globe*, April 1, 1991, p. 13.

New Jersey

A	B	C	D	E	F
$	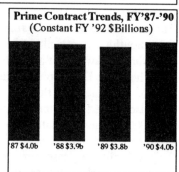			VI	DDI
+	+	+	↑	!	✂

Benchmarks	No.	Rank	Benchmarks	No.	Rank
A. Total DoD $	$5.4bil.	10	Def.-Dependent Jobs ('000), '90	301	10
B. Personnel Payroll	$1.7bil.	18	Change in Def.-Dep. Jobs, '89-'91	+6.0%	42
C. Prime Contracts (PC)	$3.7bil.	11	Unemployment Rate, '90-'91	6.1%	29
D. PC Change, FY '87-'90	+1.0%	41	Unemp. Rate Change, '89-'91	+2.6%	9
E. Vulnerability Index	8.2	34	Per Capita Income	$24,968	2
F. Defense Disloc. Index	1.05	23	Population ('000)	7,730	9

Little Falls
Picatinny Arsenal
Wayne / Nutley
Madison
Princeton
Oceanport
Ft. Dix
Moorestown
McGuire AFB

▲ Army ■ Navy
● Air Force ○ Other

Prime Contract Trends, FY'87-'90
(Constant FY '92 $Billions)

'87 $4.0b | '88 $3.9b | '89 $3.8b | '90 $4.0b

Top 5 Contractors	$ Millions
General Electric	$826.5
ITT	419.7
General Electric PLC	134.0
Astronautics	130.2
Allied Signal	119.5

Top 10 $ Sites[a]	Congressional Dist., Representative	1989 Rank	Total DoD$[c]	Payroll[c]	Prime Contracts[c]	Per-sonnel[d]
1-Moorestown (57)	12-Zimmer,r	71	$654.0	$0	$654.0	--
2-Nutley (72)	8-Roe,d	96	503.1	2.3	500.8	--
3-Oceanport (88)	3-Pallone,d	131	448.8	332.9	115.9	--
4-Fort Dix (142)	13-Saxton,r	99	277.3	247.3	30.0	9.5
5-Picatinny Ars. (156)	11-Gallo,r	166	249.5	203.1	46.4	5.2
6-Madison (164)	"	--	224.2	0.3	223.9	--
7-Little Falls (195)	8-Roe,d	252	176.5	2.1	165.5	--
8-McGuire AFB (199)	4-Smith,r	198	172.5	153.4	19.1	6.3
9-Princeton (235)	12-Zimmer,r	175	130.2	2.2	128.0	--
10-Wayne (238)	8-Roe,d	--	126.0	0	126.0	--

[a]Rating in parentheses is out of 511 sites, the top ten in each state and PR, plus D.C.
[b]Multidistrict r-Rep, d-Dem. [c]$Millions (figures may not add due to rounding) [d]Thousands

New Jersey

The New Jersey economy underwent remarkable growth throughout the 1980s. Economists predicted that New Jersey businesses will become less competitive in the1990s because of a tight labor market, but the labor force has been expanding at a healthy pace. The state's unemployment rate ranked 29th in April 1991 and its change in unemployment over the previous two years 9th (employment decreased while the labor force increased). The state's manufacturing sector declined in the late 1980s, while the services sector, although still strong, has lost some momentum. Like other Northeastern states, New Jersey faced budgetary pressures at the start of the 1990s that have not been wholly alleviated by the largest income tax increase in the state's history.[1]

Defense and the Economy

The Department of Defense spent more than $5 billion in New Jersey in 1990, making it the 10th highest site of expenditures. Defense spending accounts for 2.6 percent of gross state product and over 26,000 civilian jobs. The diverse base of the New Jersey manufacturing sector, along with the moderate unemployment rate, reduces the state's vulnerability to defense cutbacks. The program to be cut most severely is the F-15 fighter, though jet-fighter sales to Saudi Arabia make the final outcome difficult to estimate. Other programs in New Jersey affected by cuts are the M-1 tank and the F-14 fighter.

The most important defense-related industry in New Jersey is production of high-tech electronics and communications equipment, which received 30 percent of state defense dollars. Defense experts contend that such high-tech equipment, produced by many medium-sized firms in New Jersey, will remain vital to future defense needs. Other important industries include textiles (N.J. firms were 5th in the nation), missiles, and aircraft parts. The closing of the Philadelphia Naval Shipyard will affect 8,700 New Jersey residents and cost the state $12 million in annual tax revenue. Although some small-sized computer and high-tech firms could increase their military contracts in the coming years, Wall Street analysts predict most New Jersey contractors will lose business.[2]

Community Surveys

Dover. Expecting layoffs in the next five years, hiring and promotion freezes have already taken place at the Picatinny Arsenal. Officials at the arsenal contend that most of the personnel reductions can be achieved through retirement and attrition. An Army spokesman at Picatinny predicted that as few as 50 jobs will be lost, as some positions will be shifted elsewhere in the arsenal, but others fear that up to 600 civilian jobs could be lost.[3]

Eatontown. Analysts expect small contracting firms specializing in high-tech computer services, such as Vitronics in Eatontown, to continue to have significant Department of Defense business. Vitronics has expanded from 25 employees and $2 million in revenues in 1983, to 170 employees and $10 million in revenues in 1989.

Allied-Signal's Bendix Electric Power Division in Eatontown stands to lose a major generator contract should Congress cancel the V-22 Osprey program. The plant employs 850 workers and also produces the F-14 and F-15 fighters. Allied-Signal decided to cut back in the preparation of its military-related contracts and diversify its base in 1987. Today, the company is considered to be among the least vulnerable contractors.[4]

Lakehurst. The Naval Air Engineering Center is likely to be merged with the Naval Air Warfare Center's Aircraft Division centered at Patuxent River, MD. The Navy estimates that the move will eliminate 460 positions.[5]

Nutley. Due to cutbacks in military spending, particularly in orders for an electronic jamming system, ITT Avionics has announced it will reduce its workforce after 1991. The company, which employs 2,600 people in Clifton and Nutley, has already cut 300 personnel since 1987.[6] An Economic Adjustment Task Force is in place under the auspices of the Burlington County Office of Economic Development.

Raritan. Throughout the first half of the century, Raritan Arsenal was one of the government's most important supply and storage depots. Its conversion to a business park, which began in the mid-sixties and culminated around 1985, represented a huge economic step forward for the area. The park is home to 250 corporate tenants who employ over 10,000 people. Plans are underway to expand office space and residential acreage in the 1990s.[7]

Red Bank. The Communications-Electronics Command (CECOM) at Fort Monmouth, which provides tactical communications and electronic systems and equipment for the Army, was slated for reductions in 1990. In April 1991, the Department of Defense announced that it would move the Electronic Technology Device Laboratory from Fort Monmouth to Adelphi, MD. In an agreement in early 1990 between the fort and the state of New Jersey it was decided that Fort Monmouth would open its laboratory facilities to academic and industry researchers. The fort will work with the New Jersey Commission on Science and Technology on use of the Army's labs for joint research ventures with universities and private companies.[8]

Trenton. The Naval Air Propulsion Center will merge with the Aircraft Division of the Naval Air Warfare Center based in Patuxent, MD. An estimated 360 employees will be transferred or laid off.

Wrightstown. Under the 1989 Base Closure Act, the plan is for Fort Dix to move down to "semi-active" status by 1995, including relocation of basic and advanced training facilities. Dix is to be used as a training site for the National Guard and Reserve troops.[9] This cutback at Fort Dix would affect close to 2,500 civilians working directly for the Army, and an additional 1,300 working for contractors. This represents a loss of 1.8 percent of local jobs.

Rep. James Saxton and other New Jersey politicians support a job training program, a job search allowance, and a policy giving priority to laid-off workers for securing positions in other Federal agencies. The Burlington County Economic Development office has organized an area adjustment effort, in part with the help of a $67,000 Office of Economic Adjustment planning grant.

Re-use efforts may include making Dix a major Reserve training center, using fort facilities for oil-spill-cleanup operations, and developing plans for a commercial center.[10]

Notes

1. *1990 Economic Outlook for New Jersey*, Economic Policy Council and Office of Economic Policy, State of New Jersey, December 1989, pp. 16, 17.

2. *Prime Contract Awards by Region and State, Fiscal Years 1989, 1988, 1987*, Department of Defense, p. 48. Mark Dillon, "Retreat! Area Defense Industries Face Cutbacks," *Monmouth News*, Dec. 17, 1989, p. B1. *Economic Impact of the Philadelphia Naval Base and Shipyard on the Philadelphia Metropolitan Area*, October 1990, the Pennsylvania Economy League and the WEFA Group, Inc., pp. vi, ix. Contacts: (1) New Jersey Governor's Office, State House, Brenda Davis, Director-Policy and Planning, Trenton, NJ 08625; 609-292-6000. (2) Monmouth County Administrative Division, Edward J. McKenna, Jr., Mayor, Borough of Red Bank, P.O. Box 868, Red Bank, NJ 07701; 908-530-2750. (3) New Jersey Department of Commerce, Borden Putnam, CN 820, Trenton, NJ 08625; 609-292-2444. (4) New Jersey Department of Labor, Arthur O'Neal, John Fitch Plaza, CN 110, Trenton, NJ 08625; 609-292-2643. (5) New Jersey Office of Economic Development, Ben Ferrara, Director, CN 823, Trenton, NJ 08625; 609-292-7757.

3. Kevin Coughlin, "Defense Workers Face Cutbacks at 2 Bases," *Newark-Star Ledger*, May 9, 1990, p. 14.

4. *Loc. cit.*

5. *Base Closure and Realignment Report*, Department of Defense, April 1991, p. 74.

6. Joseph Perone, "ITT Avionics to Cut Workforce After 1991," *Newark Star-Ledger*, February 8, 1990, p. 45.

7. Samuel G. Nowell, Peter Cook and Howarth Gilmore, "Two Decades at Raritan Center," *25 Years of Civilian Reuse*, May 1986, p. 29.

8. "Army to Open Ft. Monmouth Labs for Civilian Research Under New Pact," *Newark Star-Ledger*, February 28, 1990, p. 22. The New Jersey Commission on Science and Technology, 122 West State Street, CN 832, Trenton, NJ 08625-0832. 609-984-1671. Edward Cohen, Executive Director for Academic and Industrial Collaborative Research and Technology Transfer with Fort Monmouth.

9. "Fort Dix: Future in Reserves," *Willingboro Daily*, January 5, 1990.

10. "Bush Official Cool to Dix Aid," *Willingboro Daily*, June 28, 1990. Letter to the Council on Economic Priorities from John Lynch, July 1990. Joseph D. McCaffrey, "Saxton Maps Strategy in 'Battle' for Ft. Dix," *Newark Star-Ledger*, April 24, 1991, p. 6.

New Mexico

A	B	C	D	E	F
$	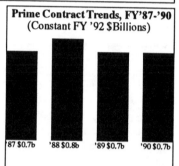			VI	DDI
+	+	+	↑	!!	✄

Benchmarks	No.	Rank	Benchmarks	No.	Rank
A. Total DoD $	$1.6bil.	33	Def.-Dependent Jobs ('000), '90	78	34
B. Personnel Payroll	$0.9bil.	29	Change in Def.-Dep. Jobs, '89-'91	+2.6%	39
C. Prime Contracts (PC)	$0.7bil.	32	Unemployment Rate, '90-'91	7.6%	8
D. PC Change, FY '87-'90	+3.5%	42	Unemp. Rate Change, '89-'91	+0.6%	32
E. Vulnerability Index	12.1	12	Per Capita Income	$14,228	47
F. Defense Disloc. Index	1.52	18	Population ('000)	1,515	38

▲ Army ■ Navy
● Air Force O Other

O Los Alamos
O Santa Fe
O Gallup
O Sandia
O Albuquerque
● Kirtland AFB
Cannon AFB ●
O Alamogordo
● Holloman AFB
O Las Cruces

Prime Contract Trends, FY'87-'90
(Constant FY '92 $Billions)

'87 $0.7b	'88 $0.8b	'89 $0.7b	'90 $0.7b

Top 5 Contractors	$ Millions
Dyncorp	$88.3
Honeywell	81.0
General Electric	28.9
Ford	27.4
State of New Mexico	25.0

Top 10 $ Sites[a]	Congressional Dist., Representative	1989 Rank	Total DoD$[c]	Payroll[c]	Prime Contracts[c]	Per-sonnel[d]
1-Albuquerque (110)	1-Schiff, r	111	$357.2	$141.2	$215.9	1.6
2-White Sands (121)	2-Skeen, r	137	325.8	157.3	168.5	4.6
3-Kirtland AFB (139)	1-Schiff, r	125	285.0	203.8	81.1	6.9
4-Holloman AFB (175)	2-Skeen, r	190	209.6	150.7	58.9	5.8
5-Cannon AFB (232)	"	269	131.4	94.0	37.4	4.5
6-Alamogordo (377)	"	374	31.4	20.2	11.2	--
7-Las Cruces (379)	"	360	30.7	19.2	11.5	0.1
8-Santa Fe (408)	3-Richardson, d	395	21.1	20.3	0.8	0.2
9-Sandia (427)	1-Schiff, r	--	15.2	15.1	.06	--
10-Gallup (433)	3-Richardson, d	--	13.8	0.3	13.5	--

[a]Rating in parentheses is out of 511 sites, the top ten in each state and PR, plus DC.
[b]Multidistrict r-Rep, d-Dem. [c]$Millions (figures may not add due to rounding) [d]Thousands

New Mexico

The New Mexico economy was only slightly behind the nation as a whole during the boom period of the 1980s. Both non-agricultural employment and personal income grew just below the national averages (1.85 percent to 1.91 percent and 7.8 percent to 8.1 percent, respectively). Unemployment from 1985-1989 was 8.3 percent, compared to a national average over the same period of 6.2 percent. In 1989, the state economy grew at the same rate as the nation, with a strong 7.4 percent rise in personal income due to increases in interest and farm income. While the economy was boosted by the large growth in defense expenditures to the state, it was adversely affected by declines in the mining and construction sectors. In April 1991 the state's unemployment rate ranked 8th worst and its change in unemployment ranked 32nd (an increase in the labor force exceeded an increase in employment). Manufacturing and tourism are potential growth areas, and the scientific research facilities are in a position to capitalize on technology transfer.[1]

Defense and the Economy

Much of the growth in New Mexico employment in the last ten years can be traced to defense expenditures and almost 15 percent of state employment is tied to defense money. Most of the money went for SDI and nuclear weapons research, which also had the related effect of helping attract private firms. The government spent $2.49 billion and employed 54,678 workers at the labs in FY 1988.[2]

State Legislative Initiatives

The New Mexico state legislature has been working to develop a plan that would assist in diversifying the state economy. It approved a measure urging the economic development and tourism departments to work with other agencies toward diversification. In the document, the legislature expressed concern over the state's "continuing dependence on the defense industry."[3]

Community Surveys

The research funding on which New Mexico depends is not liable to immediate cuts, but in the long term the state could be severely adversely affected. Los Alamos, the birthplace of the atomic bomb, and Sandia are two of the most important nuclear weapons and SDI research labs in the country.

Alamogordo. Defense Secretary Dick Cheney has proposed moving all 56 of the F-117A Stealth fighters to Holloman Air Force Base from Nevada. The plan would bring 1,812 jobs and $11 million in construction to the state.

However, he has also called for the disassembling of the 479th Tactical Training Wing at Holloman, which would cost 1,000 jobs.[4]

Albuquerque. The Inspection and Safety Center will be moved from Norton AFB in California, bringing 486 personnel to nearby Kirtland Air Force Base. In addition, 550 special operations personnel and 13 helicopters are being added to Kirtland's 1550th Combat Crew Training Wing. The Department of Defense also plans to cut 350 personnel from the Air Force Contract Management Division at Kirtland.

The Defense Avionic Army Helicopter Improvement Program is located in Albuquerque. Ten percent of the local workforce is involved in manufacturing and 5.7 percent work for the Federal Government. New Mexico's congressmen have warned of the need to diversify away from government work.[5] The Naval Weapons Evaluation Facility will close. Approximately 110 jobs will be lost or transferred.

The Albuquerque Citizens for Economic Conversion and Diversification (Edith Lennenberg, CEC/D, PO Box 53370, Albuquerque, NM 87153; 505-898-7589) has been working for several years in educating legislators on alternative industrial applications. The group helped to introduce a bill in early 1991 addressing the commercialization of technical development, and has worked with Sandia Labs on "technology transfer"—commercializing research—as well.

Gallup. An ammunition depot employing 86 people, Fort Wingate, will be closed in three years.[6]

Las Cruces. New Mexico Citizens Task Force on Economic Diversification, 1330 Evans Drive, Las Cruces, NM 88001. Charlotte Lowrey.

Los Alamos. The warming of U.S.-Soviet relations causes great concern at this isolated research institute, because almost every wage-earner works for the National Laboratory. Most of the research is devoted to nuclear weapons and SDI, and increases in expenditures for these programs are unlikely. With the city so dependent on Federal expenditures, some residents believe that other industries, like tourism, should be promoted. Others believe, however, that technology transfer is the answer. The Stevenson-Wydler Act of 1980 opened Federal labs to private entrepreneurs, and Los Alamos' future may lie in programs such as medical spectroscopy and radioisotopes. "For every $100 spent marketing a product, only $10 is required to produce it, and only $1 to discover it in the first place. These national laboratories are an undiscovered investment," states Ronald Barks, a physicist hired by Los Alamos to work toward technology transfer. Concerned Citizens for Nuclear Safety (Jay Coghlan, John Stroud, or Michele Merola, 412 W. San Francisco St., Santa Fe, NM 87501; 505-986-1973) recently received a multi-year grant for assisting the development of alternative uses for the Los Alamos labs through the Project for Economic Conversion of Los Alamos National Laboratory.[7]

Sandia Labs. The Sandia Labs should benefit from technology transfer, with an average of 20 business owners visiting the labs daily in 1988. "Nine hundred companies have drawn technology from our labs during the past five years," says Robert Stromberg, a technology transfer officer at Sandia Labs.[8]

Notes

1. Lawrence Waldman, "The New Mexico Economy in the 1980s and Beyond," *New Mexico Business*, 11:1, January-February, 1990, pp. 1-3. *New Mexico Labor Market Review*, published by New Mexico Department of Labor, 19:4, May 31, 1990, p. 9. "New Mexico and Albuquerque Economy: Review and Outlook," *1990 Albuquerque Business Outlook*, p. 1.

2. Waldman, *loc. cit.*

3. "State Efforts —Too Dependent," *Municipal Foreign Policy*, Autumn 1989, p. 47. Contacts: (1) New Mexico Governor's Office, John Dendahl, Cabinet Secretary, State Capitol, Santa Fe, NM 87503; 505-827-0305. (2) Albuquerque Mayor's Office, Mayor Louis Saavedra, City Hall, Albuquerque, NM 87103. (3) New Mexico Department of Economic Development, Alan Richardson, Director, 1100 St. Francis Drive, Santa Fe, NM 87503; 505-827-0279. (4) New Mexico Economic Research Bureau, Larry Blackwell, State Capitol, Santa Fe, NM 87503.

4. David H. Morrissey, "Defense Budget Cuts to Add, Subtract Jobs in N.M.," *Albuquerque Journal*, January 30, 1990.

5. Interview in March, 1990 with David Scott, Director, Economic Development, City of Albuquerque, NM, 505-764-3750.

6. Morrissey, *op. cit.*

7. William Charland, "Converting to Non-Defense," *The Christian Science Monitor*, November 29, 1988, p. 3. Janet Stone, *Conversion Organizers' Update* (Mountain View, CA: Center for Economic Conversion, October 1991, advance copy), p. 8.

8. *Loc. cit.*

New York

A	B	C	D	E	F
$				VI	DDI
+	+	+	↓	−	✄

Benchmarks	No.	Rank	Benchmarks	No.	Rank
A. Total DoD $	$8.6bil.	6	Def.-Dependent Jobs ('000), '90	502	5
B. Personnel Payroll	$1.8bil.	17	Change in Def.-Dep. Jobs, '89-'91	-0.2%	33
C. Prime Contracts (PC)	$6.8bil.	5	Unemployment Rate, '90-'91	7.3%	13
D. PC Change, FY '87-'90	-36.1%	9	Unemp. Rate Change, '89-'91	+1.7%	17
E. Vulnerability Index	7.6	42	Per Capita Income	$21,975	5
F. Defense Disloc. Index	5.42	6	Population ('000)	17,990	2

▲ Army ■ Navy
● Air Force ○ Other

Prime Contract Trends, FY'87-'90
(Constant FY '92 $Billions)

'87 $11.6b   '88 $9.0b   '89 $7.4b   '90 $7.4b

Top 5 Contractors	$ Millions
Grumman	$2,491.9
General Electric	985.3
Unisys	478.0
IBM	449.3
Int'l Marine Carriers	190.9

Top 10 $ Sites[a]	Congressional Dist., Representative	1989 Rank	Total DoD$[c]	Payroll[c]	Prime Contracts[c]	Per-sonnel[d]
1-Bethpage (10)	4-Lent, r	12	$2,376.7	$9.4	$2,367.3	--
2-New York (47)	(6-19)[b]	35	771.2	212.9	558.3	--
3-Syracuse (64)	27-Walsh, r	54	587.4	26.0	561.4	--
4-Great Neck (79)	8-Scheuer, d	91	484.5	5.7	478.8	--
5-Owego (90)	28-Mchugh, d	123	445.4	3.1	442.3	--
6-Ft. Drum (127)	26-Martin, r	114	316.8	290.0	26.8	11.3
7-Schenectady (132)	23-McNutly, d	116	305.3	13.1	292.2	--
8-West Point (152)	20-Lowey, d	144	258.6	231.7	26.9	8.5
9-Rome (170)	25-Boehlert, r	178	214.1	180.0	34.1	--
10-Mineola (184)	(3,5)[b]	--	192.1	1.1	190.9	--

[a]Rating in parentheses is out of 511 sites, the top ten in each state and PR, plus DC.
[b]Multidistrict r-Rep, d-Dem. [c]$Millions (figures may not add due to rounding) [d]Thousands

New York

The average annual increase in the state personal income from 1983 to 1990 was 7.6 percent, outpacing the nation, but slower than the rest of the Northeast at the end of the 1980s. The service sector was New York City's largest job generator in 1989. The financial-services sector has played an important role in New York's economic growth during the decade, but profits began to decline after the October 1987 crash, forcing large numbers of layoffs that have continued into the 1990s. The state's 1990-91 unemployment rate was 7.3 percent, 13th highest; this figure was up 1.7 percentage points from two years before (employment fell more than the labor force declined). The region of the state most dependent on defense contracts, Long Island, is also hit with other declines in the job market, a weak real estate market, and tight consumer spending. The economic weakness in 1990-91 is a big adjustment for an area that experienced rapid growth in the 1980s. The New York State deficit for FY 1991 could exceed $1.5 billion, reflecting the economic slowdown in the Northeast, increases in state expenditures, and a decrease in revenues from a cut in the personal income tax and changes in the tax code.[1]

Defense and the Economy

Total Defense Department spending in the state is $8.6 billion, sixth in the country. Long Island received over half of New York's defense awards. Of the $6.8 billion in New York State prime defense contracts in 1990, Department of Defense data show Grumman Corp. winning $2.5 billion, more than 95 percent of which went to the company's headquarters in Bethpage, Long Island, though the work itself was distributed beyond the headquarters, including some to Grumman facilities outside of New York State.[2]

State Legislative and Executive Initiatives

Gov. Mario Cuomo formed a Defense Advisory Panel, which surveyed 2,000 defense contractors in the state on their conversion needs. The state committed more than $600,000 in resources to help these companies technically and financially with the diversification process. But the state legislature in the summer of 1991 eliminated the $150,000 in the budget for conversion, the same amount that much the much smaller state of Maine is investing in conversion and a fraction of the millions of dollars that Connecticut has committed.

The Department of Economic Development and the State of New York Industrial Cooperation Council (ICC) are examining a number of diversification possibilities. The ICC, in conjunction with the national Electronic Industries Association is also conducting a defense-cut impact study. Other measures include an Industrial Effectiveness Program (by the Department of Economic Development) — offering financial support for defense dependent firms to find new markets — as well as a $170,000 grant given to a consortium of firms to boost the State's chances of winning a $600 million contract in the Federal government's Supercollider program.

The state is also committed to assisting ten Long Island defense firms to develop alternative applications. See the Long Island writeup below.[3]

Community Surveys

While overall Long Island is weakened by defense cuts, a strong foundation for a high-tech future resides in some excellent regional research institutes, e.g., such as those at Brookhaven and Cold Spring Harbor.

Some significant cuts are occurring outside Long Island. In late April 1990, General Electric's Aerospace Division announced layoffs of 4,200 people between Binghamton and four other GE plants in Syracuse and Utica, NY, and Camden and Moorestown, NJ.

A good example of a company that had the foresight to convert on its own before economic catastrophe was Frisby Airborne Hydraulics in Freeport. At the height of its dependence on military spending in 1980, 95 percent of Frisby's production was for military-related products. Now 80 percent of production is for commercial jets. "It was a real test. We had to re-evaluate every method, every cost, every operation to see where we could take some fat out of the operation and go heavily into participatory management," says Greg Frisby, chief executive.[4]

Albany. Physicians for Social Responsibility (R.D. 3, Box 1002, Selkirk, NY 12158; 518-767-9624) sponsored a Northeastern New York Economic Diversification Conference in 1989. In 1991, the Economic Conversion Coalition of the Capital Region (Clifford Tepper, 518-374-8213) is focusing on the regional economy and has proposed statewide legislation to study the impact of defense cuts and consider alternative economic activities.

Bethpage (Long Island). Grumman is based here and has many facilities throughout Long Island and elsewhere in the country. It is heavily dependent on defense contracts and has over the years announced various plans to diversify into commercial aviation parts and data systems, as well as develop a shopping center and hotel. In early 1991, the Department of Defense announced it intended to terminate the F-14D fighters, which were only in production at Congressional insistence, and instead would buy F/A-18 Hornets from McDonnell Douglas. Grumman will deliver its last 24 new F-14Ds to the Navy at the end of 1992 if Congress decides against another attempt to prolong continued production of the F-14. Grumman's problems are alleviated by several smaller Department of Defense contracts that could be continued, including deals for new E-2C radar warning planes and contracts for upgrading and manufacturing more EA-6B Prowler planes. In June 1990 Grumman announced it was offering early retirement to 6,000 employees.[5]

By the start of 1991, the company's workforce nationally was down to 25,000 from 33,700 in 1987 (within Long Island, the company's work force dropped from 25,000 to 14,000 jobs) and in April 1991 it announced plans to cut 1,900 more positions by the end of the year. Grumman sent about 300 workers in Oyster Bay back to school for retraining, using a $1 million grant from the Department of Labor. The program serves former workers anywhere on the island, and has found jobs for 90 percent of the applicants, though most take pay cuts when they restart. As is true in many other defense companies, some employees want to marshal development resources to compete for scarcer defense contracts; others would abandon defense in favor of sunrise industries such as bio-tech enterprises. In September 1991 the new chief executive of Grumman announced where he stood, that his company, with 70 percent of its income from defense work and 20 percent from other Federal contracts, would continue to rely on defense contracts as its mainstay. One of Grumman's dreams is to build a new stealthy plane for the Navy, the AX, to be built in conjunction with its old rival McDonnell Douglas.[6]

P.V. Tool Company, in Westbury, saw a drop in its 1990 revenues of almost 40 percent because of defense cuts. The company derives 80 percent of its business from Grumman subcontracts, and the scaling back of such Grumman programs as the F-14 fighter and the A-6 attack plane is crippling P.V. Tool's precision-tool business.

Long Island (Other Than Bethpage). Four other companies besides Grumman based in Nassau County—AIL (Deer Park), Hazeltine, Harris Corp., and Fairchild Republic—have seen cuts or will face them in coming years. Even though the Long Island economy has a strong defense component, it became more diversified and less defense-dependent in the latter half of the 1980s. Military contracts for Long Island (Nassau and Suffolk Counties) firms totaled $3.4 billion in FY 1989, down from $5. billion in 1987. Approximately 12,000 defense-industry workers have lost jobs in the Long Island area, and the Long Island Regional Planning Board expects at least another 10,000 jobs to be terminated in the next five years.

A group of Long Island military subcontractors has united for a lobbying effort called the "Long Island Coalition for the C-17." The C-17 is a cargo plane built by St. Louis-based McDonnell Douglas, but Long Island subcontractors, including Telephonics, have more than $450 million at stake in the program.

In March 1990, officials from the Departments of Commerce and Defense criticized Long Island business and political leaders for not preparing the region for the effects of the impending defense cuts. Nassau and Suffolk County Executives have since formed a BiCounty Commission on Peacetime Economics, which prepared a report on A Peacetime Economy. A $370,000 grant was given to the Long Island Association by the Defense Department and the State Economic Development Department to contract for a study of diversification issues, with the idea of developing models for diversification; in September 1991 the Long Island Association awarded the contract for the first phase of the study to Ernst & Whinney. A $2 million financial aid package was awarded to Hazeltine Corp. by the Department of Economic Development to strengthen its ability to compete for defense and non-defense contracts. Consultants on

Long Island include the Center for Practical Solutions, Cotilla Associates, Suite 206, 88 Sunnyside Blvd., Plainview, NY 11803 (516-349-0720), which assists defense workers through transition of unemployment.[7]

AIL Systems in Deer Park is the third-largest defense contractor on Long Island, and it saw 135 layoffs in July, 1990. The company also announced plans to eliminate another 600 jobs through early retirement and attrition.

General Instrument Corp. in Hicksville is considering the sale of its defense subsidiary, which has plants on Long Island and in six other states. The Hicksville division, with 700 employees, produces surveillance equipment for the Navy, and it is one of Long Island's larger military manufacturing companies. The military business of General Instruments makes about $200 million to $250 million in sales. The major problem facing the company is finding a buyer for the defense division after the recent cuts in military spending.

Unisys in Great Neck is affected by the Navy's decision to cancel a contract with Unisys in Great Neck to build a transmitter for the Aegis SPY-1D. The repercussions could be felt by the 4,000 workers at Unisys' plant.[8]

The Long Island Alliance for Peaceful Alternatives, 38 Old Country Road, Garden City, NY 11530 (Megan O'Handley, 516-741-4360), has held community forums on the conversion problem and helped fund a study by Martin Melkonian and Russell Moore of the Hofstra University Business Research Institute (516-463-5594) on Long Island's military dependence.[9]

New York City. In addition to the massive layoffs hitting the major defense contractors in New York such as Grumman and GE, many small businesses are affected by defense cuts. Cavalier Clothes Inc. in Jamaica, Queens, expected to lay off many of its 400 workers employed in making military clothing. New York City is not very defense-dependent, but it does receive close to $750 million from the Department of Defense in prime contracts to 465 different companies, organizations and universities.[10]

The two largest defense contractors in the city are Loral Corp. and EDO Corp. Both companies are very reliant on Department of Defense business. EDO, producer of anti-submarine warfare equipment, bomb racks for fighter aircraft, and sensors for satellites, is somewhat less vulnerable to the budget cuts, but it must expand into more commercial-oriented business if it wants to save its workforce of 720. Loral makes radar-warning receivers for aircraft and, bucking conventional wisdom, has created a cash-cow in the inner-city. "Whatever the defense budget is going to be in the 1990s, it's going to be dominated by electronics," says Loral Chairman Bernard Schwartz in explaining the company's philosophy. While most defense-related companies have become more conservative and are hoarding cash, Loral is "thinking acquisition," expanding its electronic base. Many feel that Loral will also be fairly safe in the midst of budget slashing; its labor force of 1,000 in Manhattan and the Bronx should remain fairly stable.[11]

Niskayuna (Schenectady County). A former CONDEC plant, supplier of tanks during the 1950s and defense contractor till its closure in 1985, is to be converted into a transit bus assembly site. The plant has been leased by North America's largest bus builder, TMCI Inc., a subsidiary of Greyhound Corp. TCMI intends to recruit an initial group of 50 employees, and expects to employ approximately 200 once the facility is in full production.[12]

Rochester. Two active community groups are the Rochester Economic Conversion Task Force, c/o Lloyd Lill, P.O. Box 1188, West Bloomfield, NY 14585, and the Rochester Nuclear Free Zone, 50 N. Plymouth Avenue, Rochester, NY 14614, headed by Robert Sandgrund. A nuclear-free zone ordinance was narrowly defeated in the Rochester City Council.

Staten Island. Tensions were building in 1990 over the Staten Island homeport, as a group of 10 New York City Congressional representatives, all Democrats, and Mayor David Dinkins urged the Defense Department to cancel the $188 million project at Stapleton. Another congressional group of 17 Republicans and 3 Democrats from New York State and New Jersey were urging the Secretary of Defense to complete the project. The homeport's supporters won in 1991. The naval station appeared on the Base Closure Commission's June 1991 hit list but was reprieved.[13]

Watertown. Fort Drum was expanded from a minor Army Depot in 1985 when the 10th Light Infantry Division was relocated, revitalizing the economy of the North County region and creating over 8,000 civilian jobs. But it appeared on a closure/realignment list in early 1991.[14]

Watervliet. The town's economy is dependent on the Watervliet Arsenal, which produces guns for battleships and tanks. Approximately 300 layoffs were averted by a surge of orders at the end of 1990 because of the Gulf War.[15]

Notes

1. *Meeting New York State's Fiscal and Budgetary Challenges*, Committee on Fiscal Management of the Council on Fiscal and Economic Priorities, December, 1989, pp. iii, 5-6, B2-B4. New York's economic difficulties were predicted in John Tepper Marlin, "What the Market Crash Says About New York City," *The New York Times,* October 24 (4 days after the crash), 1987, Op. Ed., p. 31, when some people were arguing with a false optimism that the employment impact of the crash would be slight. Philip S. Gutis, "Slowdown in Growth Forcing L.I. to Regroup its Economy," *The New York Times*, August 24, 1989, p. A1.

2. Contract data from *Atlas/Data Abstract for the U.S. and Selected Areas Fiscal 1990*, Department of Defense, Washington Headquarters Services, Directorate for Information, Operations and Reports, p. 83. Contacts: (1) New York State Department of Economic Development, Vincent Tese, Commissioner, 1515 Broadway, New York, NY 10004; 212-930-0200. Raymond R. Gillen, Director, Procurement Assistance Unit, New York State Department of Economic Development, Albany, New York, 518-474-7756.Albany, NY; 518-474-7756. (2) New York State Department of Labor, Jeremy Schrauf, State Campus, Building 12, Albany, NY 12224.; 518-457-6181. (3) Brad Johnson, Office of New York State, Hall of the States, 444 North Capitol, N.W., Washington, DC 20001. (4) Howard Cort, New York State Department of Labor, 518-457-1973.

3. Defense Advisory Panel: Raymond Gillen, letter to John Tepper Marlin, 1990. Defense cut impact study: The Electronics Industry Association, 2000 I Street, N.W., Washington, DC, 202-457-4900.

4. Mike Sante, "Defense Contractors Face Adapting to Leaner Times," *Myrtle Beach Sun-News*, April 8, 1990. Janet Stone, *Conversion Organizers' Update* (Mountain View, CA: Center for Economic Conversion), February 1991, p. 9 and October 1991 (advance copy), p. 8. James Bernstein, "LI Firms Lobby For Ex-Rival," *Newsday*, June 13, 1991, p. 49. John Rather, "L.I. Economy Reeling Anew After Defense Setbacks," *The New York Times*, July 29, 1990, sect. 12, p. 1. Bernstein, "Nassau Defense Plant May Be Sold," *Newsday*, July 10, 1990, p. 35.

5. Nick Ravo, "Local Military Contractors Cautiously Brace for Peace," *The New York Times*, January 3, 1990, p. B4. Richard Halloran, "Cheney Takes on Long Island Lobby in F-14 Dispute," *The New York Times*, July 10, 1989. James Bernstein and Earl Lane, "Why the Ax Fell on F-14," *Newsday*, February 4, 1991, p. 7. Charles Zehren, "Defense Workers on the Offensive," *Newsday*, June 25, 1990, p. 5. Richard W. Stevenson, "Suppliers Brace for Arms Cuts," *The New York Times*, June 18, 1990, p. D1. Numbers on employment drop within Long Island from Martin Melkonian, Economics Department, Hofstra University. Schmitt, "Price of Freedom and Budget Cuts: Retraining on L.I.," *The New York Times*, p. B-1.

6. Rick Wartzman, "Grumman Corp. Plans to Cut 7 Percent of Workforce," *The Wall Street Journal*, April 3, 1991, p. 8. Bernstein, "It's Business as Usual," *Newsday*, September 18, 1991, p. 5. The new Grumman Chairman and CEO is Renso L. Caporali; this was his first major speech to the Long Island business community. The AX: Information from Martin Melkonian, September 1991.

7. Charles Zehren, "U.S.: No Defense for LI Leaders," *Newsday*, March 15, 1990, p. 51. Hazeltine: Gillen, *loc. cit.*

8. Bernstein, "Unisys Loses Key Navy Contract," *Newsday*, April 11, 1990, p. 3.

9. Dena Barisano, "Defense Views Will Be Voiced," *The Hofstra University Chronicle*, October 26, 1989, p. 1. Carol Steinberg, "Military Suppliers Plan for Civilian Markets," *The New York Times*, July 14, 1991, p. 12-1.

10. Bernstein, "Casualties of Peace: City Feels Chill of Cold War Cutbacks," *Newsday*, June 25, 1990, p. 3.

11. Andy Pasztor and Rick Wartzman, "As Defense Industry Shrinks, Suppliers Face Widely Varying Fates," *The Wall Street Journal*, p. A-7. Bernstein, "2 Big Firms are Dodging the Bullet," *Newsday*, June 25, 1990, pp. 2-3.

12. State of New York, Executive Chamber press release, August 29, 1990. See also Janine Kava, "Bus Maker to Open in Ex-ConDiesel Plant," *The Daily Gazette*, August 30, 1990 and Michael Lopez, "Bus Maker Moves to Niskayuna," *The Times Union*, August 30 1990.

13. Jack Sirica, "Washington Briefing: SI Homeport Under Siege," *Newsday*, May 21, 1990, p. 14.

14. Gillen, *loc. cit.*

15. Elizabeth Kolbert, "Town Hopes for Peace but Is Reassured It Won't Last," *The New York Times*, February 27, 1991, p. B1.

North Carolina

A	B	C	D	E	F
$				VI	DDI
+	+	+	→	–	✌

Benchmarks	No.	Rank	Benchmarks	No.	Rank
A. Total DoD $	$4.2bil.	17	Def.-Dependent Jobs ('000), '90	190	18
B. Personnel Payroll	$3.0bil.	6	Change in Def.-Dep. Jobs, '89-'91	-10.0%	15
C. Prime Contracts (PC)	$1.2bil.	25	Unemployment Rate, '90-'91	5.6%	37
D. PC Change, FY '87-'90	-12.0%	32	Unemp. Rate Change, '89-'91	+1.5%	20
E. Vulnerability Index	7.8	40	Per Capita Income	$16,203	36
F. Defense Disloc. Index	0.11	39	Population ('000)	6,629	10

▲ Army ■ Navy
● Air Force ○ Other

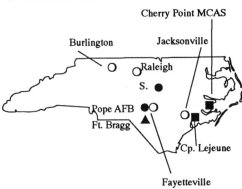

Prime Contract Trends, FY'87-'90
(Constant FY '92 $Billions)

'87 $1.5b '88 $1.5b '89 $1.2b '90 $1.3b

Top 5 Contractors	$ Millions
AT&T	491.5$
KKR Associates	30.0
Hoechst	27.1
Car. Pwr. & Light	27.0
Exide Electronics	26.5

Top 10 $ Sites[a]	Congressional Dist., Representative	1989 Rank	Total DoD$[c]	Payroll[c]	Prime Contracts[c]	Per-sonnel[d]
1-Ft. Bragg (34)	7-Rose, d	20	$924.7	$830.0	$94.7	36.3
2-Camp Lejeune (52)	3-Lancaster, d	47	724.9	688.5	36.5	20.3
3-Greensboro (91)	6-Coble, r	105	438.8	19.4	419.5	--
4-Cherry Point (106)	1-Jones, d	103	377.4	330.2	47.3	12.0
5-Jacksonville (207)	3-Lancaster, d	193	163.3	155.9	7.4	4.5
6-Fayetteville (218)	7-Rose, d	246	144.3	131.5	12.8	--
7-S. Johnson AFB (230)	3-Lancaster, d	227	134.4	119.9	14.5	5.2
8-Pope AFB (257)	7-Rose, d	--	107.8	102.3	5.5	4.1
9-Raleigh (279)	4-Price, d	299	91.2	41.4	49.8	0.9
10-Burlington (297)	6-Coble, r	--	78.1	4.7	73.4	--

[a] Rating in parentheses is out of 511 sites, the top ten in each state and PR, plus DC.
[b] Multidistrict r-Rep, d-Dem. [c] $Millions (figures may not add due to rounding) [d] Thousands

North Carolina

The state enjoyed an economic boom for much of the 1980s, including widespread corporate investment and relocation, especially in the Charlotte and Piedmont Triad areas. Although the production and electronic equipment sectors of the economy have declined slightly, the trade, biotechnology-pharmaceutical, and service sectors have grown fairly rapidly. Manufacturing accounts for almost 30 percent of total employment.[1] The state's unemployment rate in April 1991 ranked 37th in the country and its change in unemployment over the past two years ranked 20th (there was a slight increase in the labor force that was more than offset by a decline in employment).

Defense and the Economy

North Carolina has always figured prominently in U.S. national security spending, with research and development in the Raleigh-Durham-Chapel Hill triangle and many strategic bases. The Department of Defense spent more than $4 billion in North Carolina in 1990, making it one of the largest recipients of defense funds.[2] Despite the large military presence, the state's strong economy and low unemployment should protect it from the full impact of defense cuts.

Community Surveys

About 70 percent of Department of Defense money spent in North Carolina goes toward the state's massive payroll. Fort Bragg is the fourth largest site of military personnel in the nation; fellow North Carolina base Camp Lejeune is fifteenth. No bases in the state are targeted for closure in the near future, however, and a few might even be expanded. Several local politicians have stressed that the training and rapid deployment capabilities of Fort Bragg, as well as other installations in the state, are likely to remain central to the defense needs of the 1990s. State firms do a significant amount of research and development contracting, which is vulnerable to cutbacks. Some of the most important defense contracting industries in the state are textiles and clothing, the demand for which is not likely to change significantly in the near future.[3]

Charlotte. The Air National Guard was scheduled to receive $14.2 million for facilities and improvements at Douglas International.

Goldsboro. Seymour Air Force Base was due to receive $2.5 million for expansion and construction.[4]

Greensboro. The community is dependent on the AT&T Federal Systems Division which has so far weathered defense cuts well. There is the possibility that AT&T will shift more of its work from New Jersey to Greensboro.

Fayetteville. Fort Bragg is ranked 34th nationally in total military expenditures. The Department of Defense will spend $31.8 million to build a new maintenance facility there.[5] Jacksonville—In response to budgetary pressures, Camp Lejeune implemented a hiring freeze and announced layoffs for 122 civilian employees. Although these measures will have economic effects in the area, local politicians contend that the camp is not facing major cutbacks. Indeed, the new budget allows $29.2 million in construction contracts and $3.2 million in new dental and medical facilities.[6]

Notes

1. *State Labor Summary*, Employment Security Commission of North Carolina, April 1990, p. 1.

2. *Atlas/Data Abstract for the U.S. and Selected Areas Fiscal 1990, Department of Defense*, Washington Headquarters Services, Directorate for Information, Operations and Reports, p. 85.

3. "N.C. Military Bases to Feel Pentagon's Budget Cuts," *The Region*, January 31, 1990. Contacts: (1) Governor's Office, Nancy Temple, Chief of Staff, State Capitol, Raleigh, NC 27603; 919-733-4240. (2) Greensboro Mayor's Office, Thomas L. Stapleton, Manager, Business Assistance and Development, P.O. Box 3136, Greensboro, NC 27402-3136. (3) North Carolina Department of Economic and Community Development, 430 North Salisbury St., Raleigh, NC 27603; James Broyhill 919-733-4962, Gordon Corcoran 919-733-4973. (4) North Carolina Employment Security Commission, Ann Duncan, 700 Wade Avenue, Raleigh, NC 27605; 919-733-7546.

4. "N.C. Military...," *loc. cit.*

5. *Loc. cit.*

6. *Loc. cit.*

North Dakota

A	B	C	D	E	F
$				VI	DDI
–	–	–	↓	–	✌

Benchmarks	No.	Rank	Benchmarks	No.	Rank
A. Total DoD $	$0.4bil.	45	Def.-Dependent Jobs ('000), '90	22	45
B. Personnel Payroll	$0.3bil.	42	Change in Def.-Dep. Jobs, '89-'91	-8.8%	18
C. Prime Contracts (PC)	$0.1bil.	46	Unemployment Rate, '90-'91	3.7%	49
D. PC Change, FY '87-'90	-43.6%	6	Unemp. Rate Change, '89-'91	-0.5%	45
E. Vulnerability Index	7.2	44	Per Capita Income	$15,255	40
F. Defense Disloc. Index	0.06	46	Population ('000)	639	48

▲ Army ■ Navy
● Air Force ○ Other

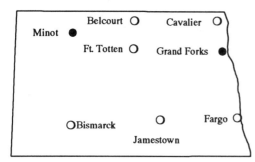

Prime Contract Trends, FY'87-'90
(Constant FY '92 $Billions)

'87 $0.2b   '88 $0.1b   '89 $0.1b   '90 $0.1b

Top 5 Contractors	$ Millions
Turtle Management	$24.4
Black & Decker	5.2
Devils Lake Sioux Tribe	4.9
Nodak Rural Electric	4.4
Dakota Tribal Industries	4.3

Top 10 $ Sites[a]	Congressional Dist., Representative	1989 Rank	Total DoD$[c]	Pay-roll[c]	Prime Contracts[c]	Per-sonnel[d]
1-Minot AFB (217)	1-Dorgan,d	221	$145.1	$124.1	$21.1	5.7
2-Grd. Forks AFB (226)	"	220	137.9	117.7	20.2	5.3
3-Fargo (389)	"	399	26.9	22.4	4.5	0.4
4-Belcourt (395)	"	444	25.6	0.1	25.5	--
5-Bismarck (428)	"	423	14.7	14.4	0.3	0.2
6-Ft. Totten (444)	"	378	10.5	.01	10.5	--
7-Grand Forks (448)	"	446	9.4	7.8	1.6	.03
8-Minot (456)	"	417	8.1	7.4	0.7	--
9-Cavalier (468)	"	470	6.2	0.7	5.5	.04
10-Jamestown (493)	"	461	3.8	1.0	2.8	--

[a]Rating in parentheses is out of 511 sites, the top ten in each state and PR, plus DC.
[b]Multidistrict r-Rep, d-Dem. [c]$Millions (figures may not add due to rounding) [d]Thousands

North Dakota

North Dakota, like most of its neighbors, has a resource-rich but not very industrialized economic base. Agriculture, particularly beef cattle and wheat, is one of the most important pillars of the North Dakota economy, accounting for about 8 percent of the Gross State Product and 14 percent of total employment. Crude oil, lignite coal and natural gas are some of the many natural resources upon which the North Dakota economy relies. This dependence on resources has led to a boom or bust economic history throughout the decade. The service sector has been growing tremendously. In 1985, services-producing industries accounted for 75 percent of the Gross State Product. The economy has relatively weak finance, manufacturing and construction sectors, which tends to make the state less resistant to recession. The April 1991 unemployment rate ranked a low 49th and change in unemployment ranked 45th (a decline in the labor force outpaced a decline in employment).[1]

Defense and the Economy

The $419 million spent in the entire state of North Dakota in 1990 was less than 10 percent of Defense Department spending in the city of San Diego. Most proposed cuts involve the M-88A2 recovery vehicle program, which could be reduced by over $1 million in North Dakota alone. State firms received over $10 million from the Department of Defense in 1989 for vehicle production. Other important defense industries include construction and clothing/equipage. The Devil's Lake Sioux Indian Tribe, the state's third largest contractor, in FY 1990 received over $5 million for camouflage clothing and equipment. The two most important military presences in the state are the strategic Grand Forks and Minot Air Force Bases. These two bases, which collectively employ over 1,000 civilians, are not targeted for reductions.[2]

Notes

1. *Job Service North Dakota 1990 Annual Planning Report*, Research and Statistics, October 1989.

2. *Atlas/Data Abstract for the U.S. and Selected Areas, Fiscal 1990*, Department of Defense, Washington Headquarters Services, Directorate for Information, Operations and Reports, p. 87. *Prime Contract Awards by Region and State, Fiscal Years 1989, 1988, 1987*, Department of Defense, Washington Headquarters Services, Directorate for Information, Operations and Reports, p. 52. Contacts: (1) Governor's Office, Janis Cheney, Director of Special Projects, State Capitol, Bismarck, ND 58505; 701-224-2200. (2) North Dakota Economic Development, Bill Patrie, 604 E. Boulevard-Liberty Memorial Bldg., Bismarck, ND 58505; 701-224-2810. (3) North Dakota Intergovernment Affairs, Shirley Dykshoorn, Director, 600 E. Boulevard, Bismarck, ND 58505; 701-224-2094. (4) North Dakota Job Services, Mike Diesz, Director, 1000 E. Divide, Box 1537, Bismarck, ND 58505; 701-224-2836.

Ohio

A	B	C	D	E	F
$	🪖	🔧	▦	VI	DDI
✚	✚	✚	➡	!	✂

Benchmarks	No.	Rank	Benchmarks	No.	Rank
A.Total DoD $	$6.4bil.	9	Def.-Dependent Jobs ('000), '90	355	9
B. Personnel Payroll	$2.0bil.	11	Change in Def.-Dep. Jobs, '89-'91	-14.0%	8
C. Prime Contracts (PC)	$4.4bil.	8	Unemployment Rate, '90-'91	7.1%	16
D. PC Change, FY '87-'90	-13.3%	29	Unemp. Rate Change, '89-'91	+2.1%	11
E. Vulnerability Index	8.9	30	Per Capita Income	$17,473	25
F. Defense Disloc. Index	3.72	8	Population ('000)	10,847	7

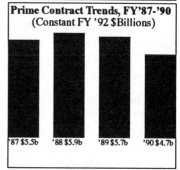

Prime Contract Trends, FY'87-'90
(Constant FY '92 $Billions)

'87 $5.5b   '88 $5.9b   '89 $5.7b   '90 $4.7b

Cleveland
Akron
Lima
Columbus, Whitehall
Dayton ◗ Wright Patt. AFB
Cincinnati

▲ Army ■ Navy
● Air Force ○ Other

Top 5 Contractors	$ Millions
General Electric	$1,490.1
General Dynamics	444.1
CFM Int'l	318.6
Westinghouse	276.6
Loral	173.1

Top 10 $ Sites[a]	Congressional Dist., C.D.-Representative	1989 Rank	Total DoD$[c]	Payroll[c]	Prime Contracts[c]	Per-sonnel[d]
1-Cincinnati (12)	(1,2)[b]	13	$2,071.5	$40.7	$2,030.7	0.7
2-Wright Pat. AFB (21)	(3,7)[b]	27	1,225.6	905.0	320.7	26.0
3-Cleveland (96)	(20,21)[b]	109	417.5	85.7	331.8	2.7
4-Dayton (102)	(3,7)[b]	122	386.0	61.7	324.3	0.3
5-Akron (129)	14-Sawyer, d	172	307.2	14.7	292.5	--
6-Lima Tank Ctr. (135)	4-Oxley, r	44	289.8	0	289.8	--
7-Columbus (173)	(10,12,15)[b]	164	212.3	113.3	99.0	3.1
8-Lima (174)	4-Oxley, r	--	210.3	4.9	205.4	--
9-Whitehall (237)	12-Kasich, r	240	128.9	128.9	0	4.0
10-Newark (277)	10-Miller, r	270	92.6	84.2	8.5	2.7

[a]Rating in parentheses is out of 511 sites, the top ten in each state and PR, plus DC.
[b]Multidistrict r-Rep, d-Dem. [c]$Millions (figures may not add due to rounding) [d] Thousands

Ohio

Manufacturing is the most important sector of the Ohio gross state product, but the fastest growing sectors have been services, wholesale trade, finance, insurance, and real estate, while construction dropped sharply.[1] Ohio's unemployment rate in April 1991 ranked 16th highest and its change in unemployment ranked a worrisome 11th (the labor force grew faster than employment).

Defense and the Economy

Only eight other states received more defense money in 1990 than Ohio. The state has a relatively high defense dependence, especially in the areas around Cincinnati and Wright-Patterson Air Force Base—Cincinnati's $2 billion-plus in defense money ranks it 12th nationally and accounts for more than 30 percent of Ohio's defense income. Defense Secretary Dick Cheney wants drastic cutbacks for spending in Ohio, particularly regarding the tank contractors in the western part of the state. Most of Ohio's defense money is granted for prime contracts, and the state ranks high in receipt of money for research and development. About 200,000 people in Ohio are employed in military contracting. Ohio firms lead the nation in prime contracts for aircraft-engine production, as well as both combat and non-combat vehicles. Of particular importance is the M-1 tank program, produced by the General Dynamics Land Systems plant in Lima. Tank contracts all over the country are extremely vulnerable to cutbacks, and Ohio firms have already lost significant contracts for M-88 A2 tanks.[2]

Heavy industry is of greatest importance in Ohio defense contracting. The small but busy military subcontractor High Tech Castings, Inc., which produces fuel pump housings for the B-1 and precision castings for the cooling systems for the F-15 Eagle, will be greatly hurt by the cuts. As 80 percent of its business is in military subcontracting, High Tech Casting will be forced to undergo major layoffs.[3]

Columbus. The Rickenbacker Air Guard Base will close. The Department of Defense decided on the move because of the probable savings of realigning Guard units to larger active bases. Some of Rickenbacker's units will move to nearby Wright-Patterson AFB in Dayton and others will be inactivated. The government projects employment loss of 6,700 and regional income loss of $41 million annually.[4]

Dayton. Wright-Patterson Air Force Base, which employs almost 26,000 workers and is the seventh largest site of personnel in the U.S., directly contracts $1 billion yearly to local firms. Most of these companies are small and medium-sized operations which will be the most hurt from cutbacks in Federal spending. It is estimated that Wright-Patterson's economic effect will be felt throughout the state.[5] The terminating of the B-2 Stealth bomber program by Congress would have an immense impact on Wright-Patterson.

Lakewood. The Lakewood Manufacturing Co. makes fenders and other metal parts for the M-1 tank, which is in danger of being cut. The company derives half of its $6.5 million in annual sales from subcontracting work on the M-1 from General Dynamics, and 95 workers are employed on the program. Lakewood is already looking to diversify into commercial markets.[6]

Lima. The government-owned/contractor-run plant here produces the M1 series Abrams battle tank. With a $100 million payroll and 5 percent of Lima's workforce, General Dynamics Land Systems, which operates the plant, is the second largest employer in a manufacturing-based local economy. The company decided to lay off 500 employees in 1990 due to production declines. The workforce is unionized, skilled, and highly paid. Large-scale dislocations such as auto restructurings have been handled with retraining under JTPA Title III. This may not work for General Dynamics' uniquely-skilled welders and other specialists in demand only in other regions of the country.[7]

Secretary Cheney's proposal to consolidate M-1 tank production at the Lima facility (a similar plant exists in Warren, MI) by September 1991 and to discontinue U.S. purchase of the tanks in March 1993 will jeopardize the remaining 2,170 jobs at the Lima Army Tank Plant, unless sufficient international orders to justify continued production. Congress may allocate funds to purchase some more M1A2 tanks and upgrade others to M1A2 status.

Notes

1. *The Final Market Value of Ohio Goods and Services: Gross State Product By Division: 1971-1986.* Prepared and distributed by the Ohio Data Users Center, Ohio Department of Development, January, 1989, p. 1. Don Larrick, Principal Analyst.

2. *Atlas/Data Abstract for the U.S. and Selected Areas Fiscal 1989*, Department of Defense, Washington Headquarters Services, Directorate for Information, Operations and Reports, p. 89. "The Challenge of Change in Ohio," *Municipal Foreign Policy*, Spring 1990, p. 23. *Prime Contract Awards by Region and State, Fiscal Years 1989, 1988, 1987,* Department of Defense, Washington Headquarters Services, Directorate for Information, Operations and Reports, p. 53. Laura Livan, "Defense Firms Try to Save Programs,"The Washington Times, February 9, 1990, p. C5.

3. "The Challenge of Change in Ohio," *loc. cit.* Contacts: (1) Ohio Department of Development, Donald Jakeway Director, 77 South High St., 29th Floor, Columbus, OH 43215; 614-466-2718, Small and Developing Businesses Division 614-466-2718. (2) Lima Mayor's Office, Mayor David J. Berger, 50 Town Square, Lima, OH 45801; 419-228-5462.

4. *Base Closure and Realignment Report*, April 1991, pp. 106-107.

5. *Loc. cit.*

6. Richard W. Stevenson, "Suppliers Brace for Arms Cuts," *The New York Times*, June 18, 1990, p. D1.

7. Interview in March, 1990 with Bill Bassitt, President, Chamber of Commerce, City of Lima, OH; 419-222-6045.

Pennsylvania

A	B	C	D	E	F
$	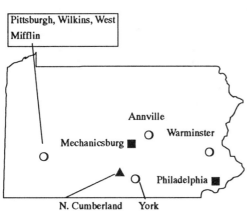			VI	DDI
+	+	+	↓	–	✂

Benchmarks	No.	Rank	Benchmarks	No.	Rank
A.Total DoD $	$5.3bil.	12	Def.-Dependent Jobs ('000), '90	280	12
B. Personnel Payroll	$2.4bil.	10	Change in Def.-Dep. Jobs, '89-'91	-2.4%	31
C. Prime Contracts (PC)	$2.9bil.	14	Unemployment Rate, '90-'91	6.8%	21
D. PC Change, FY '87-'90	-33.7%	13	Unemp. Rate Change, '89-'91	+2.8%	8
E. Vulnerability Index	8.1	36	Per Capita Income	$18,672	19
F. Defense Disloc. Index	1.37	20	Population ('000)	11,882	5

Pittsburgh, Wilkins, West Mifflin

Annville

Warminster

Mechanicsburg ■

Philadelphia ■

N. Cumberland   York

▲ Army ■ Navy
● Air Force ○ Other

Prime Contract Trends, FY'87-'90
(Constant FY '92 $Billions)

'87 $4.6b   '88 $3.9b   '89 $3.2b   '90 $3.1b

Top 5 Contractors	$ Millions
Westinghouse	$432.4
Boeing	372.7
General Electric	240.5
Harsco	141.4
Boeing/Sikorsky JV	103.9

Top 10 $ Sites[a]	Congressional Dist., Representative	1989 Rank	Total DoD$[c]	Payroll[c]	Prime Contracts[c]	Per-sonnel[d]
1-Philadelphia (15)	(1-3,7,13)[b]	17	$1,699.4	$893.4	$806.0	25.6
2-West Mifflin (154)	20-Gaydos, d	147	255.5	0.9	254.6	--
3-Mechanicsburg (158)	19-Goodling, r	148	245.8	227.4	18.3	7.1
4-Pittsburgh (181)	14-Coyne, d	188	194.2	50.2	144.0	1.3
5-York (187)	19-Goodling, r	214	187.0	6.7	180.4	--
6-Wilkins Tnshp. (216)	20-Gaydos, d	209	145.6	0	145.6	--
7-Letterkenny (242)	9-Shuster, r	229	118.7	110.4	8.3	4.7
8-N. Cumberland (244)	19-Goodling, r	--	117.2	98.0	19.3	3.6
9-Warminster (246)	8-Kostmayer, d	251	115.6	115.6	.07	2.9
10-Annville (258)	16-Walker, r	--	107.6	107.6	.06	--

[a]Rating in parentheses is out of 511 sites, the top ten in each state and PR, plus DC.
[b]Multidistrict r-Rep, d-Dem. [c]$Millions (figures may not add due to rounding) [d]Thousands

Pennsylvania

The recent growth of the Pennsylvania economy has paralleled the overall economic development of the nation. The state economy is shedding its former reliance on the manufacturing sector in favor of services-producing industries. The services sector will be the engine of Pennsylvania's job expansion into the next century: it is expected to account for 9 out of every 10 new jobs through 1995. The state's unemployment rate ranked 21st in April 1991 and its change in employment rated 8th worst (the labor force expanded in the past two years while employment fell). The unemployment rate is predicted to be around 5.2 percent by 2000.[1]

Defense and the Economy

Pennsylvania receives over $5 billion a year from the Department of Defense, and has a relatively defense-dependent economy. The programs slated for cuts in Pennsylvania include the F-14 fighter and the M-1 tank. Pennsylvania received over $617 million from the Department of Defense in 1989 for ship construction alone, representing 6.1 percent of total Defense Department ship contracts. State firms accounted for over half of total defense-related construction equipment procurement. Other important defense industries include aircraft, electronic equipment and petroleum.[2]

State Legislative Initiatives

Pennsylvania has a long history of economic development initiatives under the auspices of the state's Department of Commerce and Industrial Development Authority; concerned about the state's defense dependence, the Pennsylvania House Labor Relations Committee unanimously passed the Economic Adjustment Act. A bill, HB 135, was introduced by Rep. Allen Kukovich (717-787-6260) to create an economic adjustment board within the Department of Labor and Industry to develop a conversion strategy and identify alternative business activities. Its proposed budget of $2 million ended its life in the Pennsylvania House Appropriations Committee.[3]

Pennsylvania Jobs with Peace (Barbara Smith, Tyrone Reed, 924 Cherry St., Philadelphia, PA 19107; 215-925-3758), lobbied for the Economic Adjustment Act and held a statewide Economic Conversion Conference in late 1990, in which a major theme was the importance of grassroots protests and confrontations to achieve change. Pennsylvania Jobs with Peace is looking for its model at the campaigns in Maine and Baltimore. In May 1991 Jobs with Peace began publishing its *Pennsylvania Economic Conversion Bulletin*.[4]

Community Surveys

Expenditures in Pennsylvania are most heavily concentrated in three areas: the southeast (including Philadelphia and King of Prussia); the Harrisburg area

(Mechanicsburg and York); and the southwest (Wilkins, West Mifflin, and Pittsburgh).[5]

Chambersburg. Letterkenny Army Depot is to be realigned. The Material Readiness Support Activity will probably not move to Letterkenny as specified in the Base Closure Act of 1989. Additionally, the Depot Systems Command Headquarters will move from Letterkenny to Rock Island Arsenal. Although employment losses will be partially offset by the transfer of other functions to the depot, the Department of Defense still expects employment to decline by 2.2 percent.

Delaware County. The Delaware County Jobs with Peace Economic Conversion Committee (Robin Lasersohn, 215-872-7565) has begun discussions with local labor leaders to find areas of mutual interest with community group leaders so that progress can be made in the long term toward conversion.

Philadelphia. This metropolitan area will be one of the hardest hit sites in the country since the historic Philadelphia Naval Station and Shipyard are on the Department of Defense base-closure list. The Naval Complex accounts for 35,000 jobs (13,000 civilians and 6,000 military directly, 2,000 indirectly, and 14,000 induced). The Base Commission has recommended that only a few small functions at the port be retained; these account for 1,859 civilian and 19 military jobs. Since the Navy is the most important single defense contractor customer in Pennsylvania, the impact of the closure is likely to be profound. A study entitled "Economic Impact of the Philadelphia Naval Base and Shipyard on the Philadelphia Metropolitan Area," commissioned by the states of Pennsylvania and New Jersey and overseen by the Philadelphia Industrial Development Corporation (PIDC), estimates that 23,000 Pennsylvania and 8,700 New Jersey residents will lose their jobs when the Naval Complex closes. Philadelphia area unemployment is expected to jump 30.4 percent. The two states depend on $37 million in tax revenue from the Navy site. Since the state lost manufacturing employment during the 1990/91 recession, it is unlikely that the regional economy will be in a good position to absorb displaced Navy engineers. Pennsylvania Members of Congress vowed to try to keep the base open indefinitely by making sure that a $405 million overhaul of the carrier USS Kennedy (which should take till 1996 to complete) proceeds as planned. They are also filing a lawsuit that charges that the Navy and the Base Commission failed to use objective and complete standards in evaluating the base's military value. Pennsylvania Jobs with Peace (Tyrone Reed, 215-925-3758) is attempting to move the debate on to conversion issues, including requiring the Navy to clean up toxic wastes at the site before it leaves.[6]

The Tacony Warehouse is scheduled to close by 1993.

MCI Communications Corp. landed a five-year, $375-million contract in May 1990 to install pay phones at Navy, Marine and Coast Guard facilities in the U.S. Bell Atlantic Corp. of Philadelphia will be a subcontractor in the deal.[7]

Warminster. The Naval Air Development Center, specializing in aircraft technology, could be realigned. Most of its functions would move to Patuxent,

MD, and the airfield would close. The Navy estimates that 2,250 positions would be transferred or eliminated. Although the facility appeared on the Base Commission's final list of recommended realignments in July 1991, there is a possibility that consolidation may not occur. Congress has formed a separate commission to investigate the consolidations of military labs. Its conclusions, due in September, are only advisory, but could persuade the Base Commission to alter its decisions. Maryland Members of Congress are considering a lawsuit should closure plans proceed.[8]

York County. Defense accounts for 15-18 percent of the local economy. BMY is engaged in defense-related activities only, most significantly in the M-88 Recovery Vehicle project. The current workforce of 1,800 at BMY is a small fraction of the county-wide employment of 182,000. The county feels that it is well-positioned to withstand cuts.[9] Jobs With Peace is undertaking a study of the effects of defense cuts on the area.

Harsco Corp. mainly produced infantry apparatus designed to be used by the Army in a European land war. The company took over $110 million in write-offs on defense work, and laid off 1,200 workers from its plant between 1988 and 1990.[10]

Notes

1. *Labor Market Trends Through the Year 2000, Pennsylvania Profile*, Commonwealth of PA, Department of Labor Industry, Research and Statistics Division, Spring 1988, p. 2.

2. *Atlas/Data Abstract for the U.S. and Selected Areas, Fiscal 1989*, Department of Defense, Washington Headquarters Services, Directorate for Information, Operations and Reports, p. 95. *Prime Contract Awards by Region and State, Fiscal Years 1989, 1988, 1987*, Department of Defense, Washington Headquarters Services, Directorate for Information, Operations and Reports, p. 56. For sale by the Superintendent of Documents, U.S. Government Printing Office, Washington, D.C. 20402. DTIC and NTIS identification number for this publication is DIOR/PO6-89.

3. *Economic Conversion Briefs*, Center For Economic Conversion, Winter 1988-9. Anne Hoskins and Keith Cunningham, *Economic Initiatives*, produced by the Center for Policy Alternatives, July 1991, p.15.

4. Janet Stone, *Conversion Organizers' Update* (Mountain View, CA: October 1991, advance copy), p. 9. Contacts: (1) Governor's Policy Office, Charles Lyons, 506 Finance Building, Harrisburg, PA 17120; 717-787-1954. (2) Pennsylvania Department of Commerce, Raymond Christman, Secretary, Forum Building, Harrisburg, PA 17120; 717-783-3840. (3) Pennsylvania Department of Labor and Industry, Carl Thomas, Research Director, Harrisburg, PA 17120; 717-787-3265. (4) PIDC/Development Management Corporation, Carolyn Wallis, 22nd Floor, Fidelity Building, 123 S. Broad St., Philadelphia, PA 19109; 215-735-5050.

5. Where not otherwise cited, information that follows is from *Base Closure and Realignment Report*, April 1991, pp. 47-48, or Stone, *op. cit.*, pp. 8-9.

6. *Economic Impact of the Philadelphia Naval Base and Shipyard on the Philadelphia Metropolitan Area*, October 1990, the Pennsylvania Economy League and the

WEFA Group, Inc., pp. v, vi, ix. Kimberly J. McLarin, "Congressmen Urge Hope on Workers at Base," *Philadelphia Inquirer*, July 2, 1991, p. 4B.

7. John Burgess, "MCI Wins $375 Million Navy Contract," *The Washington Post*, May 2, 1990, p. G1.

8. *Base Closure and Realignment Report*, Department of Defense, April 1991, p. 73. Michael L. Rozansky, "Action on Bucks Navy Facility to Hit Contractors, Others Hard," *Philadelphia Inquirer*, July 2, 1991, p. 4B.

9. Interview in March 1990 with David Carver, President, York County Industrial Development Authority, York, PA, 717-846-8879.

10. Andy Pastzor and Rick Wartzman, "As Defense Industry Shrinks, Suppliers Face Widely Varying Fates," *The Wall Street Journal*, p. A-7.

Puerto Rico

A	B	C	D	E	F
$	🪖	🏭	📈	VI	DDI
–	–	–	↑	‼	✌

Benchmarks	No.	Rank	Benchmarks	No.	Rank
A.Total DoD $	$0.7bil.	42	Def.-Dependent Jobs ('000), '90	38	39
B. Personnel Payroll	$0.2bil.	47	Change in Def.-Dep. Jobs, '89-'91	+40.7%	50
C. Prime Contracts (PC)	$0.5bil.	37	Unemployment Rate, '90-'91	16%	1
D. PC Change, FY '87-'90	+27.5%	51	Unemp. Rate Change, '89-'91	+2.0%	13
E. Vulnerability Index	17.3	1	Per Capita Income	$5,591	52
F. Defense Disloc. Index	0.07	43	Population ('000)	3,286	28

▲ Army ■ Navy
● Air Force ○ Other

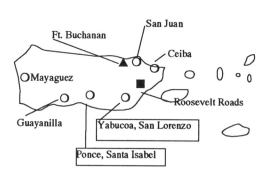

Prime Contract Trends, FY'87-'90
(Constant FY '92 $Billions)

'87 $0.4b '88 $0.3b '89 $0.3b '90 $0.5b

Top 5 Contractors	$ Millions
Peerless Petrochemicals	$68.2
Propper International	48.5
Sun Company	39.0
General Electric	38.2
Dillingham Construction	32.8

Top 10 $ Sites[a]	Congressional Dist., Representative	1989 Rank	Total DoD$[c]	Payroll[c]	Prime Contracts[c]	Per-sonnel[d]
1-Roosevelt Rds. (227)	Fuster, d	--	$135.7	$26.2	$109.5	2.1
2-Mayaguez (309)	"	--	70.1	2.8	67.3	--
3-Guayanilla (311)	"	--	68.3	0.1	68.2	--
4-Ponce (326)	"	--	51.6	6.0	45.6	--
5-Ft. Buchanan (355)	"	--	39.0	32.6	6.3	1.0
6-Yabucoa (356)	"	--	39.0	0	39.0	--
7-San Lorenzo (366)	"	--	35.1	0.3	34.8	--
8-San Juan (383)	"	--	29.5	17.9	11.6	0.3
9-Ceiba (406)	"	--	21.3	21.3	.05	0.8
10-Santa Isabel (419)	"	--	18.0	0.2	17.8	--

[a]Rating in parentheses is out of 511 sites, the top ten in each state and PR, plus DC.
[b]Multidistrict r-Rep, d-Dem. [c]$Millions (figures may not add due to rounding) [d]Thousands

Puerto Rico

As Puerto Rico's estimated per capita income (ranking 52nd out of 52) indicates, the Commonwealth is poor. Its high unemployment rate of 16 percent (No. 1) makes it the most vulnerable of the 52 "states" to defense cuts. The economy is based on tropical agricultural crops; poultry and livestock; oil refining; some manufacturing; cement production; fishing; and tourism (including gambling).[1]

Defense and the Economy

Puerto Rico has a relatively small uniformed services base, about 4,000 personnel at the main sites. Prime-contract awards were significant in 1990, about $500 million, an extremely important source of revenue for the Commonwealth. In addition, the contracts were up substantially between 1987 and 1990, the 2nd highest increase of the 52 "states."[2]

Community Surveys

Defense spending is surprisingly well distributed throughout the Commonwealth. The largest contract is for fuel, from Peerless Petrochemicals in Guayanilla, as is the No. 3 contract from Sun Company in Yabucoa. The No. 2 contractor, Propper International, is not identified in the National Register's 1990 *Directory of Corporate Affiliations*, but it sold special-purpose clothing to the Department of Defense.

Roosevelt Roads Naval Station. The high level of prime-contract awards at this base suggests that the $38 million to General Electric for operating facilities and the $33 million award to Dillingham Construction to build a dam are primarily for this site.

Notes

1. We had up-to-date U.S. Government data for the per capita incomes of the other 51 "states," but not for Puerto Rico. We estimated the Commonwealth's 1990 per capita income by applying to a 1985 figure for per capita income in the Commonwealth an inflation rate based on the growth of U.S. per capita income in the period 1985 to 1990.

2. Contacts: (1) Resident Commissioner Jaime B. Fuster (D-PR), 427 CHOB, House of Representatives, The Capitol, Washington, DC 20515-5401; 202-225-2615. (2) Puerto Rico Chamber of Commerce, 100 Tetuan, P.O. Box S-3789, San Juan, PR 00904.

Rhode Island

A	B	C	D	E	F
$				VI	DDI
−	−	+	↑	!!	✂

Benchmarks	No.	Rank	Benchmarks	No.	Rank
A. Total DoD $	$1.0bil.	38	Def.-Dependent Jobs ('000), '90	48	37
B. Personnel Payroll	$0.4bil.	40	Change in Def.-Dep. Jobs, '89-'91	+17.1%	46
C. Prime Contracts (PC)	$0.6bil.	34	Unemployment Rate, '90-'91	8.2%	6
D. PC Change, FY '87-'90	+4.5%	43	Unemp. Rate Change, '89-'91	+4.5%	2
E. Vulnerability Index	12.0	13	Per Capita Income	$18,841	16
F. Defense Disloc. Index	0.39	32	Population ('000)	1,003	44

▲ Army ■ Navy
● Air Force ◯ Other

Pawtucket
Esmond
Portsmouth
Providence
Warwick
Davisville
N. Kingstown
Middletown
Newport

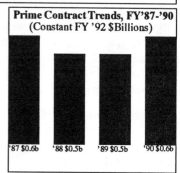

Prime Contract Trends, FY '87-'90
(Constant FY '92 $Billions)

'87 $0.6b   '88 $0.5b   '89 $0.5b   '90 $0.6b

Top 5 Contractors	$ Millions
Raytheon	$340.0
Robert Derecktor	21.3
McLaughlin Research	16.5
Mine Safety Applications	15.3
Technology Applications	14.6

Top 10 $ Sites[a]	Congressional Dist., Representative	1989 Rank	Total DoD$[c]	Payroll[c]	Prime Contracts[c]	Per-sonnel[d]
1-Portsmouth (113)	1-Machtley, r	218	$348.8	$9.3	$339.5	.03
2-Newport (118)	"	118	336.4	290.3	46.0	7.2
3-Middletown (282)	"	282	89.0	2.9	86.1	--
4-Providence (359)	(1,2)[b]	323	37.0	26.0	11.0	0.3
5-Naval Und. Sys.(412)	1-Machtley, r	394	20.2	0.0	20.2	--
6-Warwick (420)	2-Reed, d	411	17.7	8.8	8.9	.02
7-Esmond (422)	1-Machtley, r	340	16.7	1.4	15.3	.04
8-North Kings. (424)	2-Reed, d	433	15.9	12.8	3.1	0.3
9-Davisville (465)	"	462	6.7	6.7	.01	0.2
10-Pawtucket (481)	1-Machtley, r	--	4.7	3.4	1.3	--

[a]Rating in parentheses is out of 511 sites, the top ten in each state and PR, plus DC.
[b]Multidistrict r-Rep, d-Dem. [c]$Millions (figures may not add due to rounding) [d]Thousands

Rhode Island

In 1990-91 the state was severely affected by the recession. Unemployment was 8.2 percent in 1990-91, 6th highest; change in unemployment ranked 2nd worst (the labor force declined and employment plummeted even more rapidly—a huge 7.1 percent over the previous two years). The service sector is the strongest and fastest growing part of the economy. Manufacturing and farming, while expected to grow at a slow rate, are steadily losing their importance.[1]

Defense and the Economy

The people most reliant on the military's presence in the state today are highly skilled engineers, craftsmen and technicians who are residents of Rhode Island, whereas 20 years ago the relatively low-paid sailors who lived aboard the ships were most defense-dependent.[2] Another consideration not reflected in Department of Defense figures is that many residents of Rhode Island communities are employed on defense contracts in Connecticut or Massachusetts.

The job loss in Rhode Island from defense cuts between 1990 and 1995 has been estimated in a range of from 2,500 to 5,500.

State Legislative and Executive Initiatives

Gov. Sundlun has embarked on a major study of the impact on his state of defense cuts. The research is primarily the responsibility of the Rhode Island Division of Planning and the University of Rhode Island. Some pilot projects are under way at the Economic Innovation Center of Rhode Island. The National Governors Association is taking an interest in the work for possible transfer of technology to other states. The project is being paid for by the Office of Economic Adjustment of the Department of Defense and by the state's Department of Economic Development.[3]

Community Surveys

Rhode Island's defense dependence is centered on the submarine industry, primarily the Trident and Seawolf programs. The General Dynamics plant at Quonset Point, the Naval Underwater Systems Center in Newport, Raytheon in Portsmouth, and more than 100 firms doing subcontracting work provide nearly 20,000 Rhode Island jobs—4 percent of the state's total employment—directly linked to submarine production. Jobs indirectly dependent on the industry may be as many as 60,000. The General Dynamics plant alone buys an estimated $25 million worth of local goods and services annually.[4]

Davisville. The Naval Construction Battalion Center will probably close, affecting 5 military and 133 civilian jobs.[5] The facility is on the EPA's National

Priorities List due to its contamination by PCBs, lead, and petroleum oil. Civilian re-use must await cleanup.

Newport. Over 50 percent of employment on Aquidneck Island is defense-related. The Newport County Chamber of Commerce invested $250,000 to launch the Aquidneck 2000 program designed to promote economic diversification. The Defense Conversion Program of Aquidneck 2000 is a three-year program designed to serve about 7,000 workers in 50 defense-related firms at an estimated cost of $2.8 million.[6]

The Trident Command and Control Systems Maintenance Activity and the Naval Underwater Systems Center will probably be realigned to merge with the Combat and Weapon Systems Division in Newport, putting 1,160 jobs at risk.[7]

Portsmouth. Three decades ago, pastoral Portsmouth was famed mainly for its Benedictine Abbey and Catholic preparatory school headed for years by a nuclear physicist monk who had once worked at Los Alamos. Raytheon's Submarine Signal Division's contracts moved Portsmouth to $349 million in defense revenue, the largest site in Rhode Island, up from No. 8 in 1989, taking in more defense money than Newport with its naval base.

Providence. Despite possible cuts in two of its biggest projects (the M-1 tank and V-22 Osprey), Textron Inc. has spread investment among all of its various business segments, so minimizing damage from periodic defense cuts. Although the defense component of the company's revenue was up to 28 percent in 1989 from 19 percent in 1985, that was low in comparison to General Dynamics at 85 percent and Northrop Corp. at 91 percent.

Notes

1. *Rhode Island Occupational Projections to 1995*, RI Department of Employment Security, April 1989.

2. *Ibid.*, p. 6.

3. *Defense Spending After the Cold War and Rhode Island Economy: A Preliminary Report*, June 30, 1990, RI Department of Administration, Division of Planning, p. 8. Janet Stone, *Conversion Organizers' Update* (Mountain View, CA: Center for Economic Conversion, October 1991, advance copy), p. 10. Contacts: (1) Governor's Office, J.R. Pagliarini, Policy Associate, State Capitol, Providence, RI 02903; 401-277-2080. (2) Rhode Island Department of Economic Development, Henry W. Fazzano, 7 Jackson Walkway, Providence, RI 02903; 401-277-2601. (3) Rhode Island Department of Administration, Robert K. Griffith, Chief, Office of Strategic Planning, One Capitol Hill, Providence, RI 02908; 401-277-1220. (4) Rhode Island State, John Kane, Director, Administration, State House, Providence, RI 02903; 401-277-2280. (5) Rhode Island Department of Employment Security, John Renza, Director, 24 Mason Street, Providence, RI 02903; 401-277-3732. (6) Ric McIntyre, Economics Dept., University of Rhode Island, Kingston, RI 02881; 401-792-2858. Other groups and programs within Rhode Island seeking to assist companies in conversion and adjustment include: the Rhode Island Federal Procurement Assistance Center, the Rhode Island Small Business Development Center, the state Department of Economic Development's International

Trade Center, and the Rhode Island Occupational Information Coordinating Committee.[3]

4. William Donovan, "The Sub: New England's Weapon," *Providence Journal*, October 29, 1989, p. F-1.

5. "Military Bases: Look of Future," *USA Today*, July 1, 1991, p. 8A.

6. "The Aquidneck 2000 Program," as printed in *Defense Spending After the Cold War...*, *op. cit.*, Appendix D.

7. *Base Closure and Realignment Report*, Department of Defense, April 1991, pp. 85-86.

South Carolina

A	B	C	D	E	F
$		🏭	📅	VI	DDI
+	✚	+	⬆	!	✂

Benchmarks	No.	Rank	Benchmarks	No.	Rank
A. Total DoD $	$3.1bil.	20	Def.-Dependent Jobs ('000), '90	125	24
B. Personnel Payroll	$2.4bil.	9	Change in Def.-Dep. Jobs, '89-'91	0.0%	34
C. Prime Contracts (PC)	$0.7bil.	31	Unemployment Rate, '90-'91	5.7%	35
D. PC Change, FY '87-'90	+10.1%	47	Unemp. Rate Change, '89-'91	+1.4%	22
E. Vulnerability Index	10.4	21	Per Capita Income	$15,099	43
F. Defense Disloc. Index	0.59	29	Population ('000)	3,987	23

▲ Army ■ Navy
● Air Force ○ Other

Ft. Jackson
Columbia ○ ▲ ○
Mullins ○
Shaw AFB ○   Myrtle B.AFB ●
Charleston
■ ●
Beaufort, Parris Is.

Prime Contract Trends, FY'87-'90
(Constant FY '92 $Billions)

'87 $0.7b	'88 $0.7b	'89 $0.6b	'90 $0.8b

Top 5 Contractors	$ Millions
Unaka	$80.5
FN Manufacturing	44.7
Blue Cross/Blue Shield	42.6
Fluor	27.2
State of S. Carolina	21.0

Top 10 $ Sites[a]	Congressional Dist., Representative	1989 Rank	Total DoD$[c]	Payroll[c]	Prime Contracts[c]	Per-sonnel[d]
1-Charleston (24)	1-Ravenel, r	28	$1,121.8	$1,025.1	$96.7	20.0
2-Fort Jackson (137)	2-Spence, r	90	286.9	250.4	36.5	9.5
3-Columbia (177)	"	186	201.4	103.2	98.2	0.8
4-Shaw AFB (182)	"	206	193.0	150.8	42.3	6.2
5-Ch'leston AFB (211)	1-Ravenel, r	235	156.1	125.2	30.9	5.1
6-Beaufort (252)	"	262	113.3	107.0	6.3	3.7
7-Parris Island (269)	"	185	100.3	91.7	8.6	7.2
8-Myrtle Beach (274)	6-Tallon, d	278	94.0	86.4	7.6	3.7
9-Mullins (316)	"	354	63.2	2.8	60.4	--
10-N. Charleston (334)(1,6)[b]		329	46.2	1.9	44.4	--

[a] Rating in parentheses is out of 511 sites, the top ten in each state and PR, plus DC.
[b] Multidistrict r-Rep. d-Dem. [c] $Millions (may not add due to rounding) [d] Thousands

South Carolina

South Carolina's economy benefited from the boom enjoyed by the Southeast for most of the 1980s, and its prosperity is expected to continue. Retail sales were up by over 10 percent from 1987 to 1988, and per capita income grew 6.1 percent. South Carolina ranked fifth in the nation in 1989 for receiving new manufacturing investments and tied for first in new foreign investment. Although the state has lessened its dependence on the manufacturing sector, these industries remain the backbone of the South Carolina economy. The primary non-durable manufacturing industry is textiles and apparel. The state's unemployment rate at 5.7 percent ranked 35th in April 1991 and its change in unemployment 22nd (labor force growth outpaced employment growth).[1]

Defense and the Economy

Five percent of gross state product is in the form of defense dollars, and nearly 20,000 South Carolina civilians are directly on the Department of Defense payroll. Despite this fairly high defense dependence, the state's healthy economy will help it to absorb the effects of cutbacks.

Community Surveys

South Carolina serves the military primarily as a base site. Four-fifths of its defense revenue in 1989 and 1990 came from personnel payroll. The prime sites of civilian military employment are Charleston, Columbia (including Fort Jackson), Myrtle Beach, and Sumter (Shaw AFB). Shaw Air Force Base alone, the fourth largest site of defense spending in South Carolina, puts an estimated $344 million into a 15-county, 50-mile area around Sumter. The largest prime contracts are for food, health insurance, and housing. Construction contracts in the state came to $121 million in 1989. South Carolina firms also win a fair amount of ordnance contracts, with F.N. Manufacturing, Inc. receiving $36 million for gun production in 1989 and $38 million in 1990.[2]

Charleston. As of mid-1991, the Naval Electronic Systems Engineering Center seems likely to close. Its functions will be transferred to Portsmouth, VA along with 360 positions. Reduced activity is expected at the Charleston Naval Shipyard as the defense budget shrinks.

Columbia. Fort Jackson was targeted for realignment by the Department of Defense in 1988.

Myrtle Beach. Defense Secretary Dick Cheney has announced that the Myrtle Beach Air Force Base will be shut down. The base, which employs 3,792 military and civilian personnel, could close as early as 1992. Although some local officials contend that the community would be better served by civilian facilities on the site, Myrtle Beach Mayor Bob Grissom says that closing the base would be a terrible blow to the area's economy.[3] The closure would affect the base's 4,000 employees as well as 20,000 jobs indirectly dependent on the air facility in a region with 100,000 available jobs.

Sumter. Lt. Gen. Charles Horner announced that 120 jobs will be eliminated at Shaw Air Force Base. The cuts, representing 30 percent of the headquarters staff but less than 2 percent of Shaw's total personnel, will occur mostly by attrition. Horner expects that the cuts will have a minimal economic impact on the community and will improve the efficiency of the base headquarters.[4]

Notes

1. *1989 Economic Report, State of South Carolina*, South Carolina Board of Economic Advisors, December, 1989, p. 16. *Economic Developments*, S.C. State Development Board, March, 1990, p. 3.

2. Marge Barber, "Shaw's Local Impact: $344 Million," *Item*, February 18, 1990, p. 1A. *Prime Contract Awards by Region and State, Fiscal Years 1989, 1988, 1987*, Department of Defense, Washington Headquarters Services, Directorate for Information, Operations and Reports, p. 58. *Atlas/Data Abstract for the U.S. and Selected Areas, Fiscal 1989*, Department of Defense, Washington Headquarters Services, Directorate for Information, Operations and Reports. Contacts: (1) Governor's Office, Douglas McKay, Executive Assistant for Economic Development, State House, P.O. Box 11369, Columbia, SC 29211; 803-734-9818. (2) South Carolina Budget and Capital Board, Jesse Coles, P.O. Box 12444, Columbia, SC 29211; 803-734-2320. (3) South Carolina Development Board, Wayne Sterling, P.O. Box 927, Columbia, SC 29202; 803-737-0400. (4) South Carolina Labor Market Information, David Laird, P.O. Box 995, Columbia, SC 29202; 803-737-2660.

3. Joseph Serwach, "Base Closing Anticipated," *Sun News*, January 29, 1990.

4. Marge Barber, "Reduced Threat May Mean Fewer Shaw Employees," *Daily Item*, January 9, 1990, p. 1A.

South Dakota

A	B	C	D	E	F
$				VI	DDI
–	–	–	↓	–	✌

Benchmarks	No.	Rank	Benchmarks	No.	Rank
A.Total DoD $	$0.3bil.	49	Def.-Dependent Jobs ('000), '90	13	48
B. Personnel Payroll	$0.3bil.	46	Change in Def.-Dep. Jobs, '89-'91	-13.3%	9
C. Prime Contracts (PC)	$.04bil.	52	Unemployment Rate, '90-'91	3.4%	50
D. PC Change, FY '87-'90	-44.4%	5	Unemp. Rate Change, '89-'91	-0.5%	45
E. Vulnerability Index	5.8	50	Per Capita Income	$15,872	37
F. Defense Disloc. Index	0.00	49	Population ('000)	696	46

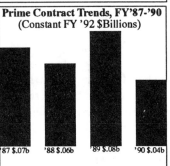

Prime Contract Trends, FY'87-'90
(Constant FY '92 $Billions)

'87 $.07b   '88 $.06b   '89 $.08b   '90 $.04b

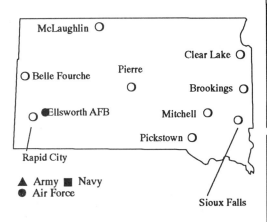

McLaughlin ○

Clear Lake ○

○ Belle Fourche   Pierre
                    ○

Brookings ○

○ ◼Ellsworth AFB   Mitchell ○
                            ○

Pickstown ○

Rapid City

▲ Army ◼ Navy
● Air Force

Sioux Falls

Top 5 Contractors	$ Millions
Raven Industries	$2.7
Technical Ordnance	2.5
Farmers Union Co-op	2.0
Dunn & Sons Maint.	1.7
MDU Resources	1.6

Top 10 $ Sites[a]	Congressional Dist., Representative	1989 Rank	Total DoD$[c]	Payroll[c]	Prime Contracts[c]	Per-sonnel
1-Ellsworth AFB (188)	1-Jackson, d	187	$186.3	$170.9	$15.4	7.1
2-Rapid City (386)	"	405	28.3	25.5	2.8	0.2
3-Sioux Falls (421)	"	367	17.6	14.0	3.6	0.3
4-Pierre (482)	"	481	4.7	3.8	0.9	.08
5-Brookings (489)	"	489	4.0	3.0	1.0	.03
6-Mitchell (498)	"	495	2.9	2.3	0.6	.04
7-Clear Lake (500)	"	--	2.7	0.2	2.5	--
8-Pickstown (503)	"	--	2.2	1.7	0.5	.05
9-Belle Fourche (504)	"	497	2.0	1.7	0.3	.06
10-McLaughlin (505)	"	--	2.0	0.0	2.0	--

[a]Rating in parentheses is out of 511 sites, the top ten in each state and PR, plus DC.
[b]Multidistrict r-Rep. d-Dem. [c]$Millions (may not add due to rounding) [d] Thousands

South Dakota

The South Dakota economy grew at an annual rate of 6.1 percent from 1980 to 1986. Like the rest of the nation, the state enjoyed a period of strong expansion following the deep recession of 1982, as the gross state product increased from $6.9 billion in 1980 to $9.8 billion in 1986. The largest industries in South Dakota are finance, insurance, real estate, wholesale and retail trade, services, agriculture, forestry, and fisheries.[1] In April 1991, South Dakota's unemployment was a low 3.4 percent and ranked 50th in the country; its unemployment declined over the past two years and the state ranks 45th in change in unemployment (a small increase in labor was accompanied by a slightly larger increase in employment).

Defense and the Economy

With a Vulnerability Index rank of 50th and a low Defense Dislocation Index, South Dakota is relatively safe from defense cuts. It receives only $296 million from the Department of Defense. A little more than 87 percent of defense expenditures in the state is payroll, and the top prime contractor in the state receives only $2.7 million. The payroll at Ellsworth Air Force Base is more than 50 percent of the state defense total.

Community Surveys

The attempted conversion of the Black Hills Army Depot in Edgemont, SD, in the 1970s is an example of an unsuccessful conversion effort. The base, which once employed some 512 civilians and a dozen soldiers, is now an eight-employee hog farm.[2]

The Army Corps of Engineers facilities in Yankton, Pickstown, and Fort Thompson are likely to be affected by defense cuts.[3]

Notes

1. *Statistical Abstract of the U.S., 1989*, Bureau of the Census, U.S. Department of Commerce, pp. 429, 431.

2. Center for Economic Conversion, "Opportunity Knocks," *Base Conversion News*, Summer 1990, p. 2.

3. Contacts: (1) South Dakota Governor's Office, Ruth Henneman, Special Assistant to the Governor, State Capitol, Pierre, SD 57501; 605-773-3212. (2) South Dakota Department of Labor, Peter de Hueck, Secretary of Labor, Kneip Building, Pierre, SD 57501; 605-773-3101. (3) South Dakota Economic Development, Darrell Butterwick, Capitol Lake Plaza, Pierre, SD 57501; 605-773-5032.

Tennessee

A	B	C	D	E	F
$	👷	🏭	📅	VI	DDI
+	+	+	↑	−	✂

Benchmarks	No.	Rank	Benchmarks	No.	Rank
A. Total DoD $	$2.1bil.	28	Def.-Dependent Jobs ('000), '90	100	30
B. Personnel Payroll	$0.9bil.	30	Change in Def.-Dep. Jobs, '89-'91	0.0%	34
C. Prime Contracts (PC)	$1.2bil.	26	Unemployment Rate, '90-'91	5.7%	35
D. PC Change, FY '87-'90	8.7%	45	Unemp. Rate Change, '89-'91	0.7%	31
E. Vulnerability Index	7.9	38	Per Capita Income	$15,798	38
F. Defense Disloc. Index	1.58	17	Population ('000)	4,877	17

▲ Army ■ Navy
● Air Force

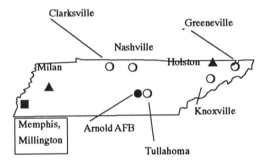

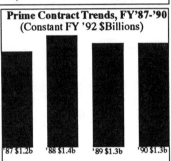

Prime Contract Trends, FY'87-'90
(Constant FY '92 $Billions)

'87 $1.2b '88 $1.4b '89 $1.3b '90 $1.3b

Top 5 Contractors	$ Millions
Fed Ex, Pan Am, et. al.	$253.5
Schneider Holdings	110.8
Martin Marietta	105.7
Ebasco-Newberg Joint Vent.	85.6
Eastman Kodak	74.2

Top 10 $ Sites[a]	Congressional Dist., Representative	1989 Rank	Total DoD$[c]	Payroll[c]	Prime Contracts[c]	Per-sonnel[d]
1-Memphis (80)	(7-9)[b]	158	$475.9	$160.8	$315.1	4.5
2-Arnold AFB (108)	4-Cooper, d	160	367.3	13.7	353.6	0.4
3-Millington (157)	8-Tanner, d	162	248.1	215.3	32.7	8.5
4-Milan AAP (262)	"	307	106.1	0	106.1	.06
5-Nashville (287)	5-Clement, d	274	85.0	72.0	13.0	1.6
6-Holston AAP (301)	1-Quillen, r	266	76.7	0	76.7	--
7-Knoxville (317)	2-Duncan, r	312	57.9	35.9	22.1	0.4
8-Clarksville (337)	7-Sundquist, r	342	44.6	43.9	0.7	--
9-Tullahoma (373)	4-Cooper, d	388	33.0	5.7	27.3	--
10-Greeneville (394)	1-Quillen, r	--	26.2	0.8	25.4	--

[a]Rating in parentheses is out of 511 sites, the top ten in each state and PR, plus DC.
[b]Multidistrict r-Rep. d-Dem. [c]$Millions (may not add due to rounding) [d] Thousands

Tennessee

Tennessee's economy is driven by a strong manufacturing sector. The state notes that the state is within one day's delivery of 76 percent of major U.S. markets. Memphis, the second largest inland port on the Mississippi, is already the sixth most important U.S. distribution center.[1] Tennessee's unemployment rate ranked 35th in April 1991 and its change in unemployment 31st (the labor force increased slightly faster than employment).

Defense and the Economy

The Department of Defense spent slightly over $2 billion in Tennessee in 1989, a relatively low amount. State firms accounted for 2 percent of U.S. missile-procurement programs in 1989.

Community Surveys

The future of the Maverick missile, and so the future of defense work in Bristol, is unclear. Other important defense industries in the state include ammunition production (Eastman Kodak and Martin Marietta) and textiles (10 percent of the 1989 Department of Defense textiles/clothing budget was spent in Tennessee).[2]

Bristol. Raytheon's plant in Bristol is a major production site of the Maverick. The main competitor is Hughes, in Tucson, AZ.

Nashville. The Tennessee Alliance for Strong Communities (Chris Atwood, P.O. Box 121333, Nashville, TN 37212; 615-244-4353) is a statewide coalition of over 35 community organizations researching the impact of military spending on state and local needs.

Oak Ridge. The fate of the Energy Department's Y-12 uranium plant will soon be decided. One plan is to merge its nuclear functions with those of facilities in other states and sell its non-nuclear manufacturing operations.[3]

Notes

1. *Tennessee: Where the World Comes to Work*, Department of Economic and Community Development, September, 1989.

2. *Atlas/Data Abstract for the U.S. and Selected Areas, Fiscal 1989*, Department of Defense, Washington Headquarters Services, Directorate for Information, Operations and Reports, p. 103. *Prime Contract Awards by Region and State, Fiscal Years 1989, 1988, 1987*, Department of Defense, p. 60. Contacts: (1) Tennessee Governor's Office, Jim Hall, Executive Assistant, State Capitol, Nashville, TN 37219; 615-741-4131. (2) Tennessee Department of Employment Security, Joe Cummings, 500 James Robertson Parkway, Volunteer Plaza, Nashville, TN 37219; 615-741-2284. (3) Tennessee Economic Development, Carl Johnson, Rachel Jackson, 8th Floor, Nashville, TN 37219; 615-741-1888.

3. Keith Schneider, "Study Foresees Closing Most Nuclear Arms Plants," *The New York Times*, February 7, 1991, p. B12.

Texas

A	B	C	D	E	F
$	🧍	🏭	📊	VI	DDI
✛	✛	✛	↑	‼	✂

Benchmarks	No.	Rank	Benchmarks	No.	Rank
A. Total DoD $	$15.8bil.	3	Def.-Dependent Jobs ('000), '90	822	2
B. Personnel Payroll	$6.7bil.	3	Change in Def.-Dep. Jobs, '89-'91	-6.2%	27
C. Prime Contracts (PC)	$9.1bil.	2	Unemployment Rate, '90-'91	6.9%	20
D. PC Change, FY '87-'90	-5.1%	38	Unemp. Rate Change, '89-'91	-0.1%	40
E. Vulnerability Index	11.5	16	Per Capita Income	$16,759	33
F. Defense Disloc. Index	9.07	2	Population ('000)	16,987	3

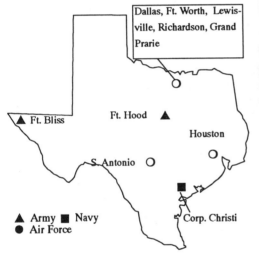

Dallas, Ft. Worth, Lewisville, Richardson, Grand Prarie

Ft. Bliss ▲   Ft. Hood ▲   Houston

S. Antonio ○

▲ Army ■ Navy
● Air Force   Corp. Christi

Prime Contract Trends, FY'87-'90
(Constant FY '92 $Billions)

'87 $10.4b	'88 $10.5b	'89 $10.4b	'90 $9.9b

Top 5 Contractors	$ Millions
General Dynamics	$2,940.2
LTV	855.8
Texas Instruments	674.5
Textron	258.2
Rockwell	248.9

Top 10 $ Sites[a]	Congressional Dist., Representative	1989 Rank	Total DoD$[c]	Payroll[c]	Prime Contracts[c]	Per-sonnel[d]
1-Fort Worth (3)	(6,12,26)[b]	3	$3,594.4	$274.9	$3,319.4	--
2-San Antonio (17)	(20,21,23)[b]	18	1,496.2	1,046.3	449.9	--
3-Fort Hood (31)	11-Edwards, d	21	971.6	839.3	132.4	37.4
4-Dallas (43)	(3-5,24,26)[b]	30	816.2	138.1	678.1	--
5-Grand Prarie (58)	(6,24,26)[b]	--	649.9	20.3	629.6	--
6-Houston (65)	(7-9,18,22,25)[b]	--	582.1	96.0	486.1	--
7-Corpus Christi (77)	(15,27)[b]	79	493.2	264.9	228.3	7.6
8-Lewisville (94)	26-Armey, r	70	425.9	4.7	421.1	--
9-Fort Bliss (104)	16-Coleman, d	61	380.0	341.8	38.2	14.7
10-Richardson (105)	(3,26)[b]	133	377.9	14.3	363.6	--

[a]Rating in parentheses is out of 511 sites, the top ten in each state and PR, plus DC.
[b]Multidistrict r-Rep. d-Dem. [c]$Millions (may not add due to rounding) [d] Thousands

Texas

The 1980s saw oil playing a decreasing role in the Texas economy. The oil industry accounted for over 27 percent of the Texas economy in 1981, and declined to 15 percent in 1987. The 1986-7 collapse of the oil and real estate market caused a severe economic crisis in Texas, and the recent rebound has been led by the strong manufacturing sector. The unemployment rate is improving, but in 1990-91 was still 6.9 percent, 20th highest. The state's change in unemployment ranked 40th (employment growth slightly outpaced labor force growth). Gross state product, personal income, and employment figures should all improve in the next decade, as the construction and trade sectors grow at faster rates, and the state product growth rate is predicted to surpass the national rate. It is expected that the growth of the 1990s will be evenly spread across all regions of the state.[1]

Defense and the Economy

One bright spot in the generally gloomy economic picture of the Lone Star State in the 1980s was the booming defense business. Only two states, California and Virginia, received more funds than Texas' $15.8 billion in 1990. In recent years, the defense sector has grown four times faster than the overall state economy. Department of Defense-related business employed 4.2 percent of all Texans and accounted for 4.8 percent of the state product in 1989. Eight of Texas's top ten sites in total expenditures are in the national top 100. Proposed defense cuts will cost Texas an estimated total loss of 68,000 jobs by 1994 (1 percent of the state non-farm workforce), and a possible consequent drop in the gross state product of 0.5 percent in 1991 and another 0.2 percent in 1992.[2]

Despite the fact that Texas is the third largest recipient of Department of Defense funds, one study suggests that Texas was the biggest loser in the arms buildup. It contends that the state employs 288,000 fewer people today than it might have had the money been spent in more civilian programs proportional to expenditures in the rest of the defense budget. Now, with military reductions a political and economic necessity, Texas may lose an additional 75,000 jobs, 38,000 in the near term and 37,000 more in the long term.

State Legislative and Executive Initiatives

Gov. Ann Richards has appointed a Task Force on Economic Transition, which has been meeting regularly since July 1991. It is studying the state's defense dependence and is planning to make proposals to help dislocated workers.

As an indicator of likely future legislative activity, the Texas Populist Alliance (Gary Keith, 512-482-8724) in September 1991 focused on conversion as a key issue for attention as part of the political agenda of 45 activists from around the state.[3]

Community Surveys

Of the bases to be closed by the defense reduction plans, four are located in Texas, and Fort Hood will face serious reductions (although cuts were frozen when the Gulf War began). Bell Helicopter Textron has already laid off workers, and in 1990, General Dynamics announced that 7,000 jobs will be lost by the mid-1990s. In early 1991, dashing hopes of a possible reverse of fortune, General Dynamics announced that its plan to cut its national workforce from 90,000 to 63,000 in the next few years will proceed despite the fact that the company had just won a contract to produce 648 F-22 Advanced Tactical Fighters from the Air Force.

The bulk of the state's defense dollars flows into the Dallas-Ft. Worth area, site of huge plants operated by Bell Helicopter Textron Inc., E-Systems Inc., General Dynamics, LTV, Rockwell, and Texas Instruments. According to the State of Texas office in Washington, about 500,000 Metroplex jobs are tied. directly or indirectly. to weapons procurement, which is an estimated 40 percent of all defense spending in Texas.

Texas firms accounted for more than twice as much Department of Defense petroleum business, 31 percent, as the next highest state. The state also received 22 percent of military-aircraft contracts, second only to Missouri. Overall, the state received over 7.7 percent of Department of Defense prime contracts.[4]

Austin. Bergstrom Air Force Base was recommended for closure by the Base Commission in July 1991. If the base closes, 8,000 civilian and military jobs will be lost. Local leaders and observers are confident that Bergstrom and the community around the Air Force base will be able to set up an effective plan to make the transition away from defense-oriented functions.[5] In addition to the direct closing of the base, many high-tech businesses in Austin will be greatly hurt by defense cuts.

One working group is the Move It To Bergstrom Organization or MITBO (Ray Reece, coordinator, P.O. Box. 3057, Austin, TX 78764), a city-wide coalition of groups and individuals committed to building the new Austin airport at the site of the Bergstrom Air Force Base. In 1987, Austin passed a $728 million bond initiative to construct a new airport in Manor. MITBO believes that converting Bergstrom into a commercial airport would avoid the expense of building a new one and would result in the airport being completed sooner. This would also give a tremendous economic boost to the area, particularly in Southeast Travis County, which they believe has been excluded from Austin's economic growth. The conversion would work to offset the loss of jobs resulting from closing the base. MITBO is busy campaigning for supporters.

The Austin Campaign for Global Security (Roxanne Elder, 227 Congress Avenue, Suite 220, Austin, TX 78701-4021, or Ruth Roberts, 4043 Turnberry, Houston, TX 77025; 512-863-7635) is the Texas affiliate of SANE/Freeze. Its

Peace Economy Campaign is an attempt to make communities aware of their defense dependence and how they can effectively convert their economies. It is active in planning for diversification of the Bergstrom AFB.

The Texas Economic Conversion Network (Don Gardner or Carin Watts, P.O. Box 2304, Austin, TX 78768; 512-471-1122 or 512-263-2585), was instrumental in the appointment by local officials of an Austin Citizens' Task Force, which has held public hearings on the future of Bergstrom. The news from the FAA in the fall of 1991 was good for those who want to re-use the site for an airport; the Federal Aviation Administration approved the Federal cost-share for building a commercial airport on the Bergstrom site.[6]

Beeville. Chase Field Naval Air Station was on the Base Closure Commission's final list of closures announced in July 1991. Chase was targeted because of the feasability of shifting many of its functions to a similar base in Kingsville, TX. The Navy's estimate is that 27.4 percent of area employment will be lost. Annual savings will amount to $22 million. Local money loss should be partially offset by the opening of a new state prison nearby in 1992 and several firms have already expressed interest in acquiring aircraft maintenance facilities. However, the future remains murky: property values are dropping, businesses are leaving, and no one knows when or if the Defense Department will offer the base to private developers.[7]

Dallas. High-tech jobs account for two-fifths of all workers in the area, and when Ft. Worth included, the area receives two-thirds of Texas' defense spending. The breadth of local employment is a plus; the continued real estate slump is a minus. Texas Instruments, anticipating a soft defense market (the company stands to lose the Chaparral missile), laid off 1,700 employees from its Defense Electronics group in 1989 and an additional 340 in April 1990. Approximately 1,500 of those laid off in 1989 opted for the company's "voluntary" retirement program. All the others were offered job placement assistance and received full salary and other benefits for 60 days. In June 1990, Texas Instruments announced that it would eliminate a further 1,000 jobs from its Defense Systems and Electronics Group in the next year. The company employs about 22,000 people in Texas.[8]

The uncertain future of the Stealth bomber has moved LTV Corp. to implement reductions of its workforce. Out of LTV's approximately 11,000 workers, about 4,000 are involved in work related to the ever controversial B-2; all these jobs could be threatened by the House of Representatives' wish to cut the B-2 altogether. In August 1990, in an effort to lessen the damage of these and other employee reductions, the Texas Department of Commerce awarded a Dallas County agency more than $3 million in Federal funding for use in assisting laid-off workers.

The Dallas League of Women Voters Economic Conversion Committee (Tricia Sullivan or Jim Frost, 214-688-4125), in conjunction with the Leagues of Plano and Tarrant County, published *Economic Conversion: Facts and Issues*, following on a conference on conversion in January 1991. The Leagues are urging the North Texas Council of Governments to establish a long-range diversification-planning committee.[9]

Ft. Worth. Ft. Worth ranks third in its dollar dependence on the Department of Defense, after St. Louis and San Diego, and it is in a much more perilous situation than San Diego because it has a higher proportion of defense contracts and some are vulnerable. Bell Textron stands to be hit hard by cuts in the V-22 and the Army Helicopter Improvement Program (AHIP). Despite Department of Defense and Marine pressure and independent studies that the V-22 Osprey is a better value than the alternatives, Defense Secretary Dick Cheney wants to cancel the program. This will result in the loss of 2,000 jobs at Bell Textron. Nearly one-fifth of the city's quarter-million workforce is involved in defense. The city is worried about firms tied to Bell and General Dynamics and expects them to look for state aid to retrain employees (but meanwhile Bell lobbies for contract renewals).[10] Furthermore, Texas legislators and officials of Bell Helicopter-Textron are contending that the V-22 has potential commercial uses.

Despite a tough fight by Texas Congressmen and Fort Worth officials, Carswell Air Force Base — home to B-52 bombers — remained on the Base Closure Commission's final list of recommended shutdowns. The economic impact could be severe, especially since other defense cuts will also be affecting the Fort Worth area. The Department of Defense estimates job loss of 12,000 in an area with 600,000 jobs. Additionally, about 100,000 military retirees and their dependents rely on Carswell for services. Fort Worth Mayor Kay Granger announced plans to name a task force for base conversion. The city is applying for a conversion-planning grant from the Office of Economic Adjustment in the Defense Department. Local officials are considering the creation of an airport, an expanded Air Force Reserve center or an industrial park with free-trade-zone status. They worry though that their plans will be put on indefinite hold as the Federal government seeks to clean various contaminated sites at Carswell.[11]

General Dynamics is the largest single employer in Tarrant County with 32,000 workers. The Department of Defense wants to terminate its Fort Worth-made F-16 fighter. General Dynamics has a $4.6 billion contract with the government to build 150 planes a year from 1990 to 1993, but it is expected that the Department of Defense will request only 96 planes in 1992, dropping to 72 in 1993, 48 from 1994 to 1997, and closed by 1998. "Moments after" the announcement by Secretary Cheney in early 1991 that he would terminate the Navy's A-12 attack jet, General Dynamics announced it would begin laying off 4,000 workers in Fort Worth and Tulsa. The Defense Department sought repayment of $1.35 billion from General Dynamics, and its partner in the A-12 project, McDonnell Douglas, but shelved that plan and instead extended $1.3

billion in loan guarantees to the two companies when their tight financial situation became apparent.[12]

Galveston. The Naval Station is slated to be closed, with the loss of 492 military and 45 civilian jobs. An additional 11 military bases and reserve units face cuts.

Grand Prairie. LTV Aircraft Products Group is involved in the production of the B-2 bomber. The company has 4,000 employees devoted to the project, although increasing pressure to curtail production of the expensive bomber has led to layoffs. Officials contend that a Congressional decision to eliminate the B-2 project would produce a catastrophic economic backlash throughout the area.[13]

Killeen. Secretary Cheney backed a proposal to reduce troop levels at Fort Hood by up to 12,000 soldiers, representing a tremendous blow to the local economy. The businesses of the Killeen area, indeed much of central Texas, are dependent on the base: around 70 percent of the area's 100,000 population is tied to the base. "We are basically a one-industry town and that industry is Fort Hood," said Rick Murphy, president of the Greater Killeen Chamber of Commerce. Local businessmen and politicians fear that the tremendous loss of revenue resulting from the cutbacks will not be accompanied by a strategy ensuring the economy's healthy transition to a civilian-based market. Fort Hood, a 350-square-mile post with an $850-million-a-year payroll, generates $1 billion per year of economic activity in the central Texas area ($250 million in Killeen alone).[14]

The Second Armored Division was originally to be replaced by the 1st Armored Division (currently at Ansbach, West Germany). Faced with tighter budgets, however, the Army began considering just "removing the troops from the force structure." The dismantling was temporarily halted due to the Gulf Crisis. Fort Hood is also home to the First Cavalry Division, which, with its 26,000 troops, will remain at Hood. Additionally, Hood could eventually gain troops as other bases close around the country, mandating force realignments. Killeen is developing an economic diversification strategy.

San Angelo. Goodfellow Air Force Base appeared on a base closure hitlist in June 1991.

Notes

1. Bob Bullock, "Texas to 2000," *Fiscal Notes*, February, 1990.

2. Bullock, "Texas Defense Boom Cooling Off," *Fiscal Notes*, April, 1988. Memo from Tom Plaut and Mickey Wright to Bob Bullock, Texas Comptroller of Public Accounts. Economic Analysis Center, February 5, 1990. "Army puts Fort Hood cutbacks on hold," *Dallas Morning News*, August 22, 1990 p. D-1.

3. Janet Stone, *Conversion Organizers' Update* (Mountain View, CA: Center for Economic Conversion, October 1991, advance copy), p. 11.

4. Marion Anderson, Michael Frisch, and Michael Oden, *The Empty Pork Barrel: The Employment Cost of the Military Build-up 1981-1985*, p. 2. Dave Montgomery,

"70,000 Texas Jobs Threatened," *Fort Worth Star-Telegram*, May 13, 1990, p. 1. *Prime Contract Awards by Region and State, Fiscal Years 1989, 1988, 1987*, Department of Defense, Washington Headquarters Services, Directorate for Information, Operations and Reports, p. 61. Contacts: (1) Office of State-Federal Relations, Randall Erben, c/o Governor's Office, State Capitol, Austin, TX 78711; 512-488-3927. (2) Killeen Mayor's Office, Mayor Blair, P.O. Box 1329, Killeen, TX 76540. (3) Texas Department of Commerce, William Taylor, P.O. Box 12728, Austin, TX 78711; 512-472-5059. (4) Texas Employment Commission, Horace Goodman, 1500 Congress Ave., Austin, TX 78778; 512-463-2222. (5) Winsome Jean, Director of Finance and Business Development, Office of the Governor, Sam Houston Building, PO Box 12428, Austin TX 78711.

5. Don Gardner, "Bergstrom: It's Time Austin Started Thinking About Life Without the Air Force Base," *Austin American-Statesman*, May 13, 1990. Gardner is Chairman of the Texas Campaign for Global Security, the Texas affiliate of SANE/Freeze, 512-263-2585.

6. Gardner, "The Chair Talks Politics for the 90s," *Campaign for Global Security Newsletter*, Winter 1989. Stone, *op. cit.*, p. 10.

7. *Base Closure and Realignment Report*, April 1991, pp. 57-58. Lee Hancock, "Beeville's Future Uncertain Without Navy Training Base," *Dallas Morning News*, July 3, 1991, p. 27.

8. John Tepper Marlin, *Cities of Opportunity* (New York: MasterMedia, 1988), pp. 242, 247. Julie Truck, "TI Adds 150 More to Defense Group Layoffs," *Ft. Worth Star-Telegram*, April 25, 1990, p. II-1. "Two Military Contractors Plan Layoffs," *The New York Times*, June 9, 1990.

9. Mary Gugliuzza, "Program for Laid-Off Workers Gets $3 Mil," *Grand Prairie News*, August 4, 1990, p. 1. Stone, *loc. cit.*

10. Interview in March, 1990 with Tom Higgins, Director of Economic Development, Fort Worth, 817-870-6117.

11. Bob Mahlburg, "Carswell Allies Quietly Explore Options for Imperiled Base," *Fort Worth Star-Telegram*, April 26, 1991, p. B1. Mahlburg, "Post-Carswell Era Begins," *Fort Worth Star-Telegram*, July 2, 1991, p. 1.

12. Kathryn Jones, "F-16 Cuts Reportedly Sought," *Dallas Morning News*, April 10, 1990, p. 9. Eric Schmitt, "Pentagon Scraps $57 Billion Order for Attack Plane," *The New York Times*, January 8, 1991, p. A1.

13. Dave Montgomery, "N. Texans Linked to Shape of B-2 Project" *Fort Worth Star-Telegram*, May 20, 1990, p. 3.

14. Roberto Suro, "Army Town in Texas Pays the Price of Peace," *The New York Times*, July 22, 1990, p. 1. Hugh Aynesworth, "Fort Hood Neighbors Oppose Closing, Fear Economy Will Collapse," *The Washington Times*, February 6, 1990. Julie Morris, "Base Closings: Towns Fear the Worst," *USA Today*, January 29, 1990, p. 9. Todd Gillman, "Texas Leaders Set to Battle Proposed Military-Base Cuts," *Dallas Morning News*, January 30, 1990. p. 9.

Utah

A	B	C	D	E	F
$	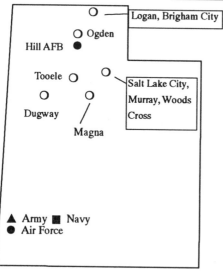			VI	DDI
+	+	+	↓	!	✂

Benchmarks	No.	Rank	Benchmarks	No.	Rank
A.Total DoD $	$1.9bil.	30	Def.-Dependent Jobs ('000), '90	103	29
B. Personnel Payroll	$1.0bil.	25	Change in Def.-Dep. Jobs, '89-'91	-7.2%	23
C. Prime Contracts (PC)	$0.9bil.	29	Unemployment Rate, '90-'91	4.6%	47
D. PC Change, FY '87-'90	-30.5%	16	Unemp. Rate Change, '89-'91	-1.1%	50
E. Vulnerability Index	10.3	22	Per Capita Income	$14,083	49
F. Defense Disloc. Index	0.69	28	Population ('000)	1,723	36

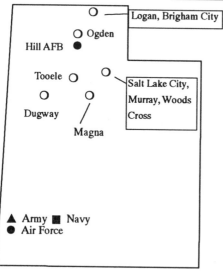

Logan, Brigham City

Ogden

Hill AFB ●

Tooele ○

Dugway

Magna

Salt Lake City, Murray, Woods Cross

▲ Army ■ Navy
● Air Force

Prime Contract Trends, FY'87-'90
(Constant FY '92 $Billions)

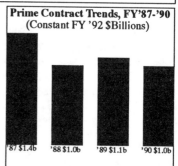

'87 $1.4b   '88 $1.0b   '89 $1.1b   '90 $1.0b

Top 5 Contractors	$ Millions
Thiokol	$159.4
Hercules	110.7
Amoco	75.1
Facilities Sys. Eng.	74.1
Unisys	72.0

Top 10 $ Sites[a]	Congressional Dist., Representative	1989 Rank	Total DoD$[c]	Payroll[c]	Prime Contracts[c]	Per-sonnel[d]
1-Hill AFB (62)	1-Hansen, r	64	$608.6	$530.5	$78.2	18.4
2-Salt Lake City (147)	2-Owens, d	181	269.6	51.8	217.8	0.7
3-Tooele (160)	1-Hansen, r	203	242.3	118.0	124.4	3.7
4-Brigham City (206)	"	134	164.2	6.5	157.6	--
5-Ogden (225)	"	256	138.1	72.7	65.4	2.3
6-Magna (247)	2-Owens, d	208	115.6	3.5	112.1	.07
7-Logan (325)	1-Hansen, r	361	51.8	4.4	47.4	--
8-Murray (330)	(2,3)[b]	326	48.3	48.0	0.3	--
9-Dugway (382)	1-Hansen, r	295	30.4	30.4	.05	1.0
10-Woods Cross (391)	"	382	26.6	1.1	25.5	--

[a]Rating in parentheses is out of 511 sites, the top ten in each state and PR, plus DC.
[b]Multidistrict r-Rep. d-Dem. [c]$Millions (may not add due to rounding) [d] Thousands

Utah

Utah has a relatively strong economy, but it is changing. Manufacturing will not be as important to its economy in 2000 as it was in 1980. Taking its place will be trade, service, and government sectors, with construction expected to make a comeback from a late-1980s decline.[1] In 1991 Utah's unemployment was a low 4.6 percent, ranking 47th. The state's change in unemployment over two years ranked 50th (the increase in employment exceeded that of labor).

Defense and the Economy

The Department of Defense spends almost $2 billion in Utah, a significant figure for a small state. Over 6 percent of total state revenue is from the defense, and 4 percent of the civilian labor force. This relatively high defense dependence partially offsets the low unemployment rate and increases the state's vulnerability to defense cuts. Defense cuts would affect spending on the F-15 fighter program in the state. State firms receive a good deal of defense-related aircraft production and maintenance contracts, as well as almost half a million dollars for missile systems. Fuel accounted for almost 10 percent of military business in the state. Utah firms in 1989 were the 3rd highest recipients of defense contractors for non-petroleum fuels and lubricants. Defense expenditures are heavily concentrated in the northwest portion of the state around the Great Salt Lake, with Hill Air Force Base in Clearfield receiving the most funds.[2]

Clearfield. Employment reductions are planned at Hill AFB due to budget constraints.[3]

Salt Lake City. Fort Douglas was recommended for closure by the Department of Defense in 1988. Commercial redevelopment is limited by two factors: part of the fort is a National Landmark site and hazardous waste cleanup is required.

Notes

1. *State of Utah Economic and Demographic Projections, 1988.*

2. *Atlas/Data Abstract for the United Stated and Selected Areas, Fiscal 1990*, Department of Defense, Washington Headquarters Services, Directorate for Information, Operations and Reports, p. 107. *Prime Contract Awards by Region and State, Fiscal Years 1989, 1988, 1987*, Department of Defense, p. 63. Contacts: (1) Utah Governor's Office, Douglas Bischoff, Deputy Chief of Staff, 210 State Capitol, Salt Lake City, UT 84114; 801-538-1000. (2) Utah Budget & Planning, Michael Christensen, Deputy Director, 116 State Capitol, Salt Lake City, UT 84114; 801-538-1027. (3) Utah Department of Economic Development, Stanley Parrish, Three South State St., Salt Lake City, UT 84114; 801-538-3700.

3. *Economic Report to the Governor 1991*, State Economic Coordinating Committee, p. 145.

Vermont

A	B	C	D	E	F
$				VI	DDI
–	–	–	↓	–	✂

Benchmarks	No.	Rank	Benchmarks	No.	Rank
A. Total DoD $	$0.2bil.	52	Def.-Dependent Jobs ('000), '90	6	52
B. Personnel Payroll	$0.1bil.	52	Change in Def.-Dep. Jobs, '89–'91	-50.0%	1
C. Prime Contracts (PC)	$0.1bil.	48	Unemployment Rate, '90–'91	7.4%	10
D. PC Change, FY '87–'90	-40.4%	7	Unemp. Rate Change, '89–'91	+3.4%	7
E. Vulnerability Index	7.1	45	Per Capita Income	$17,436	26
F. Defense Disloc. Index	5.45	5	Population ('000)	563	50

Burlington, Shelburne, Winooski, Essex Jtn., Colchester, Jericho

○ Vergennes

○ Northfield

○ Rutland

Bennington

▲ Army ■ Navy
● Air Force

○

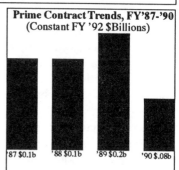

Prime Contract Trends, FY '87–'90
(Constant FY '92 $Billions)

'87 $0.1b	'88 $0.1b	'89 $0.2b	'90 $.08b

Top 5 Contractors	$ Millions
General Electric	$49.9
Hercules	10.6
Arrowsmith Shelburne	2.9
Norwich University	2.0
Faribank Scales	1.0

Top 10 $ Sites[a]	Congressional Dist., Representative	1989 Rank	Total DoD$[c]	Payroll[c]	Prime Contracts[c]	Per-sonnel[d]
1-Burlington (305)	1-Sanders, Indep.	239	$71.6	$19.3	$52.4	0.4
2-Vergennes (441)	"	409	11.2	0.6	10.6	--
3-Colchester (469)	"	--	6.1	5.9	0.2	0.1
4-Northfield (480)	"	487	4.8	2.7	2.0	.04
5-Shelburne (494)	"	460	3.8	0.8	3.0	--
6-Winooski (495)	"	419	3.8	3.4	0.4	.04
7-Jericho (496)	"	491	3.7	3.3	0.4	.03
8-Rutland (497)	"	492	3.7	2.9	0.8	.02
9-Essex Junction (506)	"	--	2.0	1.9	0.1	--
10-Bennington (507)	"	473	1.6	1.3	0.4	--

[a]Rating in parentheses is out of 511 sites, the top ten in each state and PR, plus DC.
[b]Multidistrict r-Rep. d-Dem. [c]$Millions (may not add due to rounding) [d] Thousands

Vermont

Per capita personal income in Vermont is below the U.S. figure, and more than 21 percent below the New England states' average. The manufacturing sector has declined since 1988, while services have grown, employing more than 31 percent of the 1989 Vermont workforce;[1] tourism is a major component of the services sector. The state's unemployment rate was a high 7.4 percent in 1991, 10th highest; its increase in unemployment over the past two years was 7th highest (a small decrease in the labor force was accompanied by a much larger decrease in employment).

Defense and the Economy

Vermont received the fewest Department of Defense dollars in 1990. The $151 million spent in Vermont barely accounted for 0.07 percent of total Defense Department expenditures. However, Vermont will be strongly affected by proposed cuts in the F-15 fighter program. Over 41 percent of military procurement in Vermont is related to the production of airframes or aircraft-related equipment. State firms also received $6.4 million worth of weapons contracts in 1989, which was approximately 4 percent of the state's share of total Department of Defense weapons procurement. Defense spending is most heavily concentrated in the relatively defense-dependent Burlington area, which is the home of an important General Electric facility.[2]

According to Doug Hoffer of the Community and Economic Development Office (CEDO) in Burlington, many of Vermont's defense contractors do significant subcontracting work that is likely to be impacted indirectly by cuts in weapons systems. Other firms, including GE, depend on sales abroad, which are in danger as many foreign nations re-evaluate their defense needs.[3]

State Legislative Initiatives

The Vermont Legislature considered two conversion bills during the 1990 session, both proposed by Burlington's CEDO. The first was to direct the state's Agency of Development and Community Affairs develop a statewide plan for economic conversion. The Economic Adjustment Act (S 303) calls for both industry and unions or worker representatives to be involved in conversion planning. The state agency would look into alternative use planning and potential growth industries to which workers could be transferred. The second (S 350) required companies to give 60 days notice to both workers and local governments of any plant closures affecting 50 or more employees. This would apply to more plants that the Federal plant-closing law and the 1990 Conversion Law, which relate only to plants of 100 or more employees. The bill would have extended the safety net to an additional 14,000-15,000 Vermont employees. Employers would also be required to provide benefits and assistance to the laid-off workers. Neither bill was reported out of committee, because of a state revenue shortage, but state and local legislators were reportedly interested in the issue and the bills.

Community Surveys

The Burlington CEDO initiatives are of special interest.

Brattleboro. Vermont SANE/Freeze helped coordinate a statewide Town Meeting Resolution Campaign, calling for at least a 5 percent cut in military spending to provide additional funding for community needs. The resolution was passed by 110 of 120 town meetings.

Burlington. Burlington receives over half of Vermont's defense money. The General Electric plant is the single largest taxpayer in Burlington. The workforce at the plant, however, is currently one-third the size it was 15 years ago, with the most recent layoffs coming in February 1990 when 275 people were laid-off. Plant closure is a possibility. The Burlington facility produces rapid-fire machine guns which are mounted on fighters and helicopters, many of which are being cut.

CEDO (Doug Hoffer, City of Burlington, VT 05401; 802-658-9300) undertook a study of opportunities for General Electric to diversify into more civilian-related work. It was directed by the City Council in August 1988 to "assess the vulnerability of GE's Burlington operations and the opportunities for converting them to non-military production." GE was fairly uncooperative in the study, according to CEDO officials. CEDO formulated a report to the Burlington Council recommending that a Mayoral Task Force be established to achieve a consensus on how to proceed in local adjustment activities. The proposed Manufacturing Task Force has been formed with representatives from local government, GE management, and local unions. Thus far, in the fall of 1991, GE has only consented to work toward attracting other manufacturers to the area to diversify the economy.[4]

Notes

1. *Vermont Selected Statistics*, Planning Division, Agency of Development and Community Affairs, December, 1989.

2. *Atlas/Data Abstract for the U.S. and Selected Areas, Fiscal 1990*, Department of Defense, Washington Headquarters Services, Directorate for Information, Operations and Reports, p. 109.

3. Contacts: (1) Governor's Office, Dr. Arthur Woolf, Economist, 109 State St., Montpelier, VT 05602; 802-828-3326. (2) Vermont Department of Employment & Training, Michael Griffin, 5 Green Mountain Drive, Montpelier, VT 05602; 802-229-0311. (3) Burlington Community and Economic Development Office, Doug Hoffer, Room 32, City Hall, Burlington, VT 05401, 802-658-9300. (4) Vermont Development & Community Affairs, Pavilion Building, Montpelier, VT 05602; 802-828-3221. (5) Vermont Economic Development, Pavilion Building, Montpelier, VT 05602; 802-828-3221.

4. Doug Hoffer, "Planning for a Change," *Plowshare Press*, Summer 1990, p. 8.

Virginia

A	B	C	D	E	F
$				VI	DDI
+	+	+	↑	!!	✌

Benchmarks	No.	Rank	Benchmarks	No.	Rank
A. Total DoD $	$17.5bil.	2	Def.-Dependent Jobs ('000), '90	805	3
B. Personnel Payroll	$9.6bil.	2	Change in Def.-Dep. Jobs, '89-'91	+14.0%	45
C. Prime Contracts (PC)	$7.9bil.	4	Unemployment Rate, '90-'91	5.4%	39
D. PC Change, FY '87-'90	-8.7%	35	Unemp. Rate Change, '89-'91	+1.9%	15
E. Vulnerability Index	17.2	2	Per Capita Income	$19,746	13
F. Defense Disloc. Index	0.18	36	Population ('000)	6,187	12

▲ Army ■ Navy
● Air Force

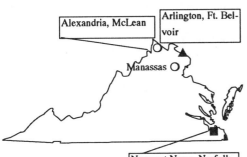

Alexandria, McLean

Arlington, Ft. Belvoir

Manassas ○

Newport News, Norfolk, Virginia Bch., Portsmouth, Hampton

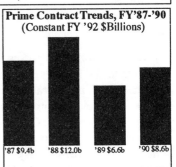

Prime Contract Trends, FY '87-'90
(Constant FY '92 $Billions)

'87 $9.4b | '88 $12.0b | '89 $6.6b | '90 $8.6b

Top 5 Contractors	$ Millions
Tenneco	$2,389.4
IBM	446.2
General Motors	239.5
Unisys	237.0
Hercules	209.5

Top 10 $ Sites[a]	Congressional Dist., Representative	1989 Rank	Total DoD$[c]	Payroll[c]	Prime Contracts[c]	Per-sonnel[d]
1-Newport News (5)	1-Bateman ,r	23	$2,744.8	$328.4	$2,416.4	--
2-Norfolk (6)	2-Pickett, d	7	2,741.3	2,236.1	505.2	34.0
3-Arlington (7)	10-Wolf, r	10	2,525.3	1,938.5	586.8	44.7
4-Virginia Beach (27)	2-Pickett, d	34	1,059.6	880.0	179.6	14.0
5-Alexandria (33)	8-Morgan, d	39	952.2	499.0	453.2	12.4
6-Portsmouth (59)	4-Sisisky, d	62	644.9	530.6	114.3	17.9
7-McLean (60)	10-Wolf, r	63	644.9	49.5	595.5	--
8-Hampton (68)	1-Batemen, r	73	515.2	440.3	74.8	--
9-Manassas (84)	7-Slaughter, r	68	462.6	9.7	452.9	--
10-Ft. Belvoir (95)	8-Morgan, d	108	418.1	308.2	109.9	9.3

[a]Rating in parentheses is out of 511 sites, the top ten in each state and PR, plus DC.
[b]Multidistrict r-Rep. d-Dem. [c]$Millions (may not add due to rounding) [d] Thousands

Virginia

For the sixth consecutive year in 1989 Virginia added over 100,000 new jobs. During that six-year period, non-farm employment increased by 4.5 percent, well above the national increase rate of 3.1 percent. Although the manufacturing part of that figure declined with decreased big-ticket Navy procurement, it was more than compensated for by growth in services, trade, government, construction and transportation.[1] Other employment-growth sectors are finance-insurance-real estate and publishing-printing. Unemployment was 5.4 percent in 1991, ranking a low 39th. However, its increase over the previous two years ranked 15th highest (an increase in the labor force exceeded an increase in employment).

Defense and the Economy

Only California surpasses Virginia in defense income. Per capita defense spending in the nation's 12th most populous state ranks third, behind Alaska and Hawaii.[2] Virginia ranks second on the Vulnerability Index.

Defense-related employees in Virginia number an estimated 250,000 in the private and government sectors, and defense-related jobs account for 8.6 percent of Virginia's total employment, a higher percentage than any other state. Tenneco, IBM, Unisys, Hercules, and GM are the leading contractors, accounting for over 60 percent of the state's contract awards in 1988. Tenneco builds aircraft carriers and submarines at its Newport News drydocks.[3]

State Legislative Initiatives

Virginia's JR 433, enacted in March 1991, calls for a Joint Subcommittee to plan for the state's economic recovery. The Joint Subcommittee is proceeding with eight working groups. Economic conversion is being considered by one of them dealing with the role of government in promoting recovery. The Joint Subcommittee will hold five meetings around the state in the fall of 1991.

The Virginia Economic Recovery Commission was created in 1991 after Virginia was badly hit by the economic downturn. The Commission found the cause in defense cuts, observing that about 24 percent of state income is defense-related. The Commission decided to present diversification initiatives to the state legislature in October 1991.[4]

Community Surveys

Newport News, Norfolk, and Arlington rank first, second, and third in contract and payroll dollars in Virginia; all are in the top ten expenditure sites in the nation. Standing to lose the most from defense cuts in the state are the Washington suburbs of northern Virginia and the Virginia shipyards (since 1982, 43 shipyards, or 39 percent of the nation's total, have shut down and 34,000 jobs have disappeared). IBM's defense line, including anti-submarine devices and general training aids, is not expected to be greatly affected by the cuts. Overall, firms in northern Virginia are 73 percent defense-dependent. Northern Virginia accounts for 46 percent of all defense spending in the state and the Hampton Roads area accounts for 42 percent.

The Virginia Task Force on Economic Conversion (Louis Tremaine, c/o Richmond Peace Education Center, 14 N. Laurel St., Richmond VA 23220; 804-358-1958; or John Accordino, 804-367-1134) aims to bring together representatives from the military, defense contractors, state officials and legislators and academics to discuss conversion. A Task Force member was appointed to one of the working groups of the Joint Subcommittee. During the summer of 1991 several members of the Task Force participated in roundtable discussions on economic conversion as part of a national project organized by the National Governors Association.[5]

Alexandria. Alexandria's Cameron Station will be closed. Although the base employs over 700 civilians, many of the employees are not residents of Alexandria. Deputy City Manager Henry Howard says that the base actually generates little economic activity for Alexandria, and he foresees conversion of the facilities to primarily residential and some commercial/retail uses. The closing of the base can also provide some affordable housing units for the community.[6] The Alexandria City Council has approved a facility re-use plan for Cameron Station.

Charlottesville. The Charlottesville-Albemarle Taskforce on Economic Conversion (Jay Worrall, 1104 Forrest St., Charlottesville, VA 22901; 804-293-5060), associated with the statewide Task Force on Economic Conversion, published a report on defense-dependence in the Charlottesville area that is being acted on by Charlottesville officials. Its work is receiving attention from the Lt. Governor and was the subject of a video produced by the Center for Defense Information.

Fairfax. Under the 1989 Base Closure Act, Fort Belvoir was scheduled to receive part of the Army Material Technology Lab's functions from Watertown, MA. Under a revision of that legislation recommended by the Base Commission in 1991, the move will not take place and instead materials elements and part of the Center for Night Vision and Electro-Optics will move from Belvoir to Maryland. Implementation of the revision is on hold until a separate Congressional commission charged with investigating laboratory consolidations makes its advisory report to the Base Commission in September 1991.

Herndon. DMA Herndon was targeted for cuts in 1988. Functions will move to a site in nearby Maryland.

Newport News. Newport News Shipbuilding, a Tenneco subsidiary, appears to be the strongest of the 13 Hampton Roads shipyards, because of its high degree of diversification. This is a strength common to the shipyards, some of which are even starting ventures unrelated to ships. For now, Newport News is keeping itself busy repairing old SSN-688 attack submarines. It is also under contract to build three new aircraft carriers, one each for 1992, 1995, and 1998.

The Newport News Shipyard is the only U.S. yard capable of handling aircraft carriers and is one of two that build submarines. Not everyone is optimistic that the state's single largest private employer, with 27,000 workers, will survive. One reason is that the company lost a Navy contract to build a second Seawolf nuclear submarine, the next generation of attack submarines, to its rival, Connecticut-based Electric Boat. Some feel that this will eventually spell the end of Newport's $2.1 billion submarine business, which provides jobs for 12,500. The company filed a lawsuit in June 1991 charging that the Department of Defense's awarding of the contract was tainted by political lobbying, against the Navy's wish to give the project to Electric Boat and Newport jointly.[7]

Portsmouth. The town may become the headquarters for the Naval Command, Control, and Ocean Surveillance Center's East Coast In-Service Engineering Directorate. As such it will probably gain positions through realignments.[8]

Woodbridge. The Harry Diamond Laboratories Research Facility is likely to close. Its functions will shift to facilities in Adelphi, MD. About 90 civilian positions will be directly impacted.

Yorktown. The Naval Mine Warfare Activity will be moved to Dam Neck, VA. An estimated 230 jobs will be transferred or eliminated.[9]

Notes

1. *Economic Assumptions for the U.S. and Virginia*, Virginia Employment Commission, November, 1989, pp. 10-12.

2. Robert Griffis, *Interim Report: Defense Expenditures in Virginia, Fiscal Year 1989*, Virginia Employment Commission, May 1990, p. 6.

3. Griffis, *op. cit.*, p. 7, p. 8.

4. Contacts: (1) Governor's Office, the Honorable Lawrence H. Framme III, Secretary of Economic Development, State Capitol, Richmond, VA 23219; 804-786-7831. (2) Virginia Economic Recovery Commission, Debbie Kelso, Office of the Lieutenant Governor; 804-786-2078. (3) Virginia Department of Finance, the Honorable Paul W. Timmreck, Secretary, 635 9th St. Office Building, Richmond, VA 23219; 804-786-1148. (4) Virginia Employment Commission, Ralph Cantrell, 703 E. Main Street, Richmond, VA 23219; 804-786-3001. (5) Virginia Department of Economic Development, Hugh D. Keogh, 1021 E. Cary Street, Richmond, VA 23219; 804-371-8100.

5. Nan Powers, "With Defense Cuts Looming, Va. Shipyards Prepare for Hard Times Ahead," September 4, 1989, p. 1. Stephen Goldstein, "Military Cuts Menace N. Virginia," *The Washington Times*, December 5, 1989, p. C-1. Griffis, *op. cit.*, p. 4. Stone, *op. cit.*, pp. 11-12.

6. Center for Economic Conversion, "Opportunity Knocks," *op. cit.*, p. 1.

7. "Cheney Considering Cutting Newport News from Sub Buying Loop," *Defense Daily*, July 6, 1990, p. 25, *op. cit.* Robert Weisman, "Newport News Fighting EB for Livelihood," *The Hartford Courant*, July 6, 1991, pp. 1, 14.

8. *Base Closure and Realignment Report*, April 1991, pp. 75-76.

9. *Ibid.*, p. 81.

Washington

A	B	C	D	E	F
$	🧑‍🔧	📠	📅	VI	DDI
✚	✚	✚	➡	!	✂

Benchmarks	No.	Rank	Benchmarks	No.	Rank
A.Total DoD $	$5.3bil.	11	Def.-Dependent Jobs ('000), '90	251	15
B. Personnel Payroll	$2.9bil.	7	Change in Def.-Dep. Jobs, '89-'91	-15.2%	6
C. Prime Contracts (PC)	$2.4bil.	15	Unemployment Rate, '90-'91	6.3%	26
D. PC Change, FY '87-'90	-29.1%	18	Unemp. Rate Change, '89-'91	0.0%	38
E. Vulnerability Index	10.3	23	Per Capita Income	$18,858	15
F. Defense Disloc. Index	0.47	30	Population ('000)	4,867	18

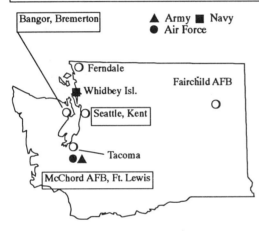

Bangor, Bremerton
▲ Army ■ Navy ● Air Force
Ferndale
Whidbey Isl.
Fairchild AFB
Seattle, Kent
Tacoma
McChord AFB, Ft. Lewis

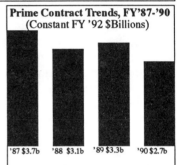

Prime Contract Trends, FY'87-'90
(Constant FY '92 $Billions)

'87 $3.7b   '88 $3.1b   '89 $3.3b   '90 $2.7b

Top 5 Contractors	$ Millions
Boeing	$1,246.9
Arco	389.9
Alcoa	100.4
Honeywell	55.3
Hewlett Packard	28.6

Top 10 $ Sites[a]	Congressional Dist., Representative	1989 Rank	Total DoD$[c]	Payroll[c]	Prime Contracts[c]	Personnel[d]
1-Seattle (20)	(1,7)[b]	15	$1,347.4	$157.2	$1190.2	2.8
2-Bremerton (54)	6-Dicks, d	65	691.6	648.2	43.4	15.2
3-Fort Lewis (75)	"	48	496.2	433.2	63.0	19.2
4-Ferndale (100)	2-Swift, d	117	391.3	1.4	389.9	--
5-Kent (159)	(7,8)[b]	130	243.6	8.9	234.7	--
6-Whidbey Is. (165)	2-Swift, d	165	223.6	208.4	15.2	4.2
7-Bangor (198)	6-Dicks, d	217	172.7	166.3	6.4	4.3
8-McChord AFB (208)	"	212	162.9	132.4	30.5	5.0
9-Fairchild AFB (228)	5-Foley, d	213	135.2	116.1	19.1	5.0
10-Tacoma (229)	6-Dicks, d	201	134.5	96.5	38.0	2.5

[a]Rating in parentheses is out of 511 sites, the top ten in each state and PR, plus DC.
[b]Multidistrict r-Rep. d-Dem. [c]$Millions (may not add due to rounding) [d] Thousands

Washington

Compared to other areas of the country, Washington is booming. The region is coming back from a slump in timber production. Fueling the expansion are the rapidly growing computer sector (Microsoft is based in Seattle) and Boeing's commercial aircraft building business (profiting from decade-long growth in air travel). An abundance of natural resources and worker migration from California are also contributing. Washington's unemployment rate was 6.3 percent in 1991, practically unchanged in two years.[1]

Defense and the Economy

Defense spending in 1990 was 5 percent of the economy and falling, due partly to the growth of the other sectors of the Washington economy, particularly housing and the commercial-aviation industry.[2]

Prime-contract spending fell about 12 percent between 1987 and 1990, affecting several thousand jobs. The services sector, followed by trade, aerospace and finance, will be the most affected by defense cuts. In the 1980s, growth in the defense-dependent sector accounted for a huge 15.5 percent of total new jobs in the state.[3] Washington's Vulnerability Index is ranked an average 23rd. Boeing, which attracts four times as much defense money as the next largest contractor in the state, has a thriving commercial-aircraft division but a money-losing military business.

The state has at least $7 billion worth of contracts linked to the controversial B-2 bomber program. Congress wants to terminate the program after 15 already-ordered planes are delivered, while the Bush Administration is seeking $30 billion for 60 more planes. Boeing has $4 billion and Northrop's subcontractors in Washington have $3.4 billion riding on the program.[4]

State Legislative Initiatives

Washington State was the first to enact a comprehensive conversion program. In March 1990 the law (SHB 2706, "Relating to the Promotion of Economic Diversification for Defense-Dependent Industries and Communities")[5] created a program in the state's Department of Community Development to help cope with defense cuts. The state bill received bipartisan support in both houses and was quickly signed. The three key provisions of this model bill direct the state to:

- Fund a yearly study to identify communities reliant on Department of Defense spending and track shifts in Federal spending priorities;
- Set up an office to notify and assist communities in utilizing state and Federal programs and in coordinating adjustment efforts; and

- Create a statewide plan for economic development to be drafted by a task force representing local governments, business, non-government community interests, and the military.[6]

A Community Diversification Program was created pursuant to the law in the State Department of Community Development, and in September 1990 a broadly representative Community Diversification Advisory Committee was appointed. The Committee met roughly bimonthly and produced a work plan for the first year's activity, the focus of which will be on a Diversification Plan for the state, drawing on models from throughout the U.S. and from abroad.

The main problem with this legislation is that its funding is susceptible to cuts. Approximately $400,000 was initially allocated for a two year period, but Gov. Gardner halved that funding under budgetary pressures. Activists have been lobbying state legislators to restore the original funding.[7]

Community Surveys

King County is the most reliant in the state on defense contracts, accounting for over 70 percent of total defense spending in the state. However, it has a varied economy capable of absorbing modest changes in military spending.

Benton-Franklin County. The Tri-Cities Diversification Project was ordered by the state (Chapter 501 of the Laws of 1987) in anticipation of the shutdown of the nuclear reactor at Hanford by the Department of Energy. Nuclear materials production and defense-related nuclear waste storage are handled at Hanford. The report was by the Washington State Department of Trade and Economic Development (101 General Administration Building, Mail Stop AX-13, Olympia, WA 98504-0613). The nuclear reactor was subsequently shut down, with the loss of approximately 2,500 jobs in 1988, and with the possibility of another 2,100 jobs being lost.

Everett. Budget cuts were considered at the new Everett Homeport/Naval Station in both 1988 and 1991. Cuts would stall the Navy's long-planned project (dating from the Reagan-era heyday of defense spending) of building a $294 million naval center with piers for an aircraft carrier and six other ships. The project is likely to remain on course if for no other reason than that the Navy has already spent $104 million.[8]

Kent. A small community of 23,000 people, it is one of the top three in prime military contracts, with $235 million in 1990. According to an official of a neighboring community, it may well have trouble absorbing cuts in its contracts.[9]

Keyport. The Naval Undersea Warfare Engineering Station will merge with the Naval Warfare Center's Weapons Systems Divisions also headquartered in Keyport. The consolidation of these facilities for the depoting of weapons and management of Pacific ranges will eliminate 700 positions.[10]

King County. Total 1986 Department of Defense expenditures in King county (which includes Seattle) amounted to $2.2 million, representing 43 percent of total military spending in Washington. In October 1988, the County Council established a committee "to conduct research to identify the potential impacts of military spending cutbacks, and recommend steps to diversify the local economy and markets for local firms, to prevent business and job loss." The action was to be an amendment to the King County Economic Development Plan. The committee, at the urging of County Council Chair Gary Grant, was to be composed of citizens, labor, and business representatives.[11]

Oak Harbor. The Whidbey Island Naval Air Station and its supporting Naval Hospital were originally slated for closure. The move would have eliminated 11,700 jobs (58.3 percent of regional employment).[12] However, the Base Commission decided to keep Oak Harbor off its final list of recommended closures so the base seems secure for the time being.

Renton. This Seattle suburb (40,000 pop., 40,000 workers because many commute in) near the airport is home to Boeing's Non-Line-of-Sight Missile. However, the Mayor of Renton's Executive Assistant feels that any worries about possible cuts in defense contracts must be weighed against the fact that Boeing has located the headquarters of its commercial aircraft division in Renton. He expects any layoffs to be through attrition and selective moves of military employees to the civilian side of the business.[13]

Seattle. The Sand Point (Puget Sound) Naval Station was realigned under the 1989 Base Closure Act. It is likely that the remaining half of the station will shutdown due to lack of a long-term mission requirement. Approximately 1,800 jobs will be affected but some of these will be transferred to nearby Everett.[14]

In 1989, Seattle firms alone. mostly Boeing. accounted for more than half of Department of Defense prime contracts in Washington. The city is enjoying commercial growth almost completely independent of military presence. Much emphasis is being put on diversifying into foreign trade and computer technology.[15]

The Sea-Lance Anti-Submarine Weapon is produced by Boeing in Seattle. Boeing in Seattle has been hiring thousands of workers who are being fired from defense contracting companies in California, such as from McDonnell Douglas or Northrop. The company has added 50,000 workers since 1985 and although employment expansion has leveled off, it gives no indication of significant decline. The company also recently announced that it reached a settlement with Grumman in Long Island, NY, to produce JSTARS planes. Although it has significant defense business, Boeing has been doing astoundingly well. It had a record $102.5 billion backlog of orders in 1990 that is leading the company to expand its facilities and plants in the Seattle area. Additionally, the firm is the main subcontractor to Northrop in the development of the Department of Defense's next generation of missiles. The Department of Defense's $15.1 billion contract is for the manufacture of 8,650 Stealth missiles. At the start of 1991, the company reached an agreement with two foreign competitors, Thomson-CSF S.A. of France and Deutsche Airbus of Germany, to coordinate efforts in the development of supersonic planes and military opportunities. Boeing management believes that such international alliances for risk sharing will be key to the company's survival in an era of reduced defense spending.[16]

The University of Washington's Institute for Public Policy and Management is doing a survey commissioned by the state that is intended to maximize the probability of entrepreneurs succeeding. The idea is to take a local inventory of resources and their use, then operate a three-fold campaign to raise private capital locally for new start-ups, to create small-business incubators, and, in particular, to create centers of excellence (Federally supported) to develop models for breeding new businesses.

Washington SANE/Freeze (Sara McCoy or Bill Patz, 5516 Roosevelt Way N.E., Seattle, WA 98105; 206-364-9112) has been pushing for further cuts in defense spending to up to 50 percent in five years and active in conversion initiatives. The group did much work toward the passage of the Defense Conversion Act, especially in efforts to get labor involved in formulation of the legislation and, subsequently, in the conversion process.[17] SANE/Freeze also lobbied for the amendment to the King County Economic Development Plan.

Tacoma. On a 1989 election initiative, 65 percent of Tacoma voters supported a call for reductions in defense spending, with 10 percent of the defense budget to be spent on domestic and social needs and deficit reduction. The initiative also instructed the Mayor of Tacoma to send these results to President Bush and to Washington's Members of Congress. Michael Collier of Sixth Sense (2603 1/2 Sixth Avenue, Tacoma, WA 98406, 206-272-5204), co-chaired the campaign.[18]

The 7th Infantry Division, currently at Fort Ord, CA, and several other smaller units in that state, will be transferred to Fort Lewis, bringing 12,300 personnel. An additional 2,370 will come from bases in Germany, and 680 positions will be created with eight new units. Overall, Fort Lewis will grow in personnel by 75 percent by 1995. Fort Lewis, in the district of Rep. Norm Dicks, a member of the House Appropriations subcommittees on defense and military construction, is to receive $7.9 million for the addition of an education development center under a bill that passed the House in May 1991.[19]

Notes

1. *State of Washington Economic and Revenue Forecast*, Economic and Revenue Forecast Council, June, 1989, p. 3. Timothy Egan, "Northwest's Fortunes, Once Grim, Thrive Despite National Recession," *The New York Times*, March 14, 1991, pp. A1, B6. *Statistical Abstract of the U.S. 1989*, Bureau of Census, U.S. Department of Commerce, pp. 429, 431, 433.

2. Dave Holland and Philip Wandschneider, *Impact of Military Expenditures on the Washington Economy*, Department of Agricultural Economics, Washington State University, June 1989, pp. viii-x.

3. *Ibid.*, pp. 33-34.

4. Eric Schmitt, "U.S. Weapons Makers Intensify Lobbying Efforts as Budgets Fall," *The New York Times*, August 6, 1991, p. D6.

5. For more on the bill, contact Bill Patz, Washington State SANE/Freeze, 5516 Roosevelt Way, NE, Seattle, WA 98105; 206-527-8050.

6. Lee Smith, Executive Director, New York State Industrial Cooperation Council, 1515 Broadway, 52nd Floor, New York, NY 10036; 212-930-0111.

7. Janet Stone, *Conversion Organizers' Update* (Mountain View, CA: October 1991, advance copy), pp. 12-13. Contacts: (1) Governor's Office, Claude Lakewold, Executive Policy Assistant, Legislative Bldg., Olympia, WA 98504; 206-586-2464. (2) Institute for Public Policy and Management, Daniel Carlson, Research Consultant, 324 Parrington Hall, MS DC-14, Seattle, WA 98195; 206-543-0190. (3) Northwest Policy Center, Dr. Paul Sommers, Research Director, 327 Parrington Hall, DC-14, University of Washington, Seattle, WA 98195 (also economics professor, Graduate School of Public Affairs at the University). (4) Community Diversification Program, Washington Department of Community Development, Paul Knox, Ninth and Columbia Building, MS/GH-51, State of Washington, Olympia, WA 98504; 206-586-8973. (5) Washington Department of Employment Security, Isaiah Turner, Commissioner, 212 Maple Park, KG-11, Olympia, WA 98504; 206-753-5114. (6) Washington Department of Trade & Economic Development, John Anderson, Director, 101 General Administration Bldg. AX-13, Olympia, WA 98504; 206-753-7426. (7) Washington Economic Development Office, Michael Alvine, Senior Development Specialist, King County Planning and Community Development Division, 707 Smith Tower, Seattle, WA 98104; 206-296-8684 or 206-344-4100. (8) Washington State SANE/Freeze, Bill Patz, 5516 Roosevelt Way NE, Seattle, WA 98105; 206-527-8050.

8. John Davies, "Everett's Plans Proceed Despite Navy Uncertainty," *Journal of Commerce*, June 4, 1991, p. B1.

9. Interview in January 1991 with the Executive Assistant to the Mayor of Renton. The Mayor of Kent, Daniel Kelleher, is at 206-872-3300 but was not reached for comment.

10. *Base Closure and Realignment Report*, April 1991, pp. 83-85.

11. Holland and Wandschneider, p. 28. Information provided by Louise McNeilly, Center for Economic Conversion, 222C View Street, Mountain View, CA, 94041; 415-968-8798.

12. *Base Closure...,* April 1991, pp. 69-71.

13. Interview in January 1991 with Jay Covington, Executive Assistant to the Mayor of Renton, 206-235-2500.

14. *Base Closure...*, April 1991, pp. 67-68.

15. *Atlas/ Data Abstract for the U.S. and Selected Areas, Fiscal 1989*, Department of Defense, Washington Headquarters Services, Directorate for Information, Operations and Reports, p. 115. Susan Rasky, "Congressman Is Seeking to Balance Constituent Jobs and Military Budget," The New York Times, December 11, 1989.

16. Egan, p. B6. "Boeing Agrees to Pact With 2 Competitors," *The New York Times*, March 21, 1991, p. D4.

17. Bill Patz, SANE/Freeze, *Proceedings: National Strategy Retreat on Economic Conversion, Block Island, June 11-13, 1990*, pp. 3-4.

18. "New Haven and Tacoma: Yes to Military Cuts," *Municipal Foreign Policy*, Winter 1989/1990, p. 17.

19. Ed Offley, "Despite Ebbing Army, Ft. Lewis Expects a Flood of New Soldiers," *Seattle Post-Intelligencer*, September 13, 1991, p. B7. Garrett, p. 5.

West Virginia

A	B	C	D	E	F
$	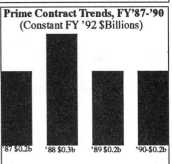			VI	DDI
–	–	–	↑	!	✌

Benchmarks	No.	Rank	Benchmarks	No.	Rank
A.Total DoD $	$0.4bil.	46	Def.-Dependent Jobs ('000), '90	18	46
B. Personnel Payroll	$0.2bil.	50	Change in Def.-Dep. Jobs, '89–'91	+20.0%	49
C. Prime Contracts (PC)	$0.2bil.	44	Unemployment Rate, '90–'91	9.7%	2
D. PC Change, FY '87–'90	+35.0%	52	Unemp. Rate Change, '89–'91	+1.1%	24
E. Vulnerability Index	10.4	19	Per Capita Income	$13,747	50
F. Defense Disloc. Index	0.06	44	Population ('000)	1,793	35

▲ Army ■ Navy
● Air Force

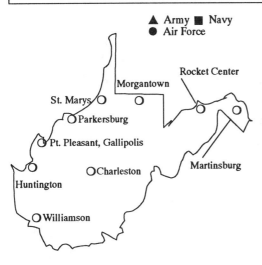

Prime Contract Trends, FY'87–'90
(Constant FY '92 $Billions)

'87 $0.2b   '88 $0.3b   '89 $0.2b   '90-$0.2b

Top 5 Contractors	$ Millions
Phoenix Petroleum	$76.9
Groves	44.0
Hercules	33.4
Newberg	11.2
OHM	4.9

Top 10 $ Sites[a]	Congressional Dist., Representative	1989 Rank	Total DoD$[c]	Payroll[c]	Prime Contracts[c]	Personnel[d]
1-St. Marys (299)	1-Mollohan, d	353	$77.0	$.06	$76.9	--
2-Gallipolis (338)	3-Wise, d	400	44.5	0	44.5	.05
3-Rocket Center (371)	2-Staggers, d	358	33.4	0	33.4	--
4-Huntington (378)	4-Rohall, d	368	31.2	24.6	6.6	0.6
5-Martinsburg (410)	2-Stagger, d	422	20.6	12.9	7.7	0.3
6-Charleston (414)	3-Wise, d	413	19.8	15.4	4.4	0.4
7-Point Pleasant (457)	"	--	7.9	2.6	5.3	.05
8-Williamson (461)	4-Rohall, d	435	7.4	0.9	6.4	--
9-Morgantown (462)	2-Stagger, d	454	7.3	4.4	2.9	.05
10-Parkersburg (464)	1-Mollohan, d	439	6.7	6.6	0.2	.06

[a]Rating in parentheses is out of 511 sites, the top ten in each state and PR, plus DC.
[b]Multidistrict r-Rep. d-Dem. [c]$Millions (may not add due to rounding) [d] Thousands

West Virginia

West Virginia has long been one of the poorest states in the nation. The trade and services sectors of its economy are the largest, 45 percent. Coal mining still employs 30,000 people, almost 5 percent of the state's employment. Although both the construction and finance sectors are relatively small (each employs only 4 percent of the total labor force), they are considered to be two of the strongest economic pillars. The state's unemployment rate was 9.7 percent in 1991, 2nd highest. West Virginia ranked 24th in change in unemployment over two years (the labor force grew twice as fast as employment).[1]

Defense and the Economy

In 1990 the state received only $412 million in defense money, the 7th smallest amount. But West Virginia's weak economy contributes to the state's having the19th highest Vulnerability Index. Defense Secretary Dick Cheney has proposed cuts in the Chaparral missile program in West Virginia.

Considering the importance of the mining industry to the state economy, it is not surprising that fuel is one of its main defense industries, 27 percent of 1989 defense spending in the state. The largest state contractor is Phoenix Petroleum Co. of St. Marys, which got nearly all the state's petroleumcontracts. Other important defense-related sectors include construction, which received over $48 million in 1989, and ammunition production, which received $31 million.[2]

Rocket Center. Rocket Center is the third largest site in West Virginia and the 371st largest of the 511 we compared in the nation. Sen. Robert C. Byrd (D-WV) altered a supplemental spending bill to direct the Army to continue developing 105mm rocket-assisted kinetic energy (RAKE) tank ammunition. The Army wants to cut the program due to its low priority in times of shrinking funding. The program, run by Hercules Corp's Allegheny Ballistics Laboratory, has a classified budget, making savings estimates impossible.

Notes

1. *1988 Population and 1987 Per Capita Income for Counties and Incorporated Places*, U.S. Department of Commerce, Bureau of Census. *West Virginia Data Profile*, Governor's Office of Community and Industrial Development, March 1990. *West Virginia Economic Summary*, Division of Employment Security, April 1990, p. 2.

2. *Prime Contract Awards by Region and State, Fiscal Years 1989, 1988, 1987*, Department of Defense, Washington Headquarters Services, Directorate for Information, Operations and Reports, p. 62. Contacts: (1) Existing Industry Services, Lori Walker, Director, Building 6, Room 517, Charleston, WV 25305; 304-348-2234. (2) Governor's Office of Community and Industrial Development, Ann M. Johnson, Director, State Capitol Complex, M-146, Charleston, WV 25305; 304-348-0400. (3) West Virginia Department of Employment Security, Ed Merrifield, Director, State Capitol Complex, Charleston, WV 25305; 304-348-2660.

Wisconsin

A	B	C	D	E	F
$	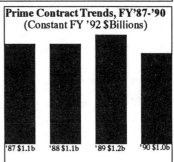			VI	DDI
–	–	+	→	–	✌

Benchmarks	No.	Rank	Benchmarks	No.	Rank
A. Total DoD $	$1.3bil.	35	Def.-Dependent Jobs ('000), '90	67	35
B. Personnel Payroll	$0.4bil.	39	Change in Def.-Dep. Jobs, '89-'91	-14.1%	7
C. Prime Contracts (PC)	$0.9bil.	27	Unemployment Rate, '90-'91	5.8%	34
D. PC Change, FY '87-'90	-11.5%	33	Unemp. Rate Change, '89-'91	+1.4%	22
E. Vulnerability Index	6.1	49	Per Capita Income	$17,503	23
F. Defense Disloc. Index	0.11	38	Population ('000)	4,892	16

▲ Army ■ Navy
● Air Force

Sturgeon Bay
Appleton ○
Ft. McCoy ▲
Oshkosh ○
○ La Crosse
Madison ○   Pt. Wash. ○
Milwaukee, Waukesha ○
Janesville ○

Prime Contract Trends, FY'87-'90
(Constant FY '92 $Billions)

'87 $1.1b   '88 $1.1b   '89 $1.2b   '90 $1.0b

Top 5 Contractors	$ Millions
Oshkosh Truck	$259.0
Peterson Builders	211.3
Astra Holdings	53.0
Trak International	46.3
Wisconsin Physicians Ins.	36.9

Top 10 $ Sites[a]	Congressional Dist., Representative	1989 Rank	Total DoD$[c]	Payroll[c]	Prime Contracts[c]	Per sonnel[d]
1-Oshkosh (148)	6-Petri, r	106	$266.4	$5.2	$261.1	.03
2-Sturgeon Bay (169)	8-Roth, r	171	216.6	4.4	212.2	0.1
3-Fort McCoy (223)	6-Petri, r	250	138.6	113.6	25.0	1.4
4-Milwaukee (248)	(4,5)[b]	243	115.5	50.4	65.2	1.4
5-Madison (280)	2-Klug, r	309	90.2	23.0	67.2	0.5
6-Ft. Washington (332)	9-Sensenbrenner, r	379	46.4	0.3	46.2	--
7-Janesville (354)	1-Aspin, d	352	39.3	0	39.3	--
8-Waukesha (387)	(4,9)[b]	383	27.5	3.4	24.1	--
9-Appleton (405)	(6,8)[b]	--	21.6	4.4	17.2	--
10-La Crosse (413)	3-Gunderson, r	386	20.0	4.0	16.1	--

[a] Rating in parentheses is out of 511 sites, the top ten in each state and PR, plus DC.
[b] Multidistrict r-Rep. d-Dem. [c]$Millions (may not add due to rounding) [d] Thousands

Wisconsin

The forecast for Wisconsin's economy is moderate growth. Total non-farm employment was predicted to grow by 11 percent between 1987 and 2000, adding 274,000 jobs. Non-farm employment should grow a little less than the national rate of 17 percent because of slower population growth. The manufacturing growth rate until 2000 should be around 2.2 percent, creating 12,000 new jobs. Top employment growth sectors are expected to be services, government, retail trade, finance and wholesale trade areas, while mining and farming will probably decline. Agriculture and tourism are also very important to the economy of Wisconsin. Tourism generates close to $5 billion a year, as approximately 6 million people visit the state a year.[1] Slow labor growth will adversely affect output growth. Wisconsin's unemployment ranked 34th at 5.8 percent in April 1991; its change in unemployment over two years ranks 22nd (employment shrank faster than the labor force).

Defense and the Economy

Wisconsin is not very defense dependent, and it will not be hit particularly hard by defense cuts. A small fraction of Wisconsin's prime contracts are at risk of being cut. No bases or personnel cuts are expected in the near future. The Vulnerability Index ranks Wisconsin 49th among the states, indicating Wisconsin's relative safety from defense cuts.[2]

Community Surveys

Rep. Tom Petri (R-WI-6) has more at stake in the defense budget among his constituents than Rep. Les Aspin (D-WI-1), Chairman of the House Armed Services Committee. Two of the top three sites are in his district, Oshkosh (145th nationally) and the army's Fort McCoy, the largest base in the state. Rep. Aspin's top site, in Janesville, ranks 350th out of 511 sites we ranked nationally.

Oshkosh. Oshkosh Truck racked up more than a quarter of a billion dollars in orders in 1990.

Sparta (Fort McCoy). Fort McCoy was considered for cuts at the start of 1991 but by the end of the summer seems likely to survive the latest round of defense cuts intact.

Notes

1. *Wisconsin Economic Profile*, Wisconsin Department of Administration, 1989.
2. Contacts: (1) Governor's Office, Bob Seitz, Governor's Policy Advisor, State Capitol, Madison, WI; 608-266-0100. (2) Wisconsin Department of Economic Development, Randall Wede, 123 W. Washington Ave., Madison, WI; 608-267-7214. (3) Wisconsin Department of Economic Development, Rolf Wegenke, 123 W. Washington Ave., P.O. Box 7970, Madison, WI; 608-266-3203.

Wyoming

A	B	C	D	E	F
$				VI	DDI
–	–	–	↑	–	✌

Benchmarks	No.	Rank	Benchmarks	No.	Rank
A. Total DoD $	$0.2bil.	51	Def.-Dependent Jobs ('000), '90	10	51
B. Personnel Payroll	$0.2bil.	51	Change in Def.-Dep. Jobs, '89-'91	-9.1%	17
C. Prime Contracts (PC)	$.06bil.	51	Unemployment Rate, '90-'91	5.3%	41
D. PC Change, FY '87-'90	+19.7%	49	Unemp. Rate Change, '89-'91	-0.8%	49
E. Vulnerability Index	7.1	48	Per Capita Income	$16,398	34
F. Defense Disloc. Index	0.00	49	Population ('000)	454	52

▲ Army ■ Navy
● Air Force

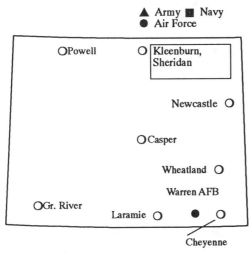

Prime Contract Trends, FY'87-'90
(Constant FY '92 $Billions)

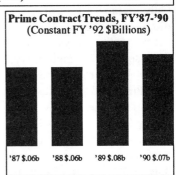

'87 $.06b   '88 $.06b   '89 $.08b   '90 $.07b

Top 5 Contractors	$ Millions
Hermes Consolidated	$25.1
Frontier Oil	10.4
Sinclair Oil	10.1
Bowman	2.8
Growling Bear	1.1

Top 10 $ Sites[a]	Congressional Dist., Representative	1989 Rank	Total DoD$[c]	Payroll[c]	Prime Contracts[c]	Per- sonnel[d]
1-Warren AFB (249)	1-Thomas,r	241	$114.9	$100.5	$14.4	4.2
2-Cheyenne (331)	"	335	46.6	35.2	11.4	0.4
3-Newcastle (396)	"	389	25.4	0.3	25.1	--
4-Casper (432)	"	483	14.0	3.7	10.3	.01
5-Laramie (488)	"	474	4.1	3.6	0.6	.01
6-Sheridan (501)	"	498	2.6	2.4	0.2	.00
7-Powell (508)	"	496	1.4	1.5	.09	.07
8-Kleenburn (509)	"	--	0.6	0	0.6	--
9-Green River (510)	"	--	0.5	0.4	0.1	--
10-Wheatland (511)	"	--	0.4	0.4	.04	.00

[a]*Rating in parentheses is out of 511 sites, the top ten in each state and PR, plus DC.*
[b] *Multidistrict*   *r-Republican*   *d-Democrat* [c] *$ Millions (rounded)* [d] *Thousands*

Wyoming

The Wyoming economy has been heavily influenced by the booms and busts of the national petroleum industry. The state experienced economic decline or slow growth for much of the 1980s and in 1991 was in a relatively weak position. The unemployment rate was up to 5.3 percent in 1991 and ranked 41st. The state's change in unemployment over a two-year period ranked a healthy 49th (employment growth kept ahead of rapid labor-force growth).

Defense and the Economy

The end of the alphabet seems also to get the tail end of the defense budget. Only Vermont received fewer defense dollars than Wyoming in 1990, another difference being that Vermont was in a free fall downward off the defense-budget map, whereas Wyoming saw an substantial increase in its defense revenues. Even so, the $228 million Wyoming received from the Department of Defense in 1990 barely represented 0.1 percent of total U.S. defense expenditures[1] On the other hand the state economy isn't very large, so these low figures actually add up to a surprisingly high defense dependence. Fortunately, so long as the Defense Secretary is Dick Cheney, former U.S. Representative from Wyoming, he is unlikely to let the nickels and dimes that go from the defense budget to his home state get lost in the shuffle as the big states battle over their share of the billions that are cut and the billions that will remain.

Community Surveys

The only significant defense-related industry in Wyoming is petroleum production and distribution. The three largest prime contractors in 1990 were all petroleum companies; they brought in $46 million in revenues, up from $38 million in 1989. The largest supplier, Hermes Consolidated, is based in Newcastle. These contracts represent the bulk of Wyoming's prime contracts. The other two of the top five contractors, Bowman and Growling Bear, are involved in modest military-construction contracts (offices and housing).[2]

Warren Air Force Base. Warren AFB is the only major defense facility in the state, accounting for virtually all of the military personnel in the state.

Notes

1. *Atlas/Data Abstract for the U.S. and Selected Areas, Fiscal 1990*, Department of Defense, Washington Headquarters Services, Directorate for Information, p. 121.

2. *Prime Contract Awards by Region and State, Fiscal Years 1989, 1988, 1987*, Department of Defense, Washington Headquarters Services, Directorate for Information, Operations and Reports, p. 68. Contacts: (1) Wyoming Department of Labor, Jack Wolff, Director, Herschler Bldg., Cheyenne, WY 82002; 307-777-7261. (2) Wyoming Economic Development Department, Steve Schmitz, Director, Herschler Bldg., Cheyenne, WY 82002; 307-777-7287. (3) Wyoming Economic Development Department, Anne McGowan, Herschler Building, Cheyenne, WY 82002; 307-777-6430.